A HANDBOOK OF CHAPLAINCY STUDIES

Chaplaincy is uniquely positioned to serve the ever-present spiritual needs of a society that is increasingly unfamiliar with formal religion. This handbook is therefore timely, revealing the cutting-edge value of a ministry that adjusts to people in the real world, reminding both individuals of their God-given value and institutions of the need to exercise power with humanity. Through its close examination of chaplaincy in a range of settings, not fudging the tensions of being inclusive yet challenging, pastoral yet prophetic, this book promotes a model of ministry that has considerable relevance and impact.
Jonathan Chaffey, Chaplain-in-Chief, Royal Air Force

This volume brings a wealth of valuable insights. I wholeheartedly commend it to anyone who works as a chaplain or who is seeking to better understand the role.
Mark Burleigh, President, College of Healthcare Chaplains, UK

Gathers together high level theological understanding with deeply reflective pastoral experience and so offers the reader a fresh and nourishing account of both the fundamentals and particularities of chaplaincy. Especially welcome is the inclusion of detailed and intelligently reflective case studies. At a time when so many mainstream churches are being drained of energy by issues of maintenance and keeping up numbers, these essays provide all interested in the church's life a vision of other ways of being church: ways of mission and embeddedness and care. The great insight, beyond the essential accounts the work gives to those involved directly in chaplaincy, is that it is precisely in these 'secular' and 'marginal' places that today's church can rediscover itself. A must-read for those involved in practical theology and pastoral ministry.
Clare Watkins, University of Roehampton, UK

A feast for those who are interested in chaplaincy – contributors bring their unique approaches to a range of areas on the subject. This book provides description and interpretation of current practices of chaplaincy and highlights the challenges facing the area. It makes a valuable contribution to the expanding literature on chaplaincy.
Ataullah Siddiqui, Markfield Institute of Higher Education, UK

A Handbook of Chaplaincy Studies explores fundamental and critical issues in chaplaincy, spanning key areas of health care, the prison service, education and military chaplaincy. Leading authors and practitioners in the field present critical insight into the challenges and opportunities facing professional spiritual care, setting out how the phenomenon of chaplaincy can be better understood in an era of religious complexity. Offering an invaluable compendium of case-studies, academic reflection and critical enquiry, this pioneering handbook presents fresh understandings of traditional, contemporary and innovative forms of spiritual practice as they are witnessed in the public sphere.

Ashgate Contemporary Ecclesiology

Series Editors
Martyn Percy, University of Oxford, UK
D. Thomas Hughson, Marquette University, USA
Bruce Kaye, Charles Sturt University, Australia

Series Advisory Board
James Nieman; Sathi Clarke; Gemma Simmonds CJ; Gerald West;
Philip Vickeri; Helen Cameron; Tina Beattie; Nigel Wright; Simon Coleman

The field of ecclesiology has grown remarkably in the last decade, and most especially in relation to the study of the contemporary church. Recently, theological attention has turned once more to the nature of the church, its practices and proclivities, and to interpretative readings and understandings on its role, function and ethos in contemporary society.

This new series draws from a range of disciplines and established scholars to further the study of contemporary ecclesiology and publish an important cluster of landmark titles in this field. The Series Editors represent a range of Christian traditions and disciplines, and this reflects the breadth and depth of books developing in the Series. This Ashgate series presents a clear focus on the contemporary situation of churches worldwide, offering an invaluable resource for students, researchers, ministers and other interested readers around the world working or interested in the diverse areas of contemporary ecclesiology and the important changing shape of the church worldwide.

A Handbook of Chaplaincy Studies

Understanding Spiritual Care in Public Places

Edited by

CHRISTOPHER SWIFT
Leeds Teaching Hospitals NHS Trust, UK

MARK COBB
Sheffield Teaching Hospitals NHS Foundation Trust, UK

ANDREW TODD
Cardiff Centre for Chaplaincy Studies, UK

ASHGATE

© Christopher Swift, Mark Cobb and Andrew Todd and the Contributors 2015

Christopher Swift, Mark Cobb and Andrew Todd have asserted their right under the Copyright, Designs and Patents Act, 1988, to be identified as the editors of this work.

Published by

Ashgate Publishing Limited
Wey Court East
Union Road
Farnham
Surrey, GU9 7PT
England

Ashgate Publishing Company
110 Cherry Street
Suite 3-1
Burlington, VT 05401-3818
USA

www.ashgate.com

British Library Cataloguing in Publication Data
A catalogue record for this book is available from the British Library

The Library of Congress has cataloged the printed edition as follows:
A handbook of chaplaincy studies : understanding spiritual care in public places /
[edited] by Christopher Swift, Mark Cobb and Andrew Todd.
   pages cm. – (Ashgate contemporary ecclesiology)
   Includes index.
   ISBN 978-1-4724-3405-0 (hardcover – ISBN 978-1-4724-3406-7 (pbk)
– ISBN 978-1-4724-3407-4 (ebook) – ISBN 978-1-4724-3408-1 (epub)
   1. Chaplains. 2. Pastoral care. I. Swift, Christopher, 1965– editor. II. Cobb, Mark, editor. III. Todd, Andrew, 1961– editor.
   BV4375.H36 2015
   253–dc23

2015004396

ISBN 9781472434050 (hbk)
ISBN 9781472434067 (pbk)
ISBN 9781472434074 (ebk – PDF)
ISBN 9781472434081 (ebk – ePUB)

MIX
Paper from
responsible sources
FSC
www.fsc.org   FSC® C013985

Printed in the United Kingdom by Henry Ling Limited,
at the Dorset Press, Dorchester, DT1 1HD

Contents

List of Contributors

Mohammed Arshad graduated in Islamic theology from Darul Uloom Al-Arabiyyah Al-Islamiyyah Bury, Lancashire and BA(Hons) QTS from Bradford University. He was appointed as a Muslim chaplain for Bradford Teaching Hospitals NHS Trust in 1999. Gradually the role developed to include delivering cultural competency training and advising specific areas and departments on cultural and religious issues. By 2003 his work expanded in the areas of training and advising to a regional and national level. He has produced religious and cultural awareness information leaflets for Bradford Teaching Hospitals NHS Foundation Trust, the Islamic Perspective on Grief and Loss, Pregnancy Loss, When a Child Dies in Hospital and Chronic Pain. In 2005 Mohammed Arshad won a first prize in the West Yorkshire NHS Modernisation Awards for the information leaflet and patient assessment process 'Taking Care of Your Health, Islam and Chronic Pain for Muslim Patients', which was also given the Special Commendation Award at the Bradford Council Community Harmony Awards 2006. Mohammed Arshad lectures on the MSc Rehabilitation Studies programme on the Management of Chronic Pain in Musculoskeletal Practice module and BSc(Hons) Physiotherapy course at Bradford University and Leeds University. In April 2013 he became Head of Chaplaincy, the second Muslim chaplain in UK to lead a multifaith team.

Alan Billings is an Anglican priest. He has trained clergy in two theological colleges in Oxford and Birmingham and is a former Director of the Centre for Ethics and Religion at Lancaster University. His latest books are *Lost Church* and *The Dove, the Fig Leaf and the Sword: Why the Church Changes its Mind about War* (SPCK). He is a former Deputy Leader of Sheffield City Council and was elected Police and Crime Commissioner for South Yorkshire in 2014.

John Caperon read English as his first degree, and taught English in a range of secondary schools. In mid career he studied in Oxford for the Anglican priesthood, and has worked as a self-supporting priest since the early 1980s. He became head and chaplain of a Church secondary school, and later an educational consultant, before taking on the leadership of the educational charity the Bloxham Project (now SCALA, the School Chaplains' and Leaders' Association). He holds higher degrees in English literature, education, and theology, and researched chaplaincy in Church of England schools for his doctorate in practical theology. His interests focus on the interplay between theology, literature and education as vehicles for human flourishing.

Jeremy Clines is the Anglican Chaplain at the University of Sheffield and author of the 2008 *Faiths in Higher Education Chaplaincy* report. He has contributed to the *Religious Literacy Leadership in Higher Education* project since its inception in 2009 and his most recent work is a chapter on chaplaincy with Sophie Gilliat-Ray for *Religious Literacy in Policy and Practice* by Adam Dinham and Matthew Francis (Policy Press, 2015). His research interests include chaplaincy practice, spiritual development, liberation and contextual theologies and church liturgy.

Mark Cobb is a Senior Chaplain and a Clinical Director at Sheffield Teaching Hospitals NHS Foundation Trust. He holds honorary academic posts at the University of Sheffield and the University of Liverpool and his primary research interests are in the fields of health-related spirituality, palliative care and service design. Mark is widely published in the fields of chaplaincy, palliative care and spirituality, and his books include *The Hospital Chaplain's Handbook* (2005), and the *Oxford Textbook of Spirituality in Healthcare* (2012) which he co-edited with Christina Puchalski and Bruce Rumbold.

David Coulter has been an army chaplain for over 25 years. He assumed the appointment as Chaplain General to Her Majesty's Land Forces in September 2014. He undertook his theological training at St Andrew's University prior to ordination into the Church of Scotland in 1989. His PhD was completed in 1997 in ecclesiastical history with the University of Edinburgh, writing a thesis on the Church of Scotland army chaplains of the Second World War. He continues to have a keen interest in military and church history and most recently published a chapter on the religion of Field Marshall the Earl Haig.

Frank Cranmer is a Fellow of St Chad's College, Durham and an honorary Research Fellow at the Centre for Law and Religion, Cardiff Law School. His particular interests are religion and human rights, religion and employment law, and the interactions between secular law and religious law generally. With David Pocklington he co-edits the *Law & Religion UK* blog.

Andrew Crompton is Chairman of St Peters House management committee, providing chaplaincy services to the universities in Manchester, as well as a researcher at Liverpool School of Architecture interested in the design of interfaces such as fonts, human faces, GUIs and multifaith spaces.

Helen Dearnley studied law at university and spent a year working at St Albans Cathedral and volunteering at HMP Holloway before training for ordination in the Church of England. After serving her curacy she became the Coordinating Chaplain of HMP Leicester, a post held for seven years, before becoming a Chaplaincy Headquarters Adviser with responsibility for the oversight of prison chaplaincies in the East Midlands and Eastern regions, as well as being the chaplaincy lead on female prisons and prisons within the private sector.

Rosie Deedes spent 16 years, 1999–2015, in the prison service as an Anglican chaplain. Alongside her pastoral and managerial responsibilities as a full-time chaplain, she did qualitative research about the experience of women leaving prison, interviewing a sample group before and after release to consider whether their expectations were matched by their experience. She did a further study for The Griffins Society, with women who had been recalled to prison for breaching their licence conditions. As a practitioner at HMP Downview, Rosie devised a programme of experiential group work, 'First Timers in Custody'. At HMP Isle of Wight she set up a training course for new volunteers working with male sex offenders. Through speaking engagements she has sought to inform community groups and churches about prisoners and prison life, encouraging people to volunteer in the establishments where she has worked. She has an active interest in restorative justice.

Sophie Gilliat-Ray is Professor of Religious Studies at Cardiff University, and the Director of the Centre for the Study of Islam in the UK. She has been undertaking research about chaplaincy since 1994, and has published numerous books, articles and book chapters on this subject including, most recently, *Understanding Muslim Chaplaincy* (with Mansur Ali and Stephen Pattison, Ashgate, 2013).

Asim Hafiz graduated from an Islamic college in England as an Imam and Islamic scholar in 1999, and later gained an MA in contemporary Islamic studies at the University of London. He has held positions in a range of religious and secular organisations, including as a chaplain in health care and the Prison Service. In Oct 2005 he was appointed as the first and only Muslim chaplain to the Armed Forces. In 2010–2011 Asim carried out a number of short visits to Afghanistan, performing his military chaplaincy duties and providing religious advice to UK and US commanders. In 2011 Asim led the UK cross-government team on religious engagement and outreach in support of stability and reconciliation in Southern Afghanistan. In 2012 he was deployed for a full six-month operational tour of Afghanistan as part of UK/ISAF's effort to increase the role of religious understanding to promote peace, stability and conflict termination. He is now employed as an Imam and dedicated Islamic religious adviser to the Chief of the Defence Staff and Service Chiefs. This new role seeks to enhance the Armed Forces' engagement with and understanding of Muslim communities in the UK as well as overseas. Imam Asim was awarded an OBE in the 2014 New Year Honours list for services to defence, especially in support of Afghan operations. and was named the Religious Advocate of the Year at the British Muslim Awards in 2015.

Chris Hewson is currently a Knowledge Exchange and Impact Officer at the University of Manchester (Faculty of Humanities), assisting in the management and externalisation of academic projects and facilitating research impact across 11 discipline areas. Previously, he was a researcher at the Manchester Architecture Research Centre (MARC): at the outset, on the EPSRC Carbon Reduction in Buildings, EcoCities and Sustainable Consumption Institute programmes; from 2010, on the AHRC/ESRC Religion and Society project 'Multifaith Spaces: Symptoms and Agents of Religious and Social Change'. Previously, Dr Hewson worked on a series of consultancy and research projects around social enterprise and skills policy. His PhD entitled 'Technologies of Citizenship: Local Media and Public Service' considered the rise of community media projects within the context of New Labour's policy programme.

Michael Kavanagh has been ordained as an Anglican priest for 27 years. Before ordination he worked as a clinical psychologist and retains chartered membership of the British Psychological Society. He has an MSc in clinical psychology from the University of Newcastle and bachelor's degrees in both psychology from the University of York and theology and religious studies from the University of Leeds, obtained whilst a student at the College of the Resurrection, Mirfield. He is especially interested in the relationship between psychology and spirituality and has publications relating to the spiritual care of the dying and bereaved, reflecting on his work as chaplain at Martin House Hospice for Children, and in the field of the rehabilitation of offenders, building on his work within the National Offender Management Service.

Ewan Kelly has been involved in health care chaplaincy for 20 years as a practitioner, educator, researcher and in strategic leadership roles. He is currently the strategic lead for spiritual care across health and social care in the Dumfries and Galloway area of Scotland, where he is seeking to collaboratively embed national programmes of work, which he was responsible for initiating, into local community contexts across sectors. He is the author and co-author of four monographs which relate to spiritual and pastoral care provision. Such writing, reflection on lived experience and research has afforded Ewan the opportunity to lecture in different parts of the globe.

Peter Kevern is Associate Professor in Values in Care in the Faculty of Health Sciences, Staffordshire University. Originally a theologian by background and training, he taught candidates for ministry at the Queen's Foundation for Theological Education for nine years before moving to the university to pursue his research interests in the theological and religious dimensions of dementia. With Professor Wilf McSherry, he has recently completed a two-year project researching the efficacy of a primary care 'chaplains for wellbeing' service in the Midlands.

Giles Legood is a Church of England priest, serving as a chaplain in the Royal Air Force, currently as Senior Chaplain of RAF Brize Norton. After working as a curate, he was a university chaplain for 12 years and also served as a Reservist Chaplain in the air force, immediately prior to joining the RAF full-time. He has written or edited a number of books in the areas of pastoral theology and ethics. He has served on flying and training units, and in Iraq. In 2014 he was appointed MBE for an operational tour as hospital chaplain at Camp Bastion, Afghanistan.

Wilf McSherry was appointed Professor in Dignity of Care for Older People in August 2008; this is a shared appointment between the Faculty of Health Sciences, Staffordshire University and the Shrewsbury and Telford Hospital NHS Trust. Wilf is also a part-time professor at Haraldsplass Deaconess University College, Bergen, Norway. In 2012 he was made a Fellow of the Royal College of Nursing for his unique contribution to nursing in the areas of spirituality and dignity.

Garry Neave is an Anglican priest and the Church of England's National Adviser for Further Education and Post-16, where his remit includes chaplaincy in schools and further education. He began his teaching career in a large bilateral school (a secondary modern with a grammar stream) and has been an FE chaplain, a senior manager in further and higher education institutions and Education Director for The Girls' Day School Trust. With Michael Camp, he is the author of *The Public Face of God* (2014), a study of chaplaincy in Church of England secondary schools and academies. His professional interests include counselling and pastoral care, and the development of educational leadership and governance within church schools and colleges.

Steve Nolan has been chaplain at Princess Alice Hospice, Esher, since 2004. His areas of research and professional interest include non-religious spiritual care, including the relationship between spiritual care and psychotherapy and spiritual care in a secular environment. His books include *Spiritual Care at the End of Life: The Chaplain as a 'Hopeful Presence'* (Jessica Kingsley Publishers, 2012); *A–Z of Spirituality* (Palgrave, 2014, co-authored with Margaret Holloway) and *Spiritual Care in Practice: Case Studies in Healthcare Chaplaincy*

(Jessica Kingsley Publishers, 2015), a collection of chaplains' case studies co-edited with George Fitchett.

Michael Paterson is a health care chaplain, psychotherapist, theological educator and pastoral supervisor. Within NHS Scotland he is the lead trainer for values-based reflective practice and holds responsibility for the initial formation and continuing professional development of chaplains in health and social care.

Stephen Pattison is Professor of Religion, Ethics and Practice and HG Wood Professor of Theology at the University of Birmingham, where he directs the practice-based Doctor of Practical Theology programme. He also holds an honorary chair in medical humanities at Durham University. A former health care chaplain, his study of mental health chaplaincy was published as *Pastoral Care and Liberation Theology* (Cambridge University Press, 1994). Pattison has long-standing interests in practical theology, chaplaincy, spirituality, ethics and management. His most recent major publications are *Seeing Things; Deepening Relations with Visual Artefacts* (SCM Press, 2007) and *Saving Face: Enfacement, Shame, Theology* (Ashgate, 2013). He was co-researcher on a project that produced *Understanding Muslim Chaplaincy* (Ashgate, 2013) and is presently researching chaplaincy in ports while also working on the topics of waste and disgust. Pattison is the lay chair of the ethics committee of the United Kingdom Council for Counselling and Psychotherapy.

Peter Sedgwick has been an Anglican parish priest in East London and County Durham (1974–1979); taught theology at the universities of Birmingham (1979–1982) and Hull (1988–1994); been the Ecumenical Theological Consultant to the North East Churches (1982–1988); been national policy officer for the Church of England in criminal justice and mental health (1996–2004); and been Principal of St Michael's College, Llandaff, Wales (2004–2014), where he also taught theology at Cardiff University. In all of this he has interacted with chaplains, as lecturer, consultant or policy officer. He has written or edited about six books, and many articles on social ethics. He is now retired and lives on an estate in Cardiff where his wife is the Anglican parish priest. He is on the board of the William Temple Foundation and a member of the Anglican Roman Catholic International Commission (ARCIC III).

Victoria Slater is a practical theologian, researcher and Visiting Scholar at The Oxford Centre for Ecclesiology and Practical Theology. She has been involved with chaplaincy for 25 years as a health care chaplain and in chaplaincy research, education, training, consultancy and professional development. Recent research projects include the development of chaplaincy in community contexts and the

Church of England's involvement in chaplaincy. Her academic interests include the development and contribution of chaplaincy in contemporary society, and spiritual care, health, well-being and contemporary spirituality. She currently works part-time in the NHS for Macmillan in cancer care.

Chris Swift is Head of Chaplaincy Services in the Leeds Teaching Hospitals NHS Trust. Chris is a former President of the College of Health Care Chaplains and has taught on the Masters courses at Cardiff and Leeds. In 2014 he was seconded by NHS England to lead a project to establish new national guidance for the NHS in England. His 2009 title *Hospital Chaplaincy in the Twenty-first Century* was published in a second edition in 2014.

John Swinton is Professor in Practical Theology and Pastoral Care in the School of Divinity, Religious Studies and Philosophy at the University of Aberdeen. He has a background in mental health nursing and health care chaplaincy and has researched and published extensively within the areas of practical theology, mental health, spirituality and health, and the theology of disability. He is the Director of Aberdeen University's Centre for Spirituality, Health and Disability (http://www.abdn.ac.uk/sdhp/centre-for-spirituality-health-and-disability-182.php). His publications include: *Dementia: Living in the Memories of God* (Eerdmans/SCM Press, 2012); B.R. Brock and J. Swinton, *Disability in the Christian Tradition: A Reader* (eds) (Eerdmans, 2012); *Living Well and Dying Faithfully: Christian Practices for End-Of-Life Care* (Eerdmans, 2009;)edited text with Richard Payne); *Raging With Compassion: Pastoral Responses to the Problem of Evil* (Eerdmans, 2007); *Spirituality in Mental Health Care: Rediscovering a 'Forgotten' Dimension* (Jessica Kingsley Publishers 2001).

Andrew Todd is Director of the Cardiff Centre for Chaplaincy Studies (a partnership between Cardiff University and St Michael's College). Andrew has 20 years' experience of theological education. He is a practical theologian and ethnographer of religion and has led several funded research projects investigating chaplaincy and the issues it raises for religion and public life. Amongst other publications, he was editor of *Military Chaplaincy in Contention: Chaplains, Churches, and the Morality of Conflict*, published by Ashgate Press in 2013.

Andrew Totten was ordained in the Church of Ireland in 1990 and is currently Assistant Chaplain-General with the 1st (United Kingdom) Division. He has served as a chaplain during military operations in Bosnia, Kosovo (afterwards appointed MBE), Northern Ireland, Iraq, and Afghanistan. He was a contributor to *Military Chaplaincy in Contention: Chaplains, Churches, and the Morality of Conflict*, published by Ashgate in 2013.

Fraser Watts is Emeritus Reader in Theology and Science at the University of Cambridge, where he was Director of the Psychology and Religion Research Group. He is a former president of the British Psychological Society and of the International Society for Science and Religion. He has published extensively on psychology and religion and his recent books include *Evolution, Religion and Cognitive Science* (with L. Turner, Oxford University Press, 2014); *Head and Heart: Perspectives from Religion and Psychology* (with G. Dumbreck, Templeton Press, 2013); and *Spiritual Healing: Scientific and Religious Perspectives* (Cambridge University Press, 2011). He remains Research Director of the Cambridge Institute for Applied Psychology and Religion.

Linda Woodhead is Professor of Sociology of Religion in the Department of Politics, Philosophy and Religion at Lancaster University. She was Director of the £12m AHRC/ESRC Religion and Society Programme between 2007 and 2013, Chair of the Theology and Religious Studies REF 2014 sub-panel, and is a member of the ESRC Council. Her books include *Christianity: A Very Short Introduction* (2nd edition, Oxford University Press, 2014), *Prayer in Religion and Spirituality* (with Giuseppe Giordan, Brill, 2013), *Everyday Lived Islam in Europe* (with Nathal Dessing and Nadia Jeldtoft, Ashgate, 2013), *Religion and Change in Modern Britain* (with Rebecca Catto, Routledge, 2012), *A Sociology of Religious Emotion* (with Ole Riis, Oxford University Press, 2010), *Religions in the Modern World* (Routledge, 2009), *The Spiritual Revolution* (with Paul Heelas, Wiley, 2005). She is the co-founder and organiser of the Westminster Faith Debates and a regular commentator on religion on radio and television.

Foreword

Chaplaincy and the Future of Religion

Linda Woodhead

Imagine that Parliament and public opinion declared that Britain's current rather haphazard religious landscape was no longer 'fit for purpose' and should be re-engineered. A 'Future Religion' task force is set up. Expectations are raised. Objections are lodged and small protests are staged. Something more suitable for early 21st-century Britain must be designed. What will it look like?

The task force decides to start with an enquiry addressing the crucial question: what functions must religion serve in 21st-century Britain? Its answers fall into four categories.

First, and perhaps most obviously, it is decided that religion must serve people's spiritual needs. This covers many things: putting people in touch with the divine – with higher truth, beauty, power and goodness; supporting devotion; providing meaning and motivation; offering ways of coping with life's hard knocks by offering various forms of healing and restoration; offering inspiration and empowerment; enabling self-transcendence as well as self-anchoring and stabilisation. Given that human well-being consists not just in physical health and material wealth but also in 'meaningfulness', all these spiritual functions must be engineered into the new religious landscape.

Secondly, religion must continue to provide *communitas* – that sense of close community and common purpose which is especially important to those who are active members of religious groups. For some, like first-generation migrants, religion provides a home from home, offering everything from a network of social support to employment opportunities. The benefits of group belonging are also important to some members of longer-settled minority religions, as well as to ethnic-majority members of churches and other religious congregations. Whilst active membership and *communitas* will never be everyone's cup of tea, even very inclusive 'low demand' kinds of religion like irregular-attendance Anglicanism offer something special when people gather for special rituals like weddings or funerals, a Christmas service, or a service for a national figure. The Future Religion task force recognises this.

Thirdly, religion must function as an engine of altruism and a motor for social sentiment. No society can survive on the basis of individual self-interest alone, not even on the basis of care for one's own family. Even Adam Smith, who took an optimistic view of the way in which the market could coordinate individually self-interested motives, knew that 'moral sentiments' were needed – and wrote a book on the subject to complement his other volume on the wealth of nations. All religions, including Christianity, emphasise the importance of care for others, even to the point of heroic self-sacrifice. Although it can be objected that religion is not necessary for altruism, and that secular people are just as likely to do good, what counts isn't just the motivation to altruism, but the narratives, symbols, rituals and social support which support it, and the structuring of altruism by way of appropriate institutions. An individual may be filled with goodwill towards others, but without structured ways of acting in a coordinated, purposeful and accountable way, may have no effective outlet, so good intentions may turn to dust.

Finally, as Emile Durkheim and his more recent disciple Robert Bellah emphasise in the discussions of 'civil religion', religion allows societies and whole nations to hold up a higher vision of who they are and to reflect on their better selves. Sometimes this can be comforting, sometimes it can be powerful and prophetic – as when Archbishop Robert Runcie preached against triumphalism over the Falklands 'victory'. Events like coronations, state funerals, jubilees, national mourning rituals and so on continue to hold us together as a nation, as well as to entertain. The Future Religion task force thinks we still need civil religion, and wants to secure religion's role in the transmission of memories, the preservation of material and cultural heritage, and the support of civic values.

So much for the ends that religion must serve. To have a realistic chance of achieving them, the task force also has to be clear-sighted about the nature of the religio-cultural landscape within which it is working. Consideration of the existing research base helps it identify some salient features.

The group notes that although 'Christian' is still the largest self-identification in the country, the situation is rapidly changing, with every generation under 50 being more likely than the previous one to identify as having 'no religion'. Amongst young adults aged under 30, almost half now identify as having no religion, and if the trend continues 'no religion' will become the majority identity within these people's lifetimes (Woodhead 2014a, 2014b). This doesn't mean that most people are becoming non-believers: only about one in five identify as atheist. No, what people are rejecting in large numbers is 'religion', including established religious groups and leaders – but fewer are turning their backs on God or spirituality. Organised secularism is in as much trouble as organised religion (Woodhead 2014a, Woodhead and Catto 2012). Future Religion also notes that Britain is unusual in retaining established religion – the Church of England and the quasi-established Church of Scotland – despite the fact that minority religions account for nine per cent of the population and growing (according to the 2011 Census: Office for National Statistics 2012). Growth is particularly evident for Islam, with British Muslims having a youthful age profile and high birth rate, and being much more successful than Christians in transmitting faith from parent to child.

Finally, the task force is very aware of the new legal landscape for religion, in which the equal status of all religious identities – and some non-religious identities – is protected not just by human rights legislation but by the recent Equality Law and duties of non-discrimination.

Armed with this information about the 'fitness landscape' in which a new religious settlement has to be engineered, the group retreats to a remote northern hotel for a period of creative reflection. It gathers evidence from people with creative visions of religious futures, and it pays close attention to existing religious initiatives of a pioneering kind – to the religious 'outliers' who may provide the clues as to where a new paradigm is emerging.

To the surprise of some, including many church leaders, the Future England task force becomes more and more interested in chaplaincy. Indeed, when it publishes its initial recommendations, the chaplaincy model looms large. Closer inspection of the group's final report reveals why this was the case, and explains why it found in chaplaincy such an important clue to the future.

One of the first things that had caught the task force's attention was that when it came to the construction of new religious spaces, it was multi-faith spaces, quiet rooms and prayer rooms which proved to be the area of vitality, with many hundreds having emerged in recent decades (see Chapter 9 of this volume). The group was impressed not just by the novelty and variety of these spaces, but by the fact that they had emerged organically without direction by state or, in many cases, organised religion. They seemed to have come into being to meet genuine need and to be an initiative of civil society – often some combination of enthusiastic individuals and local organisations, both commercial and non-profit, ranging from shopping centres to airports to schools and universities. True, they were often rather ugly, relegated to some dingy corner next to the toilets, and a world away from the grandeur of ancient cathedrals and mosques. True too that their uses had not yet been properly investigated. But they seemed nevertheless to offer clues about how religion could develop in a positive relationship with diversity.

Chapels led to chaplaincy. Here the first thing that impressed the task force was the way in which chaplaincy was so enmeshed with society. It seemed to exist in a healthy partnership relationship with the institutions and parts of society to which it was related. This was very evident in the way it had developed in recent decades to become more reflective of Britain's changing religious and non-religious landscape. The group was surprised to find Muslim chaplains in ever greater numbers and positions of seniority (reflecting their increasing integration in society), as well as pagan chaplains, humanist chaplains, Hindu chaplains and many more. They liked the fact that some of these titles reflected the communities that the chaplains served as much as their own orientation. They also liked the way that chaplains often worked in teams, engaged with people across organisations, and consisted of lay and clerical workers, full-time and part-time. Reading some of the research on the topic, they noted how chaplaincy had become a space of religious reinvention and development in its own right – in prisons, for example, creating new forms of Islamic law which cross the boundaries of the traditional law schools (Gilliat-Ray et al. 2013). They also admired the way in which some large multifaith chaplaincies become educational and knowledge resources on which various professional groups – from mental health professionals to lawyers and prison governors – draw in their professional practice. They considered all this worth investing in and building upon.

Looking at the historical development of chaplaincy, the task force also appreciated its ability to grow and adapt to changing socio-political conditions. They understood its origins, its roots in established religion, and its entanglements with social privilege (Oxbridge, public schools, Parliament, the Law, etc.), as well as its links to the growth of the professions. They understood that it had been carried along with the post-war welfare state project, and been linked to centralised public and religious power (Swift 2009). But they also saw how quickly it had been able to adapt to the mixed economy of the 21st century in which private providers of welfare, education and other services had a growing role, in which public–private partnerships of various kinds were increasingly prominent, and in which more educated and entitled 'clients', 'customers, 'consumers' and 'citizens' (rather than patients, pupils, 'laity', 'sheep', or children of a clerical 'Father') expected more choice and responsiveness from 'service providers' than ever before.

The Future Religion task force liked this model of a more equal relationship between religious professionals and those whose lives they helped resource, and thought it should be central to the new paradigm of religion. They liked the teamworking model. They recognised that chaplaincy still had to fight for its position in some organisations and institutions, and was often underfunded. But they also noted a number of new institutions – including some secular ones – which considered chaplaincy important to their healthy functioning. They highlighted the fact that many new Academies were employing chaplains, for example, and that these chaplains were seen as serving the whole institution, from the head to the students and the cleaners. This 'holistic' aspect of chaplaincy, the chaplain's ability to be a connector in an increasingly differentiated and fragmented society – and across large institutions – was considered a major strength. Whilst chaplains might need to achieve appropriate professional standards in various settings, their ability not to be subsumed into professions and to retain their independence and critical voice was considered important. They could cross divides which others couldn't, view things whole, spot problems and moral failures, and act as bridging, bonding and integrating agents.

As for the equality and diversity agenda – well, chaplaincy seemed to have much to offer here as well. This was obvious when it took the form of a multifaith team. But it was also apparent when there was a single chaplain whose role was to serve the whole community for whom she was responsible, serving their 'spiritual needs' – a usefully inclusive concept (Sullivan 2014). It was appreciated that chaplains were themselves a diverse bunch – in terms of ethnicity, gender, sexuality and other markers. Some said chaplaincy attracted people that mainstream religion couldn't comfortably accommodate: this was felt to be a positive sign.

The task force also believed that chaplaincy had the potential to build robust forms of transparency and accountability, in a way which had so far eluded traditional forms of religion. The Church of England, for example, had dealt with both the equality agenda and the freedom of information agenda by fighting to be exempted.

All this meant that when it came to rebooting religion, the Future Religion group found in chaplaincy a 'stub' on which it was able to grow the kind of religion that Britain today really needed. It looked back at its initial checklist of functions, and found that chaplaincy scored rather well. Serving the spiritual needs of an increasingly diverse society – tick. Motivating and structuring altruism, connecting people, supporting relationships, dealing with troubled ones, building trust and social capital and acting as a moral and spiritual witness – tick. Providing *communitas*? The task force was less convinced that this would normally be chaplaincy's strength, but felt that this was in any case best left to existing – and new – religious groups to do in their own ways. Supporting civic virtues, memory and heritage? Again, not a primary function of chaplains, but one which was felt to be well covered by the great cathedrals and abbeys plus a host of new 'secular' ritual providers (they cited, for example, the popular poppy display at the Tower of London to mark the centenary of the First World War, and the ceremonies around the London Olympics and Glasgow Commonwealth Games).

But how was this new religious paradigm to be funded? Here the chair of Future Religion had a stroke of luck when she recruited William Hague and Angelina Jolie as project representatives. Somehow Angelina managed to persuade the men who ran the Church of England to restructure some of their current operations, and donate some of the Church's estimated £11 billion assets to the new religious settlement. The Church of Scotland followed suit. They were national churches after all, and could see that this was best for their communities. The other major faiths came on board too, with money and support. So did the humanists. All agreed to change their recruitment and training in order to adapt to the new model.

In the longer term, the task force saw that chaplaincy had to become largely self-financing, albeit with enough central support and coordination to mean that it served all parts of society, including the least privileged. Once people began to see that religion was now for *them* and the whole of society, rather than just for 'religious people', their attitudes began to change. It wasn't just that more organisations began to employ chaplains, but that more people were willing to make regular donations of money and help to chaplaincy, especially when they could see the good it was doing in their own institutions and communities (more like the model in many Scandinavian countries and Germany, though not using the tax system to deliver the money).

With hindsight many agreed that an important reason the Future Religion task force faced so little resistance was that it didn't recommend major cuts or closures. The British don't like throwing things away, they prefer to let them die quietly or take a new form. The group was quite happy to let religious groups continue to meet and do their own things, including worship and other congregational and community activities; it was in any case genuinely committed to religious freedom, including freedom of association and expression. Interestingly, the task force also decided not to abolish establishment, but to expand and extend it – as a vehicle for rolling out the new paradigm. Britain had never had a constitutional separation of state and religion, so why impose one now? Better to allow religion and state to work together in a constructive way for the good of everyone. So established religion became truly inclusive.

The Queen was happy, and so was Prince Charles – he would get to be what he had always dreamed of: Defender of Faiths. Privately, the task force was a little disappointed. It had hoped that he would accept their preferred title 'Defender of Religion or Belief', or even 'Defender of Spirituality'. But they decided not to push it.

References

Gilliat-Ray, S., M.M. Ali and S. Pattison (2013), *Understanding Muslim Chaplaincy*. Aldershot: Ashgate.

Office for National Statistics (2012), *2011 Census*. [Online]. Available from: www.ons.gov.uk/ons/rel/census/2011-census/key-statistics-for-local-authorities-in-england-and-wales/rpt-religion.html (accessed 31 August 2014).

Sullivan, W. (2014), *A Ministry of Presence: Chaplaincy, Spiritual Care and the Law*. Chicago: University of Chicago Press.

Swift, C. (2009), *Hospital Chaplaincy in the Twenty-first Century*. Aldershot: Ashgate.

Woodhead, L. (2014a), *'No Religion' is the New Religion*. Available at: http://faithdebates.org.uk/wp-content/uploads/2014/01/WFD-No-Religion.pdf (accessed 1 December 2014).

—— (2014b) *What British People Really Believe*. Special issue of *Modern Believing*, Vol. 55, No. 1, 2014.

Woodhead, L. and R. Catto (eds) (2012), *Religion and Change in Modern Britain*. London: Routledge.

Chapter 1

Introduction to Chaplaincy Studies

Mark Cobb, Chris Swift and Andrew Todd

The presence and place of chaplains in contemporary society is a phenomenon that persists without much systematic inquiry, explanation or understanding. Those who practise chaplaincy are rightly concerned with fulfilling their responsibilities and accomplishing their tasks, consequently praxis in the demanding contexts of chaplaincy can easily outweigh any scholarly activity. This unquestioned pull towards practice and the requirements of the profession means that the scholarship within chaplaincy is often in the form of applied studies from other disciplines, for example moral philosophy and its application to ethical dilemmas. Whilst this appropriated knowledge and understanding is valid and relevant it cannot be the totality unless chaplaincy is content with becoming the sum of a set of derived insights and skills. This is not to imply that chaplains themselves are uninterested in their own practice and learning; but this can often go no further than a narrative of experience. Describing and discerning a situation is a vital first step that can lead on to critical interpretation, but this needs to be brought into reflective deliberation with theory if a general knowledge of chaplaincy is to exist and develop. What this points to is the need for a disciplined endeavour of chaplaincy studies that this book attempts to illustrate in its various modes.

It is our contention that rigorous inquiry and the creative work of scholarship can contribute to the self-understanding of the profession and its ways of interpreting the needs and contexts of those it seeks to serve, the development and refinement of good practice, and the derivation of sound guiding principles, core knowledge and critical theory. Chaplains do this in part through their commitment to reflexive practice as they seek to reason what it is best to do and how to respond to the unique circumstances of certain individuals in particular places and specific situations. Chaplaincy studies builds on this phronesis (Walton 2014) and tacit knowledge by identifying or generating sources of knowledge that can be scrutinised and brought into critical dialogue in ways that enable knowledge to be shared, fresh insights gained and new explanations, concepts and theories proposed. It is this habitual curiosity that is the characteristic of chaplaincy studies, evident in the chapters contained in this book, which has the potential to sustain and enrich not only the community of praxis, but also our knowledge of human flourishing.

What is the Object of Study?

The core of this book consists of the critical reflections of a set of people who are designated as chaplains and who practise chaplaincy. This is the ontological and evidential basis for the study of chaplaincy: the people who think and act in ways associated with being a chaplain. It is the presence and practice of designated chaplains in communities and institutions that constitute a social reality which can be the subject of observation, inquiry and analysis. It will be clear from many of the chapters in this book that what constitutes the kin of chaplaincy is a diverse family, located across a range of contexts and institutions, occupying different structural positions and inhabiting various roles. This complexity represents the first challenge in the study of chaplaincy in terms of where to draw the boundaries of the field. It is evident that mapping the location of chaplains across the social terrain can provide an outline derived from the function of chaplains and the contexts in which they work. However, one of the distinctive characteristics of chaplains is that they also represent and manifest claims about the nature of reality that inform the way they interpret and respond to human experience, such as prayer and meditation. These are typically the beliefs and practices of religious communities where chaplains have developed their spiritual disciplines and pastoral practices. This represents the second challenge for the study of chaplaincy in that a purely functional approach is insufficient and needs pairing with a substantive approach that refers to the kind of metaphysical commitments or superempirical realities found in religions (Schilbrack 2014). By implication, some forms of inquiry will require a methodological strategy capable of dealing with objects and properties that are not directly observable but which may be inferred from experiences, beliefs and practices.

It will be evident that some studies of chaplaincy concentrate more on the functional than the substantive aspects of chaplaincy, but supporting a coherent field of study we propose a definition that incorporates both elements. A definition is a useful but provisional statement that explains a phenomenon to support a common understanding. In terms of the aims of this book a definition of chaplaincy is useful to distinguish the object of chaplaincy studies from objects that might be regarded as similar, such as religious studies; it is provisional in that a definition is always open to being replaced by alternatives that perform the same function better. Here then is our definition of chaplaincy that is intended to apply across all sectors:

> Chaplaincy is a practice of care involving the intentional recognition and articulation of the sacred by nominated individuals authorised for this task in secular situations.

Chaplaincy is a practical discipline in the same way that psychiatry or the practice of the law is a practical discipline based upon a body of knowledge and involving skilled actions, reasoning and judgements about a set of particular circumstances with a degree of uncertainty. In the case of chaplaincy the practice is intended to be conscientiously caring and supportive of the particular interests of those cared for. The practice of care is relational and depends upon the capacity to understand the needs of those being cared for and accepting a responsibility for meeting some or all of those needs. Care-giving and caring relationships therefore involve personal and social ethics that are necessary for people and societies to flourish (Held 2006). The following is an example from the National Association of Chaplains to the Police that illustrates the context-specific practice of care that is offered:

> Working in today's police service is increasingly challenging. More than ever, members of the police service need to be able to keep things in perspective. Police chaplains recognise that much of police work, by its very nature, is stressful and dehumanising. We understand that everybody is a complete person – body mind & spirit – and care for them in this holistic way. We also care for the organisation, acting as critical friends within the decision making processes. (NACP 2014)

Care to individuals and organisations is provided by many different professional groups trained in distinctive paradigms and practices of care. We argue that the distinctiveness of chaplaincy is found in its attentiveness to the sacred, a term that itself could easily be the subject of a whole book. The adoption of the term sacred is a carefully chosen signifier of those fundamental qualities of life that go beyond the material and mundane by which people orientate and make sense of their lives. The sacred can be expressed in all aspects of human thought and behaviour including beliefs, values and practices, and in artefacts, symbols, places and environments. Critically in relation to our definition, it is an object that, as Lynch argues, ' ... is regarded as a grounding or ultimate source of power, identity, meaning and truth' (Lynch 2007: 138). In other words, and to follow Lynch further, the sacred is ' ... what people take to be absolute, normative realities that exert claims on the conduct of social life'(Lynch 2012: 5). An example of the sacred is life itself which has normative significance for most people in terms of absolute meaning and value. This finds its expression in the principle of the sanctity of life and the moral inhibitions this raises about intentional killing that may have a religious and non-religious basis. This term therefore admits a wide range of forms including but not limited to those mediated through religious traditions and practices. Consequently the term sanctity has a strong utility for the practice of chaplains because of the gamut of religions they are associated with and the diversity of people that they serve, including those with non-theistic, humanistic and atheistic beliefs and practices.

Chaplains have a unique licence within an organisation or institution to deal with the sacred, to handle sacred symbols and narratives, celebrate and express its manifestations, operate within sacred spaces, and deal with the consequences of disruptions to and violations against what is held to be sacred. This places chaplains in situations at the intersections of worldly and transcendent realities that they must negotiate with extreme care and absolute trust. As with any distinctive role, and in particular ones that deal with powerful values and meanings, chaplains are clearly designated and authorised for this task so that they cannot be confused with those who share a similar interest in promoting human welfare and flourishing. This raises interesting questions for chaplaincy studies about how chaplains are identified and authorised in distinction to, say, counsellors or visiting ministers of religion.

This leads us to the final distinguishing term of our definition that locates chaplains in secular situations. This is most evident from the binomial nomenclature of chaplaincy, for example airport chaplaincy and street chaplains, and is indicative of a practice that operates at the intersection of the sacred and the profane. Chaplaincy is largely at the service of institutions and organisations that are secular and pursue aims that are not contingent upon exclusively religious or non-religious worldviews, such as justice or health. Secularity here goes beyond simple neutrality and implies both a freedom of conscience to hold different beliefs and a mutual respect and equality between people regardless of their sacred orientations. It is this socio-political context that is a feature of most public domains and institutions in which chaplaincy operates, where it has been argued that:

> Secularity promises an arena which is neutral, and at any rate plural and inclusive of all members of the political community: those who believe, those who do not, those who have not made up their minds, and those who are not interested in the discussion. (Jiménez Lobeira 2014: 397–8)

Why Study Chaplaincy?

Whatever the self-interests and curiosity of chaplains in reflecting on their roles and developing their knowledge and understanding, chaplaincy also reflects something about the way society and particular organisations deal with sacred meanings, identities and truths. In simple terms there is an internal motivation to understand the profession and practice of chaplains and an external motivation about the ways in which society and the state authorise and respond to the sacred through chaplaincy. There is an interest therefore both in the 'black box' of chaplaincy and in the relation of chaplains to the wider community and society. However, before such aspirations can be realised we have to acknowledge that chaplaincy studies is a relatively undeveloped field of enquiry. This is evident when we question the reliability and accuracy of the empirical maps of the chaplaincy landscape and realise that there remain many gaps and incomplete features. For example, there are no comprehensive national inventories of chaplaincies, the concrete and symbolic forms they take, how they represent themselves and are identified, what their organising principles and structures consist of, and how they behave and practise. A recent research report, commissioned by the Church of England, for instance, included an objective to map its current involvement in chaplaincy through the analysis of extant data. The researchers reported that:

> It is a significant challenge for researchers to find accurate, reliable quantitative data about the number and type of chaplaincy roles that exist, the number of people in chaplaincy ministry, the amount of time spent in chaplaincy ministry and how that ministry is resourced. There are two main reasons for this. The first reason is that there is no conceptual clarity about what constitutes chaplaincy. For example, people may use the term 'chaplaincy' as a familiar term of convenience for any ministerial role that takes place in a non-church context without there being a clear understanding of what makes the role a chaplaincy. The second reason is that no accurate diocesan or central Church of England statistics are kept for chaplaincy. This fact says something in itself. (Todd et al. 2014: 14)

A report by the think tank *Theos* in partnership with the Cardiff Centre for Chaplaincy Studies attempts to overcome some of these limitations by mapping the range of chaplaincy provision in one UK geographical location where it finds 169 chaplains serving in the town of Luton (Ryan 2015). However, it is safe to say that the basic empirical map of chaplaincy remains largely incomplete, and in some areas either speculative or not charted at all. This may be a particular challenge for chaplaincies without any associational representation or in settings where they remain largely out of site for either strategic or numerical reasons. Mapping the territory theoretically appears to be in no better state and there is a similar lack of definition in terms of explanatory and conceptual features and landmarks. Sociological and cultural approaches to chaplaincy studies probably lead the way in this venture, exemplified by two recent publication from the United States: Wendy Cadge's study of hospital chaplains, *Paging God: Religion in the Halls of Medicine* (Cadge 2012), and Winnifred Fallers Sullivan's examination of chaplaincy as a product of religion and the law in *A Ministry of Presence: Chaplaincy, Spiritual Care, and the Law* (Sullivan 2014). Both offer critical and extensive engagements with chaplaincy from a particular disciplinary perspective and are rare but welcome examples of the limited scholarly activity in this field. In the UK there are two notable publications that have attempted to expound on the practice and nature of chaplaincy across different sectors (Legood 1999, Threlfall-Holmes and Newitt 2011), and in addition there have been studies about particular sectors, such as hospital chaplaincy (Orchard 2000, Swift 2014), or particular faiths (Gilliat-Ray et al 2013).

We are not aware of any professional or scholarly attempt to develop a comprehensive agenda for chaplaincy studies including what key questions it should seek to address and by what means, and what scope of enquiry it should encompass. The authors represented in this book provide some of the pieces of this mosaic but clearly there remains much foundational work to be completed before any systematic attempt at assembling the whole can be considered. We suggest, therefore, that the state of chaplaincy studies is an early developmental state and requires greater focus and better linkages if it is to achieve greater traction in the professional and scholarly communities. The goal of chaplaincy studies is perhaps clearer: the creation of new knowledge and the generation of new theories and understandings about chaplaincy phenomena with the intention of making a distinct and valuable contribution to the practice of chaplaincy, the academy and society. To achieve this aim chaplaincy studies will need to draw upon a range of established disciplinary knowledge, methods and expertise such as theology, sociology, psychology and philosophy. This will result in both unidisciplinary studies (an example of which would be the history of theatre chaplains) and multidisciplinary or interdisciplinary studies that address complex topics (an example of which would be understanding the impact of chaplaincy in care homes). This is why we use the plural form of 'studies' to indicate the breadth of scholarship and disciplinary approaches that can be applied to chaplaincy inquiries.

The Layout of the Book

The first section of the book explores the wider social, political and academic contexts within which the study of chaplaincy is necessarily situated. Stephen Pattison opens this section with a perceptive and informed discussion about what he sees as the rise of chaplaincy as religion has faded, and he reflects on why this might be so. Pattison draws upon the work of Lynch, as we have done, to explain how chaplaincy has embraced contemporary social sacralities as religion seems to have abandoned them. However, he ends with a warning that can be seen as something of a challenge to the goal of chaplaincy studies as we understand it, that the more we understand and explain chaplaincy the less plausible and vital it might become. Alan Billings takes a look at chaplaincy in relation to public life in Chapter 3. He begins by considering some of the changes to the place of religion in society and the public sector over time that have presented challenges to chaplaincy in the recent past and will continue to do so in the foreseeable future. Billings then develops a case for chaplaincy in terms of the value that it adds, which he argues is derived from its distinctive understanding of the complex needs of people, its availability to all, and its context-specific contribution to each sector that it operates within. However, he also recognises the ongoing challenge to chaplains of maintaining their integrity, pastoral focus and prophetic voice when operating at the interface of the state, faith communities and the individual needs of those they serve.

How to study chaplaincy is the subject of Chapter 4. Wilf McSherry and Peter Kevern scrutinise chaplaincy from four perspectives: as representative of a religious tradition; as serving institutional values and ends; as therapy for the individual client; and as a reflective and reflexive activity. This helps them to identify some of the significant gaps in the materials and methods of chaplaincy studies and the under-representation in the research of both the voice of those that chaplains care for and the voice of chaplains themselves as researchers. In Chapter 5 Victoria Slater considers the dissonance between the dominant positivist scientific approach of evidence-based practice manifest in many secular institutions and what she describes as the interpretive relational approach characteristic of chaplaincy. She aims to resolve this tension through developing an approach to practice-based evidence in chaplaincy which is a form of qualitative inquiry that she considers can be integral to practice, particularly in the form of case studies.

The second section of the book turns its attention to some of the prominent themes and topics in chaplaincy studies that practitioners and scholars of chaplaincy have to navigate and understand. In Chapter 6 Frank Cranmer sets out the legal basis for the main sectors of chaplaincy considered in this book. He then proceeds to consider questions of a more general nature including whether chaplains are employees or office holders, the extent to which a confidential conversation with a chaplain may be regarded as privileged by the law and the application of Article 9 (Freedom of thought, conscience and religion) in the European Convention on Human Rights to chaplaincy. Peter Sedgwick, in Chapter 7, describes what he considers to be the distinctive ethical demands made of chaplains and why these arise as a result of the religious communities that chaplains belong to and the secular institutions in which they work. The critical ethical question he seeks to address is what makes a good chaplain and he explores how dichotomous demands can be held together with ethical integrity.

The consequences of religious diversity for chaplaincy and the questions this raises about equality and fairness are addressed by Sophie Gilliat-Ray and Mohammed Arshad in Chapter 8. They consider the nature and challenges of multifaith chaplaincy and describe how research has responded to this changing context, which they illustrate with examples of Muslim involvement in multifaith chaplaincy and the emerging field of Islamic pastoral theology. Another illustration of this theme is taken up by Chris Hewson and Andrew Crompton who, in Chapter 9, discuss the challenges of creating and managing sacred spaces. This leads to a reflection on the operation of multifaith chaplaincy and the ways in which secular and religious interests have to be negotiated and managed in tandem. Despite some evident difficulties, what they observe is something of an experiment under way due to the freedoms and entrepreneurship that some chaplains embrace.

The consequences of psychology for chaplaincy are the subject that Fraser Watts addresses in Chapter 10, in which he compares the psychological and spiritual perspectives on the human person when dealing with pastoral and emotional problems. He explains why it is unhelpful to abandon the distinction between the spiritual and psychological as some advocate, and instead recognises the value of different discourses when addressing multifaceted problems such as depression. Finally in this section, Michael Paterson in Chapter 11 turns to the question of how chaplains can maintain their professional and vocational commitment to care in the face of the personal demands it makes of them. He examines the role and practice of supervision in support of the caring professions, from which he advances a distinctive model that he describes as a form of courageous conversation that, importantly, recognises the indissoluble bond between the ontology and epistemology of the chaplain, a conversation that at its best is restorative. Paterson wonders why it is acceptable for some chaplains to practise without deliberately reflecting with another on the meaning and purpose of their work, and he contends that supervision ultimately is a spiritual practice in its own right.

Chaplaincy is a practice, and the study of chaplaincy cannot progress without attending to the specificity of practice, which we do through four sections that address particular sectors of chaplaincy, namely health care, the armed forces, prisons and education. These all represent contexts where significant numbers of chaplains practise and where there are objects of scholarly activity that we can engage with. Inevitably, although we consider these to be exemplars of the diverse contexts of chaplaincy, it is also a limitation of this book, in that we have not attempted a comprehensive representation of the many other sectors. Each of these four sections follows the same pattern: a critical description and interpretation of the current practice of chaplaincy; an examination of the context-specific issues and challenges facing chaplaincy; and an in-depth case study and reflection derived from the experience of a particular chaplain. Together these chapters provide a rich description and analysis of chaplaincy as it operates in major spheres of the public domain.

We conclude the book by reflecting on the expansive discourse of chaplaincy studies evident in the contributions to this volume, and we go on to consider how chaplaincy studies can be developed. We propose building upon the foundational disciplines of practical theology and ethics by expanding the range of methodological approaches and theoretical frameworks in support of the interdisciplinary study of the complex phenomenon of chaplaincy. We contend that by building this enhanced environment chaplaincy will be better understood, the reflective practice of chaplains more robust and informed, and the dialogue between the public and chaplaincy more engaging.

References

Cadge, W.A. (2012), *Paging God: Religion in the Halls of Medicine*. Chicago, London: The University of Chicago Press.

Gilliat-Ray, S., Pattison, S. & Ali, M. (2013), *Understanding Muslim Chaplaincy*. Farnham, England: Ashgate.

Held, V. (2006), *The Ethics of Care: Personal, Political, and Global*. New York, Oxford: Oxford University Press.

Jiménez Lobeira, P.C. (2014), Veils, crucifixes and the public sphere: what kind of secularism? Rethinking neutrality in a post-secular Europe. *Journal of Intercultural Studies*, 35, 385–402.

Legood, G. (1999), *Chaplaincy: The Church's Sector Ministries*. London, Cassell.

Lynch, G. (2007), What is this 'Religion' in the Study of Religion and Popular Culture? In Lynch, G. (ed.), *Between Sacred and Profane: Researching Religion and Popular Culture*. London: I.B. Tauris.

—— (2012). *The Sacred in the Modern World: A Cultural Sociological Approach*. Oxford: Oxford University Press.

NACP (2014), *National Association of Chaplains to the Police*. [Online]. Available at: http://www.police-chaplains.org.uk (accessed 29 November 2014).

Orchard, H. C. (2000), *Hospital Chaplaincy: Modern, Dependable?* Sheffield: Sheffield Academic Press.

Ryan, B. (2015), *A Very Modern Ministry: Chaplaincy in the UK*. London: Theos. Available at: http://www.theosthinktank.co.uk/files/files/Modern%20Ministry%20combined.pdf (accessed 5 April 2015)

Schilbrack, K. (2014), *Philosophy and the Study of Religions: A Manifesto*. Chichester: Wiley Blackwell.

Sullivan, W.F. (2014), *A Ministry of Presence: Chaplaincy, Spiritual Care, and the Law*. Chicago: University of Chicago Press.

Swift, C. (2014), *Hospital Chaplaincy in the Twenty-First Century: The Crisis of Spiritual Care in the Nhs*. Farnham, England: Ashgate.

Threlfall-Holmes, M. and Newitt, M. (2011), *Being a Chaplain*. London: SPCK.

Todd, A., Slater, V. and Dunlop, S. (2014), *The Church of England's Involvement in Chaplaincy*. Cardiff: The Cardiff Centre for Chaplaincy Studies; Oxford: The Oxford Centre for Ecclesiology and Practical Theology, Cuddesdon.

Walton, H. (2014), Seeking Wisdom in practical theology: phronesis, poetics and everyday life. *Practical Theology*, 7(1), 5–18.

PART I
Chaplaincy in Context

Chapter 2

Situating Chaplaincy in the United Kingdom: The Acceptable Face of 'Religion'?

Stephen Pattison

Introduction

While traditional organised religious groups like the Church of England have declined in terms of size, influence and general acceptance in the UK over the last 50 years, paradoxically, chaplaincy has grown in all these aspects. Here I will give some account of the changes that have taken place and then speculate on some of the factors that may have led to the apparently inexorable rise and increasing plausibility of chaplaincy. The traditional churches have resiled from religious presence based on Christendom-like notions of broad inclusion of the whole population and low-key pastoral presence and care in favour of a stance based on clear commitment, active membership and mission. However, this kind of inclusive religiosity has been continued and developed in chaplaincy (Pattison 2008). Chaplaincy might therefore be seen as a 'new religion' which people join and which has its own norms and practices. Or perhaps it might more properly be regarded as a distinct but continuing acceptable face of traditional, established organised religion which embraces and affirms contemporary notions of the common sacred abandoned by the churches.

My interest here lies mainly in trying to stimulate discussion as to what the vague, inchoate entity 'chaplaincy' is and has become, not in particular kinds of chaplaincy or chaplaincy practices. I make extensive reference to the sectors of chaplaincy I know best – those funded in the public arena largely in the English context.

I proceed by briefly considering the changes in the established churches, particularly the Church of England, that have led to their loss of influence and acceptability. I contrast this with the rise of chaplaincy. I then examine some factors that might contribute to the success of chaplaincy, before concluding that it may be the positioning of chaplaincy as a marginal symbolic resource that makes it an acceptable and distinctive religious expression.

The Decline of the Traditional Church and the Rise of Chaplaincy

Organised religion in the contemporary world has become toxic in public perception (Woodhead 2012b). The last decade has not been encouraging for most historic Christian churches (Woodhead and Catto 2012). Attendances at services and membership have continued to decline and overt belief in God appears to be on the wane (Woodhead 2012a: 5). Religious education is losing status in schools, and critics like Richard Dawkins and Philip Pullman seem to have the popular educated ear. There is discontent with the stance of the unelected bishops representing the established Church of England in Parliament for opposing the legalisation of euthanasia which would prevent unnecessary suffering, and for refusing to implement human rights legislation on employment in the church. Calls for disestablishment and a downsizing of ecclesiastical rights and influence are increasingly common.

This general sense of decline and discontent was exacerbated when, in 2012, the Church of England's General Synod failed to approve female episcopal ordination, to widespread anger from politicians and the public (whether churchgoers or not). In 2013 the Church of England used its public profile and episcopal power to oppose the Marriage (Same Sex Couples) Act. Incidents like these confirmed a general perception that the Church of England was no longer aligned with what the general public holds sacred. The Church was perceived as failing to be an adequate mirror of the soul of the nation; indeed it is seen now as an organisation that desecrates the common sense of what is good and right. It has joined its smaller counterparts as a partisan, sectarian interest group of volunteers with no more entitlement to a place in public affairs than any other.

This caricature of decline, marginalisation and disillusion with organised religion stands in marked contrast to the growth and flourishing of chaplaincy, including in public organisations. As churches have turned inwards to their own distinctive sacralities and certainties, chaplaincy turns outward to embrace the world and the public sacralities of civic decency.

Chaplaincy is a Christian institution with its roots firmly in establishment and in Christendom. An authoritative dictionary contains the following article written in the 1950s:

> Chaplain. Originally a priest or minister who has the charge of a chapel. He is ordinarily a cleric who performs non-parochial duties. Chaplains are often appointed to monarchs, to bishops and other high ecclesiastical dignitaries, and to noblemen; they are also appointed to serve in various institutions such as schools, colleges, prisons, workhouses, cemeteries, and at embassies, legations, and consulates abroad. (Cross 1958: 264)

A chapel, too, was a distinctively Christian institution, originally a place for keeping relics. Chaplaincy's origins, then, lie in the provision of convenient clerical, sacramental, religious and other services to those who do not wish to, or cannot, participate in parochial church life, often in restricted settings (Gibson 1997). With this origin, one might expect that, by now, chaplaincy would have declined like established Christianity. However, recently chaplaincy has expanded, diversified and flourished, even as its progenitor religious tradition has declined.

How is it, then, that a phenomenon with such a very specific background in one religion has avoided the opprobrium experienced by that religion? How has it become more pervasive, even to the extent of becoming a desired vehicle for non-Christian religions that know nothing of chapels, aristocratic patronage, or consulates?

Chaplaincy has acquired a kind of protective cloak that has allowed it to escape, slipping outside traditional Christianity and a narrow range of institutions and activities to become acceptable to many groups in different situations. A growing rhetoric of professionalisation and accountability within certain conventional kinds of chaplaincy itself (e.g., in traditional public institutions like hospitals) implies increasing specialisation, expertise, competence, accountability and hierarchical structure (UK Board of Healthcare Chaplaincy 2009). However, it seems that the words 'chaplain' and 'chaplaincy' have also been released from beneath the carapace of professional restriction to become a loosely designated role allowing all manner of people with a sense of concern, married with variable competence and intense commitment, to enter highly restricted arenas. What is it about the nature of this activity and concept that has enabled it to prosper, gaining widespread legitimacy, in what looks, prima facie, like an increasingly suspicious, hostile environment? How has it escaped the toxic miasma surrounding formal religious structures generally?

Soon, I will speculate on the factors that may have helped chaplaincy to prosper and grow. But first, a little about the rise of chaplaincy in general terms. This is a difficult thing to describe with any degree of specificity; chaplaincy work is often not well documented within, or across, sectors.

The Inexorable Rise of Chaplaincy

Cross (1958) provides a recognisable, accurate picture of chaplaincy 50 years ago. Chaplains then were almost invariably Christian, mostly ordained in the established church (therefore male), and also people who earned their living from being professional clergy (there were no officially self-supporting clergy, though some were probably teachers or academics, and some chaplains were retired clergy; (Russell 1980, Todd 2011)). While some chaplaincy appointments were honorific with minimal duties, e.g., High Sheriff's chaplain, thus combinable with another full-time clerical appointment, there were a small number of full-time and part-time chaplaincy posts in a narrow range of institutions such as hospitals, schools, prisons, colleges, the armed forces and universities. In these institutions, the actual physical chapel (often mainly used by majority established churches) with its rota of services was central to chaplains' work.

In the context of a country with an established church which aimed to offer care and religious services to everyone in the land, the existence of professional Christian chaplains in institutions would have seemed unproblematic, an extension of the parochial system (Ballard 2004, Threlfall-Holmes 2011a: 121). However, even then, more provision was beginning to be made for members of non-established churches, e.g., Methodists, Catholics, often using numbers of adherents as a measure of the amount of provision to be sought. Christianity was, however, the norm for chaplaincy provision.

Since the 1950s, chaplaincy has changed greatly. The number of chaplains has grown in many sectors (Orchard 2000, Threlfall-Holmes and Newitt 2011: xiv). Police chaplains, for example, have grown in number from 80 in 2000 to 650 in 2013, according to the coordinator of the National Association of Chaplains to the Police. The types of institutions and contexts in which chaplaincy is exercised has expanded. GP surgeries, agriculture, airports, fire stations, sports clubs, race courses, shopping centres, entertainment arenas, factories and building sites are but a few of the new places in which chaplaincy is offered; the range is increasing constantly (Heskins and Baker 2006, Legood 1999, Threlfall-Holmes and Newitt 2011: xiv).[1] Chaplains have diversified, many are lay and women (lay or ordained); furthermore, many people work as chaplaincy volunteers (Orchard 2001a). Perhaps most significantly, chaplains now come from many different non-Christian religious traditions – it is difficult to imagine entitling a book on chaplaincy 'the church's sector ministries' (Legood 1999, Gilliat-Ray 2001, Todd 2011). It is estimated, for example, that there are about 450 Muslim chaplains across a variety of contexts and institutions in the UK now; there were none in 1990 (Gilliat-Ray et al. 2013: xvii). Jews, Buddhists, Hindus, Sikhs and other religions are catered for by co-religionist chaplains, some of whom are paid full- or (more usually) part-time; there is a network for Humanist chaplaincy which removes chaplaincy from the realm of conventional religious belief and practice altogether (Humanist Chaplaincy Network 2013). Increasingly, chaplaincy is becoming a professionalised, theorised activity with chaplaincy courses springing

---

[1]   It is very difficult to get a clear notion of numbers of chaplains across all sectors as they constantly fluctuate and not all sectors keep detailed statistics, particularly outwith public institutions and in relation to volunteers. Paid chaplains may be in decline; e.g., in the health sector there may have been a decline of provision of some 8% recently (http://www.bbc.co.uk/news/uk-england-23011620, accessed 5 August 2013). However, the point that chaplains and chaplaincy have expanded since the 1960s still stands.

up at, inter alia, Leeds Metropolitan, Cardiff, Glasgow, Gloucestershire and York St John universities.

Chaplains visit institutions, befriend people, offer care and social support to individuals, provide counselling, organise rituals and services, meet religious and spiritual needs in various ways, provide information and resources about religion, deal with crises, help people and groups with ethical dilemmas, and educate and train, amongst many other things (Cope and West 2011, Gilliat-Ray et al. 2013, Mowat and Swinton 2007, Newitt 2011, Swift 2009, Todd 2013).

So diverse and varied are the types, practices, contexts and practitioners of chaplaincy now that it is difficult to characterise what they have in common. A 1990 US dictionary entry reads:

> Chaplain refers to a clergyperson or layperson ... commissioned by a faith group or organisation to provide pastoral services in an institution, organisation, or governmental entity. Chaplaincy refers to the general activity performed by a chaplain, which may include crisis ministry, counselling, sacraments, worship, education, help in ethical decision-making, staff support, clergy contact and community or church co-ordination. (Hunter 1990: 136)

This captures much of what chaplains do, but nowadays it is not clear that chaplaincy is as limited and formal as this in the UK. Chaplains are often not commissioned formally by faith groups and organisations, they may have little training or formal recognition, and they may work outside organisations and governmental entities. Chaplaincy has 'gone virtual', often having uncertain, indeterminate links with formal institutions and processes, especially when voluntarily undertaken. It might now be loosely understood to be

> the intentional provision of religious, spiritual and pastoral services to, and in the context of, institutions and circumstances that are not understood primarily to be concerned with religion, the spiritual or the pastoral.

Even this understanding is probably too specific – humanist chaplains might not recognise the need to provide religious, spiritual and pastoral services, though they would be interested in providing personal support, friendship and care in the context of existential issues (Humanist Chaplaincy Network 2013). Chaplaincy seems to have become an overall institution in itself rather than being an expression of particular faith traditions or organisations.

In an increasingly rational-instrumental, managed world in which many organisations are trying to be clear and explicit about what they do and what is expected of workers, the rise of this increasingly diffuse and indefinable activity, chaplaincy, is difficult to understand (Pattison 2007: 90–109). Why are often unskilled, but willing, sympathetic volunteers working under the aegis of chaplaincy accepted in highly professional environments like hospitals and fire stations when other members of the public without religious or ideological 'baggage' are excluded? How is it that clergy and lay people can be hired with public money to undertake primary care or community health chaplaincy when they may know little about primary care? It seems that there is something inherent in the notion and practice of chaplaincy that makes it acceptable and plausible within many contexts, including those that seem, prima facie, to have little to do with formal, organised religion.

What Makes 'Chaplaincy' Plausible and Attractive?

I want speculatively to suggest that there may be a number of factors that have contributed to the increasing plausibility and attractiveness of chaplaincy.

Chaplaincy Embodies the New Religious Sacralities of Society

When Muslims and other non-Christians first encountered the notion of chaplaincy in British institutions they found it strange (Gilliat-Ray et al. 2013). While many religions have traditions of care, support and guidance, outside Christianity there is often no tradition of formal, professional, paid or institutional ministry in secular contexts. Eventually, these non-Christian traditions adopted the designation 'chaplaincy' for their work, arguing that while the concept may not be well understood in their own communities, it is a well-understood and well-designated space in the public sphere.

This provides a clue to one of the main reasons for the rise and plausibility of chaplaincy as a concept and practice. This is that entering into the world of chaplaincy is entering a space that has come to transcend specific religions. In some ways, chaplaincy seems to have become a new umbrella religion to which members of specific religious communities are and have to be converted. However, it might be more accurate to characterise it less as a 'religion' and more as a 'third space' which embodies and commends many of the sacralities of contemporary society (cf. Swift 2009: 160–65).[2]

From research undertaken across a range of Muslim chaplaincies, it is possible to see what the constituents of the new, acceptable 'religion' or 'third space' are, but first a few words on changing sacralities and sacred forms in society (Gilliat-Ray et al. 2013).

---

[2]   'Religion' is a contested concept and its relationship to other forms of social organisation and to spirituality is complex. In many ways, we no longer have a good typology for talking about religion-like and 'spiritual' spaces. See further, e.g., Lynch (2007a, b), Pattison (2013).

Lynch, following Durkheim, suggests the following definition:

> The sacred is defined by what people collectively experience as absolute, non-contingent realities which present normative claims over the meanings and conduct of social life. Sacred forms are specific, historically contingent, instances of the sacred. Sacred forms are constituted by constellations of specific symbols, thought/discourse, emotions and actions grounded in the body. These constellations of embodied thought, feeling and action recursively reproduce the sacrality of the sacred form and constitute groups who share these discourses, sentiments and practices. The normative reality represented by a sacred form simultaneously constructs the evil which might profane it, and the pollution of this reality is experienced by its adherents as a painful wound for which some form of restitution is necessary. (Lynch 2012: 29)

Sacralities are transient, they change, and they can co-exist with each other. Sacred forms transmute over time, culture and context. Even within cultures, new sacred forms can arise that groups feel to be objectively real and compelling. Importantly, sacralities and sacred forms do not necessarily coincide with formal religions. Many social institutions can be guardians and promoters of the sacred. And in a post-secular world, where divisions between sacred and secular are increasingly recognised to be arbitrary, blurred and contestable, it can be difficult in the public sphere to identify where sacred forms are institutionally located (Graham 2013).

In this context, the infringement of ultimate values can seem like desecration which causes a wound or offence requiring restitution. Lynch (2012: 54–86) provides the case study of the Irish Catholic church's initial response to child abuse by clergy, arguing that the sacredness of the child had come to be more important by the 2000s than the earlier notion of Ireland as a sacred Catholic nation supported and embodied by the church. Its leaders failed to respond adequately to public outrage about clerical abuse; they were defending and exemplifying an alternative sacrality to that which now prevailed in 'secular' society and so appeared to outsiders to be doing or condoning evil.

I suggested at the opening of this chapter that established churches, in particular the Church of England, have gradually lost touch with some of the central sacralities of British society. In opposing gay marriage, the ordination of women, and euthanasia, the Church was seen by many to be desecrating some central sacred forms. These include the equal value of different types of sexual orientation, absolute equality of men and women, the value of individual choice in maintaining or disposing of a life riven by suffering, and the virtues of inclusion and choice. The anger felt towards the Church was a sign that this desecration (not merely offence or tasteless indiscretion) had taken place. This was probably exacerbated by the residual perception that the established church should be the guardian of the sacred in society, not its antithesis. The Church as an agent of desecration came under pressure to amend its ways.

To return to chaplaincy, when Muslims entered a variety of contexts such as hospitals, prisons and universities, structured by Christian and secular sacralities like respect for individuals and individual choice, inclusion of all, and valuing of diversity, they voluntarily, but quickly, changed some of their ways of thinking and acting (Gilliat-Ray et al. 2013). These changes reveal the kinds of norms and sacralities that chaplaincy embraces and thus reveal what sort of 'religion' or religious movement it might be.

Like Christianity, Islam is a proselytising, conversionist religious tradition; its way of life is largely structured by obedience to internal religious laws and customs. The Muslim community has no central obligation to look outside itself to non-Islamic society, nor to minister to secular institutions or to non-Muslims. In theory, then, Muslim chaplains, many of them Islamic scholars, lacking any internal religious tradition of professional chaplaincy or pastoral care, might have adopted an attitude of simply visiting members of their own communities, helping with their overtly religious needs if required, and telling them directly what needed to be done to be religiously observant and obedient in particular situations.

Instead, there is evidence that they often willingly adopted new values from the socio-religious context in which they worked (Gilliat-Ray et al. 2013). They not only valued their familiar religious tradition and scholarship, they came to value and learn from practical contemporary human experience. Rather than instructing people based on religious teaching, as an imam might in a mosque, they learned to listen to individual people and began to highly value non-directive, person-centred counselling and pastoral skills and attitudes. Thus, being non-judgemental and respectful of individuals' decisions and wishes was an important value, even if those individuals had lapsed or fallen foul of religious orthodoxy. Many chaplains came to believe they should work with people of all faiths and none in institutions, and to visit strangers and non-Muslims if that were helpful. Furthermore, chaplains valued working with colleagues from other religions; they felt honoured when adherents of other religious groups used them. They became adherents of the values of promoting equality and diversity, recognising that it was inappropriate to proselytise people in restricted situations. Some chaplains were even willing to engage in inter-faith worship and other controversial activities such as shaking hands with members of the opposite sex to make it clear that they and their faith tradition were not exclusive or stand-offish. Muslim chaplains also warmed to becoming professionally competent and training to become better at the job. There was a move from 'what I need to know' (as a representative of Islam) to 'who I need to be' (to be an effective, helpful worker with people of all faiths and none).

Muslim chaplains continue to have their own distinctive tasks and approaches to chaplaincy; they have not become detached from their faith tradition and its primary importance. But the changes that took place in their attitudes and practices point up clearly some of the fundamental values and sacralities of chaplaincy.

Chaplaincy is respectful of the secular authority and values that structure its context. It is quiescent and compliant rather than critical, for example, in being non-discriminatory, even in situations where religious taboos are threatened, e.g., about homosexuality and sexual behaviour. It embraces sacralities such as equality and diversity, with concomitant commitments to non-proselytisation and working with people of all faiths and none. Freedom of belief and practice and the inclusion of the 'other' are also part of this sacred universe. But perhaps the most important sacralities are those of valuing individuals and their experiences rather than imposing traditional 'truths' and judgements upon them. This is manifest in the commitment to non-judgemental personal care and listening. Where necessary, religious traditions are subordinated to contemporary personal needs and experiences, demonstrating a commitment to respecting the ultimate importance and sanctity of the person (Campbell 1987, Goffman 2005, Taylor 1989, 1991). Chaplaincy aims to support rather than to judge. It is judicious in giving advice or guidance in contrast to the more directive approaches that might be favoured in traditional religious communities.

Charting the rise of spirituality and the decline of formal, organised religion, Heelas and Woodhead (2005) distinguish a fundamental cultural change in British society and practices towards valuing the person and subjectivity – the 'subjective turn'. This represents 'a turn away from life lived in terms of external or "objective" roles, duties and obligations, and a turn towards life lived by reference to one's own subjective experiences (relational as much as individual)':

> The subjective turn is thus a turn away from 'life-as' (life lived as a dutiful wife, father, husband, strong leader, self-made man etc.) to 'subjective-life' (life lived in deep connection with the unique experiences of my self in-relation).

This relativises the importance of external, traditional authorities, knowledge and practices, giving importance to the subjectivities of individuals as the source of authority, significance and satisfaction as they attempt to become 'what they really are' (Heelas and Woodhead 2005: 2–4, Lynch 2007b).

The effective sacralisation of the individual and her experience has led to the rise of spiritual practices that are congenial and convenient. It has left heterogeneous religious organisations like churches, requiring conformity to authority, tradition, ritual and the past, struggling to maintain their numbers and influence. So it seems significant that chaplaincy represents person-centred, permissive, individualistic values. Chaplaincy, irrespective of the religious traditions which may have shaped its practitioners, conveys and embodies the new sacralities revered by many contemporaries. It acts as the 'acceptable face of religion', honouring subjective life, persons, autonomy and personal fulfilment and happiness. If a chaplain from any tradition were not able to adhere to these values and sacralities, e.g., by being overtly intolerant of sexual minorities, by proselytising, they probably would not be accepted as a chaplain.

Further tangential evidence for arguing that chaplaincy embodies values that are deeply consonant with sacralities now lying mainly outside traditional churches comes from research into male health care chaplains' motivations for doing the job (Hancocks et al. 2008). Many chaplains had a negative experience of the institutional church they were ordained into. They tended to be liberal by contrast with the evangelical domination of the churches, and they were critical of the attitudes of the church towards sexuality – 20 per cent of respondents were in same-sex relationships. Many chaplains appeared to be 'refugees' from the church and respected the values, work and attitudes that they found in the NHS which were more professional and personally supportive than those found in the church. Here again, chaplaincy embodies values and sacralities that are widely shared in society generally, but which are less respected in religious bodies which place less value on individuals' feelings, sexuality, relationships, thoughts and preferences.

So one possible main reason that chaplaincy is deeply acceptable in non-religious social contexts may be that its values and sacralities correspond with those of wider society with its respect for individuals and 'subjective-life'. Indeed, chaplaincy can be seen to epitomise these values. Perhaps this is one reason why it is not much appreciated or understood by the institutional religious communities from which chaplains come (Hancocks et al. 2008). It might also explain why chaplaincy generally does not produce much theological reflection or material as it is not primarily a traditional, conventional religious activity, more a humanistic one. Chaplaincy as a social movement might then be seen as either the acceptable face of religion or perhaps as a substitute for religion, even for those chaplains who continue to value their religious communities of origin, which many do. It may then act as a magnet for liberal religious people, or those who are prepared to become more liberal in their concerns and interests. In this connection, the rise of notions like 'generic chaplaincy' and 'spiritual' as opposed to religious care may be noted (Pattison 2001, Carrette and King: 2005, Lynch 2007b, Swift 2009: 125–43, Sheldrake 2010). These emphases create space for those who feel trammelled by religious orthodoxies to exercise benevolent concern for those outwith those orthodoxies. Of course, some of the values and sacralities that chaplaincy embodies such as inclusiveness, being present to all people, accepting them and caring for them are probably heavily shaped by Christian theological traditions of incarnation, love of the stranger, and grace. While some kinds of sacrality may have been devalued by traditional Christian churches, they have been carried forward into chaplaincy.

This, then, may be one reason why chaplaincy has risen and developed in contemporary society in contradistinction to the institutional churches. As they have abandoned central social sacralities, chaplaincy has moved in to partially fill the gap, both by providing a service that honours and promotes those sacred forms and providing a place where those who are uncomfortable with intolerant, narrow, 'life-as' religion can find refuge. But there are others, some closely related, with which I can now deal more briefly.

Chaplaincy is Multiply Marginal

Chaplains commonly lament the fact that they are liminal, exiled figures 'between worlds', marginal both to the institutions who employ or use them and to the religious communities from which they come (Threlfall-Holmes and Newitt 2011: xiv–xvii, Woodward 1999). Chris Swift stands for many in saying that health care chaplains are

> not simply on the margins between the parochial system central to dioceses and the medical paradigm that dominates the hospital, but between life and death, gay and straight, a Christendom past and a contemporary spirituality that has rejected the rights of external authority. (Swift 2009: 173)

One reason that chaplaincy is marginal in institutions is that chaplains are not numerous. This is because they are essentially ancillary, not directly concerned with host organisations' central tasks. In the NHS, for example, there are a few hundred full-time chaplains, but thousands of doctors, nurses and other professionals (Orchard 2000).

However, if my discussion above is correct, another reason for marginalisation, in this case marginalisation from host religious communities, may be the apparent mismatch between the different sacralities and sacred forms promoted in chaplaincy and those treasured in formal religious communities. Here again chaplains are a minority group, often too busy to communicate with their native religious communities which do not pay them for their chaplaincy work and to whom they are therefore not primarily responsible.

Chaplains tend to lament their marginality. Their thinking seems to run that if chaplaincy is a valuable activity, the more provision of it there is, the better. However, it may be that marginality is one of the real strengths of chaplaincy. Not only does it promote acceptable sacralities, it does not insist itself on the institution or exert power over it. In many circumstances, chaplains only exist at the pleasure and with the patronage of host organisations. Thus they pose no real threat to their hosts and their practices, and they cannot be dominant or coercive. Chaplaincy in its marginal form is exactly the form of religious presence that is acceptable in secular institutions.

Chaplaincy as a marginal activity helps promote and preserve the common sacred, but it also keeps it in its place, on the edge of the main activities of the organisation. If chaplains became less marginal, their work might be much more controversial, disputed and scrutinised. Part of the continuing acceptability of chaplaincy may depend on its perceived powerlessness and dispensability. It is religion put, and kept, in its place. Furthermore, this expression of religion comes to the customer rather than requiring the consumer to go to church and be forced to shape their needs and spirituality to that of a religious institution.

The Chaplaincy Mystique: Engagement in Symbolic Labour

Related to the marginal nature of chaplaincy work is its non-specific, non-essential nature. Chaplains in many fields are fond of talking about presence, attention, listening, accompaniment, creating relationships, and narrative (Cadge 2012, Newitt 2011). This sounds very vague; in many ways, there is a focus on process not on outcomes as more rational-instrumental approaches to work often are in organisations (Mowat 2008). Although chaplains in some spheres want to demonstrate their efficacy through research, there is still relatively little research into what chaplains do, much less criticism as to whether or not they are doing the right thing (Mowat and Swinton 2007). I was told by a senior governmental source that there was no problem about chaplains being employed with state funds, 'so long as the stories we hear coming back are positive'. And on a phone-in about health care chaplaincy on BBC Radio 2 in June 2013, all the callers had positive stories to tell, to the annoyance of secular critics of public employment of chaplains.

What does this sort of permissive attitude betoken? In many ways, it seems, chaplains are largely allowed to determine their own work and priorities without having to directly evidence its efficacy. They are given licence to work in ways others are not. In its many, varied, forms and activities it might be thought that chaplaincy clearly points to something; but to what? The importance of humanity? A spiritual dimension to life? The numinous? The importance of recognising individual needs and cares? The necessity of recognising the non-rational, non-instrumental aspects of life and organisation? It is not clear. Nor is it clear what the motives or aims of chaplains and chaplaincy are. Is chaplaincy a vocation, a religious witness or ministry, a career, an occupation, a service, a voluntary activity, an unwarranted interference, a hangover from the past, or perhaps a way of getting cheap labour? It is probably all these things – and more (Threlfall-Holmes 2011b).

And perhaps this general vagueness points to the fact that part of what chaplaincy offers to organisations is a place where mystery and the surd aspects of life are tolerated and dealt with. These can often include hard realities such as death, illness and bereavement, what might be characterised as the symbolic 'dirty work' of organisational life (Cadge 2012: 171–90, Lyth 1988).

It seems plausible that organisations find it useful to have a group of inexpensive workers who can help manage the bits of life and the emotional, symbolic lives of organisations and individuals in a non-specific way perceived to be beneficial and to improve morale. At worst, by attending to people on an everyday basis they probably make them feel better. Beyond this, chaplains often engage with the bits that no one else wants to address, and they do this by use of words, symbols and occasionally liturgy, formal and informal.

Chaplains are symbolic in their being and in their methods.[3] They do important symbolic work that may help legitimise the organisation and help it to function, often in the background, but sometimes very much in the foreground. Work with and around symbols is rich and complex if a symbol is understood to be

> not an object or event that serves to carry a meaning but a set of relationships between objects or events uniquely brought together as complexes or as concepts, having at once an intellectual, instrumental, and emotional significance. (Asad quoted in Riis and Woodhead 2010: 64)

As symbolic labourers primarily contributing to a symbolic economy of meanings, stories and rituals, individual and corporate, it is probably essential that their work should be somewhat opaque, indeterminate and surrounded with a helpful, necessary haze of unknowing and mystique. This contributes to the attractiveness of chaplaincy rather than detracting from it. Someone needs to do this kind of difficult labour; chaplaincy seems to provide just the right kind of under-determined space where such work can be done.

If, then, chaplains were to try to clarify their functions, efficacy and usefulness too much, to become transparent, it may be that their real symbolic effectiveness would be undermined and they would become really useless and redundant. Vague 'uselessness' and a certain perpetual liminality may be essential if chaplaincy is to retain its attraction in an over-instrumentalised world and point to the imaginative and existential spaces and absences that may be denoted by words like 'religious' and 'spiritual' (cf. Swinton and Pattison 2010). Perhaps only what is useless and apparently surplus to requirements is genuinely useful in the case of symbolic presence and work.

---

[3]   In asserting the symbolic nature of chaplaincy work, I am not suggesting that chaplains do not also provide non-symbolic labour and capital which can directly benefit the outcomes of organisations financially and in other ways, e.g. in the improvement of morale and so performance (cf. Todd 2014).

Despite calls from within chaplaincy that it become more professional and demonstrably effective, there is not much evidence that this matters crucially to its hosts (Swift 2013, UK Board of Healthcare Chaplaincy 2009). Furthermore, chaplains' own claims to promote spirituality and generic approaches to people of all faiths and none as a way of broadening their credibility seem to have little effect on increasing their acceptability. Host organisations seem viscerally to understand religion and religious needs, but find spirituality as a concept and practice mystifying (Cadge 2012). As long as chaplains do not obstruct the main aims of the organisation and are occasionally specifically helpful, they will be welcomed. Their function is not primarily to be useful in any simple sense. However, organisations cannot afford too much indeterminate uselessness, which is why chaplaincy must remain a marginal, minority activity if it is to maintain its attraction and privileges of licensed presence. Like household pets which attract similar kinds of attachment, affection and symbolic importance, they are vitally important in their essential dispensability, but only if there are not too many of them and they are not too intrusive.[4]

Conclusion

I have speculated about why chaplaincy as a social institution seems to have grown and flourished while establishment Christian religion, the rock from which chaplaincy was hewn, has diminished in its plausibility and influence. Chaplaincy embraces, embodies and promotes many of the sacred forms that are valued in contemporary British society in a way that the churches now fail to do. With a focus on the ultimate value of the person, individual autonomy and experience, inclusion and equality, chaplaincy is a vehicle for the honouring of 'subjective' life over against 'life-as' and thus serves the wider interests of a society seeking spiritual rather than narrowly religious values. This focus is compatible with the culture of consumer choice and person-centredness, now seen to be an unequivocal, sacred good in society and its constituent organisations. Chaplaincy is attractive both to secular organisations and to liberals and those of inclusive temperament within religious communities who are drawn to the need to promote 'subject-life' rather than 'life-as' religion.

In some ways, chaplaincy has become an expression of the traditional role of established religion which is to accommodate, recognise and value commonly accepted social sacred forms. In a country where there has been an established church ministering to all the people of the land, chaplaincy leans heavily on the tradition of entry to social and secular spaces created by centuries of assumed

---

[4]   This is not a derogatory comparison – pets can be enormously important to identity and belonging (Miller 2008).

ecclesiastical access. The presumed right of the parish priest to enter all homes and institutions in the parish still helpfully haunts and legitimates the place of chaplaincy today (Pattison 2000: 55–81). This is what Andrew Todd (Todd et al. 2014: 5) denotes redistributed or extended establishment. And that establishment now extends to include chaplains, institutions and clients of all faiths and none. This underlies an unconscious, latently remembered knowledge and acceptance of religious presence that allows chaplaincy to exist, expand and prosper – within limits.

Chaplains are not required to leave aspects of traditional religious belief and practice behind, so long as they are willing to embrace contemporary sacralities. However, much chaplaincy now exists at a considerable distance from formal established religions; it functions as a substitute that transcends particular religions in the name of a common, if inarticulate, sacrality. Chaplains have often lamented their position of marginality in both churches and host organisations. However, it may be the very marginality of chaplaincy and its minority status that allows it to prosper in host organisations. It represents a sacrality that can be tapped on demand but not inflicted on people. This is perhaps how modern British people like to draw on religiously related organisations which are firmly positioned as biddable servants rather than autocratic masters, as limited and optional resources, not essential suppliers.

Contrary to the perceptions of some chaplains themselves, it may be an important element of the continuing success of chaplaincy that it is non-specific and somewhat opaque. Part of its attractiveness may be its undertaking underdetermined symbolic labour that stands outside the instrumental-rationality characterising much labour today. Chaplaincy takes in and deals with the aspects and events of organisational life that other occupations and functions do not reach. If that is so, then attempts to clarify the nature, work and effectiveness of chaplaincy to make it more 'professional' may threaten its symbolic plausibility and legitimacy. Its usefulness and attractiveness may depend upon its uselessness, bound up centrally with the mostly implicit perception that it deals with the sacred, the marginal, that which is so central that it must be treated as being on the edge of working and institutional life. Only uselessness may therefore be useful, only what is inessential may turn out to be vital.

References

Ballard, P. (2004). The Clergy: An Interesting Anomaly. In Pattison, S. and R. Pill (eds), *Values in Professional Practice*. Oxford: Radcliffe, 47–55.

Cadge, W. (2012), *Paging God: Religion in the Halls of Medicine*. Chicago: University of Chicago Press.

Campbell, C. (1987), *The Romantic Ethic and the Spirit of Modern Consumerism*. Oxford: Blackwell.

Carrette, J. and R. King. (2005), *Selling Spirituality: The Silent Takeover of Religion*. Abingdon: Routledge.

Cope, P. and M. West. (2011), *Engaging Mission: The Lasting Value of Industrial Mission for Today*. Guildford: Grosvenor House Publishing.

Cross, F.L. (ed.) (1958), *The Oxford Dictionary of the Christian Church*. Oxford: Oxford University Press.

Gibson, W. (1997), *A Social History of the Domestic Chaplain 1530–1840*. London: Leicester University Press.

Gilliat-Ray, S. (2001), Sociological Perspectives on the Pastoral Care of Minority Faiths in Hospital. In Orchard, H. (ed.), *Spirituality in Health Care Contexts*. London: Jessica Kingsley, 135–46.

Gilliat-Ray, S., M. Ali and S. Pattison (2013), *Understanding Muslim Chaplaincy*. Farnham: Ashgate.

Goffman, E. (2005), *Interaction Ritual: Essays in Face to Face Behaviour*. New Brunswick, NY: Aldine Transaction.

Graham, E. (2013). *Between a Rock and a Hard Place: Public Theology in a Post-secular Age*. London: SCM Press.

Hancocks, G., J. Sherbourne and C. Swift (2008), 'Are they refugees?' Why Church of England male clergy enter health care chaplaincy. *Practical Theology*, 1, 163–79.

Heelas, P. and L. Woodhead (2005), *The Spiritual Revolution: Why Religion is Giving Way to Spirituality*. Oxford: Blackwell.

Heskins, J. and M. Baker (2006), *Footballing Lives: As Seen by Chaplains in the Beautiful Game*. Norwich: Canterbury Press.

Humanist Chaplaincy Network (2013), *What is a Humanist Chaplain?* Available at: www.humanistchaplains.org/whatisit (accessed 5 August 2013).

Hunter, R. (ed.) (1990), *Dictionary of Pastoral Care and Counseling*. Nashville: Abingdon.

Legood, G. (ed.) (1999), *Chaplaincy: The Church's Sector Ministries*. London: Cassell.

Lynch, G. (2007a), What is this 'Religion' in the Study of Religion and Popular Culture? In Lynch, G. (ed.), *Between Sacred and Profane: Researching Religion and Popular Culture*. London: I.B. Tauris, 125–42.

—— (2007b), *The New Spirituality: An Introduction to Progressive Belief in the Twenty-first Century*. London: I.B. Tauris.

—— (2012). *The Sacred in the Modern World: A Cultural Sociological Approach*. Oxford: Oxford University Press.

Lyth, I.M. (1988), *Containing Anxiety in Institutions*. London: Free Association Press.

Miller, D. (2008), *The Comfort of Things*. Cambridge: Polity.

Mowat, H. (2008), *The Potential for Efficacy of Healthcare Chaplaincy and Spiritual Care Provision in the NHS (UK)*. Aberdeen: Mowat Research.

Mowat, H. and J. Swinton (2007), *What Do Chaplains Do?* Aberdeen: Mowat Research.

Newitt, M. (2011), The Role and Skills of a Chaplain. In Threlfall-Holmes, M. and M. Newitt (eds), *Being a Chaplain*. London: SPCK, 103–15.

Orchard, H. (2000), *Hospital Chaplaincy: Modern, Dependable?* Sheffield: Sheffield Academic Press.

—— (2001a). Being There? Presence and Absence in Spiritual Care Delivery. In Orchard, H. (ed.), *Spirituality in Health Care Contexts*. London: Jessica Kingsley, 147–59.

Pattison, S. (2000), *A Critique of Pastoral Care*, 3rd edition. London: SCM Press.

—— (2001), Dumbing Down the Spirit. In Orchard, H. (ed.), *Spirituality in Health Care Contexts*. London: Jessica Kingsley, 33–46.

—— (2007), *The Challenge of Practical Theology*. London: Jessica Kingsley.

—— (2008), Is pastoral care dead in a mission-led church? *Practical Theology*, 1, 7–10.

—— (2013), Religion, spirituality and health care: confusions, tensions and opportunities. *Health Care Analysis*, 21, 193–207.

Riis, O. and L. Woodhead (2010), *A Sociology of Religious Emotion*. New York: Oxford University Press.

Russell, A. (1980), *The Clerical Profession*. London: SPCK.

Sheldrake, P. (2010), Spirituality and health care. *Practical Theology*, 3, 367–79.

Swift, C. (2009), *Hospital Chaplaincy in the Twenty-first Century: The Crisis of Spiritual Care on the NHS*. Farnham: Ashgate.

—— (2013), A state health service and funded religious care. *Health Care Analysis*, 21, 248–58.

Swinton, J. and S. Pattison (2010), Moving beyond clarity: towards a thin, vague and useful understanding of spirituality in nursing care. *Nursing Philosophy*, 11, 226–37.

Taylor, C. (1989), *Sources of the Self*. Cambridge: Cambridge University Press.

—— (1991), *The Ethics of Authenticity*. Cambridge, MA: Harvard University Press.

Threlfall-Holmes, M. (2011a), Exploring Models of Chaplaincy. In Threlfall-Holmes, M. and M. Newitt (eds), *Being a Chaplain*. London: SPCK, 116–26.

—— (2011b), Values and Tensions. In Threlfall-Holmes, M. and M. Newitt (eds), *Being a Chaplain*. London: SPCK, 127–40.

Threlfall-Holmes, M. and M. Newitt (eds) (2011), *Being a Chaplain*. London: SPCK.

Todd, A. (2011), Responding to Diversity: Chaplaincy in a Multi-faith Context. In Threlfall-Holmes, M. and M. Newitt (eds), *Being a Chaplain*. London: SPCK, 89–102.

—— (ed.) (2013), *Military Chaplaincy in Contention: Chaplains, Churches and the Morality of Conflict*. Farnham: Ashgate.

—— (2014), Religion, security, rights, the individual and rates of exchange: religion in negotiation with British public policy in prisons and the military. *International Journal of Politics, Culture, and Society*. (Online).

Todd, A., V. Slater, and S. Dunlop (2014), *The Church of England's Involvement in Chaplaincy: Research Report for the Church of England's Mission and Public Affairs Council*. Available at: http://stmichaels.ac.uk/chaplaincy-studies/centre-reports-and-publications (accessed 30 October 2014).

UK Board of Healthcare Chaplaincy (2009), *Spiritual and Religious Care Capabilities and Competences for Healthcare Chaplains*. Available at: www.ukbhc.org.uk/sites/default/files/UKBHC%20Spiritual%20and%20Religious%20Capabilities%20and%20Competences%20%202009.pdf (accessed 7 August 2013).

Woodhead, L. and R. Catto (eds) (2012), *Religion and Change in Modern Britain*. Abingdon: Routledge.

Woodhead, L. (2012a), Introduction. In Woodhead, L. and R. Catto (eds), *Religion and Change in Modern Britain*. Abingdon: Routledge, 1–33.

—— (2012b), Surveying religious belief needs social science, not hard science. *The Guardian*, 5 December 2012.

Woodward, J. (1999). A Study of the Role of the Acute Health Care Chaplain in England. Open University: Unpublished PhD dissertation.

Chapter 3

The Place of Chaplaincy in Public Life

Alan Billings

Chaplains stand at the interface between organised religion and public institutions. They do so at a time when both are in a difficult place. On the one hand, many people seem indifferent towards religion and some are openly hostile, insisting that religion has no place in public life. On the other, the size of the public sector is being reduced through a mix of financial pressures and ideological conviction; money has to be rigorously prioritised. As a result, publicly funded chaplaincy finds itself challenged from two directions – from what is happening to religion and from what is happening to public services. In this chapter I will explore each of these in turn before considering the grounds on which a case for chaplaincy can still be made. First, what has happened to religion?

The Changed Landscape of Religion

Although chaplains have a long history, modern state-financed chaplaincies essentially emerged in the period immediately after the Second World War with the coming of the welfare state and a (short-lived) revival in churchgoing. In this formative period religion was relatively unproblematic in the public arena. Chaplains in the new National Health Service, for example, largely continued to do what they had done previously in the pre-war voluntary hospitals – pastoral visits and church services. Britain was a Christian nation and having the state fund chaplains drawn from the major Christian denominations raised few issues. After all, during the war men and women in the forces had encountered chaplains (padres) who were an accepted part of military life.[1] But over the ensuing decades the religious landscape changed and this raised questions about how chaplaincy would serve not only the needs of those who were members of a Christian church but also the needs of those who were not. It took time for a sense of chaplaincy as a specialist ministry to develop, not least because clergy at first only committed themselves to a few years as whole-time chaplains and there were few of them – perhaps 28 in 1948 (Swift 2009: 41). Six factors can be

---

[1]   The Army Chaplains' Department dates from 1796.

highlighted: a decline in traditional churchgoing; the growth of non-Christian faiths; the appearance of a secular religion associated with the expanding welfare state; the liberation of spirituality from organised religion; and the increase in those who said they had 'no religion'. I will briefly consider each and the way this shaped chaplaincy.

By the 21st century it was a commonplace to speak of the death of Christian Britain (Bruce 2002, McLeod 2007). Traditional forms of Christianity were in serious decline. After a rise in church attendances in the 1950s, the number of people associated with the Church or seeking its offices began to fall decade after decade (Archbishops' Council 2014). People were not so much hostile as indifferent; they walked away from organised religion. There were many reasons for this, not all of which were directly religious. All organisations suffered decline as people used their greater prosperity and leisure time to watch television[2] or pursue activities that did not involve joining with others (Putnam 2001). There was a gradual emergence of a more educated public that found itself increasingly at odds with some of the traditional teachings of the Church and the idea of Christian morality as a morality of command (Mackinnon 1963). One of the most serious defections from the 1960s onwards was that of younger women (Brown 2001). This generation felt liberated by the sexual revolution: they were able to control their own fertility, to decide when or whether to have a family, to have an education and a career. But the issues these emancipated women wanted to talk about – artificial contraception, abortion, divorce, balancing career and family life, sexuality – were all matters that the predominantly male Church leaders were only prepared to pronounce on, not debate. Women left the Church in large numbers, taking with them their husbands and children. Sunday schools collapsed and the Church struggled to replicate itself. Churches assumed that the day schools would make up for what they could no longer do – teach the children Christian faith. But from the mid 1960s schools declined to act as agents of Christianity. Older styles of teaching – religious instruction – gave way to something broader and less didactic – religious education – and worship was often replaced by an assembly with a moral theme. The presence of growing numbers of pupils of other faiths – a consequence of immigration – made it impossible in state schools to carry on teaching Christianity as if it were the only repository of religious truth and Christian prayer the only form of religious worship. A more comparative religions approach was adopted so that most of those leaving school from about this time had only a superficial immersion in any faith and almost no experience of worship.

As people retreated from Christian observance they seemed to need something to fill the void. Many found it in the values implicit in the developing

---

[2]   In the UK there were 15,000 households with television in 1947, 1.4 million in 1952 and 15.1 million by 1968.

secular philosophy that undergirded the newly created welfare state.[3] This had many of the characteristics of religion, and the new secular priesthood – those who worked in the health, welfare, social and counselling services – helped to promote it (Morgan 1985). Many that had little time for Christian doctrine or the Church, welcomed the welfare state as the embodiment of the Christian ethic, which made some say the National Health Service was the nearest the English get to a religion.[4] But in one fundamental respect the new religion/ morality of the welfare state and its servants began to part from its Christian progenitor. As long as one person's choices did not interfere with another's, the new morality was non-judgemental; it did not condemn. This became a fundamental requirement for everyone who worked for the state – from the teacher to the midwife. They would help people in need without making moral judgements as to their character or chosen way of life. In contrast, clergy could be highly judgemental, condemning aspects of modern lifestyles, voicing their opposition to abortion, pre-marital sex and gay relations. But welfare practitioners were in tune with the changing attitudes of the population as a whole; indeed they were shaping them. A gulf opened up between the religion/ morality of what became the majority of people and the religion/morality of the Church. Eventually most of the churches shifted their position on some or all of these issues; but by then, damage had been done. The general public had formed an impression of the Church as unwelcoming towards those who fell short of its standards, unsympathetic on matters that deeply affected many lives, and, above all, unwilling to debate the issues with anything like an open mind. But chaplains learned to reflect in their practice a non-judgemental approach.

Some of the men and women that walked away from the churches from the 1960s discovered that what they had valued in Christianity was what now began to be called 'spirituality'. This was not the traditional spirituality of the Church – the liturgical calendar, Bible study, retreats, set patterns of worship and prayer – but new ways of finding the inner, spiritual self and/or meaning and purpose in life. New groups began to meet or organise not under Church control, such as Sea of Faith groups or Christian ashrams.[5] All kinds of spiritual exercises began to evolve, many of which have been called 'holistic' because they were about bodily practices as much as mental exercises. Diana, Princess of Wales, illustrated in her brief life the attraction of many of these to women in particular (Richards et al. 1999). Spirituality lost its exclusive moorings in conventional religion.

[3]   The values were made explicit in the NHS Constitution from 2009 (NHS 2009).

[4]   Attributed at different times to Nigel Lawson and Norman Lamont, both former Conservative chancellors.

[5]   Sea of Faith groups were inspired by the writings of Don Cupitt, Dean of Emmanuel College, Cambridge and his 'non-realism'. Ashrams were started in Sheffield under the auspices of the Urban Theology Unit and its Director, Revd Dr John Vincent, at one time President of the Methodist Conference.

It became detached and free-floating, migrating from places of organised religion and reappearing as formless religiosity flowing through numerous non-traditional channels – from circle dancing to yoga (Heelas and Woodhead 2005). Chaplains learned not to dismiss these new expressions of spirituality.

This largely unstructured and demotic movement did, however, have an impact on the Church. It led evangelicals in particular to explore patterns of prayer and worship that made the needs of the spiritual self more central than the rituals and traditions of the Church. This became the burden of their singing and praying. However, they differed from the holistic forms of spirituality in keeping activities under the control of a (usually male) leadership, both lay and ordained. Paradoxically, they also managed to hold ethical conservatism in tension with the idea that however wretched your life was or you felt it to be, you were still the object of God's undivided attention and love. Shame and guilt – aspects of traditional Christianity that had often burdened people – were lifted at a stroke (Luhrmann 2012). These 'charismatic' and sometimes 'fundamentalist' churches continue to grow even as more traditional ones continue to struggle. But how far were their members comfortable with the way chaplaincy was accommodating to the other changes in the religious scene? There is an unresolved and possibly growing tension here.

Finally, there was a rapid growth of those with no religion. If we compare the 2001 and 2011 National Census, both of which asked questions about people's religious beliefs, we find something startling. In 2001 8.5 million people said they had 'no religion' – as against 41 million that ticked the Christian box. By 2011 this had become 14.1 million with no religion and 33.2 million Christian. The direction of travel seemed clear. The decade between the two censuses also saw an aggressive and sustained attack on religion by so-called 'New Atheists'. Their contempt for religion was summed up in the subtitle of a book by Christopher Hitchins, *How Religion Poisons Everything* (Hitchins 2007, Dennett 2007, Dawkins 2007). From the 1990s onwards they became vocal and influential. However, at the start of the current century a strain of atheism appeared that began to re-evaluate religion. The atheist philosopher, Alain de Botton, said that religions were 'intermittently too useful, effective and intelligent to be abandoned to the religious alone' and suggested that many of their practices should be emulated by non-believers (de Botton 2012). As a result, Sunday congregations of atheists have begun to appear in London and elsewhere. Inevitably, this raises questions for chaplaincy if chaplaincy is inclusive of all beliefs whether traditionally religious or not.

As far as religion is concerned, therefore, the contemporary chaplain is faced with a complex kaleidoscope of traditional religion, new spiritualities, many faiths, non-believers and aggressive secularists within a public institution that has its own ethic, the ethic of the welfare state – hospitable, inclusive, tolerant and non-judgemental, where the interests and well-being of the individual are paramount (Thompson 2013). Ministering to people who could come from any of these backgrounds might seem like mission impossible, but over the years chaplaincy has evolved to do exactly that. Chaplains have come to recognise that spiritual and pastoral needs include, but are not exhausted by, the religious needs of people from particular faith backgrounds. In this way, chaplaincy became a distinctive form of ministry, though the implications of this were not always understood by those whose ministries centred on churches, and chaplains did not always take the trouble to explain themselves through their denominational structures.

The Diminished State

Religion has changed; so has the public sector. The dream of a welfare state meeting needs 'from the cradle to the grave' (the phrase is Churchill's) now seems impossible, even if still thought desirable. As a result chaplaincy finds itself challenged not only by religious change but also by changes affecting public services driven partly by ideology and partly by financial necessity.

Today's welfare state has its origins in the publication in 1942 of the report *Social Insurance and Allied Services* by the economist and civil servant William Beveridge (1879–1953). He believed that if the five evils of Want, Disease, Ignorance, Squalor and Idleness that blighted people's lives were to be decisively overcome, it would require state and not just individual action. As well as a system of benefits, there would also have to be free, universal education, commitment to full employment, a national health service and a major house building programme. A series of acts of Parliament between 1944 and 1948 brought most of this into being – what David Gladstone has called 'the defining moment' in the transition from an ideology of welfare, where the state simply responded to problems as they arose, to one where public finances would be used to improve society (Gladstone 1999). The shift was from a *welfare society*, where families, the commercial sector and the voluntary societies met most needs (the position pre-war), to a *welfare state*, where government provided the principal services. The belief that the state could be trusted to do this was based on people's wartime experiences when the state had acted for the common good and no one begrudged making their contribution. While Beveridge and others saw all this as a matter of social justice, there were also economic arguments: an educated and healthy workforce would be a more productive one.

Not everyone agreed with this, either then or now. There were economic arguments *against* the welfare state: it was an unaffordable burden for an exhausted and indebted nation to take on. Some thought that if Britain had opted for a mixed economy of welfare, with the commercial and voluntary sector playing a continuing role, we might have experienced the same economic miracle that happened in post-war Germany. We would have avoided creating what the journalist Matthew Parris has called 'a central state monolith' and 'one of 20th century Britain's most far-reaching mistakes' (Parris 2014). There were other objections. Some believed that too much state intervention would undermine both personal initiative and family responsibility, creating a benefits culture and 'welfare dependency'. (Some contemporary critics would say they had been proved right.) Others thought the welfare state would reduce individuals to mere numbers. Roger Lloyd, the historian of the Church of England, writing in 1966, wondered whether 'the individual person had not been reduced to a cypher, to an impotent cog in a machine' (Lloyd 1966). (Again, some would say that this has been people's experience of welfare state bureaucracy.) But for the next 40 years, progress in welfare was equated with state intervention. The movement from individualism to collectivism, from what Jane Lewis called 'the darkness of the nineteenth-century poor law into the light of ... the post-war welfare state', was understood as linear and teleological (Lewis 1999).

The first major assault on the size and scope of the welfare state began in the 1980s when Margaret Thatcher's government started to dismantle the stock of council housing with the Right to Buy policy. But it was the need to reduce spending rather than any ideological driver that began to impact chaplaincy services during the early 2000s. NHS Trusts seemed to face regular budgetary crises and when in 2006 the Worcestershire Acute Hospitals Trust attempted to save money by axing six of its seven full- and part-time chaplains it triggered an outcry. It was a critical moment as it gradually became clear that Worcestershire was not alone. A survey by the think tank Theos suggested that other trusts also saw chaplaincy reductions as a means of balancing the books (Swift 2009: 92–4). A warning light flashed: chaplaincy was not universally valued because religion was no longer universally valued but neither the Trust nor the church leaders who took up the cause of the chaplaincy (nor the general public) seemed to understand how chaplaincy had changed. The case for and against the chaplaincy was made within a religious framework with little reference to wider spiritual and health needs. As a result, when the issues were debated in the national media it was too often understood as a contest between organised religion – principally the churches – and non-believers, with the National Secular Society putting the case against religion in the public sector. Nevertheless, some powerful testimony was heard from patients and NHS staff about the value of the chaplaincy and the difference made by the presence of chaplains within the hospital. Writing about the crisis subsequently, Christopher Swift, himself a hospital chaplain, said it was 'a struggle over the fundamental location and professional identity of chaplains' (Swift 2009: 81). Eventually the Trust relented, though whether it even then fully understood the nature of its own chaplaincy is a moot point.

But the biggest shock to the public sector came with the international banking crisis of 2007–2008. Governments committed huge sums of public money to prevent the complete collapse of the financial system. The British government had to find money not only to pay down the annual deficit (the difference between what a government spends and what it takes in by way of tax) but also to repay the debts incurred bailing out the banks. The Coalition Government (Liberal Democrat–Conservative) of 2010–2015 did this primarily by cutting public spending rather than raising tax (indeed, they cut tax for the most wealthy and raised tax thresholds for all). This period of austerity and caution is likely to continue under successive governments for many years to come.

Different strategies were used by different parts of the public sector to reduce costs. There were straightforward cuts in jobs and levels of service, especially in local government and the armed forces. The trend towards delivering services indirectly, outsourcing or commissioning from providers of services in the commercial and the voluntary sector, begun under the previous Labour Government, was accelerated. It was argued that this was both more effective and more efficient: the commercial and voluntary sectors were likely to be less bureaucratic, more focused on delivery, and cheaper. This also enabled government (national and local) to introduce other commercial means of driving down costs while (it was claimed) maintaining if not raising standards. Payment by results was one: government only paid for a service after agreed outcomes had been delivered. So, for example, programmes for rehabilitating prisoners would only become a charge to the taxpayer after agreed results – such as a reduction in reoffending – had been achieved by providers. If this were not achieved then the cost would have to be borne by the provider. This move towards commissioning and the use of the commercial and voluntary sectors and social enterprises saw a coming together of a financial imperative – the need to reduce the cost of the public sector – and an ideological one – a determination to reduce the size of the state. It also put pressure on all parts of the public sector to be clear about what the outcomes of their activities were and how they could be measured. Everything had to be 'evidence based'. Some would argue that this changes the ethos of service delivery. An older ethic of public service is replaced by the sort of contractual relationships that are more familiar in the business world. Providers do not hold themselves to account as a matter of professional pride but are held to account according to agreed contractual outcomes. This ethos, it is said, becomes all-pervading. The danger for chaplaincy was that it risked turning spiritual and pastoral outcomes into some kind of measurable commodity that could be procured for a certain price.

There is one final aspect to the changes that is important to note. All political parties are now committed to versions of what the Coalition Government called 'localism' or devolution of power. There is a strong argument for saying that decisions should be taken as near to the people who are affected by them as possible. Catholic social teaching knows this as 'subsidiarity'. But it could be argued that far from allowing local innovation, 'localism' was simply a euphemism for requiring local organisations to make the cuts in services implicit in overall cash reductions determined centrally. Whatever the truth of that, this is now the ethos and environment in which chaplaincy has to make its case: it will need to do so to local decision makers as much as national. There is one aspect of localism that has long been recognised in the NHS, namely that when chaplains are recruited they should represent as far as possible 'the belief patterns of the local population' (NHS Careers 2014).

Religion in Public Life

I have outlined some of the significant changes in both religion and the public sector that have challenged chaplaincy in the recent past and will challenge for the foreseeable future. Let me now turn directly to the question of the place of religion in public life that has been implicit throughout this narrative.

The chaplains with whom I have mainly been concerned are salaried employees of various institutions of the state, principally hospitals, hospices, universities, prisons and the armed forces. In recent years there has been a sustained attempt by secularists to force religion out of the public arena. The arguments have had many starting points: that religion is a matter of private judgement; that it is irrational and conflicts with science; that organised religion can be oppressive; that it causes wars; that in a plural society no one perspective should be privileged and receive public funding (Grayling 2001: 99–107). Inevitably chaplaincy has been caught up in this, especially over the use of public resources. The critics have used both the statistics of religious decline and the need to reduce public spending to give added weight to their case. The National Secular Society, for example, pointed out how much could be saved by axing chaplaincies in the NHS (estimated at £40 million) and what that might equate to in nurses (1,300) or cleaners (2,645). The British Humanist Association argued strongly that the state had no business supporting something that was harmful to people's welfare. This was the background to the decision of the Worcestershire Acute Hospitals NHS Trust to attempt to axe chaplaincy services in 2006–2007 (Swift 2009: 81–95). In one document they gave as a reason for their action that 'society is changing and becoming increasingly secular and diverse' (Swift 2009: 88). What, then, can we say about each of these objections (Avis 2003, Dinham et al. 2009, Trigg 2008)?

First, religion is a private matter. What the objectors mean is that religion *ought* to be a private matter and nothing more. They seek to define religion in a way that makes it easier to argue for its removal from public life. Some religions hardly fit this definition at all. Islam, for instance, would find the idea that religion was only about individual subjectivity very strange. Islam has always been a faith for living in community. It is about how society is ordered, about how people relate to one another as members of society – sharia law, Islamic finance. Similarly, Christianity is about being part of a congregation – the Body of Christ – and how to live as a member of that Body in the wider society. Of course, for both Islam and Christianity there is also an inward dimension, a personal relationship with God. But to say that only this aspect of faith is to count as religion is not something that survives scrutiny.

Second, religion is irrational and conflicts with science. The objection has in mind either historic battles between the Church and scientists such as Galileo or Darwin, or contemporary congregations that are called 'fundamentalist'. There is little point denying the history; it did take the Church some time to realise that questions about the origins of life or whether the earth is the centre of the universe are answered by science not the scriptures. But most Christians have long understood that and see no conflict between science and belief. It is lazy to assume that all Christians are fundamentalist or incapable of adjusting to new knowledge – as science has to adjust. I was taught physics by a disciple of Sir Fred Hoyle, a distinguished astronomer, who theorised that the universe had no beginning and no end: it was eternal. He was scornful of the idea that the world did have a beginning and coined the (pejoratively meant) term 'big bang' to describe these false theories. We now know that his 'steady state theory' does not fit all the empirical evidence – though Hoyle carried on believing it until he died in 2001. Science has moved on and religion also moves on when new evidence is compelling. Most Christians no longer think Genesis is science, though they do think it captures important truths about human nature and how to live well. A hermeneutic of suspicion needs bringing to science as well as religion.

Third, that religion is harmful and oppressive. Again, religion can be harmful and oppressive. Equally it can be liberating. Chaplaincy has nothing to gain from being the instrument of any oppressive form of faith. But it is important to note the growing body of empirical research that shows the (mental and physical) health benefits of having a faith (Miller and Thoreson, cited in McGrath 2005: 110).

Fourth, that organised religion causes wars. There have been and there are wars fought for religious reasons (Billings 2014). But many modern conflicts were instigated by atheist regimes – such as Pol Pot's murderous reign of terror in 1970s Cambodia. The truth seems to be that while religion may be a source of conflict, wars are rarely fought now principally for religious reasons, though religion may be used as a way of marking a difference between people who are in conflict over territory or natural resources (Martin 1997). There are also powerful traditions arguing for peace and commending peace-making in the major faiths that need to be highlighted.

The final objection is the most powerful because it would stand even if satisfactory answers could be given to each of the other objections: that in a plural society no one perspective should be privileged or receive public funding.

In order to counter it a case has to be made to show that chaplaincy not only contributes to the well-being of those who have faith, but also to others beyond the boundaries of faith. It is an argument about the value of chaplaincy as a general resource within public institutions.

Those who make decisions about chaplaincy will take account of public opinion. We noted earlier that there is indifference rather than hostility towards religion; but indifference disappears at certain moments and in particular situations. The Salvation Army's devotion to the homeless is seen as a good thing. The local vicar is supported when she arranges a memorial service for those killed in some local tragedy. Even the liturgies of the Church can be valued by non-believers. Baroness Mary Warnock, the moral philosopher and an atheist, has written movingly about how she is helped by formal liturgy:

> Moreover, some people at least, though they do not believe in a personal God watching over them, nevertheless sometimes need to behave as if there were such a being; their emotion may be a sense of generalised gratitude, a generalised remorse, a generalised sense of pity and sorrow for the sufferings of others. For many such people, of whom I am one, the rituals and the metaphorical language of religion, their traditional religion, are the most accessible and the most fitting expression. (Billings 2013: 26)

In other words, people can see value in religion even if they are not people of faith themselves, and could see value in funding chaplaincy where the resources it brings are seen to make a significant difference to the well-being of individuals and institutions.

Government indifference towards religion changed in 2001 when there were riots in a number of northern towns and cities. The country became aware of large numbers of disaffected Asian young people, mainly Muslims, in some inner-city areas. Everyone soon realised that if they were to reach these young people and their communities, they would have to do so through local mosques and their leaders. As government did this it discovered the role all faiths play in building social capital and community cohesion: they promote active citizenship (volunteering, giving, civic engagement); they make buildings and personnel available for community use; they sustain the virtues needed for good neighbourliness, including interfaith work; they are committed to their localities for the long term; and so on (Billings 2009: 26–52). All these considerations trumped any arguments the critics brought about the harm religion was supposed to do. Religion had social value again and while the assets of the state could not be used to propagate faith they could be used to support those activities that increased social and individual well-being. Chaplaincy could also be seen in this same light: it added value to what the state provided through its various institutions and activities.

Making the Case for Chaplaincy – Adding Value

What, then, of the future? Chaplains will, of course, want to argue for the truth of religion; but those who make decisions within the public sector will find functionalist and utilitarian arguments more persuasive. The overarching justification for a publicly funded chaplaincy must be that it 'adds value' – it does something valuable that no other professional group does. It offers a form of care that is best captured by the terms 'spiritual' and 'pastoral' and it is able to do this because gradually over the past half century or so chaplaincy has become a discrete professional group with its own skills and expertise. How, then, does chaplaincy add value?

First, the chaplaincy adds value because it understands some of the specifically religious needs of people from particular faith backgrounds – something that has become complex as British society has become more plural. This may be about offering certain prayers, administering sacraments, knowing about dietary requirements, being aware of certain sensitivities around the treatment of dead bodies or the relationships of men and women, and so on. Contemporary chaplaincies, by being interdenominational and interfaith, help ensure that the religious needs of individuals are met as far as possible and they help the organisation – prison, hospital, university, armed forces – to understand better what those needs might be.[6] They enable an organisation to be religiously and culturally literate and aware. Chaplains also recognise that while not everyone comes from a religious background, all human beings share a general need to find value, meaning and purpose in their lives, and they help them to do this. The training and experience of chaplains gives them the relevant skills and sympathies.

Second, the chaplaincy adds value because it has a brief to offer spiritual and pastoral care to all and does this without having to operate under some of the constraints that others have within a particular institution. In the armed forces the padre relates to service men and women of all ranks and their families and moves between them in a way that a hierarchical organisation makes impossible for others.[7] In the NHS the chaplain is concerned with 'all patients, their carers, friends and family as well as the staff'. Again, the chaplain has access to people at every level of organisation, and there may be times when this can be made to work for the good of an individual or the organisation as a whole.[8] This is skilled and sensitive work requiring appropriate training, accreditation and supervision. But critically, the chaplain is available for all.

---

[6] The first part-time Muslim chaplain was appointed in 1970 (Wilson 1971, cited in Swift 2009: 46).

[7] See, for example, the Royal Army website: www.army.mod.uk/chaplains.

[8] The role of the chaplain within the NHS: www.nhs-chaplaincy-spiritualcare.org.uk.

Third, a specific case for added value will need to be made for the chaplaincies in each public body. Consider, for example, the needs of a cancer patient within the NHS and those professionals that may be part of the care: the consultant may be constrained by pressures of time; the psychologist does not have a remit for pastoral care and may not have access to the organisation at all levels; the nurse may lack confidence or expertise when the patient seeks to explore hard questions about meaning and purpose and the point of their life. It is precisely at these points that chaplaincy demonstrates its value. Chaplains in the NHS need to draw upon the growing body of research that indicates that people's well-being is enhanced when physical, emotional and spiritual needs are addressed together. This argues for interdisciplinary working with chaplains taking a place alongside others.

Sometimes others see the value-added component of chaplaincy in ways chaplains might not or might not have predicted. A military chaplain told me in 2013 that he felt his work had been undervalued at the top of the army until the Afghanistan and Iraq wars. As men were injured and killed, as morale began to be affected, senior officers needed people who could sit with and reassure anxious young soldiers, visit and be with bereaved families, and who had some expertise in answering difficult questions about the morality of particular conflicts. This was a tall order, but as soon as the need was articulated the chaplaincy was seen as the obvious resource. 'Before those wars', the chaplain went on, 'when men and women were deployed in theatre we were only ever an afterthought. Now we are on the second plane out.' So far, military chaplaincy seems to have survived the deep cuts experienced everywhere else in the armed forces. Military chaplains have demonstrated how they add value.

Some Hard Questions

There are, however, some difficult areas for chaplaincies where the beliefs or moral judgements of the chaplains or their faith groups conflict with policies of the state. What then?

Chaplaincy is subject, for example, to the Equalities Act which forbids an organisation to exclude on the grounds of age, disability, pregnancy and maternity, gender (including gender reassignment), sexual orientation, ethnicity, beliefs or age. Most of the implications of these inclusive and anti-discrimination requirements will be uncontroversial, though they may require some chaplains to subordinate their personal views in the interests of those they seek to help. If, for example, a chaplain has a particular faith-based view of homosexuality, he or she cannot insist on expressing that in ways that would cause problems within the institution; and the faith group from which the chaplain comes needs to understand that this is a consequence of taking state funding. It also means that the chaplaincy has to assess continually whether its own organisation is sufficiently representative of the religious/non-religious beliefs present in the community it seeks to serve. It has to work with a broad and inclusive understanding of 'spiritual', an understanding that can be justified to the liberal state. Individual churches and faith groups are required, in effect, to accept that the modern chaplaincy is different from how chaplaincy would be if they alone were sponsoring it or if they were only ministering to their own members. It has to be shaped to the realities of working in a public institution in a society of many faiths and where some have 'no religion'.

But what if the institution does something or requires something that on religious grounds chaplains find hard to condone? Can chaplaincy have a prophetic voice? Thinking through such a situation requires maturity and professionalism on the part of chaplains. The maturity lies in recognising that we live in an imperfect world where few situations are ever wholly black or white; in a plural society which has to accommodate a range of opinions; and in a democratic state that will seek to reflect in its public policy the views of the majority. The professionalism is never to lose sight for one moment of the pastoral responsibility that the chaplain has for another person's welfare. This is best illustrated with a couple of examples.

Military chaplains understand very well that when they commit to the armed services they must do nothing that undermines morale. For this reason, RAF chaplains made no public comment about the area bombing of German cities during the Second World War even though that troubled some Christian consciences. The open expression of moral misgivings would have unsettled aircrews which potentially could have put lives at risk. Senior chaplains, however, did take their moral objections to senior commanders. Similarly, chaplains in the NHS may be drawn from denominations that have positions on such matters as artificial contraception or abortion that conflict with the practice of the institution, but when they are part of a chaplaincy team they must have as their overriding concern the well-being and welfare of patients and staff, acting within the legal and operational requirements laid on all employees. If an issue becomes intolerable for a chaplain's conscience then he or she should withdraw from the chaplaincy. One of the responsibilities of the chaplaincy, therefore, is to try to think through how chaplains might respond in advance of any change. For instance, the time may come when the law allows physician-assisted suicide. Before that time chaplains (in hospitals and hospices) will need to think about how they will act should this come about. Will they continue to offer pastoral and spiritual support to everyone involved (not least because the consciences of other staff may also be disturbed)? If they feel they cannot, it is hard to see how these chaplaincies or individual chaplains can continue to be funded by the state when the state has made its position clear.

Conclusion

Chaplaincies within public institutions are dependent on a number of factors, not all of which are within their capacity to influence either directly or at all. They need the support of the general public as well as politicians and mangers. That was not an issue when everyone's life was lived out under the sacred canopy of religion. Even though the future of organised religion in the west is precarious, there is evidence that chaplaincy will still be supported where chaplains are doing work that is regarded as valuable and could not be undertaken by some other group of professionals – the high regard in which military chaplains are currently held is an example. Chaplains will need to work harder at explaining what they do within faith communities as well as to the general public and raising their profiles both locally and nationally because any publicly funded work in the present financial climate will have to justify itself by showing the value it adds. But if they can do this, they will flourish.

References

Archbishops' Council (2014), *Statistics for Mission 2012*. London: Archbishops' Council Research and Statistics Department.

Avis, P. (ed.) (2003), *Public Faith? The State of Religious Belief and Practice in Britain*. London: SPCK.

Billings, A. (2009), *God and Community Cohesion. Help or Hindrance?* London: SPCK.

—— (2013), *Lost Church. Why We Must Find It Again*. London: SPCK.

—— (2014), *The Dove, the Fig Leaf and the Sword. Why Christianity Changes its Mind about War*. London: SPCK.

Brown, C.G. (2001), *The Death of Christian Britain: Understanding Secularization*. London: Routledge.

Bruce, S. (2002), *God is Dead: Secularization in the West*. Oxford: Blackwell.

Dawkins, R. (2007), *The God Delusion*. London: Black Swan.

de Botton, A. (2012), *Religion for Atheists*. London: Hamish Hamilton.

Dennett, D. (2007), *Breaking the Spell: Religion as a Natural Phenomenon*. London: Penguin.

Dinham, A., R. Furbey, and V. Lowndes (eds) (2009), *Faith in the Public Realm. Controversies, Policies and Practices*. Bristol: The Policy Press.

Gladstone, D. (1999), Editor's Introduction. In: Gladstone, D. (ed.), *Before Beveridge, Welfare Before the Welfare State*. London: IEA Health and Welfare Unit.

Grayling, A.C. (2001), *The Meaning of Things: Applying Philosophy to Life*. London: Phoenix.

Heelas, P. and L. Woodhead, (2005), *The Spiritual Revolution. Why Religion is Giving Way to Spirituality*. Oxford: Blackwell.

Hitchins, C. (2007), *God is Great. How Religion Poisons Everything*. London: Atlantic Books.

Lewis, J. (1999), The Voluntary Sector in the Mixed Economy of Welfare. In: Gladstone, D. (ed.), *Before Beveridge, Welfare Before the Welfare State*. London: IEA Health and Welfare Unit.

Lloyd, R. (1966), *The Church of England 1900–1965*. London: SCM Press Ltd.

Luhrmann, T.M. (2012), *When God Talks Back: Understanding the American Evangelical Relationship with God*. New York: Vintage Books.

Mackinnon, D. (1963), Moral Objections. In: Vidler, A. (ed.), *Objections to Christian Belief*. London: Constable.

Martin, D. (1997), *Does Christianity Cause War?* Oxford: Clarendon Press.

McGrath, A. (2005), *Dawkin's God. Genes, Memes, and the Meaning of Life*. Oxford: Blackwell.

McLeod, H. (2007), *The Religious Crisis of the 1960s*. Oxford: Oxford University Press.

Morgan, K.O. (1985), *Labour in Power 1945–1951*. Oxford: Oxford University Press.

NHS (2009), *NHS Constitution*. London: Department of Health.

NHS Careers (2014), *Chaplain*. [Online]. Available at: www.nhscareers.nhs.uk/explore-by-career/wider-healthcare-team/careers-in-the-wider-healthcare-team/corporate-services/chaplain/ (accessed 30 November 2014).

Parris, M. (2014), They weren't heroes. So why sing their praises? *The Times*, 15 March.

Putnam, R. (2001), *Bowling Alone: The Collapse and Revival of American Community*. New York: Simon and Schuster.

Richards, J., S. Wilson and L. Woodhead (1999), *Diana, the Making of a Media Saint*. London: I.B. Tauris.

Swift, C. (2009), *Hospital Chaplaincy in the Twenty-First Century: The Crisis of Spiritual Care on the NHS*. Aldershot: Ashgate.

Thompson, R. (2013), The Church as Christ's Holy/Sick Body: The Church as Necessary Irony. In Gittoes, J., B. Green and J. Heard (eds), *Generous Ecclesiology. Church, World and the Kingdom of God*. London: SCM Press.

Trigg, R. (2008), *Religion in Public Life. Must Faith Be Privatized?* Oxford: Oxford University Press.

Chapter 4

The Study of Chaplaincy: Methods and Materials

Peter Kevern and Wilf McSherry

Introduction

There can be little doubt of the need for further study of chaplaincy across a very broad front. While chaplains themselves are typically passionate about their role and contribution and can tell many stories of their impact upon individuals and events, there is still very little objective or generalisable information about what chaplains do and achieve. In an increasingly secular and instrumentalised society, in which every role is scrutinised for its contribution to the public good, chaplaincy must demonstrate its 'usefulness' in the same way as any other profession.

However, the evidence is slow in coming. The overwhelming preponderance of research, in the United Kingdom and elsewhere, is focused on the special case of hospital or health care chaplaincy. With a few significant exceptions, there is a notable lack of evidence and literature published addressing the many different types of chaplaincy that are provided within and across society in, for example, prisons, armed forces, universities, schools, airports, shopping centres and the police force. Furthermore, the many different roles and institutional relationships which chaplains adopt mean that research findings resist generalisation or transfer from one type of chaplaincy to another: a 'one size fits all' approach does not capture the uniqueness, nor the depth and the breadth, of chaplaincy within contemporary society. Finally, many chaplains are understandably resistant to having their contribution reduced to a set of measurable values or outcomes (McCurdy 2002) and they are also reluctant to carry out such research themselves or to elicit it from others. 'The reason why someone becomes a chaplain is not to conduct rigorous health outcomes research, but rather to serve the needs of those who are suffering ... 'Many chaplains are not interested in research, nor do they want to take the time to learn how to do it' (Koenig 2008: 87).

The challenge, then, is to try to capture and evaluate the impact that chaplains have in ways which are sensitive to chaplains' own frequently asserted claim that their role is nuanced, typically hidden and dealing in unquantifiable and indefinable outcomes; while recognising that they may be accountable to several different 'stakeholders' with divergent interests and needs. Given this complexity in the discourse surrounding chaplaincy, studies relating to it will inevitably take a number of different forms, and any individual study will represent just one of many non-commensurable perspectives on its object.

For the purposes of this chapter, it seems convenient and explanatorily useful to understand a chaplain as 'answerable' to four distinct sets of interests, each of which frames the study of chaplaincy in a different range of ways. We will therefore discuss the current field of research around chaplaincy under four headings which reflect these divergent sets of interests: chaplaincy as representative of a religious tradition; chaplaincy as serving institutional values and ends; chaplaincy as therapy for the individual client; and chaplaincy as a reflective and reflexive activity. As we will show, each of these perspectives imposes its own logic, priorities and values: it defines the subject to be studied in a different way, and so favours particular methodologies and methods. This in turn accounts for many of the difficulties in gaining an overview of the current state of research into chaplaincy.

Chaplaincy as Representative of a Religious Tradition

Chaplaincy has its origins and roots primarily within a Christian, religious, pastoral and theological tradition that has left an enduring legacy and host of associations and connotations. It remains the case that the majority of chaplains are practising Christians, and where they are not they are likely to be representing another religious tradition; although there is a decreasing expectation that chaplains should be 'official' representatives of a particular religion (see Cramer and Tenzek 2012, for US hospices), truly secular or non-religious chaplains are still very rare.

The relationship between the chaplain and their religious tradition may be complicated and peripheral in all sorts of ways (Scott 2000 [2013]): for example, Swift (2009) discovers that Anglican hospital chaplains include a disproportionate number of clergy whose beliefs or lifestyle would make it difficult to find employment in the normal parish context (Swift 2009: 150). Nevertheless, in order to continue to receive the support of the body they claim to represent, there must be an active dialogue between the two sides demonstrating the consonance of the chaplain's role and activities with the tradition. This is, in the broadest sense, the *theological* study of chaplaincy. It shares with theology generally a very variable and eclectic approach to methods and sources, but is best distinguished by the fact that it is addressed primarily to fellow adherents of the tradition and those sympathetic to it.

The fact that many chaplaincy teams are made up primarily of representatives of particular religious traditions may explain why a proportion of writing on the subject of chaplaincy takes the form of theological or ideological reflection on its role and status, and is directed to other members of the same faith tradition (e.g. Bunniss et al. 2013). In bringing the sacred and secular into juxtaposition, it has made a significant contribution to the life and self-understanding of those faith communities. For example, Cobb (2007: 9) identifies three distinct theological tasks for chaplains: confessional ('articulation of the faith, beliefs and practice of the religious community'); liberational ('to transform the world by releasing people from all that prevents them from becoming fully human'); and the critique of religion itself. Thus, chaplains may serve as agents in reforming their own communities; but on the face of it, this sort of activity has little to offer to those outside the religious tradition in question.

However, there are two pressures which between them encourage an attempt to engage a wider audience. In the first place, a purely religious model or representation of chaplaincy is being forced to change in response to a more diverse and secular society and to the fact that 'chaplaincy' must reflect the growing religious plurality that exists within many societies and indeed organisations (e.g. Abu-Ras and Laird 2011, Carey and DelMedico 2014). In a society where the proportion of people who report themselves as of no religion is increasing – in the UK, from 14.8 per cent in 2001 to 25.1 per cent in 2011, according to the latest Census (Office for National Statistics 2012) – and in which many hospital chaplains, for example, now have a multifaith team that is inclusive of minority faith groups (Orchard 2000, Duffin 2013), there is a need for a discourse on chaplaincy which preserves its core values but speaks to people of all religions and none. Secondly, secular organisations are justifiably suspicious of self-proclaimed religious representatives and suspect them of running a hidden agenda. Although chaplains may themselves be marginal to their own religious communities (see Mitchell and Sneddon 1999, Swift 2009) they are not perceived as such by their employers or managers and may justifiably be treated with suspicion (Leavey and King 2007): they are under pressure to explain why they value what they value in more publicly accessible terms. This leads into the methodologies of practical theology, where empirical data may be used as the starting point for a theology reflecting on and feeding back into practice; and public theology, in which reflection draws on and feeds in to a shared discourse on values and meanings that is not located in a specifically 'religious' realm. Against the assumption that we are living in an ever advancing secularism, such approaches seek to reconnect with some of the deeply held values and priorities which derive from the UK's religious past and which persist in its structures and assumptions (Ward 2003). The challenges, tensions and opportunities for chaplaincy as representative of religious tradition are further explored in Box 4.1.

Box 4.1

Two papers, both in the *Scottish Journal of Healthcare Chaplaincy*, neatly demonstrate two different approaches to this issue. In the first (Aldridge 2006), entitled 'The unique role of a chaplain', the author articulates the place of the hospital chaplain as the 'Religious Expert' in the clinical team, with particular gifts: as the bearer of the Christian Story; skilled in ritual and sacrament; representative of religious authority; as pray-er, pastoral theologian and faith developer. In addition, the chaplain is a 'spiritual expert', expressed in his/her roles as therapist, in teaching, personal development, interpretation and prophecy.

The second, entitled 'Listening as health care' (Mowat et al. 2013) steps much further from an explicit religious commitment and presents an account of 'listening' which, while clearly derived from the Christian tradition, assumes the context of chaplaincy to be secular and in so doing does not mention any links chaplains might have with a religious tradition. The idiom for this model is clearly one of public theology, in which the role of the 'spiritual' is valued, but decoupled from any particular framework of belief or practice.

In both cases, the emphasis of the account given is on its internal coherence rather than its conformity to any empirical data (although, to be fair, for Mowat et al. this is just one paper from a project which does generate and review empirical data at other points). In this respect, they are contiguous with a theological tradition based in the humanities in which the persuasiveness of the findings depends upon the characteristics of the narrative generated and the perceived authority of sources – in these cases, the scriptures, Jung, and recent thinking in theology and sociology.

Chaplaincy as Serving Institutional Values and Ends

By definition, chaplaincy is usually conducted within or answerable to an organisational structure which imposes its own criteria and values. These may be dominant and univocal in institutions such as a boarding school, prison or the armed forces; or relatively informal and occasional, such as chaplains in shopping centres or airports. In the former case, the role of the chaplain will inevitably include responsibility to uphold and propagate the institutional norms, or express the institution's commitments to its members (e.g. Sundt and Cullen 1998, 2002 for prison chaplains). A particularly egregious example would be the induction of Muslim chaplains into the Prison Service explicitly in order to combat the 'radicalisation' of prisoners – see, for example, Pickering (2014: 159), Dooghan (2006). This opens the possibility of research into the contribution of chaplaincy to institutional goals, in this case those set by national government as part of a wider political strategy. Clearly, the measure of chaplaincy in this case would be the extent to which it prevented the 'radicalisation' (however measured) of Muslim prisoners.

Perhaps more commonly and less contentiously, in fields such as health care the employment of chaplains requires resources which would otherwise be deployed elsewhere. The obvious question for the purposes of research and study is whether their employment saves more than it costs; or advances the goals of the institution in ways that would not otherwise be possible. In short, the values of large-scale institutions tend to be expressed in quantifiable forms, and as a result studies of chaplaincy on this scale lean towards quantitative analyses of empirical data. Good examples would include the two large-scale analyses of hospital chaplaincy in the New York area (Fogg et al. 2004, Vanderwerker et al. 2008, 2009, Galek et al. 2011), the study of hospice admissions by Flannelly et al. (2012) or the tendentious study of health service chaplains published by the National Secular Society (NSS 2011). However, such large-scale studies tend to be concentrated in health care chaplaincy where the numbers are sufficiently high to justify the approach. Smaller-scale studies may use questionnaires to elicit the opinions of healthcare managers, whether of staffing levels (VandeCreek and Burton 2001) or roles (Flannelly et al. 2006). A number use exploratory studies to attend to the voice of chaplains and from this derive institutional recommendations (e.g. Baker 2006, Whitehead 2011, Abu-Ras and Laird 2011). Others examine the role of the chaplain against the backdrop of the stated institutional priorities (e.g. Todd and Tipton 2011, Carey and Del Medico 2014). Finally, a case study approach was adopted to investigate chaplaincy in Queensland schools (taking each of nine services as a 'case') to identify how the services contributed to social capital and so justify their continued existence (Salecich 2002). Each of these approaches generates recommendations for the institution concerned, even if this is not their primary goal (see Box 4.2).

Box 4.2

The Role of the Prison Chaplain in Rehabilitation (Sundt et al. 2002)

This study arises out of 'an emerging research agenda to assess the effect of religious programming on inmate prison adjustment and recidivism' and some preliminary data that suggested that religious programmes reduce recidivism in the US correctional system. It used a questionnaire sent to prison chaplains nationally (n = 232), followed by a revised version sent only to chaplains in New York (n = 37) 'to examine chaplains' support for rehabilitation, the extent to which chaplains are involved in counseling inmates, and the content of chaplains' counseling sessions'.

---

continued ...

Measures of attitudes were recorded on Likert or nominal scales and summarised in tables; counselling techniques were selected from a standardised list; and two free-text answers were added in order to elicit information about what happened in the counselling sessions themselves.

The drawback of this multifaceted approach was that the data did not lend themselves to inferential analysis: the results were too complex and context-specific to yield a generalisable pattern that could provide recommendations for the future behaviour and activities of chaplains. But the advantage of the research design was that it enabled the researchers to build up a rich description of what chaplains do and the perspectives they bring to their work. In the process, they were able to establish that the majority of chaplains used styles of counselling that have been positively associated with reduced recidivism. In effect, this is presented as a proxy measure for chaplaincy effectiveness when measured against institutional goals.

Costing the Heavens: Chaplaincy Services in English NHS Provider Trusts 2009/10 (NSS 2011)

This study sets out to identify the amount spent on chaplaincy services by individual NHS provider (acute and mental health) trusts. By a fairly sophisticated process of statistical analysis, it then searches for a correlation between this figure (expressed as a percentage of total trust income) and two key national measures of quality used in hospitals: 'Standards for Better Health' and the Standardised Mortality Ratio. Finding that there was no statistically significant correlation between spend on chaplaincy services and score on either of these two quality measures, the report wisely forebears from claiming that chaplaincy services are therefore a waste of money. However, it does venture to calculate the savings that would be made by the NHS if expenditure on chaplaincy per trust were reduced to the level of the most 'efficient' (in terms of minimum chaplaincy spend and maximum quality score).

The problem with all statistical analyses is to identify the key variables, and a large-scale statistical study can lend an illusion of authority to some rather superficial analyses. Uncontrolled variables here include the proportion of chaplaincy which is carried out by volunteers in different trusts, and whether an increased spend on chaplaincy may in some cases be a response to conditions which also give rise to poor quality measures. For example, given the current health inequalities, a trust with a high proportion of ethnic minority patients is likely to perform poorly in the standardised mortality ratio measures and may benefit significantly from employing chaplains; the situation may be reversed in a wealthy teaching hospital. This study therefore illustrates some of the limitations of a large-scale statistical analysis when decoupled from more fine-grained studies.

Chaplaincy and Therapy

Within the healthcare context (which clearly dominates the field of research into chaplaincy) the clear role of the chaplain is a therapeutic one. Although few chaplains would want to claim physical or medical benefits for their intervention, there is wide acceptance that they may be offering psychological comfort. Many, if not all, would also claim that they offer a form of social, spiritual or existential 'therapy' beyond the narrowly psychological.

It is perhaps unsurprising, then, that the vast majority of research into the outcomes of chaplaincy is concerned with its effects on individuals and groups of recipients. Here, the search for objective measures of success or performance is inevitably unfruitful, and the methodologies deployed to research the patient experience tend instead to fall on a spectrum. At one end are large-scale surveys of patient expectations and experiences (e.g. Piderman et al. 2010, Winter-Pfändler and Flannelly 2013), of chaplains' activity with individual patients (Handzo et al. 2008) or of chaplains' attitudes and readiness (e.g. Abu-Ras and Laird 2011). These have the advantages of some degree of quantifiability and can make valid generalisations across a sample of chaplaincy interventions. But they inevitably miss the details of patient–chaplain interactions, as well as overlooking the synergistic effects on the patient experience of chaplains' roles within wider therapeutic teams. Since for most chaplains the focus is upon the interests of individual patients or clients and their immediate social circles, such extrapolation from these to bulk data analyses may seem to be missing the point. Most chaplains would claim that they adopted the role in order to help individuals or small groups: their raw materials are stories, prayers, rituals and gestures of loving concern rather than data. This is presumably one of the reasons (alongside, e.g., lack of time and training) why chaplains as a professional body have been slow to embrace the mantra of 'evidence-based practice' or the commitment to constant evaluation which it entails: there is something about this epistemology which runs counter to many chaplains' deepest motivations. It is therefore hardly surprising that research generated by and for chaplains themselves much more frequently leans towards small-scale qualitative interview studies. There is a natural 'fit' between the data gathered by these methods and the way in which chaplains themselves gather information.

One may expect, therefore, to find a large number of studies based upon interviews with patients or recipients of chaplaincy services in order to reproduce the patient voice in narrow, but rich and deep, accounts that uncover what chaplaincy means for *them*. However, although there is a fair body of research drawing on chaplains' own accounts of interactions with patients or clients (e.g. Budd 1999 the air force, Carey and Davoren 2008 and Coates 2013 in heath care, Whitehead 2011 in community chaplaincy), studies that interview patients/clients themselves are remarkably thin on the ground (Box 4.3).

Box 4.3

A pair of studies of a pilot 'community chaplaincy' service in Scotland represent two among a fairly limited number of studies which attempt to capture the patient/client experience of their relationship to the service. The first of these (Snowden et al. 2013) draws upon free-text responses to an item in a questionnaire (the Lothian PROM) designed to evaluate the effect of the service on patient outcomes. The responses were analysed using a qualitative framework method in order to extract key recurrent themes.

In the second paper (Bunniss et al. 2013), the study comprised an analysis of patient data along with 18 patient interviews; focus groups and questionnaires with a small sample of GPs; and interviews and paperwork from participating chaplains. The advantage of a mixed-methods study for these purposes is that it can capture dimensions from different sources that support each other to form a balanced overall picture. In the current instance, this rich set of data enabled themes to be identified in the patient interviews, for these to be cross-referenced to data on how patients used the chaplaincy service, and for this picture to be compared with that presented by the GPs and chaplains.

In terms of a formal hierarchy of evidence,[1] both of these studies would be rated rather low. There is no single coherent methodology, minimal control of variables and a high dependence on the perceptions of participants and researchers themselves. But their strength rests upon the way in which they build up, separately and together, a single picture of the patient experience which draws upon a range of sources and identifies in each some similar themes. The result is a rich picture which gives the impression of preserving the complexity of the patient voice without rushing to contain it within a single overarching structure.

This is turn raises the question of whether there are other methodologies which more closely reflect chaplains' concerns, a question which brings us inevitably to the fourth and final group of 'stakeholders', the chaplains themselves.

---

[1] There are a number of 'hierarchies of evidence' that are widely used in medical research. Typically, they treat meta-analyses, systematic reviews and randomized control trials as the most authoritative sources of information, and treat information gathered from qualitative studies with much more suspicion. Towards the bottom of the hierarchies are case studies and 'expert opinion', which between them account for much of the research conducted by chaplains themselves on their own context.

Chaplaincy as Reflective and Reflexive Activity

The final paradigm to be examined provides a different solution to the same dilemma. In answer to the question of how to conduct research in a way that values the uniqueness of individual encounters, it rejects the claims of generalisability in favour of a different mode of engagement. For many chaplains, the point of their role is, precisely, that its outcomes cannot be specified beforehand: 'The response of chaplains is shaped by the human reality they encounter, requiring them to deliver bespoke spiritual care services, which recognize the uniqueness of every situation' (Swift et al. 2012: 188). From this perspective, the fact that chaplains may have no clear definition of their own role (e.g. Mitchell and Sneddon 1999 [2013]) may be understood as an asset rather than a problem to be solved; but it implies that the study of chaplaincy should not take a definition of the role as its starting point: it is to be studied as a series of encounters and events.

The most obvious methodology for preserving the reflective and unique character of chaplaincy encounters is the case study (e.g. Cooper 2011, Risk 2013), which has the advantage of immediacy and coheres well with the perception of chaplaincy (see above) as concerned with narrative. Furthermore, it explicitly draws on the reflective and reflexive stance of the chaplain as a way of making sense of the situation.

The limitations of such an approach are the converse of its strengths. While capturing what appears to be an authentic chaplains' voice, the case study does not triangulate this against the perceptions of others. In one large-scale study (Montonye and Calderone 2010) the researchers concluded that chaplains' reports of patient needs may say more about the chaplains themselves than the needs of patients. Analogously, chaplains' perceptions of their own roles may reflect their own biases, and so subtly promote 'chaplain-centred care' rather than 'patient-centred care', unless viewed alongside studies employing different methodologies.

For some purposes, this confusion of the roles of chaplain and researcher may be seen as an asset rather than a liability. For example, in action research (e.g. Mowat et al. 2012), there is no separation of the research, its findings and its practical outworking: the point of the research is to bring about change in the present rather than to provide abstract or generalisable principles on which change may be brought about in the future. Action research tends to be very labour intensive, and there will always be uncertainty regarding the transferability of results to other contexts. But the process of repeated cycles of action and reflection may well prove more congenial to serving chaplains than more abstract or 'objective' methods; and does not necessarily preclude the drawing of some conclusions with lasting value and wider applicability (e.g., Crawley 2013).

A more academically orientated and methodologically articulate approach which seeks to preserve and be led by the voices and reflections of practitioners 'on the ground' is supplied by Grounded Theory. Properly understood, Grounded Theory emphasises the importance of approaching the data (typically from interviews) with as few presuppositions as possible; allowing any theoretical framework or model to arise from the data being pored over and then testing and refining it by actively seeking and evaluating counter-examples (e.g. Townsend 2010, Nolan 2011). Where conducted rigorously, this method successfully combines data gathering and analysis with reflective and reflexive insights to produce an account of the subject which is both academically and intuitively persuasive. But it is a lengthy and time-consuming process, and there is a growing debate about what can legitimately be counted as 'Grounded Theory': in reality, the term can sometimes turn out to be applied to a hasty analysis of some shakily conducted interviews!

It is clear from some of the examples given in this section that there are ways in which chaplains themselves may be drawn into the study of chaplaincy in ways which value their reflective and reflexive insights as individuals, do not compromise their independence from either their faith community or their employing institution, and which preserve the immediacy and narrative emphasis of some of their activity in the research process (Box 4.4). However, the fact that most research conducted by chaplains themselves is of fairly limited scope and quality raises the question of how to support and train them to conduct rigorous and robust research

---

Box 4.4

In a very detailed and rigorous example of a Grounded Theory study, Nolan (2011) investigates the experience of 19 palliative care chaplains using a mixture of unstructured interviews and group work. After listening to chaplains' own stories at length, the author identifies four related themes or ways of understanding the chaplain as intentionally 'present' with the patient: 'evocative presence', 'accompanying presence', 'comforting presence' and 'hopeful presence'. These he comes to understand as 'organic moments' in the patient–chaplain relationship that may ease the passage of the patient from their (now redundant) hope of recovery to a new hopefulness in the face of death that transcends despair while maintaining a true view of their situation.

The paradox of this study is that although it technically begins from a 'theory-free' perspective on the relationship between chaplain and patient, it is informed and 'framed' by influential theories on how hope develops in terminal illness and how psychotherapeutic 'transference' may underlie the chaplain–patient relationship. This raises a suspicion that has often been discussed in relation to Grounded Theory – that

---

the denial of the authority of any prior theoretical perspective does not render a study 'theory free' but simply unreflexive. However detached and objective the researcher seeks to be, they may be unconsciously drawing upon their areas of expertise and interest and this becomes the lens used when analysing and interpreting the data and developing the theory.

A rather different perspective is provided by Risk's (2013) case study of spiritual care of an individual patient with Parkinson's disease. As well as being explicitly a first-person account, this case study is relatively unusual in deliberately bringing a theoretical framework (narrative theory) into play as an interpretive and even therapeutic tool. As Grossoehme (2013) comments, the approach challenges the paradigm of chaplaincy as 'agenda-less' and portrays it as potentially able to draw on a repertoire of interventions. Thus, the study can be understood as something of a challenge to chaplains who would claim that their work is too intuitive and individualised to be open to either the use of explicit tools or learning from other chaplains or other disciplines; to the extent that the case study can be taken as a true account of an intervention that works, it invites reflection on what chaplaincy fundamentally is.

Conclusions and Further Possibilities

There is now a substantial body of research into chaplaincy from a range of disciplinary perspectives and with a variety of methodologies. Nevertheless, as this brief review and summary indicates, there are some significant gaps. Most obvious of these is the relative paucity of material from the perspective of the patient or client: it is paradoxical that a profession that is so explicitly focused on the 'service user' should apparently overlook the possibilities of engaging them in dialogue. Clearly, some of the reasons for this are practical – by definition, many recipients of chaplaincy are vulnerable and may be reluctant to contribute, and the process of gaining the necessary ethical approval for research with patients is notoriously tortuous and time-consuming – but there is room for further development here.

The understanding of chaplaincy might also benefit from some techniques and theoretical approaches which are as yet hardly used. Among the former, there is a whole range of tools that derive from ethnography and anthropology that have made brief appearances in the literature of chaplaincy (e.g. Baker 2006, Phillips 2013) but have yet to make a real impact. Among the latter, a few studies (e.g. Norwood 2006 in hospitals, Hicks 2012 for prison chaplains) are beginning to explore the potential of critical discourse-based studies of the categories, assumptions and fluxes of power associated with chaplaincy.

Furthermore, there is relatively little material that attempts something like a 'realist synthesis' (Pawson and Tilley 1997) of the functions and achievements of chaplains across the different domains of study that have been outlined above. It is still unnervingly the case that religious groups, institutional managers, chaplains and clients may discuss, understand and value chaplaincy in quite separate ways and without attempting to bring together their divergent insights into shared account. We hope that the current work will contribute to the development of such an understanding.

Finally, it remains the case that chaplains themselves are under-represented among those researching chaplaincy, and this may be to the detriment of the profession. As in other professions, there is an ineluctable move towards evidence-based practice in chaplaincy, which chaplains ignore at their peril: 'The future of chaplaincy is in the balance! Do chaplains move with the times ... or ... risk extinction or at best benign tolerance? More than ever, society demands that employees prove their value through research, audit and refining of practice' (Aldridge 2006: 21). The challenge for chaplains is to develop and defend methods of researching the field that reflect their self-understanding of their role(s) while satisfying the demands of their sponsors in the public, private and third sectors. A failure to engage with these demands may result in the imposition of research criteria and methods which obscure the distinctive contributions of the profession to the fulfilment of some fundamental human concerns. If chaplains consider that their work is widely undervalued and misunderstood, at least part of the solution lies in their own hands.

References

Abu-Ras, W. and Laird, L. (2011), How Muslim and non-Muslim chaplains serve Muslim patients? Does the interfaith chaplaincy model have room for Muslims' experiences? *Journal of Religion and Health*, 50(1), 46–61.

Aldridge, A. (2006), The unique role of a chaplain. *Scottish Journal of Healthcare Chaplaincy*, 9(1), 18–22.

Baker, M. (2006), The continuing professional education of police chaplains as a community of practice. Available at: https://opus.lib.uts.edu.au/research/bitstream/handle/10453/7439/2006005183.pdf?sequence=1 (accessed 11 April 2015).

Budd F.C. (1999), An Air Force model of psychologist–chaplain collaboration. *Professional Psychology: Research and Practice*, 30(6), 552–6.

Bunniss, S., Mowat, H. and Snowden, A. (2013), Community chaplaincy listening: practical theology in action. *The Scottish Journal of Healthcare Chaplaincy*, 16, 42–51.

Carey, L.B. and Davoren, R.P. (2008), Inter-faith pastoral care and the role of the health care chaplain. *Scottish Journal of Healthcare Chaplaincy*, 11(1), 21–32.

Carey, L.B. and Del Medico, L. (2014), Correctional services and prison chaplaincy in Australia: an exploratory study. *Journal of Religion and Health*, 53(6), 1786–99.

Coates, S.M. (2013). Upholding the patient narrative in palliative care: the role of the healthcare chaplain in the multidisciplinary team. *Health and Social Care Chaplaincy*, 17–21. [Reprint of a 2010 paper.]

Cobb, M. (2007), Change and challenge: the dynamic of chaplaincy. *Scottish Journal of Healthcare Chaplaincy*, 10(1): 4–10.

Cooper, R.S. (2011), Case study of a chaplain's spiritual care for a patient with advanced metastatic breast cancer. *Journal of Health Care Chaplaincy*, 17(1–2), 19–37.

Cramer, E.M. and Tenzek, K.E. (2012), The chaplain profession from the employer perspective: an analysis of hospice chaplain job advertisements. *Journal of Health Care Chaplaincy*, 18(3–4), 133–50.

Crawley, L.M. (2013), Collaborative inquiry: an accessible, relevant approach to chaplaincy research. *Vision*, 23(2). Available at: www.nacc.org/vision/mar-apr-2013/research-Crawley.aspx (accessed 11 April 2015).

Dooghan, J.K. (2006), *Muslim Prison Ministry: Hindering the Spread of the Radical, Militant, Violent and Irreconcilable Wing of Islam*. Kansas: Army Command and General Staff College, Fort Leavenworth, KS School of Advanced Military Studies. Available at: http://www.dtic.mil/cgi-bin/GetTRDoc?AD=ADA450078&Location=U2&doc=GetTRDoc.pdf (accessed 11 April 2015).

Duffin, C. (2013), Who pays for the pastor? *Nursing Standard*, 28(7), 24–5.

Flannelly, K.J., Handzo, G.F., Galek, K., Weaver, A.J. and Overvold, J.A. (2006), A national survey of hospital directors' views about the importance of various chaplain roles: differences among disciplines and types of hospitals. *Journal of Pastoral Care and Counseling*, 60(3), 213.

Flannelly, K.J., Emanuel, L.L., Handzo, G.F., Galek, K., Silton, N.R. and Carlson, M. (2012), A national study of chaplaincy services and end-of-life outcomes. *BMC Palliative Care*, 11(1), 10.

Fogg, S.L., Weaver, A.J., Flannelly, K.J. and Handzo, G.F. (2004), An analysis of referrals to chaplains in a community hospital in New York over a seven-year period. *Journal of Pastoral Care and Counseling*, 58, 225–36.

Galek, K., Flannelly, K.J., Jankowski, K.R. and Handzo, G.F. (2011), A methodological analysis of chaplaincy research: 2000–2009. *Journal of Health Care Chaplaincy*, 17(3–4), 126–45.

Grossoehme, D.H. (2013), Chaplaincy and narrative theory: a response to Risk's case study. *Journal of Health Care Chaplaincy*, 19(3), 99–111.

Handzo, G.F., Flannelly, K.J., Kudler, T., Fogg, S.L., Harding, S.R., Hasan, I.Y.H. and Taylor, R.B.E. (2008), What do chaplains really do? II. Interventions in the New York Chaplaincy Study. *Journal of Health Care Chaplaincy*, 14(1), 39–56.

Hicks, A.M. (2012), Learning to watch out: prison chaplains as risk managers. *Journal of Contemporary Ethnography*, 41(6), 636–67.

Koenig, H.G. (2008), Why research is important for chaplains. *Journal of Health Care Chaplaincy*, 14(2), 83–90.

Leavey, G. and King, M. (2007), The devil is in the detail: partnerships between psychiatry and faith-based organisations. *The British Journal of Psychiatry*, 191(2), 97–8.

McCurdy, D.B. (2002), But what are we trying to prove? *Journal of Health Care Chaplaincy*, 12(1–2), 151–63.

Mitchell, D. and Sneddon, M. (1999), Informing the debate: chaplaincy and spiritual care in Scotland. *International Journal of Palliative Nursing*, 5(6), 275–80. [Reissued 2013.]

Montonye, M. and Calderone, S. (2010), Pastoral interventions and the influence of self-reporting: a preliminary analysis. *Journal of Health Care Chaplaincy*, 16(1–2), 65–73.

Mowat, H., Bunniss, S. and Kelly, E. (2012), Community chaplaincy listening: working with general practitioners to support patient wellbeing. *Scottish Journal of Healthcare Chaplaincy*, 15(1), 21–6.

Mowat, H., Bunniss, S., Snowden, A. and Wright, L. (2013), Listening as health care. *Scottish Journal of Healthcare Chaplaincy*, 16, 35–41.

NSS (2011), *Costing the Heavens: Chaplaincy Services in English NHS Provider Trusts 2009/10*. London: National Secular Society. Available at: www.secularism.org.uk/uploads/nss-chaplaincy-report-2011.pdf (accessed 11 April 2015).

Nolan, S. (2011), Hope beyond (redundant) hope: how chaplains work with dying patients. *Palliative Medicine*, 25(1), 21–5.

Norwood, F. (2006), The ambivalent chaplain: negotiating structural and ideological difference on the margins of modern-day hospital medicine. *Medical Anthropology*, 25(1), 1–29.

Office for National Statistics (2012), *Religion in England and Wales 2011*. Available at: www.ons.gov.uk/ons/dcp171776_290510.pdf (accessed 11 April 2015).

Orchard, H. (2000), *Hospital Chaplaincy: Modern, Dependable*. Sheffield: Sheffield Academic Press.

Pawson, R. and Tilley, N. (1997), *Realistic Evaluation*. London: Sage.

Phillips, P. (2013), *Roles and Identities of the Anglican Chaplain: A Prison Ethnography*. Cardiff: Cardiff University.

Pickering, R. (2014), Terrorism, Extremism, Radicalisation And The Offender Management System in England And Wales. In Silke, A. (ed.), *Prisons, Terrorism and Extremism: Critical Issues in Management, Radicalisation and Reform*. London: Routledge, 159–67.

Piderman, K.M., Marek, D.V., Jenkins, S.M., Johnson, M.E., Buryska, J.F., Shanafelt, T.D. and Mueller, P.S. (2010), Predicting patients' expectations of hospital chaplains: a multisite survey. *Mayo Clinic Proceedings*, 85(11), 1002–10.

Risk, J.L. (2013), Building a new life: A chaplain's theory-based case study of chronic illness. *Journal of Health Care Chaplaincy*, 19(3), 81–98.

Salecich, J.A. (2002), *Chaplaincy in Queensland State Schools: An Investigation*. PhD thesis. Brisbane: University of Queensland. Available at http://espace.library.uq.edu.au/view/UQ:184700 (accessed 8 May 2015)

Scott, T. (2013), Chaplaincy – a resource of Christian presence. *Health and Social Care Chaplaincy*, 3(1), 15–19. [Reissue of a 2000 paper.]

Snowden, A., Telfer, I., Kelly, E., Bunniss, S. and Mowat, H. (2013), Spiritual care as person-centered care: a thematic analysis of interventions. *Scottish Journal of Healthcare Chaplains*, 16, 3–32.

Sundt, J.L. and Cullen, F.T. (1998), The role of the contemporary prison chaplain. *The Prison Journal*, 78(3), 271–98.

Sundt, J.L. and Cullen, F.T. (2002), The correctional ideology of prison chaplains: a national survey. *Journal of Criminal Justice*, 30(5), 369–85.

Sundt, J.L., Dammer, H.R. and Cullen, F.T. (2002), The role of the prison chaplain in rehabilitation. *Journal of Offender Rehabilitation*, 35(3–4), 59–86.

Swift, C. (2009), *Hospital Chaplaincy in the Twenty-First Century: The Crisis of Spiritual Care on the NHS*. Farnham: Ashgate Publishing Ltd.

Swift, C., Handzo, G. and Gohen, J. (2012), Healthcare Chaplaincy. In Cobb, M., Puchalski, C.M. and Rumbold, B. (eds), *Oxford Textbook of Spirituality in Healthcare*. Oxford: Oxford University Press, 185–90.

Todd, A. and Tipton, L. (2011), *The Role and Contribution of a Multi-Faith Prison Chaplaincy to the Contemporary Prison Service*. Available at: http://orca.cf.ac.uk/29120/1/Chaplaincy%20Report%20Final%20Draft%20(3).pdf (accessed 11 April 2015).

Townsend, L.L. (2010). Research report: a grounded theory description of pastoral counseling. *The Journal of Pastoral Care & Counseling*, 65(3–4), 1–15.

VandeCreek, L. and Burton, L. (2001), Professional chaplaincy: its role and importance in healthcare. *Journal of Pastoral Care*, 55(1), 81–98.

Vanderwerker, L.C., Flannelly, K.J., Galek, K., Harding, S.R., Handzo, G.F., Oettinger, S.M. and Bauman, J.P. (2008), What do chaplains really do? III. Referrals in the New York Chaplaincy Study. *Journal of Health Care Chaplaincy*, 14(1), 57–73.

Vanderwerker, L.C., Handzo, G.F., Fogg, S.L. and Overvold, J.A. (2009), Selected findings from the 'New York' and the 'Metropolitan' chaplaincy studies: a 10-year comparison of chaplaincy in the New York City area. *Journal of Health Care Chaplaincy*, 15(1), 13–24.

Ward, M.J. (2003), Off the edge? A theological assessment of Scott's 'peripheral stance' of chaplaincy. *Scottish Journal of Healthcare Chaplaincy*, 6(1), 39–43.

Whitehead, P. (2011), *Evaluation Report of Research at Six Community Chaplaincy Projects in England and Wales*. Middlesbrough: Teesside University and Community Chaplaincy Association. Available at: www.communitychaplaincy.org.uk/images/COMMUNITYCHAPLAINCY REPORTJuly2011_001.pdf (accessed 11 April 2015).

Winter-Pfändler, U. and Flannelly, K.J. (2013), Patients' expectations of healthcare chaplaincy: a cross-sectional study in the German part of Switzerland. *Journal of Religion and Health*, 52(1), 159–68.

Chapter 5
Developing Practice-Based Evidence

Victoria Slater

Introduction

Chaplains who work in the public sector are all too aware of the increasing pressure over the past two decades to 'evidence' the impact and value of what they do. Many will have wrestled with the seeming paradox of being asked to 'measure' or represent in an objective way work that is relational at its heart. For example, I have heard chaplains in a health care setting ask questions such as: how can one 'evidence' the significance or value of time spent sitting with a patient who is afraid of dying so that their fear is assuaged, or the time spent attending to a person with dementia who may forget the visit as soon as the chaplain leaves? There are, of course, quantifiable activities within any chaplaincy service such as numbers and category of people seen, services offered, how time is spent, etc., for which factual evidence can be provided. However, this factual evidence says little, if anything, about the values and relationships built by chaplains with and between individuals and across organisations which promote and sustain human and social flourishing and which are central to the contribution of chaplaincy.

Public sector chaplains are being challenged to find ways to respond to the contemporary cultural and professional demand to undertake research, to provide evidence of the effectiveness of what they do and to draw on 'evidence-based practice' in order to improve the quality of the service they provide. In a climate of financial stringency and increased pressure on public resources, if chaplaincy is to flourish, it is essential that chaplains are able to provide both a high quality service and a coherent account of the value of that service to those who use and resource it.

Some chaplains may feel ambivalent about the pressure to generate 'evidence' on which to base their practice. This chapter suggests that this ambivalence might stem from the philosophical dissonance between the positivist scientific approach that has fuelled the call for evidence and the interpretive relational approach characteristic of chaplaincy. How has this situation developed and how can chaplains find appropriate ways to generate evidence so that this dissonance can be resolved? To answer this question, the chapter will look briefly at the cultural context in which contemporary chaplaincy takes place and within which the emphasis on 'evidence-based practice' has arisen. It will then address the issue of what kind of evidence it might be appropriate for chaplains to develop so that the new practice knowledge that is generated can be used creatively to support and develop practice and to enable chaplains to articulate with integrity and confidence the value of their work.

Contemporary Chaplaincy in the Public Square

The first question that needs to be asked is: What are the social conditions that have prompted the call for chaplains to produce evidence for the value and effectiveness of their work? The public square can here be understood as 'those virtual and actual spaces in which public norms and policy are negotiated and enacted for the good of civil society' (Todd 2011). Todd argues that over recent decades, public norms have been secularised. Policy and practice are now located within a discourse of human rights and diversity of culture and morality. This has established pluralism as a norm and diversity as a good that contributes to the well-being of society. In this context, religion may be valued for its capacity to contribute to a diverse civil society but it may also be viewed as problematic because of its perceived associations with irrational fundamentalisms and its potential for proselytising. It is in this context of changing public norms and policy that chaplains have to negotiate publicly acceptable practices and the language in which to describe what they do (Todd 2011: 8).

Chaplaincy constantly has to negotiate its identity in dialogue with the context in which it is embedded, which in turn is being shaped by contemporary public norms (Slater 2013: 12). This means that, as for other professionals working in the public domain, chaplaincy identity is shaped inevitably by the contemporary impetus towards public accountability and professionalisation. This involves the development of the apparatus of professionalism such as codes of conduct, standards, professional associations and unions. It also involves encountering the prevalent move towards 'evidence-based practice' and the need to find creative ways of responding to the challenge that presents.

Contemporary Chaplaincy in the Research Tradition: The Rise of Qualitative Inquiry

If chaplaincy is to be publicly accountable it does need to generate evidence as the basis for good practice. However, the use of the term 'evidence' begs some fundamental questions: What counts as evidence? What kind of evidence is reliable and best suited to show the value of chaplaincy work? In relation to psychotherapy research, Finlay and Evans (2009) challenge the dominant assumption behind the move towards 'evidence-based practice' in health care that evidence should be 'scientific'. This assumption privileges research undertaken within the positivist, scientific research paradigm which utilises approaches such as experimentation and randomised control trials (RCTs) to produce findings that can be replicated in different contexts. In this research tradition, measurement and quantification are paramount and the kind of evidence that is generated may be viewed as the best and most reliable. Whilst this kind of quantitative research has enormous value in certain fields of inquiry, it raises similar difficulties for chaplaincy as for psychotherapy: how can a chaplain's contextually informed, complex understanding of individual and social human experience be quantified? Can the multilayered, constantly shifting and often ambiguous relational work of chaplaincy ever be measured? Although this research paradigm may be privileged in some contexts, it is clear that it has its limitations and that there are large areas of human experience in relation to which it is inadequate. Finlay and Evans point out (2009: 50) that Professor Rawlins, a former Chair of NICE,[1] suggested in a speech to the Royal College of Physicians in 2008 that RCTs had been put on an 'undeserved pedestal' and that other types of research needed to be given attention.

This acknowledgement is part of a broader movement over recent decades towards the valuing of qualitative inquiry in the social sciences and professions. For example, Simons (2009: 13) notes that in educational research and evaluation in curriculum innovation, predominant models drawn from positivist research could not provide the evidence needed to develop the programmes and explain their success or failure. Approaches were needed that could include participant perspectives, that paid attention to the process and dynamics involved, to the audience needs and to the interpretation of events in their socio-political context. A qualitative approach to inquiry is needed in uncontrolled, complex social situations in order to provide adequate evidence upon which to base action and inform policy.

Qualitative inquiry is now well established within the research tradition and the many different forms and processes are well documented, for example by Denzin and Lincoln (2011). Chaplaincy sits well within this qualitative research tradition which studies things in their natural social setting and interprets them in context in terms of the meanings that participants bring to them. This chapter will go on to suggest qualitative inquiry as an appropriate way to generate adequate 'evidence' to inform chaplaincy practice and policy. It will also suggest that this research paradigm is a particularly apt and powerful approach available to chaplains in the current cultural context which places a high value on the importance of listening and responding to the experience of service users. One of the strengths of qualitative inquiry, particularly case study research as addressed below, is that research findings can be communicated in

---

[1] NICE stands for National Institute for Clinical Excellence.

the natural language of participants (Simons 2009: 16). This ensures that the research is widely accessible and that participant voices are heard. This move towards qualitative inquiry in complex social contexts provides a recognised research tradition within which chaplains can work and from which they can present their work in a rigorous and accessible way. It also challenges the dominance of the positivist evidence-based practice approach and underpins a growing call for the development of practice-based evidence (Finlay and Evans 2009: 53).

Developing a Practice-Based Approach to Evidence

The growing recognition of the value and legitimacy of practice-based evidence is good news for chaplains for whom the ability to reflect on practice is a core skill that is central to personal, professional and service development. It is this commitment to reflective practice that is central to the practice-based approach to the development of evidence. Although quantitative and qualitative research methods can be drawn upon in this approach, this chapter pays specific attention to the value of qualitative inquiry for chaplains. The strength of qualitative practice-centred research is that it is usually fairly small scale and undertaken by practitioners themselves. This ensures that the research addresses core issues relevant to practice and is able to place service users' experience at the centre of the research process. In this way it is able to give a voice both to practitioners and research participants.

There is no one model of how to do practice-based research; what is appropriate will depend on the context, the subject of inquiry and the purpose of the research. For example, a chaplain might look at the involvement of chaplaincy in a bereavement support service by offering detailed descriptions of their work in context, providing quantitative data about the extent of their involvement and gaining feedback about the experience of working with chaplains from service users and colleagues. A different model might be to undertake auto ethnography by a chaplain engaging in an in-depth interpretive study of their daily practice in a specific context over a certain period of time (Swift 2014). It is up to the practitioner with their unique knowledge of their practice context, perhaps in consultation with academic colleagues, to discern the most appropriate approach in order to fulfil the purpose of the research. A short chapter such as this cannot cover all the possible approaches and methods. What it can do is present one effective way in which chaplains might develop practice-based evidence. I have chosen the example of case study because of its flexibility and wide applicability.

Qualitative Case Study and the Development of Practice-Based Evidence

What is Case Study?

Case study research comprises the study of a particular example of something within a bounded system (Cresswell 2007). Different methods of data collection and analysis may be employed to explore whatever is being studied within the chosen boundary. For example, the boundary could be chaplaincy involvement with a particular group of service users or staff; an individual or group chaplaincy practice; or the use of a particular policy. Case study may include the use of quantitative as well as qualitative methods, although this chapter focuses on qualitative case study. Although case study is understood in different ways in different disciplines (Simons 2009: 19), the research focus and action-oriented purpose of case study can be helpfully described as

> an in-depth exploration from multiple perspectives of the complexity and
> uniqueness of a particular project, policy, institution, programme or system in
> a 'real life' context ... The primary purpose is to generate in-depth understanding
> of a specific topic ... to generate knowledge and/or inform policy development,
> professional practice and civil or community action. (Simons 2009: 21)

Why Choose Case Study?

As the above description suggests, case study is a flexible way to define and focus on a particular area of practice in order to generate practical knowledge that can feed back into practice and/or inform policy. It is a particularly good approach to choose if the researcher wants to go beyond describing what is happening to explore *why* something is happening and *how* it is happening, the processes and relationships involved (Yin 2009). It allows the researcher to use multiple qualitative methods to elicit the different understandings that participants might bring to a situation and thus to move beyond descriptions of practice to capture the processes and relationships, the *how* and the *why* data, that is then available for interpretive analysis. This can be particularly useful if the researcher wants to look at the effectiveness or otherwise of a particular chaplaincy practice or area of involvement. The practice knowledge generated by an in-depth study can also be used to inform service development and policy at departmental or organisational level. As with all research, case study must be undertaken with appropriate ethical consideration and with the approval of relevant bodies such as research ethics committees.

The main strengths of case study can therefore be said to be:

- It enables a particular situation to be explored in depth from multiple perspectives.
- It is flexible and can use whatever epistemologies and methods are most appropriate for understanding the case.
- It enables the researcher to develop descriptions of practice and new knowledge about the processes and relationships involved. This generates new practice knowledge that can then be used to inform the ongoing development of best practice.
- It can document multiple and sometimes contested perspectives and thereby help to explain how and why things happened.
- It enables service users to collaborate with the research process.
- It enables the voices of research participants and practitioners to be represented.
- It can be written up in accessible language that uses the words of participants. This can engage a wide audience including funders, service users and other practitioners, allowing the study to resonate with the reader's own experience and to use their tacit knowledge to understand its significance in their own context.

Case Study Design

A great deal has been written about case study as a research approach, for example by Stake (1995) and Yin (2009) to name just two authors. There are many different types and taxonomies of case studies which are helpfully set out by Thomas (2011: 91). However, the main thing to think about in designing a study is purpose: what do you want your study to do? The design of the study needs to flow from the purpose of the research encapsulated in the question that you want the research to address. Stake's (1995) typology provides a helpful framework for thinking about this, though Stake acknowledges that not everything fits neatly into these categories and that the types may overlap. According to Stake, a study may be:

- *Intrinsic*: to generate understanding and knowledge about a particular case rather than a generic phenomenon;
- *Instrumental*: to generate knowledge that can provide insight into a wider issue;
- *Multiple* or *collective*: extends the instrumental to several cases in the belief that this will lead to a fuller understanding and provide the basis for possible theorising about a larger collection of studies.

The design of the study can be thought about as a process (Thomas 2011: 93): the subject is linked with the purpose, which in turn determines the approaches and processes adopted. For example, if a researcher wanted to explore what had worked well in the development of a new chaplaincy role to older people in a parish, the purposes might be *instrumental* (to understand the principles of good practice involved), *exploratory* (to describe and explore how and why the role had developed) and *evaluative* (to generate knowledge that could inform an evaluation of the project); the approach might be *interpretive* and oriented towards building a theory (what works well in the development of a chaplaincy role); the process might be that of a single case study.

If such a design were adopted, the researcher would be able to develop in-depth qualitative practice-based evidence relating to how the role had developed and what had worked well in the development of the role. She would be able to gather multiple perspectives on the role and its effectiveness, for example from service users, care home staff, any funders there may be and those to whom the chaplain was accountable. Following appropriate analysis, the data could provide insights into principles of good practice and areas where practice could be developed or changed. It could also provide the basis of reliable evidence that could inform the development of policy in relation to the resourcing and development of chaplaincy roles. It is important here to be clear (Thomas 2011: 161) that data are pieces of information whilst *evidence* refers to data that support or refute a proposition that has been developed through the interpretive process of the research.

Qualitative Methods of Data Collection

Once the design of a study has been decided, the next question to answer is: what methods of data collection are most appropriate for understanding the case? There is an extensive literature on research methods such as Thomas (2009), Bryman (2012) or Denzin and Lincoln (2011). These texts provide detailed discussions of methods available, with their strengths and limitations, in the context of social science research. This chapter can only give a brief indication of some of the most commonly used ways of collecting data for evidence as a guide for further thinking.

Interviews
This is one of the key methods of data collection within qualitative research. Interviews may be:

- Structured: using a predetermined list of questions. These are easy to administer and the responses are easily coded but they are not useful for enabling the researcher to reveal emergent issues or to probe motivations.
- Unstructured: in which the interviewee sets the agenda and the researcher role is mainly to listen and facilitate. These allow the interviewee to

explore their agenda in their own way but are not useful if the researcher needs to elicit data to help answer specific questions.

- Semi-structured: in which the researcher has a list of issues to be covered set out in an interview schedule. The schedule acts as a reminder of what needs to be covered but there is no set format for the interview. These offer the best of both worlds, providing the researcher with the freedom to follow up points and probe issues.

Observation

There are different ways in which to approach observation. The main difference is between:

- Structured observation, where the researcher watches for particular things, such as a behaviour or use of language, and finds ways to record and count those elements in a systematic way. Structured observation is replicable across different settings and the data can be analysed easily.
- Unstructured or participant observation, in which the researcher, unconstrained by prior assumptions, immerses themselves in a social situation and becomes a participant in order to understand what is happening. This approach enables things to be described or interpreted in a specific context in naturally occurring circumstances.

The disadvantage of participant observation is that the data rarely furnishes reasons for observed patterns of behaviour (Cameron and Duce 2013). This means that participant observation is widely used in a mixed-method approach.

Diaries

A diary may be kept by the researcher or by a research participant as a structured or unstructured record of thoughts, ideas, feelings, actions, conversations, etc. It may be written or be an audio or video recording. In qualitative research, diaries are useful for providing insight into the processes of the research over time.

Questionnaires

Questionnaires are a written form of questioning which may use closed questions requiring a 'yes' or 'no' answer or open questions that require a more discursive response. It may be administered face to face, by telephone, post, email or online. Questionnaires are a useful way to collect large amounts of data from a standardised list of questions. They have traditionally been used in quantitative research but can be used to gather qualitative data for interpretive studies by using a mixture of closed and open-ended questions. This enables questions to be put to a larger sample of people than is possible through interviews and focus groups but the responses may be hard to analyse. The design of effective questionnaires requires technical skill and experience.

Interrogating Documents
This entails gathering data from documents in the public domain. It may include published printed information and information online. The process can provide in-depth understanding of different aspects of the research and valuable information about the wider context. The challenge is to find the right documents.

Focus Groups
A focus group allows research participants to interact in order to generate data through spontaneous dialogue with each other as well as in response to the researcher's questions. They bring together people with a common characteristic in their lives to discuss a research topic in order to gain insight into the experience, thoughts, values and feelings of the participants. Ideas and responses are generated within the group interaction and the group psychology has an impact on the research area. The researcher's role is to listen in order to facilitate discussion between participants, often using focus material such as photographs and media stories to generate discussion. This method is not a suitable choice when a topic is sensitive or the sharing of it could harm a participant.

Image-Based Methods
Photographs, drawings, videos, etc. can be used as data sources. This can be a powerful extension of observation and can open up a variety of possibilities in case study research (Thomas 2011). Not least, it can enable participants to set the agenda, for example by giving them the opportunity to take or present images, and can thus enable research to be more inclusive. However, not everyone is comfortable with using images and their use can raise ethical issues of confidentiality and privacy.

The above represents a brief list of some of the methods available for collecting data. Choosing the right methods enables the researcher to elicit from participants the kind of data required for an analysis from which useful practice-based evidence can be developed. Important as they are, methods are only tools; what makes a case study useful is the quality of the data, the understandings that the researcher presents and how interpretations are justified (Simons 2009).

The Use of Case Study in Chaplaincy Research

A presentation of the use of case study in chaplaincy research is given in *Practical Theology and Qualitative Research* (Swinton and Mowat 2006: 156–91).

This gives a worked example of how the issues of research purpose, design and execution can be addressed in practice. It is well worth reading the full account of the complexities of this research, of which I can give only a brief and partial intimation.

Over the past decade, the National Health Service in Scotland has had a drive towards a more holistic understanding of care which recognises and respects both spirituality and religion. Although chaplaincy was recognised as providing a valuable service, there was no clarity about what role chaplains were actually expected to fulfil. The Scottish Executive recognised the need to develop an empirical base for chaplaincy and subsequently the Quality Health Care Division of the Executive funded an 18-month study exploring the role and function of hospital chaplains which involved all full-time National Health Service chaplains in Scotland. In the context of a changing culture, the purpose of the research was 'to examine the meaning and manifestation of the shifts in perspective and self-identification being experienced by chaplains in Scotland' (Swinton and Mowat 2006: 165). The main research question was: what do chaplains do? It was hoped that the data would provide insight into how chaplains saw and experienced their current and changing role and how they were managing changing perceptions and demands in practice.

The working assumption was that chaplains would not be able to give a simple account of their role. This meant that the means of exploration adopted would need to be able to capture the complexity of the accounts. The study therefore employed three stages of data collection: initial telephone interviews; case studies; second telephone interviews pursuing themes developed from the initial interviews and the case study data. Three case study sites were chosen for their variety and geographical spread. The case studies used several methods of data collection, including observation, interviews and informal discussions with chaplains, patients, staff and family members. The researchers analysed the data in relation to the research question, making sense of the categories derived from the data. A variety of important insights emerged from this analytical process, making available for reflection new understandings of and insights into what chaplains do.

Although Mowat and Swinton do not give details about the dissemination of this research in their account, given the stakeholders involved, it may be assumed that the practice-based evidence it developed was used to inform strategic thinking and policy making. It would also be available to support practitioners in developing practice and articulating the nature of the contribution that chaplaincy makes in a given context. The choice of case study in this instance enabled a complex subject to be examined from multiple perspectives and the voices of both service users and practitioners to be represented.

Using Practice-Based Evidence Developed from Case Studies

The Question of Generalisation

Given that the primary purpose of a qualitative case study is to effect an in-depth exploration of a unique case, researchers need to understand what kind of knowledge is generated and how it can be used. Unlike the replicable, transferrable knowledge that may be generated by clinical trials in the positivist tradition, the knowledge produced by qualitative case study is non-replicable knowledge: because something is found in one particular context it does not mean that exactly the same thing will be found in other contexts. Case studies depend for their meaning on the concrete particulars of the case in context: the knowledge they generate is context dependent. The findings of a case study are therefore not directly transferrable to other situations but they can resonate with the experiences of readers in similar contexts, offer insights and raise issues that have significance beyond the particular case. Moreover, if several case studies are done, a cross-case analysis can be undertaken that can identify patterns and themes that may have relevance in similar contexts. The role of the qualitative researcher is therefore to use an interpretive approach to develop theoretical propositions based on their findings which can then be tested in different situations. If there is sufficient detail and rich description, a reader can discern for themselves which aspects of the case may be applicable in their own context and which may not (Simons 2009).

At the heart of the case study approach sits a paradox which holds rich potential in relation to the development and representation of chaplaincy in particular contexts of practice and more widely. The paradox is that, as with all creative endeavour, the more in-depth the exploration and representation of the particular, the greater the potential both for the discovery of something unique and the recognition of a universal 'truth'. Think, for example, of Shakespeare's *King Lear* or a late Rembrandt self-portrait in which a particular representation reveals something universal about the human condition. At best, therefore, the case study tries, 'to capture the essence of the particular in a way we all recognize' (Simons 2009: 167).

The Usefulness of Case Studies to Inform Practice and Policy

Practice-based evidence developed through rigorous qualitative inquiry can provide an empirical basis for articulating the rationale for practice and for further reflection, leading to the identification of ways to develop and support individual and team best practice. As the beginning of the chapter noted, at a time of economic constraint, it is also particularly important that chaplains are able to develop an evidence base for their work in a way that can inform policy decision-making that may involve financial and human resources. The question that is sometimes voiced is: how can the kind of evidence developed through a case study be useful in supporting policy decision-making?

This chapter has already discussed the way in which a cross-case analysis can generate insights and themes that are relevant in different contexts, but policy can also be informed by the reading of an in-depth single study. A single study can present multiple perspectives on complex social situations through a direct encounter with a phenomenon. This can provide policy makers with a fuller understanding of a social reality that can inform future decisions. One example of the power of case studies to influence public policy is the case of Victoria Climbié, cited by Simons (2009: 170). Victoria died after years of abuse through the neglect of carers and the lack of communication between social care agencies. The policy response to the inquiry into this case was *Every Child Matters* (2003).[2] Chaplains are unlikely to be involved in such an unusual, high profile study that has a major impact on policy. However, more recently, I have been involved in a research project commissioned by the Church of England (Todd, Slater and Dunlop 2014) involving five case studies of chaplaincies in higher education, industry, the police, healthcare and the commercial sector. The project was commissioned in order to inform thinking about church policy regarding the support and development of chaplaincy.

Conclusion

This chapter has contextualised the growing imperative to develop practice-based evidence for public sector chaplaincy within the contemporary cultural drive to evidence the impact and value of services. It has suggested that, given the relational-centred focus of most chaplaincy work, the development of practice-based evidence for chaplaincy sits well within the tradition of qualitative inquiry with its emphasis on researching lived experience. Case study has been presented as one approach that can be a useful way of addressing questions that arise in complex social situations. It can enable service users and practitioners to have a voice that can be presented to a wide audience. Case studies hold the potential to generate evidence that can underpin the development of both practice and policy.

A chapter of this length could not cover this topic in depth. However, I hope that it may stimulate the reader to think about research and the development of practice-based evidence not as an esoteric activity undertaken by a few, but as something that can be integral to practice. Research, however small-scale,

---

[2]   *Every Child Matters: Change for Children* (2003). The national framework can be accessed at www.everychildmatters.gov.uk.

presents an opportunity to generate evidence to develop and support practice and to give an account of the impact and value of the work that chaplains do. It can also be a means by which the voices of service users can be heard. If it is done well, it can enable chaplains to articulate with integrity the contribution that they make in a given context. Ultimately, it is an important way in which chaplains can try to ensure that they continue to provide the best service possible.

References

Bryman, A. (2012), *Social Research Methods*, 4th edition. Oxford: Oxford University Press.

Cameron, H. and Duce, C. (2013), *Researching Practice in Ministry and Mission*. London: SCM.

Cresswell, J. (2007), *Qualitative Inquiry and Research Design*. London: Sage.

Denzin, N. and Lincoln, Y. (2011), *The SAGE Handbook of Qualitative Research*, 4th edition. Thousand Oaks, CA: Sage.

Finlay, L. and Evans, K. (eds) (2009), *Relational-Centred Research for Psychotherapists: Exploring Meanings and Experience*. Chichester: Wiley-Blackwell.

Simons, H. (2009), *Case Study Research in Practice*. London: Sage.

Slater, V. (2013), *The Fresh Significance of Chaplaincy for the Mission and Ministry of the Church in England: Three Case Studies in Community Contexts*. Unpublished thesis. Cambridge: Anglia Ruskin University. Available at: http://angliaruskin.openrepository.com/arro/handle/10540/305403 (accessed 12 April 2015).

Stake, R. (1995), *The Art of Case Study Research*. Thousand Oaks, CA: Sage.

Swift, C. (2014), *Hospital Chaplaincy in the Twenty-First Century: The Crisis of Spiritual Care in the NHS*, 2nd edition. Farnham: Ashgate.

Swinton, J. and Mowat, H. (2006), *Practical Theology and Qualitative Research*. London: SCM Press.

Thomas, G. (2009), *How to do Your Research Project: A Guide for Students in Education and Applied Social Sciences*. London: Sage.

—— (2011), *How to do Your Case Study: A Guide for Students and Researchers*. London: Sage.

Todd, A. (2011), Chaplaincy leading church in(to) the public square. *Crucible: The Christian Journal of Social Ethics*, October–December, 7–15.

Todd, A., Slater, V. and Dunlop, S. (2014), *The Church of England's Involvement in Chaplaincy*. The Cardiff Centre for Chaplaincy Studies & The Oxford Centre for Ecclesiology and Practical Theology.

Yin, R. (2009), *Case Study Research: Design and Methods*, 4th edition. Thousand Oaks. CA: Sage.

PART II
Key Themes in Chaplaincy Studies

Chapter 6
Chaplaincy and the Law

Frank Cranmer

Introduction: The Legal Basis of Chaplaincy[1]

The legal basis of chaplaincy is a complex mix of statute, secondary legislation, common law and custom. In a short chapter it is impossible to present a comprehensive treatment; what follows is a very brief overview of some of the main legal issues.

Chaplaincy takes place within a legal framework; but much of that framework is permissive rather than prescriptive. Traditionally, the basic position in English and Scots law has been that 'freedom' – not just freedom of religion but freedom of action generally – is the freedom to do as you wish, *always provided there is nothing in law prohibiting you from doing it*. Essentially, therefore, freedom of religion and belief has been largely a negative right resting on two principles:

- *freedom to act within the law*: 'every citizen has a right to do what he likes, unless restrained by the common law ... or by statute': Lord Donaldson MR in *Attorney General v Guardian Newspapers Ltd (No. 2)* [1990] 1 AC 109 at 178 (see also Hill 2005: 1131–2); and
- *certainty as to what that law is*: 'a statute means exactly what it says and does not mean what it does not say': Lord Bridge of Harwich in *Associated Newspapers v Wilson* [1995] 2 AC 454–90 at 475.

Jowitt implies that the legal basis for chaplaincy goes back at least to Henry VIII (Greenberg 2010: 370), but in modern terms it has three aspects: the right of religious organisations to undertake such ministrations, the right of individuals to receive (or reject) them and the corresponding duty of the state to accommodate their free exercise.

---

[1] I should like to thank Professor Norman Doe and Mark Cobb for their helpful comments on various drafts.

Prison Chaplaincy

Prison chaplaincy began as a peculiarly Anglican concern in England and Wales; however, the Prison Ministers Act 1863 empowered borough magistrates to pay non-Anglican clergy to minister to prisoners of their persuasions (McConville 1995: 131–2). Currently, under section 7(1) of the Prisons Act 1952 every prison in England and Wales must have ' ... a governor, a chaplain and a medical officer', and under 7(4) the chaplain must be 'a clergyman of the Church of England'. Similarly, section 53(3) requires Welsh prison chaplains to be clergy of the Church in Wales. Prison chaplaincy in England and Wales is by no means confined to Anglicans – nor, indeed, to Christians – but only those two Churches are *obliged* to appoint chaplains. Other chaplains are not statutory officers and are not bound to fulfil the statutory functions. For example, under Prison Rule 14(2), 'the chaplain shall visit daily all prisoners belonging to the Church of England who are sick, under restraint or undergoing cellular confinement; and a prison minister shall do the same, *as far as he reasonably can*, for prisoners of his denomination': so daily visits are obligatory for Anglican chaplains but not for others.[2]

The Welsh 'vestige of Establishment' merits further explanation (Watkin 1990). The Welsh Church Act 1914 disestablished the Church and the actual separation from the Church of England, delayed by the First World War, took place in 1920 – 32 years before the Prisons Act 1952. However, the 1952 legislation was '[a]n Act to consolidate certain enactments relating to prisons and other institutions for offenders and related matters with corrections and improvements made under the Consolidation of Enactments (Procedure) Act 1949' – an early example of statutory consolidation that did not, therefore, make new law. So the position of the Church in Wales in relation to prison chaplaincy, which had simply continued uninterrupted after disestablishment, remained undisturbed.

Similarly, section 3(2) of the Prisons (Scotland) Act 1989 requires each prison to have as chaplain 'a minister or a licentiate of the Church of Scotland', and section 9 makes supplementary provision for the appointment of prison ministers[3] of other denominations and other faiths where 'the number of prisoners who belong to a religious denomination other than the Church of Scotland ... ' appears to the Secretary of State (or now, since devolution, to the Scottish Government's Justice Secretary) to require it. In practice, the overall service is delivered under an Agreement between the Scottish Prison Service, the Church of Scotland and the Roman Catholic Church.

---

[2] Emphasis added; for a detailed discussion see Rivers (2010: 215–20).

[3] Non-Anglican prison chaplains in England and Wales were until recently described as 'prison ministers' rather than as chaplains; in Scotland the distinction in title is still maintained.

Rules 13 to 19 of the Prison Rules 1999 (as amended), Part 6 of the Prisons and Young Offenders Institutions (Scotland) Rules 2011 and Part VI of the Prison and Young Offenders Centres Rules (Northern Ireland) 1995 make specific provision for the practice of religion or belief in prison – including access to chaplaincy services. The Service Custody and Service of Relevant Sentences Rules 2009 make similar provision in relation to those in military detention.

Military Chaplaincy

In origin, military chaplaincy appears largely a matter of common law rather than of statute, though the power of the Secretary of State ' ... to appoint from time to time any army chaplain to perform the functions of an army chaplain in any ... extra-parochial district ... ' was set out in s 6 of the Army Chaplains Act 1868.[4] But though military chaplaincy derives ultimately from custom under the Royal Prerogative, its exercise is no less a matter of military law and its current structure is set out in Queen's Regulations (QRs) for the three services (Rivers 2010: 208–13).

There are currently chaplains to the Regular Forces, to the Reserve Forces and to the various military cadet forces. Commissioned chaplains are drawn from those Christian Churches on the list of eligible denominations endorsed by the United Navy, Army and Air Force Board and maintained by the Ministry of Defence: the Anglican, Roman Catholic, Presbyterian, Congregational, Baptist and Methodist Churches, the United Reformed Church, the Church of Scotland, the Assemblies of God, the Elim Pentecostal Church and the Salvation Army. There is also provision for five chaplains from other faith groups – Jewish, Sikh, Hindu, Muslim and Buddhist – who operate across all three services. Chaplains are appointed by the Secretary of State for Defence on the recommendation of the appropriate Chaplain General following nomination by an accredited representative of the religious organisation concerned.

Army and RAF chaplains hold a specific rank – for example, the RAF Chaplain-in-Chief ranks as an air vice-marshal – but, by tradition, Royal Navy chaplains hold no rank whatsoever; the Explanatory Note to Regulation 3 of the Armed Forces (Naval Chaplains) Regulations 2009 states that:

> A naval chaplain is commissioned as such, and is not an officer ... Although subject to service law, a naval chaplain has no rank, and is therefore outranked by no-one ... Conversely, a naval chaplain outranks no-one ...

---

[4]   Which was extended to the Royal Air Force by SR & O 1918/548 (Rev I p 896: 1948 I p 50). For the current status of Army chaplains see Bailey (1999).

The QRs for the RAF provide a useful summary of the role in general. Under QR J837 (*General – Observance of Religion*):

> (1) Christian Chaplains are commissioned ... to provide for the spiritual wellbeing, pastoral care and moral teaching and guidance of Service personnel and their families, regardless of faith or profession of no faith. They are to be given every support in the fulfilment of their ministry. They are not to be required to perform executive or operational duties save those proper to their profession. When a commissioned Chaplain cannot be made available, civilian Christian clerics of the appropriate denomination may be appointed Officiating Chaplains to the Military.

> (2) The reverent observance of religion in the Armed Forces is of the highest importance. It is the duty of all concerned to make adequate provision for the spiritual and moral needs of all personnel and dependants.

There are two points to be noted: that religious observance is 'of the highest importance' is simply a given, without justification, and that the express provision for ministry to families of RAF personnel presumably recognises that service families often lead a fairly peripatetic existence.

Under QR 114(1), RAF chaplains hold relative rank 'solely for the purpose of defining status as regards precedence, discipline and administration ... They are not, by virtue of that rank, eligible to exercise any executive command, or claim any advantage as regards emoluments (effective or non-effective)'. Their appointment, status and duties are set out in QRs 839–841.

QR 842 makes provision for worship:

> (1) In the light of local circumstances, Christian worship is to be arranged within Service churches or, if necessary, at convenient civilian churches, at suitable times ... on Sundays, Good Friday and Christmas Day to permit the greatest possible number of personnel to attend. Week-day services are also to be arranged as convenient. Similarly, adherents of the five Recognised World Faiths other than Christian[5] should be permitted to make their religious observances on the days and at the times prescribed by their faith ...

Chaplaincy in Education

Chaplaincy in higher and further education is largely a matter for the individual denominations and the individual institutions; its extent and nature vary widely between institutions because the institutions themselves vary so widely.

---

5   Judaism, Sikhism, Hinduism, Islam and Buddhism.

In a modern provincial university chaplains will most likely be provided by the Churches themselves: probably full- or half-time chaplains from the Roman Catholic Church, the Church of England and the major Free Churches supplemented by unpaid chaplains from smaller denominations. Some universities have historic arrangements with particular denominations and in many cases the costs are shared, so that the chaplain might be paid by the university but housed by the denomination in question. In some cases the chaplaincy building is provided by the university and in others by a particular Church: at Birmingham, for example, the building is provided by the Cadbury Trust – a charity established by the leading Quaker family in the city. Many universities, mainly those established after 1992, employ a chaplain directly, often regardless of denominational allegiance. Such posts are fully funded by and accountable to the university, except insofar as the chaplain is answerable to his or her own Church in purely ecclesiastical matters under its canon law.

Methodist chaplains (and this probably holds true for all denominations other than the Church of England) are funded by the Church itself in one way or another, though some universities make a financial contribution. There are a few full-time Methodist chaplains in higher education but, on the whole, a local minister will act as part-time chaplain while also ministering on the local circuit. Funding tends to be on an ecumenical basis, so at Cardiff University, for example, contributions are paid to the joint Chaplaincy Fund and the chaplains draw on it in relatively equal shares – it should be emphasised that the funding is provided for *chaplaincy activity*, not for remunerating the chaplains themselves or for maintenance costs.

In certain universities, however, financing is rather different. Most Oxford and Cambridge colleges either became Church of England foundations at the Reformation or were founded subsequent to it. Sections 7 (1) and (2) of the Universities of Oxford and Cambridge Act 1923 empower the universities and colleges to make and amend their own statutes. In effect, therefore, those statutes are a form of delegated legislation, and almost all of them stipulate that religious provision shall be Christian and Anglican (Clines 2008: 5). Because they are independent institutions with their own endowments, almost all colleges have a chapel and at least a half-time chaplain[6] funded from the college's resources and the larger colleges may have more than one. In addition, King's and St John's at Cambridge and Christ Church, Magdalen and New College at Oxford maintain Anglican choral services sung by choirs of boys and undergraduate choral scholars, but the music foundations are supported from college endowments, not from

---

6   Variously described as 'chaplain' or 'dean of chapel'. Some of the newer colleges were founded by other denominations, for example Mansfield (Congregational, now URC) and Harris Manchester (Unitarian) at Oxford and Homerton (Congregational, now URC) and St Edmund's (Roman Catholic) at Cambridge.

Government grants.[7] At Durham, the two independent colleges, St John's and St Chad's, are both Anglican foundations with chaplains on the college staff.[8] The College of St Hild and St Bede, which is maintained by the University, has a full-time chaplain funded by an independent charitable trust which also funds the College's organ scholarships. The pattern varies across the other colleges: some have their own Anglican chaplains, while others either share a chaplain or appoint local clergy as honorary chaplains. The other denominations appoint chaplains to the University as a whole.

Chaplaincy in schools is even more various. In Voluntary Aided and Voluntary Controlled schools, because the schools themselves are of a religious character chaplaincy will be supplied by the parent denomination but, it would appear from a recent study, not always by a designated chaplain (Archbishops' Council Education Division 2014). On the other hand, public schools that were originally religious foundations appoint chaplains of particular denominations by virtue of their own trust deeds.

In strictly legal terms, therefore, chaplaincy in higher and further education appears to rest on a combination of college statutes, the law of trusts (as at the University of Birmingham and the two independent colleges in Durham) and the general rule in *Guardian Newspapers Ltd (No. 2)* that actions are legal unless specifically prohibited. More generally, a fairly recent report commissioned by the Church of England, *Faiths in Higher Education Chaplaincy*, found that much of the chaplaincy work in tertiary education was voluntary, accounting for just over half of chaplaincy staff, and that the volunteers came disproportionately from minority faiths with almost one-third from the Baha'i, Buddhist, Hindu, Jewish, Muslim and Sikh faith communities.

Chaplaincy in the National Health Service

Chaplains have been a feature of the NHS since its inception in 1948, when the Ministry of Health declared that hospitals 'should give special attention to provide for the spiritual needs of both patients and staff' and that management committees 'should appoint a chaplain – or chaplains from more than one denomination – for every hospital for which they are responsible'.[9] In Scotland, Circular RHB(S) 1951/12, 'Religious services and appointment of chaplains', expressed similar sentiments. Today, neither local NHS Trusts in England nor

---

[7]   The majority of the other Oxford and Cambridge colleges and several at Durham also offer choral and organ scholarships, but sung chapel services usually take place only two or three times a week.

[8]   The Chaplain of St Chad's is also Postgraduate Director; the Chaplain of St John's is also priest-in-charge of a parish in Sunderland.

[9]   Ministry of Health Circular HMC(48)62 (1948), quoted in Johnson (2003).

Health Boards in Scotland are required to provide chaplaincy services under statute; however, they are obliged to do so as *a matter of contract*. Under the NHS England Standard Contract 2014/15 'The Provider must take account of the spiritual, religious, pastoral and cultural needs of Service Users and must liaise with the relevant authorities as appropriate in each case' (NHS England 2013: SC14). Similarly, in Scotland chaplaincy is governed by the Scottish Government's 2009 guidance, *Spiritual Care & Chaplaincy*; the covering letter reminds Health Board Chief Executives that they should appoint a senior lead manager for spiritual care, that their Board's spiritual care policy should be updated in light of the guidance and local need and that they should provide a round-the-clock service.

NHS England provides non-statutory guidance on chaplaincy for commissioners, Trusts, managers and chaplains (NHS England 2015). The guidance sets out a series of core principles, of which the most important are as follows:

- Chaplains must abide by the requirements of their sponsoring religion or belief community, their contracting organisation, the Code of Conduct and all relevant NHS/NICE standards.
- Patients, service users and staff must be made aware of the nature, scope and means of accessing the chaplaincy within their setting.
- Patients, service users and staff should be able to access chaplaincy at any time on any day of the week in facilities where urgent out-of-hours support is requested on average at least once a week.
- Where requests for support relate to a particular religion or belief the chaplaincy service should be able to access appropriate support for the patient or service user and, when this cannot be matched, other chaplaincy support should be offered.
- To ensure safety, accountability and continuity of care chaplains should maintain a record of work in a locally agreed format and in accordance with NHS policies for record keeping.
- Patients and service users have a right to expect that chaplaincy care will be experienced as neither insensitive nor proselytising.
- Compassion should always inform chaplaincy practice and is a key outcome of the patient's experience of the service being provided.

Chaplaincy and Canon Law

On chaplaincy generally the canons of the Church of England are largely silent. Canon C 5 empowers bishops to admit to holy orders 'any person who is to be a chaplain in any university or in any college or hall in the same or in any school ... ', and Rules 93 and 94 of the Clergy Discipline Rules 2005 provide for disciplinary procedures in respect of chaplains of prisons, hospitals, universities, 'schools and other institutions' and the armed forces; but canon law does not address the nature and functions of chaplaincy itself. Similarly, the Church of Scotland's Acts of Assembly make no specific, unified reference to chaplaincy but there are several mentions of specific chaplaincy roles.[10] The Methodists' *Constitutional Practice and Discipline* is rather more specific, with sections on the appointment of chaplains to the schools of the Methodist Independent Education Trust, to prison chaplaincy, to military chaplaincy, to workplace chaplaincy (Methodist Conference 2013: Standing Orders 343, 354, 355 and 355A) and to hospital chaplaincy (Standing Order 802).[11]

The Roman Catholic *Codex Iuris Canonici* (Catholic Church 1983) is much the most comprehensive, devoting a whole section to the position and duties of chaplains, of which these are the most important:

- Can. 564: 'A chaplain is a priest to whom is entrusted in a stable manner the pastoral care, at least in part, of some community or particular group of the Christian faithful ... ';
- Can. 565: 'Unless the law provides otherwise or someone legitimately has special rights, a chaplain is appointed by the local ordinary ... ';
- Can. 566§1: 'A chaplain must be provided with all the faculties which proper pastoral care requires ... ';
- Can. 566§1: ' ... [A] chaplain possesses by virtue of office the faculty of hearing the confessions of the faithful entrusted to his care, of preaching the word of God to them, of administering *viaticum* and the anointing of the sick, and of conferring the sacrament of confirmation on those who are in danger of death';
- Can. 566§2: 'In hospitals, prisons, and on sea journeys, a chaplain ... has the faculty ... of absolving from *latae sententiae* censures[12] which are neither reserved nor declared ... ';
- Can. 568: 'As far as possible, chaplains are to be appointed for those who are not able to avail themselves of the ordinary care of pastors because of the condition of their lives, such as migrants, exiles, refugees, nomads, sailors'; and
- Can. 569: 'Military chaplains are governed by special laws'.

[10]   Notably in the HM Forces (Kirk Sessions) Act (Act VIII 1952) and in the Church Courts Act (Act III 2000), as amended.

[11]   It also states in SO 526 that '[t]he pastoral oversight of Methodists in hospitals shall be regarded as part of their duty by the ministers and probationers stationed in Circuits in which such institutions are situated'.

[12]   A penalty *latae sententiae* is one that follows automatically by force of canon law itself when a law is contravened.

Though there is very little consistency between the internal rules of the various denominations, underlying all of them is this general rule: that *chaplains must be authorised by and be in good standing with their sending denomination*. That rule was highlighted recently by the case of Canon Jeremy Pemberton.

Canon Pemberton, an Anglican, was deputy senior chaplain at the United Lincolnshire Hospitals NHS Trust and in April 2014 married his partner Laurence Cunnington. The Acting Bishop of Southwell and Nottingham subsequently revoked his Permission to Officiate in his diocese because the marriage contravened the House of Bishops' guidelines (House of Bishops 2014: para 27). Sherwood Forest Hospitals NHS Foundation Trust in Nottinghamshire had offered Canon Pemberton the post of chaplaincy and bereavement manager but withdrew its offer when the Acting Bishop revoked his Permission to Officiate. The Trust's Director of Human Resources was reported as explaining that the offer had been subject to an approved licence and authorisation from the Bishop (PA/Huffington Post 2014). Canon Pemberton subsequently announced that he had filed an employment tribunal claim against the Archbishop of York and the Acting Bishop of Southwell and Nottingham, citing the Equality Act 2010.

The case raises several questions, not least whether the Equality Act 2010 applies to the situation and whether there is any kind of employment relationship between Canon Pemberton and the two bishops that might fall within the jurisdiction of an Employment Tribunal – and on those issues I take no view. But for the purposes of the present discussion, the case highlights the fact that chaplains in secular institutions may nevertheless remain bound by the ecclesiastical law of their own religious organisations in addition to their secular legal relationships.

Chaplains: Office Holders or Employees?

Canon Pemberton's experience also raises the wider question: are chaplains employees or office-holders? Traditionally, employees and workers have had full employment rights while office-holders have had very few. Traditionally also, the courts have tended to regard clergy as office-holders unless there has been very clear evidence of an intention on the part of *both* parties to create an enforceable employment relationship.

The Supreme Court held in *President of the Methodist Conference v Preston* [2013] UKSC 29 that the rights and duties of Methodist ministers derived from their status under the Church's Constitution rather than from contract (see para 20), that Methodist ministry was a vocation and that the Revd Mrs Preston's claim for unfair constructive dismissal therefore failed (Cranmer 2013). Subsequently, however, in *Sharpe v Worcester Diocesan Board of Finance Ltd & Anor* [2013] UKEAT 0243 12

2811 an Employment Appeal Tribunal (EAT) held that a lower tribunal's decision that the Revd Mark Sharpe, Anglican former incumbent of Teme Valley South, could not be a 'worker' within the terms of the Employment Rights Act 1996 was flawed and remitted the case for a fresh hearing. In an appeal against that decision, however, the Court of Appeal held in *Sharpe v Bishop of Worcester* [2015] EWCA Civ 399 that a Church of England incumbent with freehold was an office holder rather than a worker or an employee and did not, therefore, have employment rights.

In the absence of clear evidence to the contrary, however, *most* clergy in *most* chaplaincy situations would appear to be employees with employment rights: full-time prison chaplains are employed by the relevant prisons service, NHS chaplains by NHS trusts and military chaplains under the Queen's Commission – though education chaplaincy is more varied. That view would appear to be supported by *Piper v Maidstone & Tunbridge Wells NHS Trust* [2012] UKEAT 0359 12 1812, in which the lead chaplain of the NHS Trust claimed successfully for unfair dismissal; on the other hand, in *Miller v Secretary of State for Home Affairs* [2004] UKEAT 00926 03 0405 it was held that a Quaker prison minister who was paid hourly for her attendance was not in an enforceable employment relationship.

In short, the precise employment situation of any individual will depend entirely on the facts of the particular case (Cranmer 2014, Rivers 2010: 115), and overlaying the individual's specific situation is the need to be in good standing with his or her own denomination.

Chaplaincy, Religious Pluralism and Religious Minorities

Increasingly, higher and further education institutions appoint Jewish and Muslim chaplains as well as Christian ones; but funded chaplaincy in tertiary education is still very largely provided by Christian denominations. That is partly a matter of demography, partly of resources and partly of cultural history. However, it is not without its problems.

According to the 2011 Census, over 2.7 million respondents in England and Wales were Muslims (Office for National Statistics 2012), and in 2007 the Government commissioned a study of Islam within higher education from Dr Ataullah Siddiqui (2007) of the Markfield Institute of Higher Education. He suggested that '[c]haplaincy for Muslims has in general been both tentative and precarious. Muslims as a whole are only just catching on to the idea of chaplaincy' and implied that at least part of the reason was that the majority of Muslim students in the 1970s and 1980s had been foreign postgraduates whose priorities were largely 'to find *halal* food, accommodation, and places for communal meetings and gatherings'. He estimated that there were over 30 Muslim chaplains/advisers in universities in England, but almost all were volunteers with little or no specific training for chaplaincy and many were largely unsupported financially.[13] Moreover, though physical chaplaincy facilities for students (and staff) from non-Christian religions had grown there did not appear to have been any commensurate growth in paid personnel (Clines 2008: 13).

Chaplains and Confidentiality

In general terms, legal professional privilege protects confidential communications between lawyer and client and a party does not generally have to disclose privileged material during the course of legal proceedings. Privilege may also cover some communications between a lawyer and third parties for the purpose of preparing litigation; however, in *R (Prudential plc & Anor) v Special Commissioner of Income Tax & Anor* [2013] UKSC 1 the Supreme Court held by a majority of 5–2 that legal professional privilege did not extend to anyone other than the legal profession and that any change to that rule was a matter for Parliament.

It is very doubtful whether *any* other confidential communication between one party and another is privileged in such a way. Canon 113 of the Church of England's Canons of 1603/04 includes a proviso that

> if any man confess his secret and hidden sins to the minister, for the unburdening of his conscience ... we do not in any way bind the said minister by this our Constitution, but do straitly charge and admonish him, that he do not at any time reveal and make known to any person whatsoever any crime or offence so committed to his trust and secrecy (except they be such crimes as by the laws of this realm his own life may be called into question for concealing the same), under pain of irregularity.

Nevertheless, in *Anderson v Bank of British Columbia* (1876) LR 2 ChD 644 at 650–651, rejecting a submission that privilege attached to information prepared for a client in the course of litigation, Jessel MR made the following more general statement, *obiter*:

> Our law has not extended that privilege, as some foreign laws have, to the medical profession, or to the sacerdotal profession ... [I]n foreign countries where the Roman Catholic faith prevails, it is considered that the same principles ought to be extended to the confessional, and that it is desirable that a man should not be hampered in going to confession by the thought that either he or his priest may

---

[13] Siddiqui (2007: 46, 48). He cites the example of an imam who led Friday prayers at a post-1992 university as a volunteer and who for 16 years had had to pay out of his own pocket for petrol and parking.

be compelled to disclose in a Court of Justice the substance of what passed in such communication. This, again, whether it is rational or irrational, is not recognised by our law.

He reiterated this in *Wheeler v Le Marchant* (1881) 17 ChD 675 at 681:

Communications made to a priest in the confessional on matters perhaps considered by the penitent to be more important even than his life or his fortune, are not protected.

The current (2011) edition of *Halsbury* on ecclesiastical law states that while ecclesiastical authority obliges a priest hearing a confession to observe strict secrecy 'it seems unlikely that the courts would recognise such a communication as belonging to the category of privileged communications, but this remains uncertain' (Bursell and Kaye 2011: 813). So given the uncertainty surrounding confidentiality of formal confession, it is difficult to argue that a communication with a chaplain *not* in the course of a confession could attract any kind of legal privilege whatsoever.

Ethically Problematic Pastoral Cases: Is There a Right of Conscientious Opt-Out?

Section 4(1) of the Abortion Act 1967 provides that, subject to an overriding duty to participate in treatment necessary to save the life or to prevent grave permanent injury to the physical or mental health of a pregnant woman, 'no person shall be under any duty, whether by contract or by any statutory or other legal requirement, to participate in any treatment authorised by this Act to which he has a conscientious objection'. A hospital chaplain is unlikely to be under an 'overriding duty to participate': but what if a chaplain conscientiously opposed to abortion refuses as a matter of principle to minister to any woman in hospital specifically for a termination?

Again, the law is somewhat unclear. In *R v Salford Area Hospital Authority ex parte Janaway* [1989] 1 AC 537 a secretary required to type appointment letters for patients seeking abortions was not allowed the conscientious opt-out; Lord Keith declared at para 33 that the words 'to participate' meant 'actually taking part in treatment'. On the other hand, *Doogan & Anor v NHS Greater Glasgow & Clyde Health Board* [2013] ScotCS CSIH 36 unanimously upheld the claim of two Roman Catholic midwives working as labour ward coordinators at Glasgow Southern General Hospital that being required to supervise a ward in which terminations were carried out violated their declared conscientious objection to participating in abortion, only to be reversed by the unanimous

judgment of the Supreme Court in *Greater Glasgow Health Board v Doogan &
Anor* [2014] UKSC 68.

What *Doogan* and *Janaway* demonstrate is this. The Abortion Act is now
almost 50 years old and one might expect that by now we would know with a
reasonable degree of certainty what was covered by the conscientious opt-out in
section 4. We do not, but it would be very surprising indeed if that section was
held to apply to a hospital chaplain.

Chaplaincy, Article 9 and the Wider Legal and Social Context

Article 9 (Freedom of thought, conscience and religion) of the European
Convention on Human Rights protects freedom of thought, conscience and
religion and the right to manifest one's religion or beliefs 'subject only to such
limitations as are prescribed by law and are necessary in a democratic society
in the interests of public safety, for the protection of public order, health or
morals, or for the protection of the rights and freedoms of others'. So far as
chaplaincy is concerned, therefore, Article 9 protects both the right to provide
such services and the right to receive them; but those rights are not unqualified.
Almost inevitably, given that people in custody are not free agents, the relevant
Article 9 cases relate to the practice of religion in secure institutions – and with
mixed outcomes.

In *JL v Finland* [2000] ECHR 32526/96, when the applicant, a Jehovah's
Witness detained compulsorily in a secure psychiatric hospital, complained that
he had not been allowed visits by fellow Jehovah's Witnesses and had been given
meals containing blood, contrary to his beliefs, the European Court of Human
Rights (ECtHR) found the grievances unsubstantiated. Moreover, there was
no absolute right under Article 9 for a detainee to manifest his religious beliefs
outside the institution in which he was detained and, in exercising his freedom
to manifest his religion, an individual might need to take his 'specific situation'
into account.[14] In *McAree & Anor, Re Judicial Review* [2010] NIQB 79 Treacy
J rejected a prisoner's complaint under Article 9 that since his transfer to the
Harm Reduction Unit at HMP Magilligan he had not been permitted to attend
Mass: he held that the chaplain's decision to withdraw his offer to celebrate
Mass in the Harm Reduction Unit had been directly attributable to the fact
that the plaintiff was suspected of drug-dealing within the prison system (paras
57–59). In *Florin Andrei v Romania* [2014] ECHR 400 the ECtHR held that
the physical conditions under which the applicant prisoner had been held had
violated Article 3 (prohibition of torture, inhuman or degrading treatment)
ECHR but rejected his complaint about the authorities' refusal to let him see

[14] For which see *Kalaç v Turkey* [1997] ECHR 37 para 27.

a priest to make his confession on a religious festival. The Court had already ruled in *Iorgoiu v Romania* [2012] ECHR 1831/02 that Romania had a well-established chaplaincy regime for Orthodox detainees; and the fact that Mr Andrei had not been able to make his confession on a specific day had not violated Article 9.

In *Poltoratskiy v Ukraine* [2003] ECHR 216, on the other hand, the ECtHR held that refusing to allow a prisoner under the death sentence (later commuted) to attend the prison's weekly religious service or to have visits from a priest violated his Article 9 rights. Similarly, in *Vartic v Romania (No. 2)* [2013] ECHR 1296 it held that the authorities' failure to give a Buddhist prisoner vegetarian meals breached Article 9: to have done so would neither have disrupted the management of the prison nor adversely affected meals for other inmates. While not a chaplaincy issue *per se*, *Vartic* illustrates the more general requirement to strike a fair balance between applicants' Article 9 rights and the authorities' need not to be overburdened by unreasonable demands.[15]

Conclusion

Though chaplaincy is part of the wider protection of religion and belief under Article 9 its funding is a matter of some controversy. The National Secular Society has argued that hospital chaplaincy leads to unequal care because many patients do not share the religion of the appointed chaplain and that the £29m spent on chaplaincy in England in 2009/10 should have gone to medical care: 'if churches, mosques and temples wish to have representation in hospitals to visit those patients who want some religious support whilst in hospital, they should do it at their own expense' (National Secular Society 2012). The response of the Church of England's Director of Mission and Public Affairs, Dr Malcolm Brown, was that it was widely accepted within the medical profession that health care involved looking after the whole person, not just the body: 'The role of hospital chaplains in a regime of holistic care is not in doubt among serious practitioners' (Mail Online 2011).

Whether or not the National Secular Society's critique resonates with the public at large, even with those who are avowed non-believers, is unclear (see, for example, Sokol 2009). But in any event, protecting the *right* to manifest under Article 9 ECHR must surely imply giving people who have little or no control over their freedom of movement – in prisons, in hospitals and (sometimes) in educational establishments – reasonable *opportunity* to manifest. Chaplaincy

---

[15]   In *Janusz Wojciechowski v Poland* (Application no. 54511/11 currently pending), the applicant complained that while on remand he had not been able to attend Sunday Mass for an entire year. For a discussion of some of the earlier cases see Rivers 2010: 226–9.

is an important part of that opportunity; whether or not, in the final analysis, society at large should fund it is a socio-political question, not a legal one.

References

Anderson v Bank of British Columbia (1876) LR 2 ChD 644 at 650–651.

Archbishops' Council Education Division (2014), *The Public Face of God: Chaplaincy in Anglican Secondary Schools and Academies in England and Wales*. London: Church of England Archbishops' Council Education Division; The National Society.

Associated Newspapers v Wilson [1995] 2 AC 454–490.

Attorney General v Guardian Newspapers Ltd (No. 2) [1990] 1 AC 109 at 178.

Bailey, D. (1999), *Legal Regulation of the Appointment, Ministry and Episcopal Oversight of Army Chaplains*. Unpublished LLM dissertation. Cardiff: University of Wales.

Bursell, R. and Kaye, R. (eds) (2011), *Halsbury's Laws of England*, 5th edition, vol 34: Ecclesiastical Law. London: Butterworth Lexis.

Catholic Church and Canon Law Society of America (1983), *Code of Canon Law: Latin-English edition*. Washington, DC: Canon Law Society of America.

Clines, J.M.S. (2008), *Faiths in Higher Education Chaplaincy*. London: Church of England Board of Education.

Cranmer, F. (2013), Methodist ministers: employees or office-holders? *Ecclesiastical Law Journal*, 15(3), 316–25.

—— (2014), *Case-law on Church Employment* (August 2014). [Online]. Available from: www.churcheslegislation.org.uk/files/publications/CLAS_employment_of_church_workers_Nov_2014.pdf (accessed 12 April 2015).

Doogan & Anor v NHS Greater Glasgow & Clyde Health Board [2013] ScotCS CSIH 36.

Florin Andrei v Romania [2014] ECHR 400.

Greater Glasgow Health Board v Doogan & Anor [2014] UKSC 68.

Greenberg, D. (2010), *Jowitt's Dictionary of English Law*. London: Sweet & Maxwell / Thomson Reuters.

Hill, M. (2005), The permissible scope of legal limitations on the freedom of religion or belief in the United Kingdom. *Emory International Law Review*, 19, 1129–1186.

House of Bishops (2014), *Pastoral Guidance on Same Sex Marriage*. [Online]. Available from: www.churchofengland.org/media-centre/news/2014/02/house-of-bishops-pastoral-guidance-on-same-sex-marriage.aspx (accessed 31 August 2014).

Iorgoiu v Romania [2012] ECHR 1831/02.

JL v Finland [2000] ECHR 32526/96.

Johnson, C. (2003), Managing chaplaincy service delivery. *Scottish Journal of Healthcare Chaplaincy*, 6(1), 33–8.

Kalaç v Turkey [1997] ECHR 37 para 27.

Mail Online. 2011. Hospital chaplains who cost £29m a year have no clinical benefit, says controversial study. [Online]. Available from: www.dailymail. co.uk/health/article-1361357/Hospital-chaplains-cost-29m-clinical-benefit-finds-controversial-report.html (accessed 31 August 2014).

McAree & Anor, Re Judicial Review [2010] NIQB 79.

McConville, S. (1995), *English Local Prisons 1860–1900: Next Only to Death*. London: Routledge.

Methodist Conference (2013), *The Constitutional Practice and Discipline of the Methodist Church*. London: Methodist Publishing.

Miller v Secretary of State for Home Affairs [2004] UKEAT 00926 03 0405.

National Secular Society (2012), *NSS Briefing: Hospital Chaplaincy*. [Online] Available from: www.secularism.org.uk/uploads/nss-hospital-chaplaincy-campaign-briefing.pdf (accessed 31 August 2014).

NHS England (2013), *2014/15 NHS Standard Contract: Service Conditions*. London: NHS England.

—— (2015), *NHS Chaplaincy Guidelines 2015: Promoting Excellence in Pastoral, Spiritual & Religious Care*. [Online] Available from: http://www.england. nhs.uk/wp-content/uploads/2015/03/nhs-chaplaincy-guidelines-2015.pdf (accessed 20 May 2015).

Office for National Statistics (2012), *2011 Census*. [Online]. Available from: www. ons.gov.uk/ons/rel/census/2011-census/key-statistics-for-local-authorities-in-england-and-wales/rpt-religion.html (accessed 31 August 2014).

PA/Huffington Post (2014), NHS withdraws job offer to gay Canon Jeremy Pemberton over bishop's refusal to grant licence. *The Huffington Post*. [Online]. Available from: www.huffingtonpost.co.uk/2014/08/04/nhs-trusts-regret-over-being-prevented-from-recruiting-gay-clergyman-_n_5647823.html (accessed 31 August 2014).

Piper v Maidstone & Tunbridge Wells NHS Trust [2012] UKEAT 0359 12 1812.

Poltoratskiy v Ukraine [2003] ECHR 216.

President of the Methodist Conference v Preston [2013] UKSC 29.

R (Prudential plc & Anor) v Special Commissioner of Income Tax & Anor [2013] UKSC 1.

R v Salford Area Hospital Authority ex parte Janaway [1989] 1 AC 537.

Rivers, J. (2010), The Law of Organized Religions: Between Establishment and Secularism. Oxford, New York: Oxford University Press.

Sharpe v Bishop of Worcester [2015] EWCA Civ 399.

Sharpe v Worcester Diocesan Board of Finance Ltd & Anor [2013] UKEAT 0243 12 2811.

Siddiqui, A. (2007), *Islam at Universities in England: Meeting the Needs and Investing in the Future.* [Online]. Available from: www.mihe.org.uk/sites/default/files/upload/Documents/siddiqui_report2007.pdf (accessed 31 August 2014).

Sokol, D. (2009), *The Value of Hospital Chaplains.* [Online]. Available from: http://news.bbc.co.uk/1/hi/health/7990099.stm (accessed 31 August 2014).

Vartic v Romania (No. 2) [2013] ECHR 1296.

Watkin, T.G. (1990), Vestiges of Establishment: The Ecclesiastical and Canon Law of the Church in Wales. *Ecclesiastical Law Journal*, 2, 110–15.

Wheeler v Le Marchant (1881) 17 ChD 675.

Chapter 7

Chaplaincy and Ethics: What Does it Mean to Be a Good Chaplain?

Peter Sedgwick

Chaplaincy as Different from Local Religious Professionals because of the Ethical Demands of the Host Institution

The argument of his chapter is threefold, and is set out in programmatic form. First, I argue that chaplaincy based in a secular institution is different from ministry based in a parish, local mosque or other religious institution because the institution which the chaplain serves will have its own legitimate ethical demands on the chaplain as a member of that institution. However, the local expression of ministry, whether parish or synagogue, is not answerable to a secular institution in the same way. The burden of this article is that to offer a description of the topic 'ethics and the chaplain' is quite unlike a description of the topic 'ethics and the parish priest', or any other faith tradition that has its place of worship in a town, on the main street, or wherever.

My argument, following Kathryn Tanner's article (2002) is as follows. 'Ordinary' religious communities are open-ended and mediate between the ecclesial/religious and the public (public is further defined below). Tanner's defence of the ambiguity of the Christian life is that it is essentially 'messy', open-ended, ill-defined, and also intrinsically embodied, as opposed to the theologically deductive nature of Christian (again, or any other faith tradition) ethics and practice given in the academy/seminary. Religious practice in the community, as any good scholar of religious history is well aware, can only be recorded as inherently a series of compromises between the demands of community life and those of the institution. Patrick Kavanagh's poetry of mid-20th-century Ireland and the rural Roman Catholic Church captures this well.[1] Ambiguities, inconsistencies and open-endedness in the ordinary lives of faith traditions such as Islam or Christianity that are communities of worship within social communities demand theological reflection. The demand is because theological reflection has to make sense of the messiness and compromises.

---

[1] Patrick Kavanagh, 'Lough Derg', in Kavanagh (2005: 90–110).

They also enable the faith tradition to respond to its environment, which is often unpredictable, conflictual and very complex.

The Nature of those Ethical Demands put upon Chaplains by the Host Institution

Secondly, I want to argue that chaplains, unlike parish clergy (or any other religious professional), have particular, highly prescribed demands put on them by the institutions in which they work. Not only is this the case, it is good and desirable that institutions have this expectation of chaplains. Out of many years of personal experience since 1982, working first with industrial, university and health chaplains in the 1980s, both in North-East England and on Humberside (Sedgwick 1988: 1–35; 1996), working nationally with prison chaplains from 1996–2004 across the whole of England and Wales, and finally teaching a wide variety of chaplains in the last decade since 2004 (but especially military chaplains) who have taken the Cardiff MTh in Chaplaincy, I have learnt to appreciate how much secular institutions look to a chaplain to perform certain ethical tasks. I think of industrial chaplains working in Teesside, or in the coal industry, in the 1980s, helping young apprentices to become responsible employees, and having a sense of civic accountability; prison chaplains contributing to offender resettlement programmes in the 1990s (Sedgwick 1999); or military chaplains in the last decade again training young recruits in England and Wales, but also contributing to morale on operations in Iraq and Afghanistan. All this behaviour is quite properly expected of the chaplain by the host institution, and it brings a set of ethical demands on the chaplain very unlike those on the local rabbi or parish priest. Chaplaincy and the living out of ethical behaviour is different from 'doing ethics' in the practices of faith traditions that are parishes, mosques, synagogues and the like. There are, of course, equally great differences between the ethical demands on hospital, military and prison chaplains as they serve the institution in which they are set. For instance, there are very different demands contained within end of life issues in a hospital, or a fatality on operations in Afghanistan, or thirdly a SID (self-inflicted death) in custody, on the particular chaplain involved. Such a careful mapping of ethical dilemmas and expectations is very necessary.

Such ethical dilemmas arise because chaplaincy operates in settings where there is a high degree of professionalism, and a high degree of secularity. They are efficient, non-open-ended institutions that work according to bureaucratic logic. They are performance-driven institutions.[2] Chaplains who work there have

---

[2]   David Faulkner (2001) captures the change to performance-driven management in the criminal justice system very well.

to fulfil the institution's criteria, including its ethical criteria. That means two things: first, contributing to the ethical outcomes of the institution – educating the staff of the institution in ways that inform them how to achieve the ethical outcomes, and modelling ethical behaviour oneself. Secondly, the chaplain does well by contributing to the standards of an organisation (Jacobs 2008). The question of what it means to be a good chaplain raises questions about the relationship of utilitarian (or consequentialist) ethics and virtue (or Kantian) ethics, and whether the goodness of a chaplain can be understood outside of the institution in which they represent their faith tradition.

The question therefore arises as to whether being good is the same as being efficient ethically or performing well in terms of the ethical outcome. The institution demands regularity, consistency and the predictable provision of pastoral care, ethical guidance and behaviour from 'their' (the ambiguity of ownership is deliberate) chaplains. To take further the question of end of life issues, chaplains join hospital ethics committees to provide guidelines in difficult situations,[3] and accompany relatives when they face the switching off of a machine that had provided artificial ventilation (Nolan 2012); contribute to the official policy on SIDs in custody, including in one case known to me the pastoral care of those who discovered the body (Tilt 2010); provide the appropriate degree of reassurance and ethical care to the colleagues of those killed in action (King 2013); offer care to pupils or students in a school or university when someone takes their own life;[4] and so on. The very acronyms that surround a chaplain constrain the ethical behaviour and provision of education of a chaplain – and in one way this must be expected, and even welcomed. The individuals to whom the chaplain ministers are categorised, classified and have patterns of expected behavioural outcomes (good examination results; being an effective fighting power; creating an environment in which shoppers will be encouraged to spend in a retail centre) to which the chaplain must contribute – or leave.

The Second Ethical Demand on Chaplains: Maintaining the Ethical Integrity of their own Tradition

There is, however, a third stage in the argument of this chapter, and it is absolutely crucial. I wish to argue that not only are chaplains different from local rabbis, imams or parish clergy; not only do chaplains have particular

---

[3]   Among many examples, Derek Fraser is alternate Vice Chair of the Cambridge Central Research Ethics Committee as well as a member of the Clinical Ethics Forum.

[4]   See 'Students and depression: the struggle to survive', *The Guardian* 23 March 2013; Bailey (2002).

ethical demands put on them; there is also another set of ethical demands (the second ethical demand on the chaplain) which are like those of a local-based ministry, but intensified to a high degree. The chaplain has then also to maintain the ethical demands of their own religious tradition, embodying them in worship, ritual behaviour, teaching and simply being present. Such a description of a chaplain's task is about ethical integrity, whether as Christian, Jew, Muslim or whatever faith tradition is espoused. It is true that all religious professionals have to live with the demands of ethical integrity. However, the living out of that ethical integrity as a chaplain in the very secular and modern context of a 21st-century institution (such as ministering under pressure on a high-tech hospital ward, or being based for months on an aircraft carrier on operations, or working as a chaplain within a psychotherapeutic, high security prison – all of which are actual contexts known to me) is often subtle, indirect and sometimes only apparent for those with eyes to see. Unlike the first set of ethical demands, which are perfectly legitimate in secular terms, justified by secular ethical theories and measurable by quantifiable analysis (a set number of hours training young recruits according to certain standards, a measurable presence with employees of the institution when they are under stress such as soldiers at a Forward Operating Base (Sedgwick 2013), the insight of a hospital chaplain who is a trained psychotherapist and working with bereaved relatives), the second set of ethical demands are integral to the faith tradition itself, have their own logic and are much contested as to whether they are susceptible to ethical reasoning from the secular world.

Ethics is never simply that which suits an organisation. Ethics is also what is true to a faith tradition, and to the chaplain's own faith values. Such an ethical dimension in many religious traditions is never, of course, fully able to be expressed in the here and now. In an 'ordinary' faith community, on the street of a town, there are the ambiguities and compromises of daily life. For a chaplain, there are the inevitable constraints of what the institution requires. These two divergences from the ethics of a faith tradition are, I have argued, different depending on whether one is being a chaplain or a parish priest (in Anglican terms). But in both cases the religious professional has to express as far as they can their 'true' faith, above and beyond either the compromises of daily life (in a parish) or as a chaplain. Equally, for both chaplain and parish priest, the ethics they espouse will not be fully able to be expressed in any reality on earth: it is an eschatological faith, fully expressible only at some time of religious fulfilment (Christians call this the coming of the Kingdom of God). Nevertheless, the ethics of their 'true' faith must be expressed. This expression of the heart of their belief is a constant ethical demand, and a continual recalling of self to God, or to the religious tradition in which one stands.

Studying the Justification of these Ethical Demands, from both the Secular Institution and also from the Faith Tradition

How are these ethical demands actually justified, either from the institution or from the faith tradition? The first set of ethical demands is often made on many others than chaplains, and those who are also caught up in these imperatives may include a wide range of staff, such as welfare officers, training and education staff, and front-line practitioners themselves (e.g. chaplains in a hospital will certainly know about medical ethics, but so might a senior nurse manager). The ethical demands of an institution (broadly enhancing performance effectiveness, increasing ethical knowledge among staff, ensuring social cohesion, etc.) are often assimilated to a form of deontology, utilitarianism, consequentialism, or to social psychology. In the latter case, social psychology examines the efficacy of the institution and the ethical questions which may arise. For an old and very famous example, take the 1960 Tavistock study of London teaching hospitals and their high wastage rate (Menzies 1960). For a very recent example, a study by a social psychologist on the efficacy of British and American soldiers in war has updated the well-known dictum of General Marshall in the Second World War that soldiers often do not want to kill (Murray 2013).

The second set of ethical demands, however, on ethical integrity is justified by the faith tradition to which the chaplain belongs. This is about the interweaving of spirituality, ethics and practical theology, so that terms such as righteousness or holiness are applicable here. Both sets of ethical demands refer to the 'good chaplain', competent at the institution's moral demands, but also holy and walking in the way of their God. My argument, then, is first that chaplains have different ethical demands from religious professionals based in a local community; secondly, they have ethical demands put on them by an institution; thirdly, they also have particular (and very intense) ethical demands to do with their own integrity; and finally, that all of this can be, and is, studied by theologians and social scientists.

Studying How Chaplains Respond to the Ethical Demands of the Secular Institution

There is, however, one further point to make, which is that both of these sets of ethical demands not only have their own theoretical and very different set of justifications, but the response to these ethical demands and the justification of these demands can itself be studied. It is not simply that chaplains live in my view both with the ethical demands of their institution and also with sustaining the ethical integrity of their faith tradition (call this living with institutional demands, the demands of A1, and living with ethical integrity the demands of B1). When the response of a chaplain is studied, in a reflective way, the observer asks what theoretical construct can shed light on how the chaplain responded. This can be called *meta*, or *reflective*, analysis. The contributions of secular ethicists in recent years to the ethical demands (A1) of a secular institution have been very helpful here. However, the *meta-reflection* on how the chaplain responds to the ethical demands of the institution operates at a very different level both from the self-descriptions of a chaplain, or the theoretical justification of the ethical demands put upon them, and this *meta-reflection* can be called A2. So the work of the social sciences, such as ethnography or reflexive sociology, can be used to understand chaplaincy. One such theorist is the late French philosopher Pierre Bourdieu, whose influence is enormous, and whose writings have been used in the last decade by Andrew Todd, Kathryn Tanner and others in reflecting on the nature of ministry, whether as a chaplain (Todd 2014) or in a parish (Tanner 2002). Tanner is indebted to Bourdieu on his distinctions of *practices* within *fields*, and the *habitus* which makes agents engage with *fields* (Bourdieu 1977, Rey 2007, Warde 2004). They are therefore socialised, which is a term much discussed by theologians and philosophers in recent years. Chaplains are agents. They operate in *fields* as diverse as the military, prisons, car factories, private boarding schools and hospitals (to name but a few that are personally known to me over the years). Theologians have argued that creation includes the divine sustaining of sociality, and socialisation (Hardy 2001: 88). The crucial thing is that how they behave is bounded by the institution in which they operate (Tanner 2002: 232).

Furthermore, when operating in such institutions, chaplains, unlike parish clergy, ministers or any other faith professional, operate in *public*. This raises the question of what is the relationship of the concept of *public* to the concept of field: are they synonymous? Nigel Biggar is one influential English theologian who has written much on the nature of the public (2011). Questions of the Rawlsian proviso are raised by Biggar here. That is, does a chaplain have to reframe their discourse so that everything is able to be understood in the language of the secular institution? If so, can a chaplain say anything? Of course they can, and their ethical behaviour, guidance and exemplar are hugely valued. How does the chaplain contribute to the good of the organisation? The answer is, as argued above, in two ways. On the one hand there is the well-known method of ethics education and secondly by contributing to the standards of an organisation, and ministering to its members.

Studying How Chaplains Respond to the Ethical Demands of the Faith Tradition: 'Keeping Integrity'

In observing the second set of ethical demands (B1) which are about preserving the religious and ethical integrity of the chaplain and those to whom they minister, a different set of theoretical arguments come into play. In Bourdieu's terms, the *habitus* which sustains them as chaplains can be defined as engaged dispositions, or embodied socialisation. This set of theoretical arguments which come into play when a chaplain is observed maintaining their integrity can be called B2. These are the demands of a particular faith, not only of doctrine, but also of ritual, liturgy and above all spirituality. This is not about what Bourdieu called 'the power of imposing on other minds a vision' (1990: 138). It is about being true to oneself. So the question is in what way one might come to reflect on why a chaplain would be concerned with ethical integrity, and how would one study the social practices which would ensure that integrity is not lost? There are two answers to this. One is that the justification of a chaplain's concern for ethical integrity can be given in terms of the *justification* of virtue ethics. This is not the same as explaining what virtue ethics actually is about, but how one would justify its truth value, or veracity. In the mid 1950s, it was thought that no one could either justify arguments for keeping ethical integrity or indeed observe such integrity. Ethics in British philosophy in the 1950s was either about personal opinions, which were akin to personal emotional states (emotivism), or the carrying out of particular ethical imperatives, chosen for whatever reason might be of value to the person (R.M. Hare). The only valid alternatives were arguments from social utility, such as deontology, consequentialism or social psychology.

It took the rigour of the conservative Roman Catholic philosopher Elizabeth Anscombe to show how ethical integrity is constitutive of a particular way of life; such a way of life is about excellence, or *arete*, and the *aretaic turn* made sense of the daily lives of all those who sought to attain moral integrity, or religion, as a way of life. Anscombe showed that the dismissal of virtue ethics consigned religious and personal integrity to the dustbin, which was a very western, and modern, form of insularity. She was followed impressively by the British philosopher Philippa Foot (1978, 2001, 2002). Foot pointed out that those who adopted virtue ethics, with its concern for integrity, conscience and humility, did so because of their *dependence on a particular way of life* which makes virtue ethics possible, and which is only itself sustained by continually performing actions virtuously in a reciprocal way. (There is dispute among moral philosophers as to whether the ethical theories which would explain the demands put by a secular institution on a chaplain, such as deontology or consequentialism, are also compatible with virtue ethics. Martha Nussbaum would take one view, Foot and MacIntyre another. But this article is not about ethical theory per se.) Foot's arguments are of value because they justify why a chaplain would have a concern for ethical integrity of a very particular sort, such as Christian, Muslim, Jewish or Buddhist. Indeed, Christian can be broken down into Baptist, Roman Catholic, Anglican and so on, and Muslim into Shia, Sunni – the list goes on for each faith.

However, the reflective observer asking how a chaplain responds is not yet satisfied. For in giving this answer, you have to justify why *these* particular practices? How can the practices of ethical integrity, as lived out in a person or community's life, be understood? Here the great theorist is Stanley Hauerwas, who introduces into this debate a whole series of different concepts, such as worship and ritual, relationships, re-encountering and re-embodying the story by their presence and finally the nature of what he calls 'embodiment'. What do these concepts mean? How do chaplains live them out? So I offer a Hauerwasian reading of what it means for a chaplain to have a *habitus*, or to show embodied socialisation (Hauerwas and Wells 2004, Wells 2004). A different theoretical justification is that of scriptural reasoning, which speaks of 'histories of wisdom ... deep reasonings ... like kinship rules, eating practices, poetry, folk songs and the language of elusive desire' (Adams 2006: 50). Again the concern is with the integrity of a faith tradition, which includes ethical integrity. Adams (2006: 54–5) highlights a concern that the deep reasonings of the world faiths are often not made public in an accessible way, especially on issues of end of life, sexual and medical concerns. One response to Adams is that chaplains could perform just this role.

Chaplaincy is deeply about worship and ritual. Prison chaplains who practice Eucharistic reconciliation have much to contribute to restorative justice, and that in turn can feed the understanding of penitence (Berkman 2004). My own experience of this in Cardiff Prison has shown how the links can be lived out. The SORI (Supporting Offenders through Restoration Inside) course was developed by Cardiff Prison Chaplaincy following contact with the Bristol Prison project as a multi-agency project tailored to the needs and strengths of HMP Cardiff. It developed into a series of voluntary courses for offenders, victims and community representatives based on their individual needs (Liebmann 2007, Sedgwick and Jones 2002, Shaw 2010). Always the experience of worship was at the heart of those leading it, and often of those taking part in it: chaplains and prisoners being forgiven and reconciled in worship by the God who redeems us. Chaplaincy is also about embodiment. In this *habitus*, the chaplain both inhabits their institution but also is an agent who worships; meets those of their own faith tradition, other faith traditions, and none; re-encounters the overarching narrative of their tradition and re-enacts it; and behaves in a certain deeply embodied way.

Embodiment is above all about living with truthfulness and the possibility of mutual correction, as chaplains make themselves vulnerable, but also have to engage with behaviour they find deeply challenging, such as sexist or racist banter. Here again worship can point to the necessity of overcoming brokenness (Wadell 2004). Embodiment includes the nature, layout and furnishing of a chaplain's office; the mixing together of cigarettes and Holy Communion in a single act of pastoral gift by the Christian chaplain Studdert Kennedy in the trenches of the First World War to those about to die (Wilkinson 1996, Snape 2013); coaching the Cambridge University college boat as a chaplain in the ministry of Lancelot Fleming, who was college chaplain, Arctic explorer and sportsman in the 1940s; anointing with holy oil the self-harmed and weeping wounds of a woman prisoner on Good Friday in Holloway prison in the ministry of Rosie Deedes – the list is endless, and is performed in each tradition in new ways that bodily re-enact the faith tradition.

In theoretical terms, the chaplain is described as operating in a Bourdieuian field of practices. To keep their integrity they must also embody a Hauerwasian narrative. Bourdieu and Hauerwas meet in the ethical life of every chaplain, at least those who are not humanist or secular chaplains. To put it very bluntly: any institution needs chaplains to educate, care and uphold the organisation (Bourdieuian practices). To keep their faith, a chaplain must read ethics through worship, re-enact the story and embody it (Hauerwas' ethical theory). This is not a contradiction but recognition of the complexity of reality. The reality is the faith life of the chaplain. Both are ethical, but in different ways

Summary of the Arguments Above

So the theoretical argument can be simply put. The behaviour of chaplains can be understood in terms of the secular ethical demands (A1) put upon them. Those demands can be explained through theories such as utilitarianism, deontology, etc. The response of chaplains can be understood through the social theories of Bourdieu and others (A2). They also have issues of ethical integrity (B1) and this is best justified in two ways (B2): first, it can be understood from the perspective of the meta-ethics of Foot, and secondly from the reflective descriptions offered by Hauerwas. A comprehensive understanding of the question 'what makes a good chaplain?' needs both an answer from the institution (A1) and the justification of chaplain's responses (A2), but also from the standpoint of the ethical integrity of chaplains (B1) and the justification of this (B2). The study of ethics and chaplaincy is impoverished if only one set of ethical demands of them is analysed, and it is equally impoverished if the meta-analysis of how chaplains respond is ignored.

Such embodiment requires theological reflection. The argument can now be drawn together. Chaplains perform as functionaries in public institutions and are evaluated as to their ethical efficacy by standard and predictable modes of measurement. They are also members of their faith tradition by embodying within these expected ethical practices of the institution (or field) the ethical nature of their faith tradition. So I am arguing that every chaplain lives two lives, and good chaplains do this well. They perform the ethical demands of the institution to which they are a chaplain, and they also model and live out the ethical demands of their faith tradition. This is not a contradiction, but it is a delicate balance that chaplains inhabit, and they know it very well, as many have often told me.

The ethical demands of the institution are observable, measurable and rational (visit prisoners, and prevent recidivism; teach children; contribute to health, healing and wholeness). However, the ethical demands of the faith tradition are often lived out in non-linguistic ways: the ethical imperative of worship on a battlefield, or before a heart operation for all the recipients, not least the surgeon or soldier; the constant presence of relationships that do not betray those to whom they minister (the most extreme example of this known to me is Brother Bill Tomes, chaplain to the drug gangs since 1983 in the notorious housing project called Cabrini Green in Chicago, where Brother Bill, as a layman with the full blessing and permission of the Roman Catholic Cardinal Bernardin of Chicago, baptised the children of drug dealers, and anointed the dying bodies of mortally wounded gangsters – he remains an iconic figure in contemporary America[5]); the re-encountering of the story and its re-enactment in every circumstance; and above all its embodiment beyond words (again the extreme example is Fr Michael Fallon Judge, OFM (May 11, 1933–September 11, 2001), who was a Franciscan friar and Catholic priest who served as a chaplain to the New York City Fire Department. It was while serving in that capacity that he was killed, becoming the first certified fatality of the September 11, 2001 attacks. The certification of his death as casualty 0001 at the World Trade Centre on 9/11 is a recognition of the ethical example of his embodied faith (Ford 2002).

The Non-Resolvable Paradox of Chaplaincy and Ethical Demands

Ethics and chaplaincy live on the edge of the dichotomy between secular practices and faith integrity. Institutions need good chaplains. In secular practice there are moral debates and ethical dilemmas relevant to chaplaincy: What of the just war tradition? What attitude does a chaplain take to end of life issues? What should a chaplain say about consumerism if they are a chaplain in a retail mall? The moral debates behind all of these issues need to be analysed with great care. But the overarching theological point is twofold. First, such debates are within a bounded field (Bourdieu) where the institution claims the loyalty of the chaplain. Secondly, the faith tradition responds – as it always must – by a counter claim that the ultimate eschatological ethical significance is to be

5   See 'In the line of fire: Brother Bill Tomes', *Time Magazine*, August 24, 2002; 'Brother Jim', *Chicago Tribune*, December 10, 2004; 'Brother Bill', http://www.chicagoreader.com/chicago/brother-bill/Content?oid=875746 (accessed 12 April 2015).

found in the faith tradition from which this chaplain comes. How are these held together? My answer is that the performance of the narrative in terms laid out clearly by Hauerwas enables the chaplain to keep their integrity. But the living out of the faith tradition's claims is often non-linguistic, embodied, ritualised and a form of re-enacted narrative. It is in all of this nonetheless deeply ethical. How the ethics of the institution which the chaplain serves in measurable terms, and the ethics of the faith tradition which the chaplain inhabits as part of their being (and is often non-observable to the secular eye), can be held together in a coherent whole, is the supreme question to be answered. And, I would claim, every chaplain knows that.

References

Adams, N. (2006), Making Deep Reasonings Public. In D.F. Ford and C.C. Pecknold (eds), *The Promise of Scriptural Reasoning*. Oxford: Blackwell Publishing.

Bailey, A. (2002), Faith and Spirituality in Students' Mental Health. In N. Stanley and J. Manthorpe (eds), *Students' Mental Health Needs*. London: Jessica Kingsley, 227–43.

Berkman, J. (2004), Being Reconciled: Penitence, Punishment and Worship. In S. Hauerwas and S. Wells (eds), *The Blackwell Companion to Christian Ethics*. Oxford: Blackwell, 95–108.

Biggar, N. (2011), *Behaving in Public: How to Do Christian Ethics*. Grand Rapids: Eerdmans.

Bourdieu, P. (1977), *Outline of a Theory of Practice*. Cambridge: Cambridge University Press.

—— (1990), *In Other Words*. Cambridge: Polity Press.

Faulkner, D. (2001), *Crime, State and Citizen*. Winchester: Waterside Press.

Foot, P. (1978), *Virtues and Vices and Other Essays in Moral Philosophy*. Berkeley: University of California Press; Oxford: Blackwell.

—— (2001), *Natural Goodness*. Oxford: Clarendon Press.

—— (2002), *Moral Dilemmas: And Other Topics in Moral Philosophy*. Oxford: Clarendon Press.

Ford, M. (2002), *Father Mychal Judge*. New York: Paulist Press.

Hardy, D.W. (2001), *Finding The Church*. London: SCM.

Hauerwas, S. and Wells, S. (eds) (2004), *The Blackwell Companion to Christian Ethics*. Oxford: Blackwell.

Jacobs, M.R. (2008), What are we doing here? Chaplains in contemporary health care. *Hastings Center Report*, 38(6), 15–18.

Kavanagh, P. (2005), *Collected Poems*. London: Penguin Books.

King, P. (2013), *Faith in a Foxhole?* Unpublished MTh dissertation. Cardiff University.

Liebmann, M. (ed.) (2007), *Restorative Justice: How It Works*. London: Jessica Kingsley.

Menzies, E.P. (1960), A case-study in the functioning of social systems as a defence against anxiety: a report on a study of the nursing service of a general hospital. *Human Relations*, 13, 95.

Murray, L. (2013), *Brains and Bullets*. London: Biteback.

Nolan, S. (2012), *Spiritual Care at the End of Life: The Chaplain as a Hopeful Presence*. London: Jessica Kingsley.

Rey, T. (2007), *Bourdieu on Religion*. Durham: Acumen.

Sedgwick, P. (1988), *Industrial Mission and the Mission of the Church*. London: Church of England Board for Social Responsibility.

Sedgwick, P. (1996), The Enterprise Culture. In J. Rogerson (ed.), *Industrial Mission in a Changing World*. Sheffield: Sheffield Academic Press, 51–62.

—— (1999), A Theology of Vulnerability. In Church of England Board for Social Responsibility, *Prisons: A Study in Vulnerability*. London: Church House Publishing, 113–23.

—— (2013), Terrorism and Interrogation as an Issue for Chaplains on Operations. In A. Todd (ed.), *Military Chaplaincy in Contention*. Aldershot: Ashgate, 65–83.

Sedgwick, P. and Jones, C. (eds) (2002), *The Future of Criminal Justice*. London: SPCK.

Shaw, S. (2010), When SORI is not the hardest word. *Inside Times*, February.

Snape, M.F. (2013), *The Clergy in Khaki: New Perspectives on British Army Chaplaincy in the First World War*. Aldershot: Ashgate.

Tanner, K. (2002), Theological Reflection and Christian Practices. In M. Volf and D. Bass (eds), *Practicing Theology*. Grand Rapids: Eerdmans, 228–45.

Tilt, D. (2010), *The Prison Chaplain's Role in Caring for Prison Staff, with Particular Reference to their Care Following the Self-Inflicted Death of a Prisoner*. MTh dissertation. Cardiff University.

Todd, A.J. (2014), Religion, security, rights, the individual and rates of exchange: religion in negotiation with British public policy in prisons and the military. *International Journal of Politics, Culture, and Society*. (Online).

Wadell, P. (2004), Sharing Peace: Discipline and Trust. In S. Hauerwas and S. Wells (eds), *The Blackwell Companion to Christian Ethics*. Oxford: Blackwell, 289–301.

Warde, A. (2004), *Practice and Field: Revising Bordieusian Concepts*. CRIC Paper no 65. Manchester: University of Manchester.

Wells, S. (2004), *Improvisation: The Drama of Christian Ethics*. London: SPCK.

Wilkinson, A. (1996), *The Church of England and the First World War*. London: SCM Press.

Chapter 8

Multifaith Working

Sophie Gilliat-Ray and Mohammed Arshad

Introduction

Since the Second World War, European societies and major public institutions have witnessed a rapid increase in religious diversity. Muslims now constitute the second largest faith group in most parts of Europe. Although their numbers as a national percentage may be as low as three or four per cent, in some particular towns and cities that figure can rise to about 30 per cent of the local population (2011 Census of England and Wales). Furthermore, in these particular localities there are often also sizeable communities reflecting other world religions – Jews, Hindus, Sikhs and others.

This changing religious demography in many European and Western societies has had consequences for local public institutions serving such mixed faith and multicultural areas. The historic accommodation of 'belief' (including secularism) reflecting variable historic church–state arrangements has been disrupted by the need to deliver more explicitly 'multifaith' services in prisons, hospitals, the military and so on. This has come about as the right of hospital patients, prison inmates and military personnel to maintain their religious identity and observe associated practices has gradually been recognised (if not accommodated). The major variation between public institutions and different societies occurs in relation to *the degree* to which this recognition and accommodation of religious diversity is facilitated, alongside the local context and national socio-political arrangements which either enable or constrain the process.

It is a paradox that chaplaincy is both a relatively liminal arena of religious activity ('out of sight, out of mind'; 'behind closed doors') and yet the increasing religious diversity of the populations of Europe has given chaplaincy a new legal, political, economic, social and religious significance. This is because chaplaincy and the accommodation of religious services is often taking place within institutions funded via public taxes, and in the case of Britain, some forms of chaplaincy and religious provision are themselves publicly funded. In a multifaith society, this raises pressing questions about equality and fairness from political, economic, legislative, philosophic and practical perspectives.

This was the starting point for the research that James Beckford and Sophie Gilliat conducted in the mid 1990s that resulted in the book *Religion in Prison: Equal Rites in a Multi-Faith Society* (Beckford and Gilliat 1998) and a range of other publications that questioned the equity of existing arrangements around publicly funded chaplaincy and civic religion in a context of increasing religious diversity in England and Wales (Beckford 1998, 2001, 2013, Gilliat-Ray 1999, Gilliat-Ray 2001). Where increasing religious diversity in England challenged well-established assumptions about the role of the Anglican church and its personnel as the 'brokers' of religious services in public institutions, in France, increasing religious diversity challenged (and continues to challenge) the norms that surround the principle of *laïcité*, or strict separation of church and state. Consequently, as Farhad Khosrokhavar notes in France, Muslims have not yet found an 'institutionalised framework within which to agree on compromises with the government'. Increasing religious diversity in other European and Western societies has similarly challenged the religious/political status quo in one way or another. The nature of the challenge usually reflects the assumptions that have accumulated over time in relation to the socio-legal position of religion in these different societies. Ultimately, however, the extent to which the development of multifaith chaplaincy has occurred is often a reflection of the broader position of religion in society per se, and the extent to which new or more pragmatic arrangements are able to evolve within existing frameworks.

Meanwhile, the infrastructures established by Muslim and other religious minorities in order to engage with civil society and political/public bodies in different European and Western societies are highly variable; this is a reflection of their different migration histories, numeric size and human capital. But this variation has resulted in differential capacity to negotiate with authorities for recognition and more equitable treatment within chaplaincy structures, both locally and nationally. So, for example, the existence of the Muslim Council of Britain (MCB) – an umbrella body launched in 1997 – offered a structure through which the National Health Service in England and Wales could establish a dialogue about the provision and recruitment of Muslim chaplains in hospitals (Gilliat-Ray 2010). Not all European societies have equivalent 'representative' bodies such as the MCB, and even among those that do, the socio-political context for negotiation of more equitable arrangements and greater inclusion in chaplaincy will of course be different.

Mapping the Discourse

At this point, we need to clarify what we mean by 'multifaith chaplaincy' as we use the phrase in this chapter. Essentially, we are using the term to refer to the inclusion of chaplains from a range of faith communities within chaplaincy or spiritual care departments, in order that they might oversee the religious needs of individuals and families from their faith tradition. In Britain, this work is increasingly undertaken in a context where assumptions about 'teamwork' and mutual respect in relation to religious difference prevail to some degree. Consequently, there are many occasions when chaplains from different faiths can and do substitute for one another in relation to non-liturgical functions.

The evolution of multifaith chaplaincy in Britain has occurred as an outcome of a felicitous convergence of political opportunity and policy directives (e.g. the ethos of 'inclusion' and more responsive public services that characterised the late 1990s' 'New Labour' government); the pastoral and practical religious needs of growing and diverse faith communities; the availability of suitable personnel to take up new chaplaincy positions; and the willingness of extant professional chaplaincy associations to engage with the new landscape of religious diversity around them (Gilliat-Ray 2008). Since 2010, multifaith chaplaincy (at least in the UK) has been stimulated further by the evolution of equalities legislation. Religion is a protected characteristic (along with racial, gender or other identity markers) and this has helped to shape a more hospitable environment for the inclusion of chaplains from a range of religious traditions within public institutions (at least in theory).

If we map the development of social scientific research about religious diversity and chaplaincy in public institutions it is virtually impossible to find any major studies pre-dating the work conducted by Beckford and Gilliat in the mid 1990s. The publication of *Religion in Prison* was a catalyst for new academic research and writing, much of it undertaken by sociologists and anthropologists of religion, by chaplaincy practitioners and by practical theologians (nearly all Christians), and by people with a combination of these perspectives (Hansen 2012, Hunt 2011, Lie 2001, Todd 2011, 2013, 2015, Todd and Tipton 2011). This body of research and writing about multifaith chaplaincy (in particular) has been evolving within a much larger and rapidly expanding field of international study concerned with religion in public institutions and religious diversity in public life per se (of which this is a small sample: Becci 2011, 2012, 2015, Cadge 2012, Fabretti 2014, Griera and Martinez-Arino 2014, Sullivan 2011, 2014). It is of course impossible to draw distinct lines between these various fields given the obvious intersection between them, but nonetheless, the research and writing about multifaith chaplaincy (in particular) needs to be situated within this larger evolving field.

An Emerging Field of Islamic Pastoral Theology

More recently, and in parallel with these developments, there is an emergent body of work concerned with the particular accommodation of Islam and the development of Muslim chaplaincy in many European and Western institutions, largely as a consequence of the numeric size of Muslim communities and the distinctive issues that pertain (Beckford et al. 2005, Gilliat-Ray et al. 2013, Hamza 2007, Harris 2009, Khoja-Moolji 2011, Khosrokhavar 2015, Kowalski 2009, Kowalski and Becker 2015, Lahaj 2009, Levine 2009, Marranci 2009, Padela et al. 2010, 2012, Seymour 2006, Spalek and Wilson 2001). Where professional chaplaincy discourse has so far largely failed to reflect the voices and concerns of Muslims and chaplains from other minority faiths about their experiences of multifaith working, this is beginning to change. As Muslim chaplains acquire growing influence, seniority and leadership in the profession as practitioners (especially in the UK and USA) they are becoming active contributors to policy making, academic research, continuing professional development of staff, and thus the shaping of chaplaincy discourse. As a consequence of their contributions, it is clear that a new field of 'Islamic pastoral theology' is in the embryonic stages of development, as Muslim chaplains seek to interpret Islamic texts and principles in order to meet the challenging pastoral needs of 21st-century Muslims (Ali 2014). This interpretive work requires an ability to think and act contextually and with reference to the ethos of public service, equality and diversity that govern the public institutions in which they work (Gilliat-Ray et al. 2013).

The second part of this chapter goes on to illustrate this interpretive work through discussion of some concrete examples of Muslim involvement in multifaith chaplaincy work derived from practitioner perspectives. Some of the opportunities and satisfactions of chaplaincy work become evident through these examples, as well as the some of the challenges and obstacles that can frustrate the delivery of equitable pastoral care in public institutions. In many ways, these outcomes are two sides of the same coin; whether a situation is a good example of multifaith cooperation, or an occasion for hostile tension, seems to depend critically upon the quality of the human relationships involved.

Last Rites

The religious diversity that characterises many modern societies goes beyond demography and statistics; it has changed the composition and character of many households and families, some of which are now themselves 'multifaith'. This diversity can present particular challenges when it comes to marking the rites of passage associated with birth and death, and the death of a baby only magnifies the challenge of addressing an intensely painful pastoral dilemma. A scenario that is becoming more prevalent in chaplaincy in many modern societies is the need to explore the possibility of combining funeral rites from several religious traditions, in order to accommodate the needs of grieving families, or the wishes of the deceased. In such situations, urgent and immediate pastoral need trumps theological and ritual niceties, issues around professional superiority or self-protective territorialism. It gives way to an opportunity for multifaith teamwork that goes beyond policy directives or polite, but distant, mutual regard. This is illustrated through an event that took place at Bradford Royal Infirmary in 2008. One evening, an elderly female Roman Catholic patient passed away unexpectedly when her treatment for cancer could no longer be sustained. Her relatives included her two sons, both of whom had converted to Islam, and a daughter, who, like her deceased mother, was a committed Roman Catholic. Given that there are rites to be performed at the moment of death in both Roman Catholic and Islamic traditions, it was perhaps inevitable that the siblings wanted to offer their mother last rites that conformed to their own understanding of 'correct practice' at such a time. As the voices of dissension were raised, from muted whispers to far more animated and heated debate, the ward staff took the initiative of calling both the Muslim and the Roman Catholic chaplains.

Very quickly, the two chaplains recognised the need to provide for the whole family, and together they presided over the offering of last rites according to both traditions. This involved reading prayers from both faiths as the patient died, followed by establishing a consensus with the relatives that subsequent burial would be in accord with both Islam and Roman Catholicism. Because the chaplains were of different genders and different faiths, they were able to complement one another in supporting all the members of the family.

Multifaith Worship Spaces: The Politics of 'Sharing'

> Multifaith is politically significant because it is replacing Christianity as the face of public religion in Europe and America. (Crompton 2013: 493)

The ethos of 'multifaith' that now pervades many public institutions that employ chaplains has coincided with times of economic challenge and shrinking public service budgets in many European societies. In these circumstances, the repurposing of existing worship facilities into multifaith spaces, or the design of entirely new facilities 'for people of all faiths and none' (as the phraseology usually goes), poses challenges in relation to the use of a single facility by people from a wide range of religious traditions (Gilliat-Ray 2005a, b). A major study in the School of Architecture at the University of Manchester explored some of these questions – from political, economic, social and design perspectives – as part of the 'Religion and Society' programme funded by the two major UK research councils.[1] Multifaith spaces were described thus:

---

[1]   www.sed.manchester.ac.uk/architecture/research/mfs/.

usually they are mundane spaces without an aura whose most characteristic form is an empty white room ... they are the architectural equivalent of ambient noise ... there is an assumption that we should not be exposed to symbols of other people's faith if that can be avoided. The most important issue in multifaith design has become how to prevent a space becoming meaningful in an inappropriate way. (Crompton 2013: 474)

While these are issues for which architects appear to have few immediate answers, chaplains have to navigate the reality of how to share worship spaces on a day-to-day basis, and manage the 'unstable equilibrium' (ibid. 480) that inevitably arises when different traditions are using the same facility. This sometimes exposes the limits and tensions of multifaith chaplaincy relationships as different religious events jostle with one another as they share the same confined, but ultimately 'non-space'. When the occasions of congregational worship happen to coincide, perhaps when a Christmas Day service happens to fall on a Friday, thus clashing with regular Muslim Jumu'ah prayer, multifaith spaces shared by people of 'all faiths and none' become sites of inevitable (un/friendly) religious competition that can potentially test chaplaincy team relationships to breaking point. In such contexts, defined more by absence rather than presence, the smallest material or embodied artefact becomes significant (ibid.).

The physical manifestation of these conflicts can sometimes be telling. During fieldwork research for the Muslim Chaplaincy Project (Cardiff University, 2008–2011)[2] we saw material signs of subtle tensions which suggest contested understandings about multifaith working at a day-to-day level. For example, an incident recorded in field notes following a visit to a London hospital points to the difficulties of trying to accommodate different worshipping traditions within a single space, along with the fact that Muslims tend to make disproportionate use of shared worship space in public institutions.

Adil opened the cupboard where copies of the Qur'an and prayer mats were kept. He showed me an arrow on the inside of the cupboard door which had the word 'qibla' written underneath it [to indicate the direction for prayer]. He told me this is the best he can do as his team members would not allow the arrow to be placed anywhere on the walls. This would defy the purpose of a generic worship room. Adil told me that he could not understand how a line on the wall would make the room less generic. He raised the issue with his colleagues who said that maybe they should have a compass on the wall with pictures showing the direction towards

2   The Muslim Chaplaincy Project, also funded as part of the AHRC/ESRC 'Religion and Society' programme was conducted by Sophie Gilliat-Ray (Cardiff University), Stephen Pattison (Birmingham University) and Mansur Ali (Cardiff University) between 2008 and 2011; see Gilliat-Ray et al. (2013).

different faith places such as Makka, Jerusalem, India, Rome, etc. Adil told them that they were complicating matters and all that he wanted was a small arrow on the wall. He showed me how Muslim service users draw the arrow on the skirting board and how his colleagues delete it with correction fluid. The whole corner is a mess due to the over-use of correction fluid (field notes, part-time male hospital chaplain, April 2010). (Gilliat-Ray et al. 2013: 107)

But alongside these kinds of tensions, we also heard accounts of inter-religious generosity in relation to sharing of religious space. For example, a Jewish rabbi was happy that Muslims used the hospital synagogue for Friday prayers when the Muslim prayer room became too small:

we [had] permission from the Rabbi to use the synagogue, we now from the last two years, and they were happy, they said 'yes, this is a step forward towards community cohesion, let's do it'. Two years now we are doing it (full-time female hospital chaplain). (ibid. 108)

There is also evidence to suggest that chaplains of different faiths are learning about the use of religious space from one another in ways that are surprising, sometimes modelling their behaviour on that of colleagues.

[Musaddiq] first went into the multi-faith room and did a small prayer (du'a). I asked him what this prayer was about (as it is unconventional) and he told me that this is something that he picked up from his Christian line manager ... that it is good practice to go to the chapel or mosque every day and make a prayer for the sick (field notes, shadowing a full-time male hospital chaplain, July 2010). (ibid. 105)

These examples illustrate that chaplaincy departments in many public institutions have now become sites of intensive inter-religious encounter, and chaplains themselves have become important carriers of knowledge about the practical and pastoral implications of living in a multifaith society. As such, chaplaincy departments can model the kind of inter-religious cooperation that could be informative and valuable in wider society more generally.

Alongside the evolution of generic multifaith spaces shared by people 'of all faiths and none', there is a discernible assumption in some quarters that, in financially straitened times, chaplains themselves can adopt generic approaches to religious and spiritual care for people of 'all faiths and none' so that the personnel engaged in chaplaincy reflect themselves the 'non-spaces' in which they facilitate individual or corporate worship. The rather different arrangements for religion in American public life mean that the idea of 'interfaith' chaplaincy is taken as normative in many public institutions (Abu-Ras and Laird 2010,

Cadge and Sigalow 2013). Chaplains are typically hired to be 'chaplains', who happen to be Christian, Jewish or Muslim, not as 'Christian chaplains', 'Jewish Chaplains' or 'Muslim chaplains'. This side of the Atlantic, in the UK, the faith-specific approach is also under some degree of pressure – the assumption being that in a society where people increasingly self-define as 'spiritual' rather than 'religious', a member of any faith tradition can, with appropriate training, offer 'spiritual care' to people of 'all faiths and none'. Stephen Pattison warns of the consequences of this approach in much the same terms as Crompton warns in relation to the spatial equivalent. 'Pastoral care which transmutes into generic spiritual care may become a case of the bland leading the bland' (Pattison 2001: 34), the result being a 'metaphysical marshmallow that is non-specific, unlocated, thin, uncritical, dull and un-nutritious' (ibid.).

The ethos of multifaith that now pervades the delivery of pastoral care in public institutions means that chaplaincy is a sphere of contemporary religious activity that excludes those who are unable to subscribe to a 'team' approach. So where James Beckford and Sophie Gilliat established that the predominant experience of chaplains from minority faith traditions in Britain was one of exclusion, the last 20 years have seen the pendulum swing towards far greater inclusion and cooperation, making incidents of exclusion or discrimination the exception rather than the rule. A Muslim chaplain interviewed as part of the Muslim Chaplaincy project reported that his chaplaincy team was like a jigsaw puzzle:

> I think we all play an important part ... we're these pieces of the jigsaw. A Jewish piece, a Hindu piece, a Sikh, a Christian ... a Quaker, you know. And to collecting all these pieces ... actually creates a picture called the chaplaincy (full-time male prison chaplain). (Gilliat-Ray et al. 2013: 106)

If the human relations that shape multifaith chaplaincy have progressed since the 1990s, there remain significant economic and structural impediments to genuine equality of service delivery. The gradual incorporation of minority faith traditions into public pastoral care has exposed their relative strengths and weaknesses in terms of economic and human capital, and organisational capacity. This is particularly well illustrated in relation to the extent to which different faith communities can draw upon a pool of 'volunteers' who might undertake routine ward visits in hospitals, or support ex-offenders upon release from prison as part of community chaplaincy projects. With their longer history of establishment and greater human and material resources, most of the Christian churches can rely upon voluntary activity to support salaried chaplaincy; not so minority faiths, which, due to their migration history, lack this kind of resource.

The inequality of opportunity and service delivery that continues to shape day-to-day multifaith chaplaincy work is to some extent becoming rebalanced by the fact that chaplaincy is, perhaps increasingly, just one dimension of 'religion' in public institutions. Thus the increasing presence of Muslims in prisons, for example, means that the functioning of the entire regime, and the material culture of the prison – i.e. what religious artefacts prisoners are allowed to have or not have, is shaped by their presence. This is manifest in the allocation of spaces for worship, staff training requirements, decisions about menus and catering, and so on. The operational functioning of prisons now has to take far greater account of religion per se. A by-product of this is the increasing religious literacy of staff, even if this has not resulted in increasing religious tolerance.

However, it would probably be fair to say that the disproportionate consideration of Muslim religious needs in public institutions – on account of their numerical presence and distinctive requirements – has resulted in the continued marginalisation of chaplains from smaller religious traditions, such as Buddhism and Sikhism. Where volunteers or sessional chaplains from these traditions make an input to the work of chaplaincy teams, it is usually only on the basis of a few hours per week, if that. Such a limited presence restricts their capacity to make their views heard among senior managers, to shape institutional policy, or forge relationships with key staff members that might facilitate greater inclusion. There is still 'no level playing field' (Lie 2001: 183) in aspects of multifaith chaplaincy.

Conclusion

Over the last three decades, as society has become increasingly diverse in terms of faiths and cultures, research and writing about the impact of these changes upon chaplaincy and public institutions has evolved. There has been a clear shift of emphasis, with early research tending to concentrate on issues of Anglican/ Christian 'brokerage' on behalf of other faiths (Beckford and Gilliat 1998, Lie 2001). Another distinctive trend in the research field then evolved with a focus upon issues of equality and diversity (Orchard 2000, 2001), the need for religious 'justice' in chaplaincy (Noblett 2002), alongside the emergence of 'how to' literature which considered the religious and pastoral needs of patients or prisoners from particular religious traditions during their hospitalisation or imprisonment (Gatrad et al. 2004, Gatrad and Sheikh 2001, Gatrad 1992). Since the late 2000s, the research field has developed once again towards an interest in the career trajectory and work of chaplains from smaller faith traditions (especially Islam; Ali and Gilliat-Ray 2012, Gilliat-Ray et al. 2013).

This has coincided with a political and social context where concerns about religious radicalisation and extremism have become pressing. Recent research has documented some of the implications of this for the work of chaplains, especially within prisons (Todd 2011, 2013, Todd and Tipton 2011). The challenges and opportunities of multifaith chaplaincy have been severely tested in relation to the political contests that have surrounded chaplaincy since 9/11, and the increasing scrutiny placed upon chaplains to 'prevent violent extremism' and to promote 'community cohesion'.

This chapter began by noting that increasing religious diversity has given chaplaincy, as a distinctive sphere of religious activity, new political, economic, legal and social significance. However, the implications of this changing religious landscape are not limited to lawyers, policy makers, chaplains or politicians. It is notable that over the period since the mid 2000s, the academic community with an interest in undertaking research about religion in public institutions has grown significantly, alongside the growing religious diversity described at the beginning of this chapter. Consequently, there is greater reflection about research methodology, and the distinctive questions that arise from the study of religion in 'non-religious' places (Cadge and Konieczny 2014, Swift 2009).

For example, chaplaincies – operating as they do at the meso-level of society – are situated at the nexus of the private religious worlds of individuals on the one hand, and the dynamics of society and major institutions, on the other. This makes them ideal sites for mapping the evolution of new religious discourse, because of the way in which it is possible to see far larger issues in microcosm. In a recent special issue of the journal *Qualitative Inquiry* devoted to consideration of ethnography in prisons, Rod Earle cites Sharon Shalev's observation that 'prisons ... are an early warning system for society ... they constitute the canary in the coalmine, providing an omen of mortal danger that often lies beyond our capacity to perceive' (Shalev 2009, cited by Earle 2014). However, the scope for prisons or hospitals to signal possible future trends need not always point towards danger.

Thus, the felicitous convergence of social and political forces that have created the new profession of 'Muslim chaplain' has led to the development of a new kind of Islamic leadership in Britain and the USA, and, increasingly, in Europe as well. Some of the most able imams in Britain have been able to use public-funded chaplaincy positions as opportunities to think beyond the theological or legal binaries of halal or haram. For example, some Muslim chaplains working in health care are using the resources of the Islamic tradition to support clients with depression and other psychological states. But more significantly than that, they are beginning to isolate some of the religious and medical distinctions to be drawn between straightforward mental illness and spiritual disorders which are sometimes attributed by patients to the influence of evil spirits or *jinn*. Unconstrained and freed from a dependence on community elders or mosque committees, they have been empowered to forge an Islamic 'pastoral theology', if not in theory, certainly in practice. Even if they continue to hold conservative views about matters of religion, they are nevertheless usually 'playing by the rules of the game' in public institutions, and we could regard this as significant, theologically and politically, in relation to the future of Muslim leadership in European societies. In this way, multifaith chaplaincy has served as a catalyst for evolving religious professionalism and entrepreneurialism, suggesting the creation of religious specialists who can act as role models for the conduct of multifaith relationships in society as a whole.

References

Abu-Ras, W. and Laird, L. (2010), How Muslim and non-Muslim chaplains serve Muslim patients? Does the interfaith chaplaincy model have room for Muslims' experiences? *Journal of Religion and Health*, 50(1): 46–61.

Ali, M. (2014), Perspectives on drug addiction in Islamic history and theology. *Religions*, 5(3): 912–28.

Ali, M. and Gilliat-Ray, S. (2012), Muslim Chaplains: Working at the Interface of 'Public' and 'Private'. In Ahmad, W. and Sardar, Z. (eds), *Muslims in Britain: Making Social and Political Space*. London: Routledge, 84–100.

Becci, I. (2011), Religion's multiple locations in prison: Germany, Italy, Swiss. *Archives de Sciences Sociales des Religions*, 153(Jan–March), 65–84.

—— (2012), *Imprisoned Religion: Transformations of Religion During and After Imprisonment in Eastern Germany*. Farnham: Ashgate.

—— (2015), Institutional resistance to religious diversity in prisons: comparative reflections based on studies in Eastern Germany, Italy and Switzerland. *International Journal of Politics, Culture, and Society*, 28, 5–19.

Beckford, J. (1998), Ethnic and religious diversity among prisoners: the politics of prison chaplaincy. *Social Compass*, 45(2), 265–77.

—— (2001), Doing time: space, time, religious diversity and the sacred in prisons. *International Review of Sociology*, 11(3), 371–82.

—— (2013), Religious diversity in prisons: chaplaincy and contention. *Studies in Religion/Sciences Religieuses*, 42(2), 190–205.

Beckford, J. and Gilliat, S. (1998), *Religion in Prison: Equal Rites in a Multi-Faith Society*. Cambridge: Cambridge University Press.

Beckford, J., Joly, D. and Khosrokhavar, F. (2005), *Muslims in Prison: Challenge and Change in Britain and France*. Basingstoke: Palgrave Macmillan.

Cadge, W. (2012), *Paging God: Religion in the Halls of Medicine*. Chicago: University of Chicago Press.

Cadge, W. and Konieczny, M.E. (2014), 'Hidden in plain sight': the significance of religion and spirituality in secular organizations. *Sociology of Religion*. [Online].

Cadge, W. and Sigalow, E. (2013), Negotiating religious differences: the strategies of interfaith chaplains in healthcare. *Journal for the Scientific Study of Religion*, 52(1), 146–58.

Crompton, A. (2013), The architecture of multifaith spaces: God leaves the building. *The Journal of Architecture*, 18(4), 474–96.

Earle, R. (2014), Insider and out: making sense of a prison experience and a research experience. *Qualitative Inquiry*, 20(4), 429–38.

Fabretti, V. (2014), Dealing with religious differences in Italian prisons: relationships between institutions and communities from misrecognition to mutual transformation. *International Journal of Politics, Culture, and Society*, 28(1), 21–35.

Gatrad, A.R., Brown, E. and Sheikh, A. (2004), Developing multi-faith chaplaincy. *Archive of Diseases in Children*, 89(6), 504–5.

Gatrad, A.R. and Sheikh, A. (2001), Medical ethics and Islam: principles and practice. *Archive of Diseases in Children*, 84(January), 72–5.

Gatrad, R. (1992), *The Muslim Patient*. Wolverhampton: School of Health Sciences, Wolverhampton Polytechnic.

Gilliat-Ray, S. (1999), Civic religion in England: traditions and transformations. *Journal of Contemporary Religion*, 14(2), 233–44.

—— (2001), Sociological Perspectives on the Pastoral Care of Minority Faiths in Hospital. In Orchard, H. (ed.), *Spirituality in Health Care Contexts*. London: Jessica Kingsley Publishers, 135–46.

—— (2005a), From 'chapel' to 'prayer room': the production, use, and politics of sacred space in public institutions. *Culture and Religion*, 6(2), 287–308.

—— (2005b). 'Sacralising' sacred space: a case study of 'prayer space' at the Millennium Dome. *Journal of Contemporary Religion*, 20(3): 357–72.

—— (2008), From 'Visiting Minister' to 'Muslim Chaplain': The Growth of Muslim Chaplaincy in Britain, 1970–2007. In Barker, E. (ed.), *The Centrality of Religion in Social Life: Essays in Honour of James A. Beckford*. Aldershot: Ashgate, 145–60.

—— (2010), *Muslims in Britain: An Introduction*. Cambridge: Cambridge University Press.

Gilliat-Ray, S., Ali, M.M. and Pattison, S. (2013), *Understanding Muslim Chaplaincy*. Aldershot: Ashgate.

Griera, M. and Martinez-Arino, J. (2014), *The Accommodation of Religious Diversity in Prisons and Hospitals in Spain*. Augsburg, Germany: RECODE.

Hamza, D.R. (2007), On models of hospital chaplaincies: which one works best for the Muslim vommunity? *Journal of Muslim Mental Health*, 2(1), 65–79.

Hansen, K.P. (2012), *Military Chaplains and Religious Diversity*. London: Palgrave Macmillan.

Harris, R.T. (2009), Supporting your Muslim students: a guide for clinical pastoral supervisors. *Reflective Practice: Formation and Supervision in Ministry*, 29, 154–69.

Hunt, S. (2011), Testing chaplaincy reforms in England and Wales. *Archives de Sciences Sociales Des Religions*, 153(1), 43–64.

Khoja-Moolji, S.S. (2011), *An Emerging Model of Muslim Leadership: Chaplaincy on University Campuses*. Harvard University: Pluralism Project.

Khosrokhavar, F. (2015), The constrained role of the Muslim chaplain in French prisons. *International Journal of Politics, Culture, and Society*, 28, 67–82.

Kowalski, M. (2009), Names of God: practical theology for Muslim chaplains in CPE. *Reflective Practice: Formation and Supervision in Ministry*, 29, 178–86.

Kowalski, M. and Becker, W. (2015), A developing profession: Muslim chaplains in American public life. *Contemporary Islam*, 9, 17–44.

Lahaj, M. (2009), Making it up as I go along: the formation of a Muslim chaplain. *Reflective Practice: Formation and Supervision in Ministry*, 29, 148–53.

Levine, S.E.J. (2009), Muslim Chaplains in America: voices from the first wave. *Reflective Practice: Formation and Supervision in Ministry*, 29: 142–7.

Lie, A. (2001), No Level Playing Field: The Multi-Faith Context and its Challenges. In Orchard, H. (ed.), *Spirituality in Health Care Contexts*. London: Jessica Kingsley, 183–94.

Marranci, G. (2009), *Faith, Ideology and Fear: Muslim Identities Within and Beyond Prisons*. London: Continuum.

Noblett, W. (2002), Prisons: A Developing Chaplaincy. In Jones, C. and Sedgwick, P. (eds), *The Future of Criminal Justice*. London: SPCK, 89–102.

Orchard, H. (2000), *Hospital Chaplaincy: Modern, Dependable?* Sheffield: Lincoln Theological Institute.

—— (ed.) (2001), *Spirituality in Health Care Contexts*. London: Jessica Kingsley Publishers.

Padela, A., Killawi, A., Heisler, M., Demonner, S. and Fetters, M. (2010), The role of imams in American Muslim health: perspectives of Muslim community leaders in Southeast Michigan. *Journal of Religion and Health*, 50(2), 359–73.

Padela, A.I., Killawi, A., Forman, J., DeMonner, S. and Heisler, M. (2012), American Muslim perceptions of healing: key agents in healing, and their roles. *Qualitative Health Research*, 22(6), 846–58.

Pattison, S. 2001. Dumbing Down the Spirit. In Orchard, H. (ed.), *Spirituality in Health Care Contexts*. London: Jessica Kingsley Publishers, 33–46.

Seymour, S. (2006), The silence of prayer: an examination of the Federal Bureau of Prisons' moratorium on the hiring of Muslim chaplains. *Columbia Human Rights Law Review*, 37(2), 523–88.

Spalek, B. and Wilson, D. (2001), Not just 'visitors' to prisons: the experiences of imams who work inside the penal system. *The Howard Journal*, 40(1), 3–13.

Sullivan, W. (2011), *Prison Religion: Faith-Based Reform and the Constitution*. Princeton: Princeton University Press.

—— (2014), *A Ministry of Presence: Chaplaincy, Spiritual Care, and the Law*. Chicago: University of Chicago Press.

Swift, C. (2009), *Hospital Chaplaincy in the Twenty-First Century: The Crisis of Spiritual Care in the NHS*. Aldershot: Ashgate.

Todd, A. (2011), Responding to Diversity: Chaplaincy in a Multi-Faith Context. In Threlfall-Holmes, M. and Newitt, M. (eds), *Being a Chaplain*. London: SPCK, 89–102.

—— (2013), Preventing the 'neutral' chaplain? The potential impact of anti-'extremism' policy on prison chaplaincy. *Practical Theology*, 6(2), 144–58.

—— (2015), Religion, security, rights, the individual and rates of exchange: religion in negotiation with British public policy in prisons and the military. *International Journal of Politics, Culture, and Society*, 28, 37–50.

Todd, A. and Tipton, L. (2011), *The Role and Contribution of a Multi-Faith Prison Chaplaincy to the Contemporary Prison Service*. Cardiff: Cardiff Centre for Chaplaincy Studies. Available at: http://stmichaels.ac.uk/assets/pdf/Todd-and-Tipton-2011-Report-on-Prison-Chaplaincy.pdf (accessed 17 April 2015).

Chapter 9

Managing Multifaith Spaces: The Chaplain as Entrepreneur

Chris Hewson and Andrew Crompton

Introduction

> The Charity Commission had been troublesome, challenging that we were in fact
> a charity. We rewrote our mission statement not mentioning religion. We are now
> a limited company. (Airport chaplain, in conversation 31 December 2010)

In our study of multifaith spaces[1] (henceforth MFS) we have been impressed
by how often we found them being managed by Anglican clergy. In these places
individuals with a gift for casuistry and diplomacy, and there are many of them,
can express themselves in ways unavailable in regular ministry. Since there is no
standardised model of multifaith, chaplains experience difficulties and freedoms
that set them apart from the established faith apparatus; in effect a large
experiment is underway centred on managing sacred space in secular settings.[2]
In these circumstances clergy and associated laity must adapt themselves to
the organisations that support them, justifying themselves with reference to
producing measurable results, or by *adding value* (Threlfall-Holmes 2011).
Hitherto secure patterns of employment found in the church are undermined
and chaplains share in the insecurity of a deregulated market. Intolerable though
this might seem, many rise to the challenge in an entrepreneurial spirit.

Running a multifaith chaplaincy as a business may not be as radical as it first
seems. It is continuous with a tradition of workplace and industrial chaplaincy,
within the institutions of post-war modernity, which seeks to bring chaplains
into closer proximity to 'other' spaces and faiths (Torry 2010: 1050). Where
MFS are retrofitted chapels these continuities are obvious. Only where they
are deliberately designed to avoid explicitly Christian, or indeed any particular
religious imagery, could one doubt it. In extreme cases one might make the claim

---

[1]   Multi-faith Spaces: Symptoms and Agents of Religious and Social Change
(2010–2013; AHRC Religion and Society Programme, AH/H017321/1).

[2]   An institutional parallel to the forms of urban 'postsecular rapprochement' noted by
Cloke and Beaumont (2012).

that such places are not sacred, let alone Christian, and as such are harbingers of the end of formal religion. But even here there are continuities, as we will show.

The Business of Religion

Clergy and businessmen share many skills. Even when the purpose is to advance fellowship rather than accumulate capital, most ministers know about bookkeeping, fund raising, event planning, running clubs, property management, handling difficult people, and so on. The juxtaposition of worship and large scale commerce is hardly new either. Before the formation of the welfare state, Methodist Central Halls combined respectable entertainment with amenities such as employment exchanges and pharmacies, so allowing worship to continue in cities after worshippers had moved to the suburbs. Nearly 100 were built in British cities between 1886 and 1939, most of them substantial pieces of property development drawing on the skill of Methodist businessmen, with mortgages serviced through associated shops and offices. Their Christian origins could be deduced from the absence of alcohol, gambling or unsuitable performers; you might see Arthur Askey but not Max Miller. After holding their own against music hall and cinema they were gradually driven out of business by television, whose mixture of programmes like *Songs of Praise* and associated light entertainment was not so different to what Central Halls presented in a live setting (Connelly 2012). As with modern MFS, Central Halls did not look like churches and could be enjoyed without encountering formal worship.

We argue that situating worship in a commercial environment was then, and still is, a bold idea. Since the millennium a steady increase has taken place in the number of MFS in offices, airports, shopping centres, football grounds and so forth (Brand 2012). Whilst traditional chaplaincy in the armed forces, prisons, hospitals and education has taken a multifaith turn, it is in these more commercial settings that chaplaincy has taken its most entrepreneurial form. These insights have subsequently been reflected back into these more traditional spheres. With the exception of airports, these are realms where no sacred space formerly existed.

In these places chaplains address social, economic and institutional imperatives that go beyond the simple act of offering universal access to the divine (Witham 2010). They must be entrepreneurial in finding ways to be useful. A shopping centre gains a commercial advantage if it can cater to Muslims looking for a place to pray; a multifaith chaplain will be required to keep that room in order. At an airport the disaster contingency planning committee requires end of life support and bereavement counselling; a multifaith emergency response team will be written into the plan. Flight crew camaraderie generates weddings, memorials, ceremonies, scattering ashes at the airport and so on; again, the chaplain is there to preside and direct. Chaplains make themselves useful by taking on roles that evade formal job descriptions, leading to an engaged and practical form of ministry, often at odds with the wider faith establishment. Inside an airport terminal people in need do not present themselves in the MFS but must be sought out amongst the crowds. We found several chaplains covering large distances each day walking through the terminals looking for opportunities to be supportive. One chaplain was particularly keen to make it known that he was always available to talk to staff and passengers, cultivating a reputation as a dependable character witness at employment and immigration tribunals.

In another example, chaplains were part of a charitable trade, recycling goods confiscated at security and disbursing unwanted luggage to good causes. Their MFS had a bowl of pebbles which were stolen one by one. The chaplains replaced them from their store, as well as the books that vanished from their shelves.[3] In these and other ways they put themselves about, enmeshing themselves into the life of the airport. It therefore follows that what multifaith chaplaincy sets out to achieve may be ambiguous. As Swift (2009: 166) notes, 'the multi-referenced chapel has given way to the ambiguity of the prayer room and its accompanying sense of uncertainty about the role of the chaplain'. Accordingly, some chaplains effectively compartmentalise the blurred responsibilities of faith leader and chaplain, others are happy to be described as 'multifaith' or 'generic' chaplains. Sometimes this is codified in the form of an MFS mission statement. Here is the example from the airport mentioned above that caused the Charity Commission to hesitate:

> The Chaplaincy [...]: A living expression of faith through the provision of pastoral and humanitarian care for all people irrespective of race, gender, sexuality, physical and mental ability, within and beyond the airport community (2009–2015)

The Charity Commission's objection was (we speculate) that aims such as 'humanitarian care' are not precise enough to express a charitable purpose. They advise: 'Don't include your charity's motive or ethos in its purpose ... unless this means your purpose will be carried out in a specific way.'[4] While it would have been sufficient to state 'in accordance with Christian principles', multifaith cannot be sufficiently particular about its methods and so fails the test of being charitable. Correspondingly, our study noted chaplains subtly distancing themselves from both religious and institutional orthodoxies by providing services distinct from business as usual. The multifaith chaplain appeared as all things to all people; their role took on facets that were supplementary to the core goals of the institution, or at the very least beyond the capacities or job

---

[3]   *The Nation's Favourite Poems* (ed. Griff Rhys Jones) amongst the most stolen.

[4]   https://www.gov.uk/how-to-write-charitable-purposes, Charities Act 2011.

descriptions of other employees. Chaplains simultaneously belonged and did not belong: we found them wearing policemen's style Dr Martens shoes for walking, with a tie and a day-glow jacket marked 'Airport Chaplain'. They are an interface between the public and staff on the one hand and the corporate entity on the other.

Office and Religious Life Combined

Multifaith chaplains usually have their own room separate to the worship space. This will be not quite a study, rather something approximating a commercial office. Both spaces will often be windowless with a suspended ceiling. There will normally be a store in which furniture, books and other consumables can be put out of sight so that the worship space can be emptied. The ability to clear and reset, for an MFS to say nothing, is important.

The language of office furniture is international.[5] The image of desk and bookcase presents an appearance of professional power. The chaplain will have her share of report writing, personal development reviews, impressing the boss, displaying innovative thinking, 'value-added' initiatives, compliance and counselling. It would be easy to think of this as unbecoming and limited, yet chaplains share the common experience of office workers, with familiar insecurities and irritations. The rituals and liturgy of the Church of England (CofE) relate to rural life, with much of the Bible story told in metaphors relating to agriculture. It might be argued that the CofE has never truly adapted itself to the industrial, let alone the post-industrial condition. Indeed, the *Faith in the City* report (General Synod of the Church of England 1985) was premised on a vision of mass 'industrial society' that had to a large extent vanished by the time of publication. By contrast, MFS are ideally suited to the post-industrial age with its individualisation, widespread insecurity and emphasis on the consumption of goods and services.

To illustrate, on revisiting one chaplain, the first thing we were told was, 'we've been restructured'. The issue of overt religiosity at this airport was a constant backdrop, and now temporarily deprived of her MFS she was walking around the airport like a member of a mendicant order:

> I am a figure in a balance sheet ... HR knows we are useful we can help defuse situations ... I hand out sweets. At Easter I handed out eggs, I bought most of them myself. I play secret Santa ... I talked to a member of staff who had been

---

[5]   An unfortunate link with Scientology, the only other religion to make use of the office as a sacred environment (every Church of Scientology maintains an office in honour of L. Ron Hubbard).

made redundant. He said he was not hostile to Christianity. I do not mention God in the course of a week. I told him, today I shall pray for a new job for you.[6]

The purposes are Christian, the tone is secular. Happily, on a subsequent visit the MFS had been reinstated, a hybrid space in a sea of commercial outlets.[7] In other MFS, institutional choices are less zero-sum. For instance, in one North American MFS it was observed that the large room was bookable for all manner of secular activities including fraternity initiations. While it was made clear that prayerful activities would always take precedence, exactly how this would be interpreted was a matter for the current Executive Director.

It is often noted that the success of Pentecostal groups, relative to other Christian denominations, is in part because they are easy to set up and highly entrepreneurial within their own spiritual frame of reference. MFS are likewise easy to establish in out-of-the-way areas, typically places where a viable rent cannot be had. Our study points to far flung, virtually disowned MFS located near toilets or lift shafts. These spaces are generally used only by those whose faith makes prayer a necessary requirement. Chaplaincies that acquire MFS in more lugubrious surroundings often have to justify them on a daily basis. The stakes are higher, both success and failure are more likely.

Design students are often told to consider an object or area in its larger context – a chair in a room, a room in a house, a house in a neighbourhood, and so on.[8] To the extent that institutionally sited MFS represent and reflect global rather than local populations, an international style should emerge. This does in fact happen and airport MFS are at the forefront. This has the air of equality, but what is left in these circumstances? In the words of Simone Weil (1976: 244–5):

> Each religion is alone true, that is to say, that at the moment we are thinking on it we must bring as much attention to bear on it as if there were nothing else; in the same way, each landscape, each picture, each poem, etc., is alone beautiful. A 'synthesis' of religions implies a lower level of attention.

The sharing of physical space is a matter of concession and local negotiation, a set of compromises, some minor, others substantive. An analogy can be found in the urban design approach that erodes distinctions between pedestrians and vehicles, a growing feature of many UK towns and cities, (Hamilton-Baillie 2008). A mutual understanding of the trajectories and space requirements of each participant is required. Sometimes this is achieved by the total removal of

---

[6]   An airport chaplain (in conversation, 28 June 2011).

[7]   The space had not moved, but an airport redesign had moved it airside to what was now a more commercially sought-after location.

[8]   A method attributed to architect Eero Saarinen.

signage, an ironic warning that no one has precedence. An absence of symbols in MFS parallels this process; absence is itself a sign of tolerance (e.g. the absence of a cross is a sign of humility, of not giving offence). Everyone is disadvantaged, but some more than others.

The idea of the MFS as a sacred space separate from the world does not hold up. Often, with few or no services to conduct and no permanent congregation to serve, the multifaith chaplain may *rightly* start to wander. Our study is rife with examples of chaplains who would rather be in motion than tied to the upkeep of a room. The service, not the space, is the product shaped by the chaplain. Lead chaplains are not managers as might be traditionally understood, rather they are key organisational nodes or points of passage. Through the figure of the chaplain-as-moderator, the multifaceted flow of objects and ideals that make up multifaith chaplaincy are locally contested and given form. The actual MFS serves as a backdrop for this activity, although what happens in it may be of secondary importance.

Negotiations are needed to maintain a balance between the presence and absence of this or that faith: 'only if scrupulously maintained in unstable equilibrium between these modes of failure can they provide universal access to the divine. Maintaining this balance requires a diplomatic inter-faith minister' (Crompton 2013: 480). The figure of chaplain-as-moderator has three key underpinnings. First, the need to generate a modus operandi whilst both managing a diverse team of chaplains and ministering to a wide range of users. Secondly, a recognition that MFS are invariably fashioned via networks of more or less formalised relationships, with host institutions and faith spaces external to the institution (churches, mosques, temples, chapels, etc.). Thirdly, whilst MFS are very much objects of modernity, they may clash with the aims of the institution that houses them; for instance the logic of capitalist accumulation in a shopping centre, or the prevailing strictures of temporal organisation in a prison or school. To see MFS as inherently inclusive misreads their purpose. A normative programme is erroneously assumed, whereby shared and inclusive space is seen as an end-point. In reality, it is fleeting requirement that brings users into these spaces.

Established Models

Where multifaith chaplaincy emerges from a Judeo-Christian framework, as in hospitals or prisons, individual chaplains might work under a faith title such as priest or pastor. In schools, universities, offices, airports and shopping centres, a secular designation such as faith advisor or counsellor may be an alternative. Hospitals[9] and prisons are places where people in genuine distress can be found

---

[9]   For instance, the Patients' Charter (1991) called for 'quality based' provision of faith services within NHS hospitals.

needing help, and traditional chaplaincy continues. It is, however, in other possibly more inconsequential environments, that multifaith experimentation reaches its most complete form.

Like other corporate places MFS aim for stability, predictable outcomes and replaceable components. Ironically this leads to those who work in them being in an insecure position. A chaplain may be part-time, or work between sites; their role might be geographically bounded (i.e. a city and its institutions) or institutional, for example ministering to a set number of universities or hospitals. A lead chaplain may work on their own, or have a core staff and possibly volunteers. Commonly they can call on part-time representatives of other religions as required. They may answer to their own faith community or to an HR department or pastoral care manager. If the latter, they may be the manager of all the institution's faith spaces. Alternatively, they might have a wider non-operational remit, delegating responsibility for the MFS to a lead chaplain.

As with any professional role, personal proclivities are as significant as experience and outlook. Some chaplains steadfastly support their own tradition, with differing outcomes regarding the ability to effectively manage an MFS. Pastoral and material faith provision in one institution may bear no comparison with that at an ostensibly similar site. Furthermore, the locally negotiated nature of MFS can have the effect of disconnecting lead chaplains from a shared vision of multifaith chaplaincy, (if this can even be said to exist), engendering risk aversion. As Todd (2011: 101) notes:

> At issue is the shared identity of chaplaincy within a multi-faith, multicultural setting. Too great an emphasis on faith-specific provision not only risks competition for scarce resources but also a lack of professional coherence; too great a weight placed on that coherence risks a loss of distinctiveness, rooted in the riches of multiple faith traditions. A balance is necessary. ...

Consequently, sharing experiences of managing religious and secular services in tandem is undoubtedly the best form of assistance for those entering the field. In the UK, lead chaplains are often ordained or lay members of the CofE. In line with legislation – specifically the Equality Act 2010 – this *need* not be the case. Differences between Anglicans and Nonconformists are reflected in both differences of style and specific interpretations of MFS provision as a manifestation of Christian 'hospitality' (cf. CHELG 2013). The rhetoric of hospitality, as Biddington (2013: 321) reminds us, fails to recognise that 'hosting or "being at home" for the stranger is always potentially both an occasion for celebratory encounter and a risky and uncertain undertaking. By contrast, it would appear that multifaith spaces are home for no one and everyone is an outsider.' This sentiment is echoed by Barnes (2002: x, 3):

> Christian discipleship in a multifaith society can no longer afford to patronise others into a predetermined scheme of things ... It is perfectly possible for persons of faith to maintain their own integrity while yet learning how to relate responsibly and sensitively to each other.

Such integrity is seen as coherent and inherently relational, speaking to a wished-for harmony that extends beyond the physical space of the encounter, into the wider world. The idea of MFS as relational space renders multifaith chaplaincy a form of entrepreneurial and local action, rather than a set of transferable precepts. This clashes with a vision of chaplaincy defined in reference to a set of spaces and architectural forms which are largely Christian (Nolan 2008). Undeniably, the idiosyncrasy of Protestant managers providing services to a Muslim-majority client base has shaped recent debate. Albeit a model of chaplaincy has recently been fashioned from within Islam,[10] 'building upon a very well-established but less formally defined and less institutionalised understanding of pastoral care' (Gilliat-Ray 2008: 146). Islam is no longer inevitably viewed as a minority partner,[11] and a stress is placed on training within the context of locality as necessary for managing diversity in a multifaith space (see Gilliat-Ray 2003a: 15).

Chaplaincy in Public Institutions

Hospitals perhaps evince the clearest rationale for delimited faith space, with the suggestion that medical professionals are in charge of the body and its care, with the chaplain's remit stretching to all other areas; parallel theatres of the body and the soul. As Gatrad et al. (2004: 505) observe, the hospital chaplain fuses 'generic issues on diversity and specific issues on faith' in order to generate a worldview blessed with 'the requisite "insight" needed to facilitate and deliver multi-faith care to the diverse populations they serve'. These are modest yet entrepreneurial acts of creative destruction, introducing insights external to the prevailing value system. This might be guided by religious orthodoxy, but will largely focus on the reproduction of 'social benefit' (*contra* institutional reproduction) and will overlap with the non-clinical aspects of care offered by medical and nursing staff; a shared language of care, rather than 'a universally inclusive notion of spirituality ...

---

[10]   For instance, within with the certificate of Muslim chaplaincy, offered by Markfield Institute of Higher Education from 2003. In the same year, Newham University Hospital was the first to appoint a Muslim lead chaplain.

[11]   Although, Prideaux (2009: 464) notes the potential for Muslim–Christian dialogue to become 'an act of faith in itself ... deeply problematic ... because of the apparent potential for syncretism ... [in contrast] "practical dialogue" tends to be the dialogue of necessity.'

based on a particular understanding of the concept' (MacLaren 2004: 459).[12] This echoes Todd's stress on 'balance', highlighting the need for a clear spiritual position, yet not viewing the hospital as the primary conduit via which to reflect on these issues (cf. Narayanasamy 2004). It is significant that MFS perform a process of separation from the values of the host institution.

Professional role requirements, encompassing an operational sense of 'the spiritual', are held in tension with prior theological commitments and associated understandings of how faith space might operate. This is evident in prisons, where a disciplinary mode is tempered via a service-based model that has much in common with other public institutions. Prisoners have little scope to seek solitude, and are 'likely to encounter religious representatives far more frequently than in the course of daily life in the outside world' (Beckford 2001: 374). Whilst officers are the eyes and the governor the brain, chaplains are the ears of the prison with a role integrated into the routine activities of prisoners, rather than providing what Beckford et al. (2005: 94) refer to as 'a voluntary complement to the normal round of activities'. This is a supply-led model of chaplaincy, which meets latent rather than expressed demands.

Within further education, Learning and Skills Council (LSC) guidance stresses the role of chaplaincy in 'equipping individuals', observing that 'an important element of effective chaplaincy is to build in sufficient time to reflect' (LSC 2007: 29). Within this scenario, space emerges for the moral and institutional aspects of chaplaincy to be brought together on a local basis.[13] The LSC puts forward six different models of chaplaincy: coordinator, team leader, staff lead, volunteer, shared institution and chaplaincy assistants (op. cit.: 8).[14] Noting the Employment Equality (Religion or Belief) Regulations 2003, the legal personhood of the chaplain is highlighted, alongside their existing pastoral and curriculum support function. The development of an exclusive, locally derived MFS is stressed: 'it is important that, as soon as possible, the chaplaincy team reflects the make-up of the area the college serves; and develops links that reflect the religious diversity in England', with design proposals benchmarked against the requirements of these representatives (op. cit.: 22).

---

[12]   Analogous to the possibilities of negation inherent in the 'international style', as Gilliat-Ray (2003b: 337–8) warns, 'new, rather secularised, individualistic, humanistic definitions of spirituality can mean anything to anyone, regardless of their belief or lack of it, and it is questionable whether this makes them useful to anyone'.

[13]   Contrastingly, in an assessment of prayer facilities in three Midlands sixth form colleges, Parker (2009: 33) foregrounds the institutional drive towards academic attainment that sees extracurricular activities as deprioritised, and the provision of faith space being 'met by a sense of surprise and gratitude amongst students'.

[14]   Similarly, Gilliat-Ray (2000) provides a typology of universities as either: anti-religion, tolerant, anti-denominational or multifaith pragmatist. Obviously, the outlook of any chaplaincy cannot necessarily be reduced to the stance of the wider institution.

With respect to higher education, work by the Equality Challenge Unit (ECU) stresses that whilst there is no statutory responsibility to provide prayer rooms within the Equality Act 2006, MFS represent an obvious outcome, alongside associated protocols around religious etiquette, health and safety and religious timetabling (ECU 2009a, b). This guidance builds upon earlier advice stressing the need for proposed solutions to the material accommodation of faith to be allied to ongoing programmes that promote trust and respect throughout the institution. An accompanying example is structured around a fourfold process: consultation, dividing space according to need, the encouragement of local discussion and ongoing review (ECU 2005: 37–8). The key point to stress here is that whilst constructive, the implied inclusivism inherent within these guidelines elides the oftentimes individualised nature of MFS usage.[15]

Balancing Resources

In acting entrepreneurially, lead chaplains operate as obligatory points of passage, for whom facilitation shades off into brokerage (Beckford 1999: 678). The chaplain seeks a balance between institutional and extra-economic outcomes, often within a milieu that prioritises the former over the latter, or seeks to convert the latter – sometimes erroneously – into the former. Based on what we have observed, we argue that the extent to which the chaplain-as-moderator is able to perform this balance is consistent with what could be termed the effective alignment of material and non-material resources at their disposal. These include, but are not limited to: relationships with key stakeholders; the presence and absence of spaces and objects; competition within the spiritual marketplace; and tensions both creative and destructive with and within the host institution. As Chapman and Lowndes (2009: 372) suggest, faith representation blurs the line between direct and indirect democracy. Utilising the work of Saward they uphold 'non-elected' claims to legitimacy, noting their explicit nature, specificity and spatial and temporal flexibility. In the original formulation: '...none of us is ever *fully* represented; representation of our interests or identities in politics is always incomplete and partial. This implies representation is about a claim (redeemed, if at all, only partially), and not a fact or a possession' (Saward 2009: 3).

What do these observations imply for MFS? We would suggest that they serve to bolster the claim that with respect to matters of faith, the state is *ipso facto* incapable of fully serving citizens' interests. Imagine, for a moment, what

---

[15] Evidence from the Australian higher education sector suggests that chaplaincy 'needs to meet the religious/spiritual needs of an individual practicing by himself/herself more so than the needs of a group' (Possamaia and Brackenreg 2009: 361).

a state-sponsored MFS might look like. Accordingly, new forms of authenticity are likely to be found within networks where consent takes on a more apparent and consistent form: ' ... as new "governance strategies" call forth new types of representatives they are, in effect, creating new constituencies ... [and] opening up spaces for creative political agency' (Chapman and Lowndes 2009: 373). These networks presently rest upon a residual Christianity; the 'assumption that Christian chaplains take most of the responsibility for matters related to religion' (Beckford et al. 2005: 19). At the same time, there is a move away from the categorisation of multifaith space as 'sacred' (Huxley 2008), with residual Christianity counterbalanced by what one might term 'benign Islamisation'. The entrepreneurial chaplain will understand and manage this incommensurability through careful facilities management, timetabling and controlled overlap of use; religious and earthly matters are managed in tandem. This learning process is widely embraced by many chaplains, albeit to the occasional detriment of faith actors located beyond the Judeo-Christian–Islam axis.[16]

Conclusion

The duties of a multifaith chaplain are far removed from what a 19th-century vicar would have thought normal. In his book of 1882, *Duties of the Parish Priest*, Professor Blunt positions his students between Evangelicalism and Popery. At the edges of his world are other forms of Christianity, what lies beyond them is not to be thought of (Blunt 1882: 112). Surely he would have been amazed by multifaith in which clergy operate within a matrix of competing faiths. What is clear is that multifaith bears witness to multiple experiences of reality, even if the various chaplains involved do not personally accept them as true. In these circumstances one begins to wonder what success would look like; is it necessary for a space to thrive, or merely survive? Perhaps MFS cannot be successful in any recognised sense of the term but are *inherently* peripheral. The fact that we have not found any famous or model MFS in our survey speaks to this marginality.

Most MFS are *ad hoc* and insubstantial. On occasion a lot of money and energy goes into their creation, as for example at Koffler House at the University of Toronto. Here a three-storey Multifaith Centre for Spiritual Study and Practice has been embedded into the pastoral and scholarship functions of the institution. The stated purpose is to promote spiritual dialogue, first by encouraging separate practices then looking for commonalities. To mention one subtlety, the building is designed to allow the use of smoke in Hindu and First Nation ceremonies without setting off the fire alarms, or disquieting subsequent

---

[16]   For instance, within one Western European airport the Abrahamic prayer room structure merely offers those outside these faiths to 'pick a room'.

occupants. Great care has gone into the sensitive and equitable satisfaction of every religious requirement, except for this: the ability of any faith to claim that it is uniquely true. The rigour and completeness of this place is a rebuke to any such claim, but only in degree not in kind. In such places, as Don Cupitt (1991: 63) puts it, 'modern faith is unavoidably a lifestyle, fictionalist, slightly *camp*, affected. The role of a practicing Christian is now a character part, not a leading role.' The entrepreneurial chaplain is often validated through their role as counsellor or friend, standing at odds to the organisation that houses them. As such they are outsiders. Entrepreneurs similarly succeed by seeing opportunity where others do not, risking and encountering failure. It is necessary for the concept to endure that many entrepreneurs fail. That many MFS succeed without adequate institutional support, or a coherent vision, speaks well of this ongoing experiment.

Acknowledgements

AHRC Religion and Society Programme.

References

Barnes, M. (2002), *Theology and the Dialogue of Religions*. Cambridge: Cambridge University Press.

Beckford, J.A. (1999), Rational Choice Theory and prison chaplaincy: the chaplain's dilemma. *British Journal of Sociology*, 50, 671–85.

—— (2001), Doing time: space, time, religious diversity and the sacred in prisons. *International Review of Sociology: Revue Internationale de Sociologie*, 11, 371–82.

Beckford, J.A., Joly, D. and Khosrokhavar, F. (2005), *Muslims in Prison: Challenge and Change in Britain and France*. Basingstoke: Palgrave Macmillan.

Biddington, T. (2013), Towards a theological reading of multifaith Spaces. *International Journal of Public Theology*, 7, 315–28.

Blunt, J.J. (1882), *The Parish Priest, His Acquirements, Principal Obligations, and Duties*, 8th edition. London: John Murray.

Brand, R. (2012), Multi-Faith Spaces as Symptoms and Agents of Change. In Woodhead, L. and Catto, R. (eds), *Religion and Change in Modern Britain*. London: Routledge.

Chapman, R. and Lowndes, V. (2009), Accountable, authorized or authentic? What do 'faith representatives' offer urban governance? *Public Money & Management*, 29, 371–8.

CHELG (2013), *Developing and Managing Faith Space in Universities and Colleges – Guidance for Chaplains.* London: Churches Higher Education Liaison Group.

Cloke, P. and Beaumont, J. (2012), Geographies of postsecular rapprochement in the city. *Progress in Human Geography*, 37, 27–51.

Connelly, A. (2012), A pool of Bethesda: Manchester Central Hall, 1886–2010. *Rylands Bulletin (New Series)*, 89, 122–56.

Crompton, A. (2013), The architecture of multifaith spaces: God leaves the building. *The Journal of Architecture*, 18, 474–96.

Cupitt, D. (1991), *What Is A Story?* London: SCM Press.

ECU 2005. *Employing People in Higher Education: Religion and Belief (Guidance).* London: Equality Challenge Unit.

ECU 2009a. *Religious Observance in Higher Education: Facilities and Services.* London: Equality Challenge Unit.

ECU 2009b. *Religious Observance in Higher Education: Institutional Timetabling and Work Patterns.* London: Equality Challenge Unit.

Gatrad, A.R., Brown, E. and Sheikh, A. (2004), Developing multi-faith chaplaincy. *British Medical Journal*, 89, 504–5.

General Synod of the Church of England (1985), *Faith in the City – A Call for Action by Church and Nation: The Report of the Archbishop of Canterbury's Commission on Urban Priority Areas.* London: Church House Publishing.

Gilliat-Ray, S. (2000), *Religion in Higher Education: The Politics of the Multi-Faith Campus.* Aldershot: Ashgate.

—— (2003a), Ministerial formation in a multi-faith society. *Teaching Theology & Religion*, 6, 9–17.

—— (2003b), Nursing, professionalism, and spirituality. *Journal of Contemporary Religion*, 18, 335–49.

—— (2008), From 'Visiting Minister' to 'Muslim Chaplain': The Growth of Muslim Chaplaincy in Britain, 1970–2007. In Barker, E. (ed.), *The Centrality of Religion in Social Life: Essays in Honour of James A. Beckford.* Aldershot: Ashgate.

Hamilton-Baillie, B. (2008), Shared space: reconciling people, places and traffic. *Built Environment*, 34, 161–81.

Huxley, J. (2008), *Recovering the Calm: Best Practice Guide to Prayer Rooms and Quiet Space at Work.* London: Employers Forum on Belief.

LSC 2007. *Multi-Faith Chaplaincy: A Guide for Colleges on Developing Multi-Faith Student Support.* Coventry: Learning and Skills Council.

Maclaren, J. (2004), A kaleidoscope of understandings: spiritual nursing in a multi-faith society. *Journal of Advanced Nursing*, 45, 457–62.

Narayanasamy, A. (2004), Commentary on Jessica McLaren's 'A kaleidoscope of understandings: spiritual nursing in a multi-faith society'. *Journal of Advanced Nursing*, 45, 462–4.

Nolan, S. (2008), 'This chapel is a sanctuary': another place or a place for the other? *International Journal of Public Theology*, 2, 313–27.

Parker, S. (2009), Theorising 'sacred' space in educational contexts: a case study of three English Midlands Sixth Form Colleges. *Journal of Beliefs and Values*, 30, 29–39.

Possamaia, A. and Brackenreg, E. (2009), Religious and spirituality diversity at a multi-campus suburban university: what type of need for chaplaincy? *Journal of Higher Education Policy and Management*, 31, 355–66.

Prideaux, M. (2009), Muslim–Christian Dialogue: the gap between theologians and communities. *International Journal of Public Theology*, 3, 460–79.

Saward, M. (2009), Authorisation and authenticity: representation and the unelected. *Journal of Political Philosophy*, 17, 1–22.

Swift, C. (2009), *Hospital Chaplaincy in the Twenty-first Century: The Crisis of Spiritual Care on the NHS*. Farnham: Ashgate.

Threlfall-Holmes, M. (2011), Values and Tensions. In Threlfall-Holmes, M. and Newitt, M. (eds), *Being a Chaplain*. London: Society for Promoting Christian Knowledge.

Todd, A. (2011), Responding to Diversity: Chaplaincy in a Multi-faith Context. In Threlfall-Holmes, M. and Newitt, M. (eds), *Being a Chaplain*. London: Society for Promoting Christian Knowledge.

Torry, M. (2010), *Bridgebuilders: Workplace Chaplaincy – A History*. Norwich: Canterbury Press.

Weil, S. (1976), *The Notebooks of Simone Weil I*, trans. A. Wills. London: Routledge and Kegan Paul.

Witham, L. (2010), *Marketplace of the Gods: How Economics Explains Religion*, Oxford: Oxford University Press.

Chapter 10

The Interface of Psychology and Spirituality in Care

Fraser Watts

The purpose of this chapter is to introduce psychology and indicate its relevance to chaplaincy. Psychology is both a science and a profession, and holds those two together. On the one hand it studies human nature and functioning, and does so using the careful, systematic research methods that justify it being regarded as a science. On the other hand, it has developed a range of professional applications, of which clinical, educational and occupational are the best developed; they overlap with the settings in which chaplaincy is practised. Such professional applications are based on the research-based knowledge that psychology has accumulated. Equally, professional psychology also seeks to evaluate and learn from professional practice, so there is a to-and-fro between knowledge and practice. That leads to something equivalent to the theological reflection that is a core element in pastoral theology as reflective practice.

There is a wide range of applications of psychology to faith-based ministry (Watts et al. 2002), and this chapter will apply that approach to chaplaincy. That includes not only the psychological study of spirituality, but points of intersection between psychology and spirituality concerning general issues about being human, pastoral work with individuals, and the contexts in which chaplaincy is located. For a more general survey of pastoral psychology see Watts et al. (2002: Chapters 8–10) or Rose (2013).

The Psychology of Spirituality

Some of the people seen by chaplains will be explicitly religious, though many will be 'more spiritual than religious', so spirituality is important in chaplaincy. The psychology of religion has recently been extended to include the psychology of spirituality (e.g. Hood et al. 2009), providing a theoretical framework to engage with those who are spiritual but not religious. Religion and spirituality are multifaceted, and most psychologists distinguish at least three aspects: experience/feeling, behaviour/practice and belief/thinking (e.g. Loewenthal 2000). We will consider here those three facets of spirituality in turn.

Religious or spiritual *experiences*, broadly conceived, are more common than is often realised. A typical survey question is: 'Have you ever been aware of, or influenced by, a presence or power, whether you call it God or not, which is different from your everyday self?' About a third of the population say 'Yes' to that question (Hay 1982). Interestingly, that percentage is roughly the same in the US and the UK, despite very different levels of religious affiliation. Religious people report such experiences more than non-believers, though 24 per cent of atheists and agnostics also report them. Such spiritual experiences are more closely linked to thinking that the spiritual side of life is important. Many people who have had such experiences don't talk about them, perhaps because they feel they would not be understood; they may welcome an opportunity to do so.

Two aspects of spiritual experiences can be distinguished (Watts 2002). One concerns the basic experience, which may be concerned, for example, with a sense of the unity of all things. The other concerns the interpretation of the experience, which is where people's religious faith, or lack of it, shows itself. Some people want to define religious experience in terms of just one or other of these factors. My view is that core religious experiences have both features, though there can be spiritual experiences that lack any special experiential qualities, and others that do not include any explicitly religious interpretation.

There are also what can be called 'sacred emotions' such as gratitude, awe, wonder and hope, which help people to see spiritual significance in events in their lives. Cultivating such emotions is an important part of spirituality, whether or not that is framed in an explicitly religious way. For example, Robert Emmons has developed ways in which people can be trained to explicitly identify things for which they can be grateful, and has shown that people derive a range of benefits from doing so (Emmons and McCulloch 2004). That has traditionally been done in religious settings through prayers of thanksgiving, but people can cultivate gratitude in the context of a more secular spirituality. Hope is another important spiritual emotion, and much chaplaincy work is conducted in settings such as prisons or hospitals where hope does not come easily. Elsewhere (Watts 2002) I have made the distinction between optimism (in the sense of a rationally based expectation that the future will be good), and hope (in the sense of an attitude of mind that remains positive no matter how bleak the circumstances may be). Hope can be maintained in a situation where optimism is impossible, and probably does more than optimism to transform the future.

Many people have spiritual *practices* of one kind or another. Transcendental meditation, mindfulness and yoga are probably the most widely used. They are a counterpart to the prayer that is a traditional part of much religious life in the Abrahamic faiths. Meditation involves acquiring the ability to focus on present experience, rather than the cognitive multitasking in which people normally engage. It also involves drawing back from the judgemental reactions and learning to focus just on sensory experience, which in turn fosters the attitude of compassion. Mindfulness has been officially recognised as making a significant contribution to the treatment of depression (Williams et al. 2007), probably the first time that a spiritual practice has been recognised as clinically effective. This is not to claim that mindfulness is a panacea for depression, though there is strong evidence that it makes a valuable contribution, including lowering relapse rates. Meditation seems to confer a broad range of benefits, including reducing abuse of drugs and alcohol, that goes beyond just subjectively feeling better. There are measurable differences between experienced and novice meditators in brain activity, but even a 6–8-week programme produces significant changes.

However, spiritual practices go much broader. For example, forgiveness is another practice that has migrated from its religious origins to become a method of secular therapy (Watts and Gulliford 2004). Religion has much to learn from the systematic way in which therapeutic forgiveness has been developed, taking people through a series of stages: recall of a specific incident, empathy with the offender, adopting a perspective of humility, commitment to forgive, and strategies for holding on to forgiveness. Some religious commentators have been critical of therapeutic forgiveness as 'cheap grace'. However, some of it is costly, and the benefits of it are demonstrable. Nevertheless, there may be things that therapeutic forgiveness could learn from a religious perspective, such as a focus on how to receive forgiveness oneself, not just to extend it to others.

Spirituality also has its own beliefs and patterns of *thinking*. The percentage of people who believe in God remains high. However, not all would go so far as to say they believe in a personal God, and many do not attend religious worship, showing a pattern of 'believing without belonging' (Davie 1994). Though the percentage of people who believe in God has been falling, belief in an afterlife has been increasing, as has interest in angels. These are beliefs that now seem to be embraced more enthusiastically outside faith communities than within them. Perhaps the most basic distinguishing feature of those who take a spiritual worldview is the wish to interpret events in a way that discerns meaning and purpose. It is a core function of religion to support ways of making meaning out of what could seem meaningless events. There seems to be a deep-seated instinct in humans to discern transcendent meanings, and to base life around them. In that sense humans seem to be a spiritual species, if not necessarily a religious one.

Psychological and Spiritual Perspectives on the Human Person

We will now explore points of convergence and divergence between psychological and spiritual approaches to the human person, though it needs to be emphasised that neither psychology nor religion/spirituality are monolithic. In fact, one can often find parallel debates within the two domains.

The primary focus of psychology is on the individual, but psychology is both a biological and a social science and seeks to integrate those rather different perspectives. There is a tendency in some psychological circles to want to reduce everything to biology, and to see all aspects of human functioning (including religion) as a product of evolution or the physical brain; but that reductionist approach has not been universally accepted within psychology. There is a strong strand of dualist thinking in some religions which emphasises a spirit or soul that is potentially disembodied, but again this is not universally accepted. There has recently been a movement, at least within Christianity, towards a more monistic view of the human person within which different facets can be distinguished but not separated (Brown et al. 1998). Though there are differences of emphasis between psychology and religion here, there is no irresolvable conflict.

Within both psychology and religion one can find both positive and negative views of the person. There is perhaps a tendency towards a moralistic and judgemental approach within religion, and towards a more positive and accepting approach in psychology, though again there is much diversity. Something equivalent to the religious concept of inherent sinfulness seems to surface again in Freud's concept of the 'id' (the source of dark impulses) and in Dawkins' 'selfish gene'. Religion has sometimes seemed to trade on guilt, but a conflict with psychology largely disappears in the light of Freud's distinction between neurotic and realistic guilt. Psychology is mainly concerned to free people from the former, whereas religion sees value in the latter; so again there is no real disagreement.

There can also be a difference of emphasis between tough and tender approaches to managing people. Sometimes religion tends to emphasise discipline and direction, and to be judgemental, whereas psychology, especially humanistic psychology, has emphasised nurturance and acceptance. However, again, this seems only a difference of emphasis. Research has consistently supported the view that people flourish best when they receive an appropriate combination of nurturance and demands. That applies to parenting of children and to adults in the workplace. There is no reason why both psychology and religion can't both accept that keeping those in balance contributes to human flourishing.

Finally, there are issues about the unity and integration of personality. People often experience a tension between a sense of a unifying core of personality, and the fact that they have to behave differently in different situations. Psychology has been more accepting of the plurality of the self, and to see integration of personality as something to work towards, often through developing an integrative self-narrative. In contrast, some religions have put the emphasis on the unitary core of personality (Turner 2008), though religions are quite diverse on this, with Christianity probably emphasising it most and Buddhism least. From that perspective, a plural self can look like disintegration. However, once again, there seems to be no irreconcilable divergence between psychology and religion, just a difference of emphasis.

Spiritual and Religious Perspectives on Pastoral and Emotional Problems

Distinguishing between psychological and spiritual aspects of pastoral issues is a complex and subtle matter (Benner 1988). There are various possible approaches. One is to dispose of the distinction entirely, and to claim that all problems are psychological, or that they are all spiritual. My own view is that such narrowing of focus impoverishes our understanding of pastoral matters, and should be resisted. Another approach is to see it as a matter of what medicine would call 'differential diagnosis', and to try to classify pastoral issues according to whether they are psychological or spiritual. That also seems to me to be unsatisfactory, because there is both a psychological and spiritual aspect to most pastoral issues (even if the latter is not always recognised).

To some extent, we are dealing here with different discourses. The language of 'mental illness' is a relatively recent one, and the medicalisation of emotional and psychological problems remains controversial. Many see the language of possession, used for example in the Christian gospels, as just a different way of talking about what we would now call mental illness; or see what St John of the Cross called the 'dark night of the soul' as a different way of talking about depression. It is indeed helpful to recognise that we have multiple discourses for emotional and psychological problems, but it seems an over-simplification to suggest that they are all saying essentially the same thing. Different discourses make different assumptions and focus on different phenomena.

One distinguishing feature of the religious or spiritual perspective to personal problems is that it is more willing to consider moral values. The difference here may not be as stark as appears at first sight, as psychological approaches may actually embrace liberal values under the pretence of having no values at all; also, a religious approach need not handle moral issues in the form of adhering to fixed moral rules. There has recently been interest in retrieving a classical tradition of pastoral theology that includes moral considerations (Pattison 2000). Spiritual approaches (like many psychological approaches) will also avoid a completely reductionist medicalisation or biologisation of problems, though that does not preclude making space for medical care where appropriate. It is a more subtle matter how to distinguish between psychological and spiritual approaches. One helpful approach, suggested by James Hillman (1979), is that psychological approaches tend to go deeply into problems, whereas spiritual approaches tend to rise above them (Watts 2002: Chapter 5, Watts 2011: Chapter 1).

Depression is a commonly encountered problem that illustrates the interface between psychological and spiritual approaches; it is also a complex and multifaceted problem that can be seen from a variety of different perspectives. From a psychological point of view the two most important aspects of depression are social and cognitive. Experiences of loss or failure can lead to depression, but are more likely to do so in people who lack social support, especially in those who lack a confidant. Cognitively, people who are depressed tend to think negatively about themselves, the world and the future, and there is a tendency to over-generalise from particular negative events, taking them as reflecting a pervasive and enduring inability to do things right. Feeling that depression is intolerable is especially pernicious in locking people into a depressed state.

From a broader spiritual point of view, there can sometimes be long-term benefits from depression. It can lead to a helpful reappraisal of life style. It can also enable people to recognise negative things about themselves more clearly and accurately, embracing 'depressive realism' rather than an over-positive view of the self. In depression there is often a loss of sense of meaning and purpose, which may lead people to seek a framework that provides that. Religion can sometimes lead people to blame themselves for being depressed, though it can also lead people to be more accepting of periods of unhappiness without regarding them as intolerable.

Spiritual and Religious Perspectives on Therapy and Counselling

It is in connection with therapeutic and counselling psychology that there has been most tension between psychology and religion. However, I will claim that even here there is no incompatibility between the two, just a difference of emphasis that does not prevent fruitful dialogue (Browning and Cooper 2004). One of the key issues in the attitude of religion to psychology has been that of authority. There is a range of views on this among Christian thinkers (see Johnson 2010), but some have wanted to maintain the authority of scripture, and to make it clear that psychology can only be allowed a subordinate position. Conservative thinkers in other religions would probably take a similar view. However, this has not been the universal religious response to psychology, and some have sought a fruitful engagement between two approaches, despite their different preconceptions and objectives. Three main approaches to therapy will be considered here: psychodynamic or interpretative approaches, non-directive or person-centred approaches, and cognitive and behavioural approaches. In each case, there are points of both convergence and divergence with a spiritual perspective.

The relationship between psychoanalysis and religion has been an uneasy one, but has not been as uniformly negative as is sometimes imagined. Freud's critique of religion as 'illusion' (i.e. wish fulfilment) is well known (Freud 1961), though even Freud admits that it doesn't necessarily mean that religion is erroneous. One key problem with Freud's work on religion is that he allowed his personal views to intrude on what he could legitimately say as a psychologist. He also over-generalises about 'religion' and neglects the possibility that his critique might apply to some forms of religion more than others, or that it might apply to atheism.

In fact the reception of Freudian psychology in religious circles has sometimes been quite positive. In the UK, for example, church leaders such as William Temple were quite welcoming of the 'new' psychology in the inter-war years. Later, the object relations turn in psychoanalysis, in which Donald Winnicott was a key figure, led to a favourable view of religion in which it was valued as potentially good for adjustment. Religion was said to occupy a 'transitional' space that enabled it to broker an accommodation between internal and external worlds (see Meissner 1984: Chapter 7). There are also approaches derived from psychoanalysis, like that of Jung, that are readily open to spiritual factors. Indeed, many of Jung's key psychological concepts seem to have close parallels in religious and spiritual traditions (Edinger 1972).

People tend to have well-established patterns of emotional response that cut across different situations, and psychoanalysis classically looks for links between three different domains: formative childhood relationships, the person's current presenting problems, and the relationship to the professional (counsellor, chaplain, etc.) who is working with them. Psychodynamic approaches to chaplaincy may want to bring an extra relationship into consideration, i.e. how people relate to God and to religion. There is growing evidence that people's approach to religion is to some extent predictable from their formative attachment relationships in childhood. For example, people who have sudden religious conversions are likely to have had insecure attachments in childhood (Granqvist and Kirkpatrick 2004). How people experience God, and what kind of image they have of God, is often different from their explicit conceptualisation of God, which is more based on theological correctness. People are liable to experience God in a way that is shaped by their social and relational patterns; for example, people who are prone to guilt may experience God as being judgemental, when it might be more helpful for them to experience the forgiveness of God. There are promising approaches to working explicitly with people's God image in the context of pastoral care (Moriarty and Hoffman 2007).

There has probably been greatest religious hostility to humanistic approaches to counselling (e.g. Vitz 1994), which sometimes seems to set aside religious values and priorities and to focus instead just on what suits the person concerned. However, it is arguable that there may be more underlying convergence than is apparent on the surface. The lack of explicit reference to God and religion does not necessarily mean that religious values are being set aside; it is possible to pursue what are believed to be religious purposes without referring to that explicitly. Going outside theological and religious discourse is not the same as going beyond religious and spiritual objectives.

Thomas Merton is one religious thinker whose views are easily reconciled with humanistic psychology (Morea 1997). The view would be that for someone to find personal fulfilment is convergent with realising their God-given potential and God's purposes for them, whether or not that is named explicitly. In person-centred counselling, the task of the counsellor is to reflect back in a way that shows accurate empathy, positive regard, and genuineness. From a theological point of view, it has been suggested that providing these three therapeutic conditions represents something akin to the love of God, and the kind of love to which most religious people aspire (Thorne 2012).

Cognitive behaviour therapy (CBT) represents a very different approach that is more practical, specific and problem focused. Behaviour therapy was developed in the 1960s, and then broadened to include approaches to thinking as well as behaviour. Much CBT is concerned with self-regulation, and with finding ways in which people can avoid doing things that are damaging to them or which they want to avoid, and building up skill and confidence in doing things that they want to do. Though some religious people have attacked CBT for its background non-religious assumptions, there is actually much convergence between CBT and the kind of advice that has traditionally been given in pastoral care. Ways of integrating CBT with spiritual approaches are now being developed (e.g. Hodge and Hodge 2006).

Psychotherapy has often had a negative view of religion, stemming from Freud, though there has recently been a marked softening of that attitude. The growth of interest in spirituality rather than religion has been helpful here, as it has proved easier to integrate spiritual concerns about meaning, purpose and value into therapy, and there is now a growing use of spiritually integrated forms of therapy (Pargament 2007).

Psychological Aspects of Particular Chaplaincy Settings

Though chaplaincy in different settings has much in common, there are also specific psychologies relevant to particular settings, and distinct points of intersection between psychology and spirituality that arise in different chaplaincy settings. The second volume of the recent *APA Handbook of Psychology, Religion and Spirituality* (Pargament 2013) contains a helpful set of chapters on psychology of religion and spirituality as applied to health care, military, correctional and educational settings.

There is now a well-developed body of research and intervention in health psychology (e.g. Ogden 2012), looking at psychological risk factors for illness, and psychological treatments for health problems, often using the CBT approach. Religiousness is a well-established predictor of good outcomes, for both physical and mental health, though the research evidence is complex and the causal pathways are not clear (Koenig et al. 2012), and religion can sometimes be associated with poor mental health (Hood et al. 2009). Other matters have been explored, such as preparation for surgery, showing substantial benefits from careful preparation, including reduced post-operative pain and faster discharge. That illustrates the general point that how people experience illness and treatment has an important bearing on overall health care; and how people experience illness is, broadly, a spiritual issue. Health care outcomes are affected by patients' coping strategies, and coping is in turn affected by religion and spirituality (Pargament 1997).

Military psychology is less well developed, though there are points where it intersects fruitfully with spirituality and chaplaincy. There has been much controversy about including spiritual fitness in the US army's Comprehensive Soldier Fitness programme (Pargament and Sweeney 2011), with some objecting that it is framed in a way that favours beliefs in a supernatural deity. The concept of spiritual fitness is itself an interesting one. It often represents no more than an analogy with physical fitness, but there is scope for evolving patterns of spiritual practice that are integrated with physical training, which reflects the recent psychological interest in embodied cognition. Military service also raises issues about coping with injury and trauma that are similar to those found in other health care settings, but occur in particularly intense form in military service. There has been a valuable programme of psychological research into the effects of recent military deployments in Iraq and Afghanistan (e.g. Greenberg et al. 2011). The numbers of service personnel who show adverse effects of deployment is smaller than might be feared, and progress has been made in identifying risk factors such as pre-service vulnerability and perceived lack of support.

There are promising leads in the intersection between religion and forensic, criminological and correctional psychology (e.g. Duwe and Johnson 2013). Research indicates that a religious background serves to protect against delinquency to some extent. There has also been interesting research on the contribution of faith-based approaches to the prison system, such as the InnerChange Freedom Initiative in Minnesota, for which there is encouraging research support (e.g. Duwe and Johnson 2013). At least in the US, where most of the research has been carried out, a high proportion of prisoners are involved in religious programmes of one kind or another. Even simple programmes like volunteer-led Bible studies seem to reduce recidivism (Johnson et al. 1997). Conversion seems to provide prisoners with a helpful new narrative about themselves that gives them a new identity, enables them to find purpose and meaning in their imprisonment, and empowers them in relation to their future (Maruna et al. 2006). There are also issues about institutional aspects of the prison system, such as how to build a climate of trust and hope, that offer a challenge to positive psychology. There is probably no chaplaincy setting where there is such positive evidence for the value of programmes that focus on religion and spirituality.

Educational psychology is a well-established branch of professional psychology. Much of it is rather narrowly focused on specific problems in educational attainment, though there is a growing recognition that spiritual development is a legitimate topic in educational psychology and in the school curriculum (de Souza et al. 2009). The psychology of religion has contributed data on age-related changes in religion and spirituality that are relevant to educational chaplaincy, though the data is largely from the US (Hood et al. 2009). Religious affiliation in school years is mainly influenced by parental religiousness, which is most likely to transfer to children if parents are deeply religious, and if children and parents are close, and if religion is important in school as well. There is no dramatic change in religious affiliation at the start of college years, though there is the start of a significant movement towards being more spiritual than religious. Half the people who are involved in formal religion at age 18 are no longer involved at age 30 (Kinneman 2011). Educational chaplaincy in the college years needs to either seek ways of reversing the trend away from formal religion, or to connect with students who are still spiritual but not religious.

Conclusion

Psychology is both a research-based scientific discipline and an approach to professional practices that interfaces at a number of points with the concern of chaplaincy. That includes the psychological study of spirituality and the comparison of psychological and spiritual approaches to the human person, to personal and pastoral problems, and to counselling and therapy. There is also a potentially rich intersection between various particular fields of professional psychology and the principal settings in which chaplaincy is practised.

References

Benner, D.G. (1988), *Psychotherapy and the Spiritual Quest: Exploring the Links Between Psychological and Spiritual Health*. London: Hodder and Stoughton.

Brown, W., M. Nancey and H.N. Malony (eds) (1998), *Whatever Happened to the Soul?* Minneapolis: Fortress Press.

Browning, D.S. and T.D. Cooper (2004), *Religious Thought and the Modern Psychologies*. Minneapolis: Fortress Press.

Davie, G. (1994), *Religion in Britain since 1945: Believing without Belonging*. Oxford: Blackwell.

De Souza, M., L.J. Francis, J. O'Higgins-Norman and D.G. Scott (eds) (2009), *International Handbooks of Religion and Education, Volume 3: Handbook of Education for Spirituality, Care and Wellbeing*. New York: Springer.

Duwe, G. and B.R. Johnson (2013), Estimating the benefits of a faith-based correctional program. *International Journal of Criminology and Sociology*, 2, 227–39.

Edinger, E. (1972), *Ego and Archetype: Individuation and the Religious Function of the Psyche*. New York: Putnam.

Emmons, R.A. and M.E. McCulloch (eds) (2004), *The Psychology of Gratitude*. New York: Oxford University Press.

Freud, S. (1961 [1927]) *The Future of an Illusion*, J. Strachey, trans. New York: Norton.

Granqvist. P. and L.A. Kirkpatrick (2004), Religious conversion and perceived childhood attachment: a meta-analysis. *The International Journal for the Psychology of Religion*, 14, 223–50.

Greenberg, N., E. Jones, N. Jones, N.T. Fear and S. Wessely (2011), The injured mind in the UK Armed Forces. *Philosophical Transactions of the Royal Society B*, 366, 261–7.

Hay, D. (1982), *Exploring Inner Space: Scientists and Religious Experience*. Harmondsworth: Penguin.

Hillman, J. (1979), Peaks and Vales. In J. Hillman (ed.), *Puer Papers*. Dallas: Spring Publications, 54–74.

Hodge, D. and D. Hodge (2006), Spiritually modified cognitive therapy: a review of the literature. *Social Work*, 51, 157–66.

Hood, R.W. Jr., P.C. Hill and B. Spilka (2009), *The Psychology of Religion: An Empirical Approach*, 4th edition. New York: Guilford Press.

Johnson, E.L. (ed.) (2010), *Psychology and Christianity: Five Views*, 2nd edition. Westmont, IL: IVP Academic.

Johnson, B.R., D.B. Larson and T.G. Pitts (1997), Religious programs, institutional adjustment, and recidivism among former inmates in prison fellowship programs. *Justice Quarterly*, 14, 145–66.

Kinneman, D. (2011), *You Lost Me: Why Young Christians are Leaving Church and Rethinking Faith*. Grand Rapids, MI: Baker.

Koenig, L.B., D. King and V.B. Larson (2012), *Handbook of Religion and Health*, 2nd edition. New York: Oxford University Press.

Loewenthal, K.M. (2000), *The Psychology of Religion: A Short Introduction*. Oxford: Oneworld.

Maruna, S., L. Wilson and K. Curran (2006), Why God is often found behind bars: prison conversions and the crisis of self-narrative. *Research in Human Development*, 3, 161–84.

Meissner, W.W. (1984), *Psychoanalysis and Religious Experience*. New Haven, CT: Yale University Press.

Morea, P.C. (1997), *In Search of Personality: Christianity and Modern Psychology*. London: SCM Press.

Moriarty, G. and L. Hoffman (eds) (2007), *God Image Handbook for Spiritual Counseling and Psychotherapy: Research, Theory and Practice*. Binghampton, NY: Routledge/Haworth.

Ogden, J. (2012), *Health Psychology: A Textbook*, 5th edition. Maidenhead: Open University Press.

Pargament, K.I. (1997), *The Psychology of Religion and Coping: Theory, Research, Practice*. New York: Guilford Press.

—— (2007) *Spiritually Integrated Psychotherapy: Understanding and Addressing the Sacred*. New York: Guilford Press.

—— (ed.) (2013), *APA Handbook of Psychology, Religion and Spirituality. Volume 1: Context, Theory, and Research. Volume 2: An Applied Psychology of Religion and Spirituality*. Washington, DC: American Psychological Association.

Pargament, K.I and P.J. Sweeney (2011), Building spiritual fitness in the Army: an innovative approach to a vital aspect of human development. *American Psychologist*, 66, 58–64.

Pattison, S. (2000), *A Critique of Pastoral Care*, 3rd edition. London: SCM Press.

Rose, J. (2013), *Psychology for Pastoral Contexts: A Handbook*. Norwich: Canterbury Press.

Thorne, B. (2012), *Counselling and Spiritual Accompaniment: Bridging Faith and Person-centred Therapy*. Chichester: Wiley-Blackwell.

Turner, L. (2008), *Theology, Psychology and the Plural Self*. Farnham: Ashgate.

Vitz, P.C. (1994), *Psychology as Religion: The Cult of Self-worship*, 2nd edition. Grand Rapids, MI: Eerdmans.

Watts, F. (2002), *Theology and Psychology*. Farnham: Ashgate.

—— (ed.) (2011), *Spiritual Healing: Scientific and Religious Perspectives*. Cambridge: Cambridge University Press.

Watts, F. and L. Gulliford (eds) (2004), *Forgiveness in Context: Theology and Psychology in Creative Dialogue*. London: T & T Clark.

Watts, F., R. Nye and S.B. Savage (2002), *Psychology for Christian Ministry*. London: Routledge.

Williams, M., J. Teasdale, Z.V. Segal and J. Kabat-Zinn (2007), *The Mindful Way through Depression: Freeing Yourself from Chronic Unhappiness*. New York: Guilford Press.

Chapter 11

Supervision, Support and Safe Practice

Michael Paterson

Supervision and the Intentional Use of the Self

Irrespective of context, chaplains are liminal figures: there for all, accessed by some, understood by few. Chaplains handle that sense of liminality in different ways. Some deny it outright and manifest grandiose exhibitionism countering the role authority of appointed managers with their own personal and charismatic authority. Others embrace the freedom that being liminal accords them and operate from their personal strengths and aptitudes. Some defend against the estrangement of liminality by adopting contextually validated roles and turn themselves into middle managers, bureaucrats, counsellors or simply everyone's friend. Some regress and default back to earlier identities turning the shopping mall, prison or ship into 'their parish'. And some maintain a prophetic stance and use their sense of professional dislocation to free them not only to respond to individual spiritual distress but to promote spiritual care and well-being at individual, team and organisational levels, challenging practices which militate against human flourishing and 'speaking truth to power'.

Pastoral supervision, in which due attention is paid not only to praxis (the work) but also to ontology (the person of the worker) can play an invaluable role in enabling chaplains to inhabit and embrace their liminality as a vocational locus of grace. After all, 'who else with nothing in their hands, deals day in, day out with the crushed, the bruised and the defeated?' (Fraser 2013). Supervision comes into its own and becomes truly transformative when it enables chaplains to keep their hands empty and their hearts open to the unexpected and unbidden that characterises pastoral practice. Supervision moves beyond a tick box exercise to courageous conversation when it confronts chaplains with their own defences against feeling useless and inadequate and empowers them to befriend their own vulnerability as a place of deep levelling and commonality with those they encounter. Faced day in, day out with the 'crushed, the bruised and the defeated' certainly takes its toll. What van Dernoot Lipsky admits as a carer could also be found on the lips of many a chaplain:

> After years of bearing witness to others' suffering, I finally came to understand that
> my exposure had changed me on a fundamental level. There had been an osmosis:

I had absorbed and accumulated [distress] to the point that it had become a part of me, and my view of the world had changed. I realized eventually that I had come into my work armed with a burning passion and a tremendous commitment but few other internal resources. As you know, there is a time for fire, but what sustains the heat – for the long haul – is the coals. And coals I had none of. I did the work for a long time with very little ability to integrate my experiences emotionally, cognitively, spiritually or physically. (2009: 3–4)

My experience as a chaplain and as a supervisor over the last decade has convinced me that we can sustain the 'heat' of chaplaincy by regularly 'coming away by ourselves to a quiet place' (Mk 6.31) to reconnect with those 'elemental stories' which motivate us (Ryan 2004: 8) and where, in the supportive presence of another, we can courageously face the gap between who we espouse to be and what we actually do. Pastoral supervision, understood as a place where we exceed the basics of quality control and continuing professional development to monitor and tweak the internal wiring which directs our ministerial reflexes and impulses, offers an opportunity for deep personal, professional and vocational questioning, catharsis and restoration. Supervision of this kind recognises that nowhere are ontology (inhabiting the being of a profession) and epistemology (how we arrive at 'knowing' what to do and how to act) more clearly wedded together in an indissoluble bond than in the lives of those who minister and whose tools of the trade are nothing less than the intentional use of the self (Kelly 2012).

Supervision – What's in a Word?

The term 'supervision' falls victim to what Flew has coined 'death by a thousand qualifications' (Feinberg 2012). Pohly speaks for many when he observes:

supervision is a term that is loaded with baggage. It carries an image of *bossism*, of someone in authority looking over one's shoulder and controlling every move, rewarding or punishing at will. It suggests a hierarchy of superiority/inferiority and dredges up threatening associations with the past. For this reason some people suggest abandoning the term and substituting something more palatable.

Various alternatives have been proposed: *extra*-vision, mentoring, ministerial reflection, consultancy support. Notwithstanding the variations in terminology and in emphasis, the literature portrays broad agreement that supervision offers an opportunity to reflect on the past, in the present in order to improve the future (2001: 2).

The Genesis of Supervision within the Caring Professions

In 1902 Freud invited doctors to meet together to share observations on their experiences, and in 1925 supervision was woven in with personal analysis and theoretical underpinnings as the third strand in psychoanalytic training. The ensuing decades saw supervision move from the 'commendable' to the 'normative' category with the requirement in 1956 of 150 hours of supervision 'for the purpose of instruction, skill development, personal analysis and evaluation of the candidate's development' (Pohly 2001: 43). Being rooted in the psychoanalytic tradition has left a lasting imprint upon the philosophy and practice of supervision which finds expression in two hotly contested issues: i) Who is supervision for? ii) What is its focus or purpose?

Who is Supervision For?

Although this question is inextricably linked to that of purpose, what makes it worth considering in its own right is the myriad of assumptions which underpin the range of terms used to describe the parties involved. While the literature largely concurs in referring to the person who conducts the session as the 'supervisor', the origins of the practice within psychoanalysis can be detected in terming those on the receiving end as 'students' or 'trainees' rather than supervisees or practitioners. The significance is more than semantic since choosing to refer to the practitioner as 'trainee' or 'student' locates supervision within professional initiation processes rather than within a philosophy of lifelong support, and betrays a power imbalance between the two parties with all the concomitant ensuing dynamics that involves and paves the way for understanding the role of supervisor in terms of assessing performance and quality control.

Supervision as Quality Control

In contrast with the USA, Canada and Australia, where the systematic telling of professional stories in the context of supervised training programmes (such as Clinical Pastoral Education) plays a normative role in the formation of chaplains, in the UK supervision and reflective practice have, until very recently, been prime candidates for the 'all may, some should, none must' vote. Furthermore, where supervision does feature, as in the 2007 Healthcare Chaplaincy Standards, no clear definition of what is entailed or what one might expect from engaging in it is profferred. As a result models are often uncritically adopted from business management or social work with no attention paid to the underlying assumptions and implicit worldviews therein. Moreover, when supervision takes place within the worker–line manager relationship, the lens of enquiry usually favours the interests of the organisation (expressed in the focus on risk management, scrutiny and surveillance) to the neglect of the person who inhabits the role. As Weld (2012) notes, while quality control measures 'clearly strengthen the mandate' for reflective practice and clinical supervision, they simultaneously 'threaten their integrity' as a 'worker-centred and a learning-focused activity'. As a result, reflection on practice

> veers between line management aimed at compliance with procedures and checklists and safe surface exploration. This type of supervision becomes mundane with a 'must do' rather than 'want to do' energy and does not take up the learning opportunities that are possible. The investment in the relationship becomes perfunctory and tends to be corrective rather than transformative. (Davys And Bedooe 2010: 81)

Supervision as Education

The pedagogical or formational aim of supervision has a strong history within the helping professions. 'The supervisor is an instructor' writes Tarachow (1963: 15) 'whose task it is to teach and demonstrate the theory and skills the practitioner needs to acquire competence'. In more recent years the influence of educational theorists such as Dewey, Schön and Kolb is clearly detectable in writers who fundamentally understand supervision as a learning environment. More particularly, Winnicott's notion of a space in which a child feels safe enough to play is widely taken up by those who see supervision as a space conducive to learning, a space for creative play and a space for integration. The educational capacity inherent in supervision is neatly summarised in the mantra 'reflective practice turns history into learning'.

What Makes Supervision 'Good'?

Irrespective of emphasis – clinical, managerial, pastoral – the efficacy of supervision points to a combination of three factors: clarity of purpose, quality of relationship between the parties and commitment to improving the experience of those on the receiving end of care.

Clarity of purpose saves supervision from collapsing into personal therapy, spiritual accompaniment, crisis management or advice giving. It replaces opportunistic conversations which arise in reaction to what goes wrong or proves difficult with intentional, regular, boundaried space which fosters lifelong learning and professional development. Attention to the relationship (mirroring those of the chaplain/supervisee) begins with the supervisor making room for the chaplain in her heart (Is 54.2). It is no small matter to make mental, psychological or spiritual room within oneself to welcome another and yet without this radical inner hospitality, open and vulnerable to the supervisee as stranger, little of any good is likely to unfold in the session. Maintaining openness without collapsing the professional boundaries into friendship, collusion or avoidance requires supervisors to keep a steady eye on the third character of effective supervision, i.e. the commitment to improving the experience of care for those on the receiving end. Unlike counselling, which focuses on the well-being of the person in their widest social context, or spiritual direction, which explores the transpersonal dimension of a person's life, supervision has a missiological thrust in that its whole *raison d'être* is to improve the quality of presence, care, skill and resilience offered by the supervisee. To that end the word 'work' is emblazoned over the lintel of the door where supervision takes place. To be effective, supervision mindfully attends to whatever aspect of the supervisee's thinking, doing and being that is relevant at any one time *in so far as* it impacts on those on the receiving end of their care.

From Tick Box to Transformative Supervision

It is paradoxical that the contemporary promotion of reflective practice among chaplains presents a serious threat to supervision ever achieving its transformative potential. It has been my experience that while some chaplains find in supervision an invitation to integrate personal and professional personas, inner spirituality and practical skills, others now come because they need something to put in their continuing professional development plan or because it has become a requirement of the job or simply team policy. It certainly takes a brave person to risk committing professional suicide by being left behind. As a result we now see people joining reflective practice or supervision groups who have little expectation or desire to reflect and minimal willingness to change their practice as a result. Notwithstanding that, some people's personal histories have left them with a limited capacity for new learning (Carroll 2009: 212), this 'status quo' dynamic manifests itself in participants presenting polished case work to their peers which only serves to showcase their own ego rather than aspects of their work which illustrate uncertainty, intrigue or surprise. While low risk-taking is to be expected at the early stages of a supervisory relationship or a group's life, when it becomes the cultural norm, 'deeper learning' and transformative potential are 'left outside the door' (Weld 2012: 25).

However, even when all the conditions conducive to good reflection have been met – hospitality, safety, confidentiality, uninterrupted space, etc. – some chaplains simply do not have the inner spiritual or psychological resilience to engage creatively with the process. Some chaplains, for instance, seem unable to receive feedback as just that – feedback and not criticism – or to hear the impact the story they have told has had on other members of the group without feeling personally responsible or dissolving inside.

Therein lies a huge challenge. If reflective practice is to become normative rather than simply for those who are, by personality or temperament, 'that way inclined', the whole question of chaplaincy training and formation in the UK urgently requires reviewing. In contrast to the world of talking therapies in which in order to become a counsellor one has to have been a client, it is at least puzzling that someone can practise as a chaplain without ever having had to expose their soul and spirit, less still explore their sense of meaning and purpose, to the loving eye of a spiritual companion. Needless to say many chaplains do just that but the fact that it remains optional rather than a requirement of our formation is highly questionable and impacts on the quality of spiritual care delivered and on reflective practice upon that care among the chaplaincy community.

A Map for Soulful Supervision

As interest increases in supervision across disciplines outside therapy and counselling, I have developed a generic model of supervision which can be used both with individuals and with groups. It is devised with three kinds of supervising practitioner in mind: those who do not have the therapeutic hinterland with which to embrace the dominant therapeutic models that are currently available; experienced supervisors whose supervisees have little interest in the psychodynamic processes which underpin extant models; and supervisors who wish to work cross-professionally where the ability to use generic skills and hold an intentional space is of greater value than first-hand knowledge of the particular profession or sphere of activity.

As an intentional space, supervision has a clear structure characterised by six processes, as outlined in Figure 11.1.

- **Hosting and Containing** focuses on the kind of hospitality which enables transformative learning. This includes attention to the ethical framework, organisation culture, immediate environment and quality of interpersonal relationship between participants.
- **Eliciting and Focusing** is not only about getting the work into the room but about identifying the energy or impulse that will make reflection worthwhile, i.e., what is it in particular about this that makes it worth looking at here today?
- **Exploring and Imagining**. Once a focus has been established, exploring and imagining becomes a playful and creatively fertile place in which

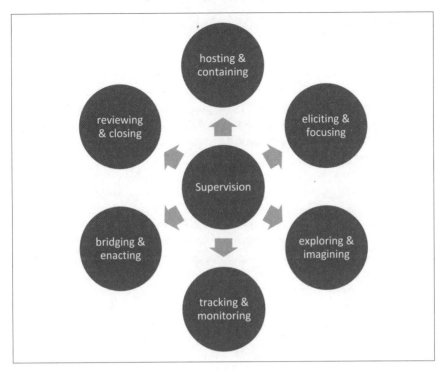

Figure 11.1

to try out ideas and ways of working. It is also the place in which stray thoughts, fantasies, images and metaphors can be aired.

- **Tracking and Monitoring**. Tracking is both a discreet moment in the reflective cycle and something that runs through the whole session. It is a way of monitoring that what is happening is matching what it is needed within the allotted time.
- **Bridging and Enacting** are reminders that we reflect on work
  - from the *past*,
  - in the *present*
  - in order to change and enhance work in the *future*.

  A bridge is built out from the reflective time and back into the world of everyday practice. Enacting names the first steps to be taken.
- **Reviewing and Closing** is the process of naming what has been learned through reflection and the drawing of a line on the exploration. In supervision, closing well is just as important as beginning well.

This model is outlined in depth in Paterson and Rose (2014: 191–214).

Benefits of Supervision

Earlier in this chapter I outlined some of the factors that militate against the efficacy of supervision. In drawing this chapter to a close I would like to highlight some of the gifts and graces that arise when supervision and reflective practice embrace rather than avoid risk-taking, allow courage to replace fear and engage in truth-telling rather than defensive self-protection. Together, I believe these gifts and graces have the capacity to lead us from reflective to 'transformative' practice.

We Are Not Alone

The first gift of courageous reflection is the discovery that far from being alone in our inadequacies, we are surrounded by others who also stumble and stutter around the workplace and become bewildered and unsure in their pastoral practice. The grace of telling the truth about our practice rather than hiding behind an intricate professional façade releases us from living in isolation and restores us to a community of flawed yet faithful practice. In so doing we recognise each other not just as 'human resources' but as human beings made in the image of God. While informational learning can happen in solitude, transformational learning requires relationship:

> What arises through this relationship becomes the vehicle for changing how we understand ourselves and each other. The quality of relationship is what allows us to feel safe enough to trust, to take emotional risks, to allow ourselves to be seen in our uncertainty and vulnerability, to uncover the biases and beliefs that we unconsciously use to construct our identities and ways of knowing and to see ourselves and others from fresh perspectives. (Shohet 2011: 10)

Risks Pay Off

There is much truth in the saying 'if you always do what you have always done, you will always find what you have always found'. Reflective practice becomes transformative according to Sheila Ryan (2004) when it 'interrupts practice', 'disturbs stuck narratives' and 'wakes us up to what we are doing'. She continues, 'when we are alive to what we are doing, we wake up to what is, instead of falling asleep in the comfort stories of our routines and daily practice' (ibid.: 47). Transformative reflection invites us into the centre of our own doubts only to be met there not by the wagging finger of condemnation but by the respectful curiosity of wondering 'what if?'

Care for the Carer

Much of what we do as chaplains takes place in noisy, public and stressful environments. Our conversations are often interrupted by passers-by, our tea breaks by pagers and our home life by on-call rotas. And yet those of us who live within the Judeo-Christian tradition live by a Story which makes Sabbath rest a commandment and not just a recommendation, and love for self the twin sister of love for neighbour. Supervision and reflective practice becomes transformative when we 'allow, albeit briefly, the doors to shut, the noise to be reduced and a quiet space for satisfying professional conversation' (Davys and Beddoe 2010: 87). In that Sabbath place, the 'rejected stone' of self-care may indeed become the 'cornerstone' that can sustain us, recharge us and propel us back into the world to face the demands of front-line practice (Karl 1988).

Vocational Renewal

While I am conscious that our work setting is multicultural and secular, I am also convinced that supervision and reflective practice can only be transformative for people of spirit if it can bring us face to face with the gap between who we say we are (vocation) and what we actually do (our practice). I have a concern that in turning too readily to counselling, nursing or business management for forms of supervision and reflection on practice, we chaplains 'have forgotten our primal language' and allowed 'other languages [to] take its place' (Brueggemann 1991: 42).

Nevertheless, in advocating the need for a conversation not only 'on the wall', in the sanctioned grammar and vocabulary of our particular work settings, but also 'behind the wall', in our native language of spiritual wisdom and practice, what I am proposing is not some neo-orthodox withdrawal or obscurantist position but rather a theology of total immersion 'in the contingencies, complexities and ambiguities' of our workplace contexts which 'seeks to do justice to [the] many contexts, levels, voices, moods, genres, systems and responsibilities' which daily face us as chaplains (Ford 2005: 761).

When reflection breaks free from its bondage to political correctness and is expansive enough to include the whole chaplain – including his or her spiritual self – then it has the transformative capacity to recover 'that which has been inwardly sequestered, abandoned or oppressed' (Coombe 2011: 182), reconnect us with the Story which underpins the work we do (Weld 2012: 115) and regenerate the 'passion [that] arises when the essence of one's life has been touched and one starts dealing with the world from that place' (Encke 2008: 23).

Summary

In this chapter we have explored the role of supervision in supporting chaplains to embrace rather than shun their liminal role and outlined that what makes supervision 'good' is attention to clarity of purpose, relationality and telos. We have explored the challenges presented by the term 'supervision' and traced the legacy which flows from its roots in psychoanalysis. We have outlined differences which variously place the emphasis in supervision on quality control, ongoing professional development and personal transformation. We have considered a map for a supervision session which combines supervision's long-standing therapeutic legacy with attention to the spiritual, pastoral and wisdom traditions that underpin chaplaincy practice. Ultimately, supervision, understood as a spiritual practice in its own right, will be judged on its ability to keep chaplains hospitable and present, learning and developing, courageous and engaging in the workplace. That responsibility lies with both parties.

References

Brueggemann, W. (1991), *Interpretation and Obedience*. Minneapolis: Fortress Press.

Carroll, M. (2009), Supervision: critical reflection for transformational learning, part 1. *The Clinical Supervisor*, 28(2), 210–20.

Coombe, N. (2011), Fear and Stepping Forward Anyway. In: Shohet, R., *Supervision as Transformation: A Passion for Learning*. London: Jessica Kingsley.

Davys, A. and Beddoe, L. (2010), *Best Practice in Professional Supervision: A Guide for the Helping Professions*. London: Jessica Kingsley.

Encke, J. (2008), Breaking the Box: Supervision – A Challenge to Free Ourselves. In Shohet, R., *Supervision as Transformation: A Passion for Learning*. London: Jessica Kingsley.

Feinberg, J. (ed.) (2012), *Reason and Responsibility: Readings in Some Basic Problems of Philosophy*. Belmont, CA: Dickenson Publishing Company.

Ford, D. (2005), *The Modern Theologians*, 3rd edition. Oxford: Blackwell.

Fraser, D. (2013), Address to the Scottish Healthcare Chaplains conference, March 2013. Unpublished.

Karl, J.C. (1998), Discovering spiritual patterns: including spirituality in staff development and the delivery of psychotherapy services. *American Journal of Pastoral Counseling*, 1(4), 1–23.

Kelly, E. (2012), *Personhood and Presence: Self as a Resource for Spiritual and Pastoral Care*. London: Continuum.

Paterson, M. and Rose, J. (2014), *Enriching Ministry: Pastoral Supervision in Practice*. London, SCM Press.

Pohly, K.H. (2001), *Transforming the Rough Places: The Ministry of Supervision*, 2nd edition. Franklin, TN: Providence House Publishers.

Ryan, S. (2004), *Vital Practice: Stories from the Healing Arts, the Homeopathic and Supervisory Way*. Portland: Sea Change.

Shohet, R. (2011), *Supervision as Transformation: A Passion for Learning*. London: Jessica Kingsley.

Tarachow, S. (1963), *An Introduction to Psychotherapy*. New York: International Universities Press.

van Dernoot Lipsky, L. (2009), *Trauma Stewardship: An Everyday Guide to Caring for Self while Caring for Others*. San Francisco: Berrett-Koehler Publishers.

Weld, N. (2012), *A Practical Guide to Transformative Supervision for the Helping Professions: Amplifying Insight*. London: Jessica Kingsley.

PART III
Health Care Chaplaincy

Chapter 12

Health Care Chaplaincy

Chris Swift

Introduction

The study of health care chaplaincy is a relatively recent development. Although the work of chaplains has been associated with the care of the sick since medieval times (Swift 2014), it was only in recent years that their work has become a topic of research and professional education. How, when and where health care chaplaincy began to be studied is intimately connected to the chaplains' sense of professional identify and occupational security. This chapter sets out the organisation, structure and form of chaplaincy care in the United Kingdom (UK), mindful of international links and comparisons. It will explore the key themes in the current practice of chaplaincy and analyse the challenges faced in both the provision of spiritual care and the ways in which it is studied.

The body of research concerning both chaplains and spiritual care has grown considerably in recent years. This phenomenon is found across the Western world, whether countries operate health services through systems of state insurance or via largely private arrangements. Although the volume of publication is limited when compared with other professions it is nevertheless evidence of increasing debate about the role and impact of the care provided by chaplains. In the UK the rise in research expresses the political context of chaplaincy, not least in the financial pressures facing all forms of public sector provisions and the relentless focus on cost, value and quality. As almost all health care in the UK remains in state control (National Health Service[1]) the fate of chaplaincy has been entwined with the place of religion in society and the varying influence of church leadership in particular. It has led the public funding of chaplaincy to be debated in the media and required its supporters to argue that chaplains are not simply the vestigial remains of religious privilege.

While recognising that there may be commonalities in all chaplaincy it is important to recognise that the local expression of spiritual and religious need is shaped significantly by context, language and history. This challenges the idea that

---

[1]   The National Health Service (NHS) was founded in 1948 by an Act of Parliament to be a universal health provision for the population of the UK financed through taxation and coordinated by the government.

a single approach can be replicated without adjustment or that research findings in one setting can be applied elsewhere without careful consideration. It is a unique feature of health care chaplaincy that such a small group of health service staff can embody a wide range of diverse identities. Religious pluralism might be the first thought connected with this diversity but research has revealed that it extends into both human sexuality and institutional disaffection (Hancocks et al. 2008). Health care chaplains effectively occupy marginal positions in multiple worlds, ranging from the community of health care professionals, to secular management structures and religious bodies. In the 20th century chaplains moved from an office-holder mentality to one of corporate identity as members of chaplaincy or spiritual care teams, although the degree of corporate identity as chaplains continues to vary between individuals and faith traditions.

As we shall go on to see, health care chaplaincy offers rich potential for deeper and more complex study. At a time when the place of religion in society continues to cause major debate, chaplains are located in a national institution of political significance. It is a setting in which all sections of society participate to some extent, and where the most advanced forms of scientific research and application are taking place. This places chaplains alongside pressing ethical questions as well as in contact with the contested visions of how public medicine can (or should) be delivered in the 21st century.

The Organisation and Provision of Chaplaincy

Chaplaincy in the UK has developed over the past century in ways which have led to considerable diversity in the way its services are provided. Typically these range from faith-specific care to patients from a particular community to pastoral support offered using skills common to all professional chaplains. For example, a Roman Catholic chaplain might focus almost exclusively on the needs of Roman Catholic patients while a Methodist minister employed as a chaplain in a mental health setting could use the skills of pastoral and spiritual care to support a patient unaligned with any religious tradition. In most cases chaplains are employed by a health provider, especially the NHS and hospice sector. However, alternative scenarios exist, including service level agreements (e.g. where a hospital pays a diocese to provide chaplaincy services) and situations where care is provided as integral to a community appointment (such as chaplaincy to a nursing home). In Scotland the NHS funded the churches to employ chaplains until 2006 when the situation changed to direct employment by the health service. There are subtle but important differences between the home nations of the UK, with Scotland in particular emphasising the approach of generic spiritual care and the role of chaplains in the community promoting good health and well-being (Bunniss et al. 2013).

Historically in England health care chaplaincy was shaped at a national level by Department of Health briefings and circulars. However, following the election of the Labour Government in 1997 chaplaincy in England became more focused on the needs of a multifaith society (Swift 2014: 57f). This accorded with declared Labour values to promote both diversity and social inclusion. Chaplaincy leadership in the Church of England's Hospital Chaplaincies Council (HCC) ensured that chaplaincy worked to reflect these values and was instrumental in the creation of the Multi-Faith Group for Healthcare Chaplaincy (MFGHC).[2] Along with the professional membership bodies this new group worked towards the publication of substantive guidelines for health care chaplaincy in England. *NHS Chaplaincy* (2003) was the fruit of this work and described in greater detail than previous official documents what might be expected from a chaplaincy service. However, these guidelines were questioned by some chaplains who noted that they were shaped to a considerable extent by the views of faith leadership rather than serving chaplains. At the same time the NHS published a workforce strategy, *Caring for the Spirit* (2003), which raised similar concerns about the degree of chaplaincy input into its approach. This latter document set out an ambitious programme of professional development but was closed by the NHS before its 10-year plan was completed.

This approach to NHS guidelines development, and the response to it by the College of Health Care Chaplains (CHCC),[3] led to disagreements within chaplaincy in England which lasted until the publication of *The Trotter Report* in 2010. This report referred to 'long-standing tensions and antipathies between different (chaplaincy) bodies' (Trotter 2010: 1). In particular, the report expressed concern about the role of the HCC in coordinating chaplaincy relations well beyond Anglican chaplains. Following the report the HCC was disbanded and its remaining functions re-allocated within the Church of England. Relations in general between the chaplaincy organisations improved. This was given particular expression in the formation of the new Panel for Professional Advisers[4] (endorsed by all parties) and, a little later, the creation of the Chaplaincy Leadership Forum (CLF).[5] The CLF provided a point of meeting for all those engaged in chaplaincy provision and was designed to enhance rapport and build trust between the parties.

---

2   The MFGHC was renamed in 2014 to become the Healthcare Chaplaincy Faith and Belief Group.

3   The CHCC has existed both as an independent membership group for chaplains and, since 1997, as an autonomous section of a trade union (currently Unite).

4   See letter to all Chief Executives of Hospital Trusts, Hospital Chaplains (NHS in England), 12 December 2011.

5   The CLF comprises: faith group representatives from the MFGHC; the Presidents of the CHCC and the Association of Hospice and Palliative Care Chaplains; the Chair of the UKBHC; and the Chair of the Panel of Professional Advisers.

There can be little doubt that the combined effect of these changes led to an improvement in relations between chaplaincy organisations. This was evidenced by the level of consultation in the CLF when NHS England[6] decided to produce new guidelines for health care chaplaincy in 2013. The resulting work led to agreement over the appointment of a project leader, regular feedback to the CLF, and reporting through CLF members to all sections of the chaplaincy community in England. This is not to say that the consultation process was without disagreement.

As noted above, health care chaplains in the UK are not a single professionally regulated group. There is a voluntary register and the possibility of formalising this with an independent regulator. Some chaplains hold a legal licence for their work, including chaplains authorised by the Church of England. This can be enforced in certain circumstances with a risk to the chaplain's employment or the prevention of movement between hospitals.[7] However, there are no commonly agreed professional entry criteria for chaplaincy, with only the Professional Advisers' Panel acting as a consistent safeguard for the support of appointments to a common standard. Compared with other professions in health care, or the operation of Clinical Pastoral Education in other countries, chaplaincy's lack of a cohesive identity can be interpreted in two ways. It can be seen as politically weak, failing to develop its shared professional practice to enhance safe care while presenting a confusing impression of its role to employers. Alternatively there are those who would argue that the absence of binding professional characteristics allows the relationship between the chaplains and their religious communities to be emphasised. In England this latter position has been expressed by the Roman Catholic Church in particular, which appears to fear that a stronger sense of chaplains' identity as health professional inevitably weakens their relationship to the Church. This fear has been heightened by research concerning Church of England chaplains which showed their sense of distance from the institutional church and a feeling of almost 'refugee' status (Hancocks et al. 2008). Contrastingly, the drive towards greater professional cohesion is led by Christian chaplains of a variety of traditions who believe that health care identity and religious belonging are not inimical. The roots of the differences in these positions are historic, ecclesiological and indicative of theological diversity. A service in the NHS constituted to reflect the range of beliefs in a hospital population is bound to present these challenges. This

---

[6]   NHS England is the national health body holding responsibility for chaplaincy between 2013 and 2015.

[7]   This is illustrated by the case of Canon Jeremy Pemberton whose marriage to Laurence Cunnington in April 2014 led to the refusal of a licence by the acting Bishop of Southwell and Nottingham when Canon Pemberton was offered a chaplaincy post by another NHS Trust. The Trust subsequently withdrew the job offer.

widening diversity will require careful attention and effective leadership if it is to avoid further fragmentation of the chaplains' identity in the coming years.

By contrast, chaplaincy development elsewhere in the UK was untroubled by the particular tensions encountered in England. Scotland made significant progress in coordinating the development of chaplains with the appointment of its own Training and Development Officer and the publication of guidance with the authority of the Scottish government (Scottish Government 2009). Drawing heavily on the model from Scotland, Wales followed a year later with its own standards (National Health Service Wales 2010) and the Northern Ireland Healthcare Chaplains' Association issued a Spiritual Care Policy in 2013. These publications share common themes but also reflect the context of each home nation. Careful study of the documents offers a rewarding insight into the similarities and divergences of spiritual health care in the UK.

National Guidelines

It is usual in the NHS for professions to receive new practice guidelines to reflect changes either within the NHS or the profession. For chaplains the history of publication in England suggested a 10-year cycle of guidelines publication.[8] By 2013 the most recent guidance (2003) was archived on the Department of Health website. Chaplains and those in positions of leadership recognised the need for updated guidelines and NHS England agreed to commission work to produce them. In October 2013 a project lead was seconded on a part-time basis for six months, later extended by a further two months.

Those unfamiliar with chaplaincy can find it surprising that making statements about such a small group of professional staff can be highly contentious. According to one study, there are fewer than 500 whole-time equivalent chaplains in the acute health sector in England (Swift 2013). During the consultation phase of the guidelines project significant criticism came from two sources. One was the Roman Catholic Church and the other the British Humanist Association (BHA) and National Secular Society (NSS). In a weekly publication, figures from the Roman Catholic Church accused the draft guidance of failing to make dedicated provision for Catholic patients:

> you get a feeling that any chaplain will do and that some patients – especially those who are elderly and very ill – might be lucky if they get the chaplain who represents their own faith. (Jim MacManus, quoted in Moorhead 2014)

---

[8] The guidance before 2003 emerged in 1992 as an NHS Management Executive Circular HSG (92)2 which was criticised for its lack of engagement with Church leaders (The Lord Bishop of Exeter, Hansard, 17 February 1992 Vol. 538 cc.983–5).

In its response the BHA lobbied for the removal of the word 'chaplain' from the document (entirely) and the NSS published a call for the secularisation of chaplaincy services in the NHS.[9] Unsurprisingly the final document could not reconcile these responses but instead both strengthened the commitment to specific religious care and also provided the option for NHS facilities to employ any qualified chaplain to address the needs of patients who do not identify with a religion. These aspects of the guidelines attempted to balance the requirements of the Equality Act (2010) to treat both religious and non-religious beliefs with equal regard. It also reflected a growing awareness within the literature of the limitations inherent within the national census and similar instruments used in health care. Typically, a host of religious identifiers (e.g. 'Sikh', 'Hindu', etc.) are set alongside a limited range of negative alternatives (e.g. 'none', 'other'). It is argued that this approach fails to recognise the positive ethical and spiritual commitments of people who do not locate themselves within a religious category (Lee 2014). However, given the difficulties ward staff appear to have in recording religious data, the complexity of screening for spiritual needs outside a religious framework is very challenging. As Swinton has observed, the 'nature of spirituality requires a plurality of approaches that recognise and respond to the complex nuances' of the spiritual (Swinton 2010: 33). This is far from easy for professional chaplains and must be a considerable challenge to those with little experience of discussing spiritual needs.

The NHS Chaplaincy Guidelines (2015) represent an attempt to describe a coherent chaplaincy provision for the NHS in England while indicating a direction of travel which may widen the range of beliefs and religions participating in service delivery. This reflects the 2010 Equality Act by extending the staffing calculation to ensure that all patients who do not declare a religious faith can have the support of chaplains who are not appointed on a religious basis. An alternative to this approach would have been to exclude all faith or belief criteria from appointments – a position advocated by the NSS.[10] If the 1990s marked a movement from Christian to multifaith chaplaincy (Department of Health 2003), the 21st century may yet witness the development of chaplaincy to include a growing number of non-religious spiritual care practitioners.

Texts, Education and Research

In the UK, publication about chaplaincy in hospitals coincided with the passing of the Act of Parliament to create the NHS. Wall's slim volume of

---

[9]   See www.secularism.org.uk/news/2014/10/call-to-secularise-nhs-chaplaincy-services (accessed 14 April 2015).

[10]   See www.secularism.org.uk/news/2014/10/call-to-secularise-nhs-chaplaincy-services (accessed 14 April 2015).

1946 was followed by a small but growing literature in the 1950s and 1960s. Notable examples of this are works by Cox (1955) and Autton (1966). It was not until 1971 that Michael Wilson undertook the first systematic study of the chaplain's role, carried out in a large hospital in Birmingham and resulting in a landmark publication. At the same time, Lambourne (1971) argued an approach, focusing in particular on mental health care, which was probably contributory to the absence of Clinical Pastoral Education from English chaplaincy. Nevertheless, the progress of publication was fitful and spanned several disciplines including theology, religious studies and health care. Peter Speck's *Being There* in 1988 sought to bridge the various identities of chaplaincy and interrogate the distinctive role of the chaplain as one of constructive presence. In the same period Stephen Pattison offered an exploration of health and illness from the perspective of practical theology (1989) and remains a critical commentator on the role of health care chaplains. Since then other professions and disciplines in health care have added their voices and research evidence concerning the role of spiritual care. A leading academic in the field of religion, spirituality and health has observed that the rate of publication 'literally exploded since the mid-1990s' (Koenig 2012: 2). However, Harriet Mowat's review of evidence for the efficacy of chaplaincy in the NHS found that most of the material was 'high grade opinion' rather than the results of research studies using validated tools (Mowat 2008: 10). While the balance of publication has shifted towards journal articles, the theological roots of chaplaincy have ensured that books remain a significant way in which practitioners interrogate ideas and develop academic argument. These range from works setting out practice guidance (Cobb 2005) to broader collections of papers dealing with multiple aspects of spirituality and health (Cobb et al. 2012). Given the size of chaplaincies the international character of the debate has been encouraging, with relevant texts emerging from the USA in particular. Wendy Cadge's astute analysis of chaplaincy (2012) and Winnifred Sullivan's observations from a perspective of law and religion (2014) are two such valuable contributions.

Given the breadth of identities in chaplaincy, and the lack of a unitary system of authorisation, education provision has been based on published competencies and national job evaluations (especially in the years immediately following the implementation of *Agenda for Change* in 2004). Some religious leaders both experience and study chaplaincy as part of their leadership formation but many have little detailed understanding of the work until they become chaplains. Introductory courses for newly appointed chaplains lasting a few days are provided on a regular basis by the Chaplaincy Centre at St Michael's College in Llandaff, Wales. Beyond this there are centres offering Masters level study from postgraduate certificates through to a full MA. Although professional registration is voluntary, the UKBHC includes in its criteria: 'evidence of undertaking postgraduate chaplaincy study for example a Postgraduate Certificate/Diploma/MSc in Healthcare Chaplaincy'.[11]

Due to the weak identity of chaplains as health professionals, some avenues of funding for further study are unavailable. For example, the list of Allied Health Professions which can be awarded doctoral grants by the National Institute for Health Research omits chaplains. At the same time, given the size of chaplaincy in the UK, the number of those interested, able and willing to engage in lengthy research is limited. Full funding for study fees can sometimes be obtained through a combination of faith-based charitable grants, employer resources for advanced study, and regional or national NHS awards open to all staff. Funding alone does not appear to be the primary obstacle to undertaking advanced study. Given that most chaplaincy departments are staffed by fewer than seven whole-time equivalent staff (in the largest Trusts), engaged in round-the-clock service provision, it is easy to recognise the challenge of identifying individuals able to engage in prolonged study. Unless funding is available in addition to fees, backfilling the chaplain's day-to-day work, it is questionable whether it will be possible to develop individuals to lead sustained programmes of research.

The result of this situation is the development of education and research in a sporadic and largely uncoordinated manner. This is not to underestimate the value of what has been achieved but to be realistic about the possibilities for understanding the chaplain's involvement in spiritual care. Without strategic planning for chaplaincy research, it is unlikely that chaplains will to be able to communicate its value and benefit to patient care. It will not be able to reshape practice to reflect the evidence of what is most helpful to patients and service users. In effect, chaplaincy will continue to be dependent on the good will and broad understanding of policy makers rather than arguing its case on the basis of evidence about its outcomes.

The common features of Masters-level health care chaplaincy education include the following: developing knowledge and critical understanding of spiritual and pastoral care; ethics; organisational structures and power; research; supervision; and bereavement. Reflective practice is promoted as a core skill in chaplaincy, and case studies are used to give contextual understanding of the chaplains' work. This approach is supported in literature concerned with pastoral care and those working in health care more generally. In the field of pedagogy the idea of 'threshold' concepts or knowledge has been helpful in designing health care chaplaincy education which can enable advanced and skilful practice. Summarising the central concerns of this, two occupational therapy academics identify the following threshold concepts for their profession: 'client-centred practice and the use of self, developing a professional self-identity and practicing

---

[11] See www.ukbhc.org.uk/chaplains/registration/registration-criteria (accessed 23 November 2014).

in the real world' (Fortune and Kennedy-Jones 2014: 295). Similar challenges face those working with chaplaincy students who are attempting to enter the world of professional spiritual care where they will often be lone practitioners expected to meet complex needs in stressful situations. Successful spiritual care involves recognising the importance of liminal and threshold knowledge.[12] The work of Meyer and Land highlights the importance of the threshold in how epiphanies are achieved which transform someone from a knowledgeable student into a skilful practitioner. The overall aim of the postgraduate experience for chaplains is therefore about developing unconscious competence, so that chaplains are well resourced in order to tailor spiritual care to the uniqueness of each pastoral encounter. The Carnegie work on clergy education has already identified this particular dynamic in the kind of pedagogy needed for ministerial formation and is arguably just as important for those becoming chaplains. It

> relies on the exercise of a teacher's imagination at every stage of designing and conducting the activities of teaching and learning ... It leads ... to the construction of pedagogical events encompassing all the ambiguity we have been describing but directed, nonetheless, toward specific expectations for student learning. (Foster et al. 2006: 59)

It is the less tangible attributes of professional demeanour that can struggle to be taught and assessed in an open, accurate and fair manner. Current thinking within chaplaincy supports the publication of case studies as the most effective way to promote education and research into the spiritual care provided by chaplains (Fitchett 2011). The case study is suited to chaplaincy as it makes visible the complex interaction of personalities and traditions within a single health care encounter. Given the significance of culture to spiritual care this attention to verbatims and non-verbal communication enables professional understanding to be advanced on a shared basis. However, it is important to recognise the limitations of case studies (Flyvbjerg 2006) and their weakness in producing generalisable evidence for the benefits of chaplaincy spiritual care. The strengths of case studies, moving people across the threshold into an awareness of specific professional practice, are also the shortcomings for producing detailed knowledge applicable to all. How chaplains are enabled to assimilate case study learning into developing their practice is therefore a key skill.

Leading chaplains have called for research to focus on outcomes (Handzo et al. 2014) and case studies offer an accessible way for many chaplains to evidence their work and offer it for wider analysis. More will need to be done

---

[12] Meyer, J.H.F. and R. Land (2010), Threshold Concepts and Troublesome Knowledge (5): Dynamics of Assessment, in Meyer, J.H.F., R. Land and C. Baillie (eds), *Threshold Concepts and Transformational Learning*. Rotterdam: Sense Publishers, 61–79.

to understand how chaplaincy care benefits patients and service users, and the education programmes currently available in the UK go some way to building the capacity for future research and leadership. However, chaplains have a lot of work to do – in partnership with academics – if they are to reveal the evidence which will shape and inform their future development.

Conclusion

This chapter has described some of the central issues for the study of health care chaplaincy in the UK, ranging from the history which has shaped its provision to the debates surrounding its future. The issues of both religious faith and non-religious beliefs have become ever more complex and nuanced in legislation. It is indicative of this trend that many of those who do not believe in a god reject the label 'atheist',[13] and someone describing their certainty that God exists says in a broadcast interview: 'No, I am not religious'.[14] What these identities mean and how they relate to spiritual needs in the context of health care will continue to be an important question for research in the coming years.

Chaplaincy services are thinly spread across clinical specialities and services making the identification of their impact on patient well-being a considerable challenge. While small in number the resources required to do thorough research into chaplains' impact are considerable. The development of a patient-reported outcome measure in Scotland is a helpful contribution to this work but will require field testing in many different contexts (Snowden et al. 2013). For the moment, case study collection and analysis offers the most helpful insight into what characteristics in chaplaincy have the most significant impact on patients, service users and staff. These are also a very useful resource for educating and developing new chaplains and those interested in becoming an advanced practitioner in spiritual care.

The progress in chaplaincy leadership in England has been encouraging but the scale of the task ahead is significant. Work needs to be done to clarify chaplains' professional identity and legitimate accountability. The new guidelines are at a best a staging point on that journey, and the responses to the consultation illustrate the range of divergent views about the service. Yet these serious challenges are also the reason why studying chaplaincy offers potentially rich insights into the wider nature of society and how matters of belief relate to our health and well-being.

---

[13]   See   http://blog.newhumanist.org.uk/2007/10/new-humanist-poll-is-sam-harris-right.html (accessed 14 April 2015).

[14]   Dr David Nott speaking on Radio 4, quoted in the 11th Norman Autton Memorial Lecture.

References

Autton, N. (1966), *The Hospital Ministry*. London: Church Information Office.

Bunniss, S., H. Mowat and A. Snowden (2013), Community chaplaincy listening: practical theology in action. *The Scottish Journal of Healthcare Chaplaincy*, 16, 42–51.

Cadge, W. (2012), *Paging God: Religion in the Halls of Medicine*. Chicago: University of Chicago Press.

Cobb, M. (2005), *The Hospital Chaplain's Handbook*. Norwich: Canterbury Press.

Cobb, M., C. Puchalski and M. Rumbold (eds) (2012), *Oxford Textbook of Spirituality in Healthcare*. Oxford: Oxford University Press.

Cox, J.G. (1955), *A Priest's Work in Hospital*. London: SPCK.

Department of Health (2003), *Religion or Belief? A Practical Guide for the NHS*. London: Department of Health.

Fitchett, G. (2011), Making our case(s). *Journal of Health Care Chaplaincy*, 17(1–2), 3–18.

Fitchett, G. and S. Nolan (2015), *Spiritual Care in Practice: Case Studies in Healthcare Chaplaincy*. London: Jessica Kingsley Publishers.

Flyvbjerg, B. (2006), Five misunderstandings about case-study research. *Qualitative Inquiry*, 12(2), 219–45.

Fortune, T. and M. Kennedy-Jones (2014), Occupation and its relationship with health and wellbeing: the threshold concept for occupational therapy. *Australian Occupational Therapy Journal*, 61(5), 293–8.

Foster, C.R., L.E. Dahill, L.A. Goleman and B.W. Tolentino (2006), *Educating Clergy: Teaching Practices and Pastoral Imagination*. San Fransisco: Jossey-Bass.

Hancocks, G., J. Sherbourne and C. Swift (2008), Are they refugees? Why Church of England male clergy enter health care chaplaincy. *Practical Theology*, 1(2), 163–79.

Handzo, G.F., M. Cobb, C. Holmes, E. Kelly, and S. Sinclair (2014), Outcomes for professional health care chaplaincy: an international call to action. *Journal of Health Care Chaplaincy*, 20(2), 43–53.

Koenig, H.G. (2012), Religion, spirituality, and health: the research and clinical implications. *International Scholarly Research Notices*.

Lambourne, R.A. (1971), Objections to a national pastoral organisation. *Contact*, 35.

Lee, L. (2014), Secular or nonreligious? Investigating and interpreting generic 'not religious' categories and populations. *Religion*, 44(3), 466–82.

Moorhead, J. (2014), New rules threaten Catholic ministry in hospitals. *The Tablet*, 7 August.

Mowat, H. (2008), *The Potential for Efficacy of Healthcare Chaplaincy and Spiritual Care Provision in the NHS (UK)*. Aberdeen: Mowat Research.

National Health Service Wales (2010), *Standards for Spiritual Care Services in the NHS in Wales*. Available at: www.wales.nhs.uk/spiritualcare (accessed 25 November 2014).

Pattison, S. (1989), *Alive and Kicking: Towards a Practical Theology of Illness and Healing*. London: SCM.

Scottish Government (2009), *Spiritual Care and Chaplaincy*. Edinburgh: The Scottish Government.

Snowden, A., I. Telfer, E. Kelly, S. Burniss and H. Mowat (2013), The construction of the Lothian PROM. *Scottish Journal of Health Chaplaincy*, .16, 3–16.

Sullivan, W.F. (2014), *A Ministry of Presence: Chaplaincy, Spiritual Care, and the Law*. Chicago: University of Chicago Press.

Swift, C. (2013), A state health service and funded religious care. *Health Care Analysis*, 21(3), 248–58.

—— (2014), *Hospital Chaplaincy in the Twenty-First Century: The Crisis of Spiritual Care on the NHS*. Farnham: Ashgate.

Swinton, J. (2010), The Meanings of Spirituality: A Multi-Perspective Approach to 'the Spiritual'. In McSherry, W. and Ross, L. (eds). *Spiritual Assessment in Healthcare Practice*. Keswick: M&K Publishing, 17–35.

Trotter, J. (2010), *Health Care Chaplaincy and The Church of England: A Review of the Work of the Hospital Chaplaincies Council*. London: Church of England Mission and Public Affairs.

Wall, B. (1946), *Visiting the Hospital: A Practical Handbook for Hospital Chaplains and Clergy who Visit Hospitals*. London: A. R. Mowbray & Co.

Chapter 13

Contextual Issues: Health and Healing

John Swinton and Ewan Kelly

At the heart of the task of chaplaincy is the search for health and well-being and the desire to find ways in which people can experience such things even in the midst of illness, disease and disability. In one sense it is this quest for health, irrespective of the presence of illness, that sets chaplaincy aside as a unique and important health and social care profession. However, such a goal can be frustrated by the needs of a health care system that often functions according to a quite different set of priorities. In a self-consciously secular health care system that tends to prioritise such things as targets, economic viability, statistical returns, reduced waiting lists and the search for cures, the call to take spirituality seriously and to reframe our understandings of health and wellness is often neither obvious nor welcomed. Current criticisms of chaplaincy as not being 'value for money' (Wynne-Jones 2014)[1] are indicative of a lack of understanding of the breadth of our understandings of health and the absence of recognition as to the crucial meaning dimensions that are central to the experience of illness and recovery from ill-health. Such critiques are also indicative of a narrowness in our cultural understandings regarding what health is and what healing actually looks like in practice. We would like to suggest that such perspectives on health are both deceiving and deceptive.

A deeper reflection on current health care practices indicates a movement that has a quite different ethos from the types of concerns we have highlighted above. More and more there is a movement towards putting patients at the forefront of thinking about good care and the nature of health, healing and well-being. Pathology or potential clinical outcomes remain important, but it is how the experience of illness is perceived and responded to by unique individuals that sits at the forefront of emerging thinking and practice. This offers a powerful opportunity for chaplains. More and more, health and social care literature evidences the significance of the impact of person-centred care and patient experience in influencing outcomes for patients. Patient safety and

---

[1] Secularists claim chaplains are a waste of taxpayers' money. *The Telegraph*, Sunday 19 November 2014. Available at: http://blogs.telegraph.co.uk/news/jonathanwynne-jones/9414557/Secularists_claim_chaplains_are_a_waste_of_taxpayers_money/ (accessed 9 November 2014).

clinical effectiveness remain important, but a focus on persons is becoming a priority (Doyle et al. 2014). There is an increasing awareness of the need to (re)humanise our health and social care systems in ways that encourage and ensure the well-being of patients, carers and staff. Health and social care policy seeks to promote the enhancement of quality in health and social care (in particular its person-centred dimension), and in so doing has enabled scope for chaplaincy and spiritual care provision to raise its profile and increase the impact it can make on health, healing and well-being. The central role of chaplaincy is becoming clearer and much more integrated within current strategies and approaches.

Illness As Meaningful

Running alongside of this movement is an increasing recognition of the importance of understanding the meaningfulness and inherent spirituality of experiences of illness. There is more to the experience of illness than simply getting rid of it. Illness is a deeply meaningful event in people's lives which can of course be tragic, but sometimes it can be quite transformative (Frank 1995: 77). Even if we make a full recovery from whatever ailment we encounter, life will never be the same again. Illness is a semiotic event (Kleinmann 1980); it is a disturbance in our life stories that requires to be properly understood, acknowledged and interpreted. Illness is a happening that is freighted with meaning and potential, both negative and positive. That being so, for chaplains, the 'health' in health care may well mean something deeper and richer than it does for others. It may be that the chaplain embodies a thick and vital dimension of the meaning of health and healing that is easily occluded by thinner more instrumental understandings.

Such a recognition of and stress upon the meaning dimensions of illness is not in any sense a push against medicine. Rather it is an enhancement of holistic care within which the personal and communal meanings of illness are recognised as being an important dimension of what illness is, how it should be conceived and the best ways in which it should be dealt with. The experience of being ill is inevitably a deeply meaningful and ultimately spiritual experience. The key spiritual questions – Who am I? Where do I come from? Where am I going to? Why? – frequently bubble to the surface in the midst of the confusion and disorientation of illness. Such meaningful experiences are not epiphenomenal to the tasks of health and social care; they are central to them. Illness can be a deeply lonely place; a strange world within which the need to be heard, understood, cared for and ultimately to find that which evokes love can often take priority over the need to be cured or discharged. Within the experience of illness, injury, accident or trauma, issues of health, healing and well-being can take on deep and vital meanings that are easily lost in the speedy, efficient, task-oriented busy-ness of our health and social care systems. Health and social care without spirituality would be a very lonely, empty and thin place for the sick and the dying. As chaplains begin to think through precisely what it might mean to be health and social care professionals, this may be a good time to reflect on precisely what our goals are when it comes to health and the meanings of health and illness.

A *Health* Service?

In the United Kingdom we have a National Health Service (NHS). The NHS is undergoing rapid change and transformation due to financial, demographic and social challenges. Health and social care services are increasingly being integrated in order to deliver supportive care within community settings, rather than seeking to admit people into institutional settings. People are not only living longer but are doing so with an increasing number of chronic long-term conditions which cannot be cured but which individuals, families and communities, supported by health and social care workers, may adjust to in order to live as well as possible with their conditions (Scottish Government 2013). Dementia, diabetes, cardiovascular disease, chronic lung disease and arthritis would be obvious examples of this. In order for this to occur professionals are learning to empower patients to enable health and well-being to be coproduced, rather than maintaining a dependency culture where professionals 'do to' rather than 'work with' patients. Put slightly differently, in terms of health, our understandings are guided not by a top down imposition of what health is and how it might be achieved, but in an ongoing conversation between lay people (patients, family, etc.) and professionals within which new definitions and understandings of health are beginning to emerge. What health is for someone with appendicitis is not necessarily what health is for someone with dementia. Health then is contextually bound; a coproduction emerging from sensitive and democratic conversations between health care professionals and those who receive their services. The meaning of health and well-being is thus seen to be shifting and changing in rhythm with movements such as these within the NHS and beyond.

The Nature of Health

Ideas about health are not things that are natural to the world. They are not the same as natural things like trees, rivers or mountains. Ideas about health are things that human beings create for different purposes in different cultures, contexts and situations. At one level one might argue that the nature of health is obvious: we are healthy when we are functioning well, when our bodies and minds seem to be in good shape and we are not encountering physical or psychological dis-ease or suffering. To be healthy is to feel good about one's self and the world. This way of thinking underpins classic descriptions of health such as the World Health Organization's definition which describes health as '[a] state of complete physical, mental and social well-being and not merely the absence of disease and infirmity'.[2] To be healthy is to be in harmony with one's self and with one's environment. The problem with such an understanding of health is that no one can actually achieve it! With this definition, everyone is always ill all of the time! A health service that is driven by such a definition will quickly find itself overpowered by the need that it generates. It may well be the case that we are healthy when we are functioning well. The question is: *precisely what do we mean by 'functioning well'?*

What Do We Expect from Health?

Our expectations and desires about the nature of fulfilled human living are deeply implicated in the ways in which we construct our models of health. Since the Enlightenment[3] the understandings of health, illness and healing that have underpinned much thinking within Western cultures have been heavily influenced by some version of the model of health that has emerged from developments within medicine (Cunningham and French 1990). The fact that it is almost impossible for Westerners to think about health, illness and healing without first thinking about medicine is indicative of the power that has been given to medicine to determine our perspectives on health, who should be responsible for healing and by what means such health and healing should be brought about. This is quite surprising, bearing in mind the fact that much if not most healing goes on elsewhere. If we are sad, most of us go to our family and friends rather than a counsellor. If we have a headache, we go to the

---

2   Preamble to the Constitution of the World Health Organization as adopted by the International Health Conference, New York, 19–22 June, 1946; signed on 22 July 1946 by the representatives of 61 States (Official Records of the World Health Organization, no. 2, p. 100) and entered into force on 7 April 1948. Available at: www.who.int/about/definition/en/print.html (accessed 29 October 2014).

3   The Enlightenment refers to a period extending from the late 16th and early 17th centuries (in the case of Europe) to the mid to late 20th century. The Enlightenment is characterised by the growth and strengthening of a specific set of social practices and ways of doing things that is deeply tied in with the philosophical assumptions of liberalism and an emphasis on science, technology and reason as the primary ways of understanding the world (as opposed to religion).

supermarket and buy an aspirin. If we encounter existential angst we might talk to a minister, a priest or a relevant faith community representative whom we think might listen well. Most of us, most of the time do not consult doctors or psychiatrists when we encounter something that challenges our perceptions of personal wellness. In reality, most definitions of health and many of society's perceptions of what healing is, take place with no necessary reference to medicine or professional health care. In other words, we live in a context where there are multiple definitions of health and healing, but one overarching perspective that tends to overpower the others.

Health As the Absence of Illness?

So what exactly do we mean when we talk about a medical approach to health and healing? We do not of course mean that all doctors think in the same way or that all doctors utilise the same model of health. By the term 'medical approach', we simply strive to capture a general mood that comprises a significant aspect of the ethos of Western health and social care practices. When we talk about 'ethos' we refer to some of the implicit and explicit assumptions that drive our understandings of what health and healing actually look like. The ethos of health and social care practices has to do with the underlying assumptions that drive the ways in which we see health and social care and consequently prioritise our actions.

Elliot Dacher notes that the goals of Enlightenment medicine (and in various ways, contemporary health care) have been shaped by three underlying assumptions and principles:

> (1) objectivism, the idea that accurate knowledge can be exclusively achieved through an impersonal assessment of sensory based information; (2) determinism, the idea that causation is exclusively characterized by an upward and linear mechanistic linkage; and (3) positivism, the idea that knowledge exclusively accumulates through the accretion of data from the positive results of sensory based experimentation. (Dacher 1995)

This perspective presumes that diseases have a specific cause which is solely located within observable pathological structures somewhere within the boundaries of the human body. It assumes that the course of a disease is predictable and that it reveals itself in fixed and identifiable signs and symptoms. Importantly, these signs and symptoms are not considered to be unique to any particular individual, but rather they manifest themselves in the same way in all people. They have predictable outcomes and can be described and formulated into diagnoses which all doctors, wherever they are and irrespective of context or culture, can use to initiate the process of healing through the appropriate use of medical technology. The task of medicine is to identify diseases and to engage in actions which will bring about cure. Here healing is specifically understood as cure, i.e. the eradication of harmful pathogenic entities or processes.

Within this perspective, health is understood as the absence (or the minimisation of the impact) of disease. Healing is presumed to relate to any actions or processes that can move a person towards such a goal or state. Colin Samson observes that this understanding of health and healing has been a major driver for the development of medical science since the Enlightenment:

> Enlightenment medicine reflected a confidence in scientific methods of observation and experimentation to control nature and intervene to correct ailments that seemed to cut short life ... The approach to sickness advocated by the medical profession has now become almost a monopoly by virtue of its legitimization by the state in all Western countries as well as other societies. (Samson 1999: 3)

Our point is not that this way of looking at the world is inherently wrong or even that it is misguided. Our point is that this narrow and rather thin view of health has come to dominate our perceptions and worldviews to the exclusion of other important ways of looking at health, ill-health and human well-being. This means that we run the risk of missing out on vital dimensions of meaningful human experience, which are crucial for a full and thick understanding of what health looks like.

Chaplaincy: Health, Healing and Well-Being

Understood in this way it is not difficult to see how the medical approach can make it difficult for health care systems to see the relevance of chaplaincy. If health is perceived primarily in terms of the absence of illness (in practice and in policy) and if the economic drivers of the system focus on fixing, mending and moving people out of the system as quickly as possible, ideas of presence, relationship, listening, meaning seeking, hope inspiring and other key chaplaincy tasks can easily be perceived as things that should be viewed as somehow quite apart from the *real* tasks of healing. However, as we have suggested, there are in fact many different models of health and healing available to us. The question then is what model of health and healing might chaplaincy contribute to the overarching healing narrative of health care? Here we will focus on two interconnected models.

Health As the Presence of Well-Being

The first is the idea that health is deeply tied in with well-being. Well-being is a subjective measure that relates, not to comparisons between perceived norms, but to the things that contribute to an individual's well-being. Well-being as a related concept to health has to do with enabling individual and communal human flourishing, which has physical, psychological and spiritual aspects. According to Webster:

> The opposite of wellbeing is not illness, but dis-ease, in the sense of unease – being ill-at-ease with ourselves. Wellbeing is not the result of 'cure' but of the incremental building of networks of relationships and human connection, self-esteem, self-belief, purpose, meaning, value and good relationships. (Webster 2002: 41)

Within this approach the polarisation of health and illness is put to one side and the focus is turned on those things that enhance resilience and increase capacity within the experience of illness. Creating well-being is primarily conceived as having to do with promoting capacity (McKnight 1995: 199) and helping others to (re)discover the resources or assets which are within them, around about them and beyond them and which help to keep them well as individuals and corporately. Such activity is counter to prevailing health care culture insofar as it moves the focus from fixing deficits to enhancing capacities even within the ongoing presence of deficits.

Understood in this way, to use Wendell Berry's expression, health-is-membership (Berry 2002). It has to do with feeling at home with one's true self irrespective of one's circumstances and recognising that one exists in and is a part of a context or a story that is greater than one's self. *Healing* relates to the means by which such well-being is achieved. Spiritually, health, in this frame, has to do with the desire to be connected to that which is beyond (transcendent and temporal). It relates to the ability to hold on to who you are and why you are in the world even in the midst of difficult circumstances and sometimes unbearable suffering. Well-being does not necessitate 'feeling good', but it does lead to feeling safe and secure. Understood in this way the idea of 'healing presence' takes on a new energy (Kelly 2012). Pain, illness and suffering become significant insofar as they are recognised not only as things to be eradicated, but as the enemies of community (Hauerwas 1993: 146). Healing has to do with overcoming such loneliness and disconnection by recognising the centrality of a person's connectedness with self, community and, for the religious, God. Only when each of these dimensions of well-being are taken into consideration can we claim to have a full understanding of health and well-being. Health-as-well-being does not require the absence of illness; it can be found even in the midst of illness.

Health As Recovery: Well-Being and Healing in the Midst of Enduring Problems

The idea of health-as-well-being offers new possibilities for spiritual care and opens the way for a rich and broad understanding of health-within-illness. It also resonates deeply with some innovative perspectives emerging within mental health care, namely *health-as-recovery*. The recovery movement was initiated by people with mental health problems (mental health service users) who wanted to push against understandings of mental health, illness, healing and recovery which demanded that such concepts should be determined by the presence or absence of recognisable diagnostic symptoms. In this approach, health, recovery and healing are redefined and reframed as achievable goals even in the midst of enduring mental health problems. Central to this way of looking at health is the reinterpretation of the idea of *recovery* (Davidson et al. 2010). The general consensus often assumes that people with conditions such as enduring schizophrenia or bipolar disorder are inevitably going to be ill for the remainder of their lives. People living with such conditions can therefore never achieve the ideal of health or the biomedical understanding of healing. Recovery in this perspective is simply not an option. The recovery movement seeks to challenge such an exclusive understanding of recovery, health and healing by shifting the locus of recovery away from disease and pathology towards an emphasis on the person bearing the diagnosis. The recovery movement emphasises recovery from mental distress as more personal and existential than medical. Recovery is measured in terms that reach wider than the simple reduction of symptoms or in-patient admissions. Success is also measured by how well people are able to pursue things that give their lives meaning (Deegan 2007). Here, mental health is not measured by the presence or absence of mental health problems or the reduction of in-patient admissions, but by the way in which the person constructively and positively reframes her symptoms in ways that bring personal fulfilment, hope and new possibilities even in the midst of severe mental health problems. Healing and recovery are measured by how well a person is able to pursue the things that give purpose and meaning to their lives. The task of healing and recovery and the movement towards mental health (with health perceived as a continuum rather than an ideal) is to find ways to move towards living fully as a human being even in the midst of serious mental illness. Such an understanding of recovery converges with recent accounts of spirituality, personalism and existentialism, while diverging from the dominant paradigm's stress on biological psychiatry.

Healing in this approach has to do with enabling people to develop the ability, the desire and to be given the opportunity to pursue those goals that give meaning and purpose to their lives, without being dependent on curative intervention as the only determinative goal. This movement does not deny the pain and difficulty of mental health problems. It simply states that through a process of renegotiating the meanings of mental distress and placing them into a different frame which includes but is not defined by the goals of psychiatry. It is possible to be well and recovered even in the midst of profound psychological distress. Thus mental health is not the *absence* of illness, but the *presence* of meaning, identity and hope. Healing relates to the various means through which such goals might be achieved. Health may or may not involve cure, but it always involves those things that sustain persons as persons. Such an approach is thus central to the types of person-centred approaches to care that we mentioned at the beginning of this chapter.

Such an understanding of health and recovery dovetails with ideas of health-as-well-being and is not confined only to a mental health care context. It could apply to any health care context where the person-centred nature of health and healing is threatened, misunderstood or in need of reframing. The point is that viewed through these two models our understanding of health does not require to be defined by cure and healing; it is, rather, defined according to a certain ways of noticing and being with people.

The Chaplain As Healer

These two perspectives (or dimensions) on health help us to come to see that health is a much broader and deeper experience than simply the absence or avoidance of illness. This opens up an important space for chaplaincy in terms of defining and working with different models of health. The chaplain might best be perceived as a 'cultural broker'. A cultural broker is a person who facilitates the crossing of borders between a person or a group of people from one culture to another culture. In the case of health and healing, the borders being crossed are the intersections between the various perspectives on health that are available within any health or social care system. In this mode the chaplain moves between the different understandings of health available in health and social care practices and embodies a variety of quite different perspectives on the nature of healing, recovery and well-being. These include understandings that focus on efficiency, safety, technology, cure and discharge. But they also include other ways of looking at health that require a relational and co-productive assets-based approach rather than a transactional approach. This will involve developing such virtues as patience, kindness, compassion, trust and modes of presence which reinforce presence.

The chaplain as the moderator between these health worlds is required to be multilingual, holding in tension aspects of each model of health in ways that encourage healing. That is not a small role to play. It is vital.

The chaplain's role is thus seen to be one of educator, resourcer and supporter of staff across disciplines and sectors; the main health and social care professional who can effectively facilitate others to understand and navigate the complexities of working out what health looks like in a variety of contexts and situations. Chaplains are thus seen to be not only moderators, but also people with the theoretical and practical skills to equip other staff to fruitfully inhabit such a health care world, deliver person-centred, holistic, spiritual care within it and to learn how to dwell healthily in the strange world of illness.

Healing As Hospitable Healing Presence

The chaplain is thus seen to be a healer insofar as she recognises that the process of health and social care has to do with interpreting and reinterpreting the experience of illness in the light of models of health that take seriously the meanings of illness and the significance of persons and seeks to enable people to find health and wellness even in the midst of extreme difficulties. Healing in this approach can be perceived as the restoration of identity and personhood after or in the midst of trauma or illness. We have already suggested that suffering can become the enemy of community insofar as it alienates us from our communities and ultimately from our selves. Elaine Scarry puts this well in her reflections on the impact of pain:

> Pain either expands to fill the whole of our universe or contracts our universe and confines it within the boundaries of our immediate experience. The inexpressibility of pain, comes unsharably into our midst as at once that which cannot be denied and that which cannot be confirmed ... whatever pain achieves it achieves in part through unsharability, and it ensures this unsharability through resistance to language. (Scarry 1985: 4)

Healing has to do with opening up the experience of pain, illness, suffering and loss and enabling people to find themselves and their communities in the midst of such experiences. In so doing people can begin to move towards spiritual health: a type of health that may desire cure, but is not defined by it. Helping the health care system to recognise the depth and breadth of health and the deep complexities of illness is a major contribution that chaplaincy brings to the health care context. Indeed, it may be that such an approach to health and well-being has the potential to enable chaplaincy to be recognised as a truly valuable health care profession in the deepest and most healing sense of the term.

References

Berry, W. (2002), Health is Membership. In *The Art of the Commonplace: The Agrarian Essays of Wendell Berry*. Berkeley, CA: Counterpoint., 144–58.

Cunningham, A. and French, R. (eds) (1990), *The Medical Enlightenment of the Eighteenth Century*. London: Cambridge University Press.

Davidson, L., Rakfeldt, J. and Strauss, J. (eds) (2010), *The Roots of the Recovery Movement in Psychiatry: Lessons Learned*. London: Wiley.

Deegan, P.E. (2007). The lived experience of using psychiatric medicine in the recovery process and a shared decision making program to support it. *Psychiatric Rehabilitation Journal*, 31, 62–9.

Doyle, C., Lennox, L. and Bell, D. (2013), A systematic review of evidence on links between patient experience and clinical safety and effectiveness. *BMJ Open*, 3, e001570. Doi:10.1136/bmjopen-2012-001570.

Frank, A.W. (1995), *The Wounded Storyteller: Body, Illness, and Ethics*. Chicago: The University of Chicago Press.

Hauerwas, S. (1993), *Naming the Silences*. Edinburgh: T&T Clark Ltd.

Kelly, E. (2012), *Personhood and Presence: Self as a Resource for Spiritual and Pastoral Care*. London: T & T Clark International.

Kleinmann, A. (1980), *Patients and Healers in the Context of Culture: An Exploration of the Borderland between Anthropology, Medicine and Psychiatry*. Berkeley, CA: University of California Press.

McKnight, J. (1995), *The Careless Society: Community and its Counterfeits*. New York: Basic Books.

Samson, C. (1999), *Health Studies: A Multidisciplinary Reader*. London: Blackwell.

Scarry, E. (1985), *The Body in Pain: The Making and Unmaking of the World*. Oxford: Oxford University Press.

Scottish Government (2013), *A Routemap to the 2020 Vision for Health and Social Care*. Available at: www.scotland.gov.uk/Resource/0042/00423188.pdf (accessed 6 May 2014).

Webster, A. (2002), *Wellbeing*. London: SPCK.

Wynne-Jones, J. (2014), Secularists claim chaplains are a waste of taxpayers' money. *The Telegraph*, Sunday 19 November. Available at: http://blogs.telegraph.co.uk/news/jonathanwynne-jones/9414557/Secularists_claim_chaplains_are_a_waste_of_taxpayers_money/ (accessed 9 November 2014).

Chapter 14
Case Study

Steve Nolan

Health Care Chaplaincy – Grace in a Brief Encounter

Early in September 2013, Den was admitted to hospice care suffering from small cell carcinoma of the lung, with liver and bone metastases. He was 80 years old. He had lived most of his life in south London, and like many boys from the city, Den's education and early work years had been disrupted: first by Nazi bombers, then by National Service. He eventually started work as a builder, retraining in mid-life as a building inspector. In the late 1950s, Den took a holiday to watch motor racing and met Connie. The couple married the following year and set up home in an unfurnished, rented flat. Four years later, Elaine completed their family.

Den was an intelligent and grounded man with wide interests. He enjoyed fishing, photography and computing, had eclectic musical tastes and followed south London football teams. With Connie and Elaine, he was a lifelong camper. Generous with his time and energies, Den was gentle and made a good friend. Now retired, he had remained very much the provider to Connie and Elaine, who, with Den's sister, Millie, showed conspicuous devotion in visiting the hospice. Connie and Millie arrived late morning every day and stayed until taken home by a friend or by Elaine, who visited several times a week, driving across London after work and returning home to Kent in the late evening. While Den had not been religious, Connie brought Elaine up within the Roman Catholic tradition that she had herself known from childhood. As a young woman, Elaine had married within the Church but had become alienated from it, following her divorce. Elaine had a teenage child of her own and was living with her long-term partner, Alan, who was very close to Den. Elaine and Alan were planning to marry but had not yet 'got around to it'.

Den was admitted to Princess Alice Hospice, an independent 28-bedded in-patient hospice, in the south of England. As an independent charity, Princess Alice Hospice provides high-quality palliative care, free at the point of need, to adults with cancer and other life-limiting illnesses. The hospice also supports families and carers during the illness, and provides bereavement care afterwards. The Princess Alice Hospice catchment area takes in over one million people across a large part of Surrey, southwest London and Middlesex.

I began work as a chaplain in this hospice in June 2004. My spiritual formation began within Roman Catholicism, but, after exploring the possibility of the priesthood and engaging with the Charismatic Renewal Movement, I left to join an independent evangelical church, whose style was Pentecostal. I spent two years in an evangelical Bible college and worked in churches in Kent and Wolverhampton. My theological understanding had begun to change, and, following a short break in 'secular' work, I trained for Baptist ministry in a liberal theological college in Manchester, my home city. Following ordination, I served seven years in a small church in northwest London, where I began to engage in interfaith work. I consider myself fluent in several dialects of Christian spirituality; I have found wisdom and spiritual nurture in eastern faiths, particularly Buddhism; I have a personal and professional interest in non-religious spirituality and spiritual care; and I am dual qualified and accredited as a counsellor/psychotherapist. I am 56, at the time of writing.

Formal permission from an ethics committee is not necessary for a case study; however, the paper on which this chapter is based was submitted to, and approved for publication by, Princess Alice Hospice, on condition that identities and identifying details are disguised. All the verbatim accounts were written up within 24 hours of the intervention.

Case Study

Initial Encounters

I visited Den and his family in response to a referral, shortly after his admission; Den's nurses felt he needed to talk. He was asleep when I arrived and I introduced myself to his wife, Connie, and his sister, Millie. They seemed pleased that I had called, but my initial sense was that they didn't particularly want any support. Indeed, when our chaplaincy volunteers visited (four times over the next ten days), they found no obvious desire to talk, certainly not from Den; although one volunteer, Geraldine Worthington, did record that Den had 'seemed to be quite stressed emotionally'. During these initial encounters, I was also asked to contact Den's daughter, who had asked staff about the possibility of arranging her wedding in the hospice. I followed this up, making several phone calls and eventually arranged a meeting to discuss what was in her mind.

With Den

Two weeks after admission, Den was referred to me again. This time, Connie expressed concern that Den had something on his mind, but would not talk to her about it. Could I help? When I visited, Den was alone in his room.

Chaplain:	How's it going Den? Can I call you Den? (*Nods*) How's it going Den?
Den:	(*Pause*) About the same as yesterday.
Chaplain:	And how was that?
Den:	(*Pause*) Muddled and confused.
Chaplain:	How are you feeling today?
Den:	(*Pause*) Well, muddled and confused!
Chaplain:	(*Pause*) Do you have anything on your mind, Den?
Den:	(*Pause*) Connie and I haven't really spoken about ... (*His voice trailed off*).
Chaplain:	Is that something you like to speak about? (*Long pause*) You and Connie have been together a long time, Den. (*Nods*) She seems a lovely lady.
Den:	The best!
Chaplain:	I met your daughter, Elaine, yesterday. She seems very nice.
Den:	(*Pause*) My sister's here, and you say you've met my daughter.
Chaplain:	Yes.
Den:	It's not the best time.
Chaplain:	It's not the best time?
Den:	I find when they're here ... It's not the best time to make decisions.
Chaplain:	Would you like me to come back tomorrow? (*Nods*) Okay, Den. I'll wish you well.

Den extended his hand to shake mine, and engaged me with a look that felt very purposeful. We held each other's gaze as I walked around his bed and towards the door. Later, I summarised our meeting in Den's notes:

> Den indicated he has things to speak about but didn't want to talk today. I offered to see him again tomorrow.

With Connie

I found Connie, a gentle, quietly spoken woman, and Millie, an equally quiet south Londoner, in the hospice coffee lounge. I joined them at their table.

Connie:	Did he speak to you?
Chaplain:	(*Although he had said little, I was protective of Den's confidentiality*) He was tired today, and said I could come back tomorrow.
Connie:	But did you say anything to him?
Chaplain:	(*I assumed Connie was referring to the wedding plans*) No, no! I wouldn't do that. That's for Elaine.
Connie:	No, I meant were you able to talk with him?

Chaplain:	No, but he said I could come back tomorrow.
Connie:	That's a shame.
Chaplain:	I'll see him tomorrow. (*Connie looked worried*) Is there something you think he needs to talk about?
Connie:	Not really. He doesn't talk to me about how things are, only about how he's feeling.
Chaplain:	Has Den always been a private man?
Connie:	(*Nods*) He has. He's done it to protect me. He's always been the one ... I'm the stupid one, the one who doesn't text, or email, or set the programme on the TV.
Millie:	But she's *not* stupid, and she's no retiring wallflower.
Chaplain:	But Den's looked after things and been the provider.
Connie:	Hasn't he just. Well, we'll go back now.

With Den

As promised, I visited Den the following day.

Chaplain:	How's it going, Den?
Den:	About the same as yesterday.
Chaplain:	So a bit muddled and confused then. (*Nods*) Can I pull up a chair and join you?
Den:	Sure.
Chaplain:	(*Pause*) Connie told me you've always been very protective and looked after her. (*Sigh*) Do you worry about Connie?
Den:	Not as much as I used to.
Chaplain:	Not as much.
Den:	She's hard.
Chaplain:	(*I was puzzled by his use of 'hard'*) She's become tougher?
Den:	More than she was. (*Den looked very tired*)
Chaplain:	Is there something you'd like to talk about?
Den:	Not really.
Chaplain:	Okay, Den. Shall I let you rest?
Den:	Yes, please.

On getting up, I noticed on Den's dresser a small picture of a man and woman.

Chaplain:	Is this you and Connie?
Den:	Yes.
Chaplain:	Can I have a look?
Den:	Yes.
Chaplain:	What a lovely picture.

Den:	It was back in the seventies.
Chaplain:	You made a very handsome couple. Thanks Den. Can I see you again?
Den:	Yes.

With Connie

Later the same afternoon, I had a phone call from Den's health care assistant (HCA): Connie would like me to come and talk with Den. Before going into Den's room, I spoke with his HCA. It was Ward Round day and Connie had received bad news: she had been expecting Den would return home, but he was now too unwell; she had been told Den would deteriorate. In speaking with his health carers, we agreed we needed to try to help Connie manage her anxieties. Den was being attended to, so I looked for Connie. She was walking alone in the garden.

Chaplain:	You've seen the doctors today.
Connie:	Yes. It wasn't good.
Chaplain:	Would you like to have a cup of tea and sit and talk about it?

We found seats in the coffee lounge.

Connie:	We were told by the cancer hospital that he might have about two years, but it doesn't look that way now. Den's happy to stay here. I don't think I'll tell Elaine.
Chaplain:	(*I thought it would be unhelpful not to tell her daughter*) Why wouldn't you?
Connie:	She has such a long drive home, and she's so tired. I think I'll tell Alan (*Elaine's partner*).
Chaplain:	That's a good idea.
Connie:	We always said we would go together. Elaine doesn't agree with that. She says what about her, but she has Alan. We didn't have many friends. (*Begins to cry*) We were always enough for each other. But it wouldn't be difficult.
Chaplain:	(*This sounded like suicidal ideation, but I wanted Connie to be more explicit*) How do you mean?
Connie:	A few sleeping tablets. A few *more* tablets.

I felt Connie had taken me into her confidence, and I was cautious about challenging her directly; nonetheless, I felt I should say something about the implications of her possible action.

Chaplain:	When that does happen, it can be very hard for those who are close to you. It can make things very difficult for them. (*Pause*) You were very close with Den. (*Nods*) When did you meet?

On reflection, I should have stayed longer with Connie's suicidal ideation and checked how serious she was; but she seemed to find respite in recounting how she and Den had met and some of their experiences together. In Den's notes, I summarised my meeting with Connie:

> Spent time with Connie. She expressed she had suicidal thoughts and spoke about not wanting to 'go on' after Den's death. I discussed this with my line manager.

With Elaine

I accompanied Connie back to Den's room and found Elaine with her dad. I had news for her about her wedding plans, and we agreed to talk. Elaine had been with Alan, her partner, for over 20 years. They had always intended to marry but they 'just hadn't got around to it'. Elaine wanted Den to 'give her away', and was eager to make the arrangements. Having contacted the Registry Office, I was advised that a registrar would not attend the hospice, because it was not the patient who wanted to marry. As a Baptist minister, I did not have the option of applying for an Archbishop of Canterbury's Special Licence, so the next best option was for Elaine and Alan to marry at a Registry Office and then have a blessing in Den's room at the hospice. However, because it was felt time was short, I agreed to have the blessing first. We set a date for a week the following Sunday and I wrote a bespoke service of blessing on their intention to marry.

With Connie and Millie

A week after the blessing, I found Connie and Millie drinking tea in the hospice dining room. By this time, Den's condition had begun to improve, to the point where there was talk of discharging him.

Connie:	You'll think we're always eating!
Chaplain:	How's Den today.
Connie:	Sleeping. He seems to sleep all the time now. The social worker hasn't been yet.
Chaplain:	Were you expecting him?
Connie:	He said he'd come today. But they said he wasn't around today. He was coming to talk to Den about nursing homes. They want to send Den out. I can't have him at home. He doesn't want that.

He'd prefer to say here. He likes it here. He doesn't want to go to a nursing home. I understand why they're saying that, but ...

Millie sat quietly, but her facial expressions supported Connie. I felt compromised. I had a strong urge to explain the hospice discharge policy, but held back in order to allow Connie the space she needed to express her feelings. In any case, Connie's sense of helplessness, evident also in Millie, silenced us all. I wanted to reach out and hold her hands, which she rested on the table. I regret that I didn't.

Later, I saw Millie sitting alone in the corridor. I sat down next to her.

Chaplain: How are you doing?

Her eyes instantly watered, and she blinked back tears. I asked about Connie, and Millie told me about the weight of the decision Connie felt she was being forced to make. She said that the family had offered to help Connie to have Den at home.

Millie: I'm a widow, so I could be there to help during the day, and Elaine and Alan could be there at the weekend!

With Den and Connie

The following day I visited Den in his room.

Chaplain: Hello Den. How are you today?

Wide-eyed, he looked like the proverbial rabbit caught in the headlights. I squeezed his hand, but with little response.

Connie: He doesn't speak now.

Den stared at the wall behind my head. Connie was pouring a tot of whisky; Millie was in search of ice. We distilled our opinions about malts, and Den nodded his preference for Irish.

Connie: The social worker hasn't been yet.
Chaplain: Were you expecting him?
Connie: He was going to come to talk about nursing homes.

We stood by Den's bed and rehearsed the previous day's conversation. Without speaking, I moved and sat beside Den. Taking his hand, I squeezed it, and he responded in kind. He closed his eyes and seemed to drift off to sleep. I looked back toward Connie. She had turned side on to me, and was dabbing her eyes with a tissue. Still holding Den's hand I stood and reached out to Connie. Millie returned without ice, and I offered to get some from the kitchen. Den was asleep when I returned.

As I needed to leave, I offered to see if my social worker colleague was available. Like me, he felt Den's condition had deteriorated, and rather than burden Den and Connie, he felt it wise to wait until the doctors had assessed whether discharge would be appropriate.

With Den, Connie and Millie

Three days later, at the morning handover meeting, it was reported that Den was unresponsive. Chaplaincy volunteer Geraldine Worthington visited and sat with Den for a while. He was quiet, and after a while Geraldine told Den, 'I'll leave you, now, but I'll come back later'. As she left the room, Den died.

Connie and Millie arrived within the hour; due to her long journey, Elaine arrived sometime later. Geraldine and a young trainee nurse waited with Den, and were there when Connie and Millie arrived. I joined them a few minutes later. Den hadn't been religious, and religion hadn't been part of my involvement with his family. They did not ask for prayers, and I didn't offer any; I felt Den would not have welcomed prayer, and I surmised that Connie and Millie would ask if they wanted it. I simply watched quietly, and witnessed his womenfolk as they anxiously caressed him, their pink-warm hands in salient contrast to the paling ochre of his now cold fingers, and I listened to the words they whispered to each other:

Connie:	I just want to be with him.
Millie:	You can't do that to Elaine.
Connie:	But she has a husband now.
Millie:	But she needs you.

Since our conversation in the coffee lounge three weeks earlier, I had been looking for an opportunity to speak with Connie about her suicidal ideation. From what I had heard, clearly Connie had expressed her thoughts, at least to Millie. I had discussed our earlier conversation with colleagues, and we agreed that, while there was nothing we could do to prevent Connie taking her own life, if she was serious, I should nevertheless try to speak further with her and also (with her permission) alert her General Practitioner (GP). Later that morning, once Elaine had arrived, I asked to have a private word with Connie.

Chaplain:	I remember a conversation we had some time ago in the coffee lounge. And you said that you didn't want to go on without Den. (*Nods*) And you mentioned in the room, just now, that you didn't want to be without him. (*Nods*) Connie, I'm very concerned about you. Have you thought about what you might do?
Connie:	No.
Chaplain:	But you are thinking about it. (*Nods*) Connie, Elaine would be devastated.
Connie:	But she has Alan.
Chaplain:	But she loves you, and needs you now. It would be devastating if you did anything.
Connie:	It's devastating for me.
Chaplain:	I know. (*Pause*) Connie, I want to speak to your doctor.
Connie:	And tell him about Den.
Chaplain:	And tell him what you've said to me.

Connie gave me permission to contact her GP, and I documented what I had done.

With Connie, Elaine, Millie and Alan

After the weekend, I found Connie, Elaine and Millie in the Sanctuary, the room in the hospice set aside for prayer and quiet reflection. They had come to light candles and write some words for Den in the message book. They were all tearful, and I sat with them for a short while. Connie's words were barely audible, but Elaine was able to ask if I would take the service for her dad. I agreed, and we arranged a time later in the week for us to plan the service together. When they arrived, I spent over an hour with them, listening and writing up their memories and anecdotes about Den, which I used to construct a eulogy. As we ended the appointment, Alan voiced: 'It's good to talk like this. Actually, it's quite therapeutic.'

A week later, I conducted Den's funeral at a local crematorium.

Commentary

As a hospice chaplain, I am a health care professional whose specialty includes belief (religious/non-religious) and ritual practice. Part of my job is to understand how belief and ritual function in people's lives, to be a resource for my colleagues in these matters, and also to be available to act in a religious and pastoral capacity as a Christian minister. An important part of my role is to provide (and model) spiritual support to people who are dying, and to their relatives and friends. To this end, I need a working concept of *spirituality*.

Definitions of spirituality are legion and at times contradictory. Nonetheless, definitions are important for a variety of reasons, not the least of which is in providing a coherent rationale for practice. Personally, I do not subscribe to the widely assumed – but unsubstantiated and essentially reductive – view that spirituality is primarily associated with the human search for meaning (Saunders 1988, Speck 1988, White 2006). I adopt the more fully developed and nuanced humanistic and phenomenological definition produced by Elkins et al. (1988), which in broad terms understands spirituality to be related to the sense we humans appear to have that we are *more than* merely physical bodies. In theological terms, I take this sense (of being *more than*) as the sense of transcendence. While at this point I find it a challenge to operationalise this understanding fully, it nonetheless enables me to interpret the variety of ways we extend our being as so many expressions of the human spirit (Nolan 2011); specifically, it gives me a perspective from which to approach spiritual care in a way that is not determined by religious factors alone.

The case presented exemplifies work in what is often described as the post-Christian era, where chaplains work with people whose religion is secularised and whose secularism is touched by the sacred. This work with Den and his family involved a range of chaplaincy interventions and practices, much of which would not be considered *religious*, and which, arguably, may have been delivered by another health care professional – for example, a social worker. However, I regard the work as pastoral care of the kind that is typical of Christian pastoral ministry, and I would argue that, because it attends to that 'extension of the conscious self' (Elkins et al. 1988: 10) that I regard as 'transcendent', it is properly *spiritual* care of the kind best delivered by a chaplain (Nolan 2011). I want now to reflect briefly on aspects of the case that highlight facets of contemporary health care chaplaincy.

Den's nurses felt he needed to talk. Like Connie, Den's nurses felt he had something on his mind, but they were unclear about what it was or how to help. The role and value of chaplaincy has been challenged by secularists (Paley 2008a, b, Christian 2011), who regard the work of health care chaplains as a relic of their religious heritage and argue that they provide care that could be provided equally well, and at less cost, by community faith leaders. Yet among colleagues on the multidisciplinary team, chaplains accrue what Pierre Bourdieu terms *symbolic capital* – a type of honour or recognition, based on observing the effects of our work over time. The chaplain's work may be formal, as in visits arranged to bring a sacrament or give pastoral support; or it may be informal, as when I was asked to 'drop in' to see if Den would like to 'chat'. But the challenge, and the skill, is to establish a relationship with a total stranger, who is informed by a set of preconceptions about chaplains, based on a mix of cultural stereotypes and personal experiences, and to do this almost instantaneously in a way that can open a safe space in which the person can talk freely.

I had a strong urge to explain the hospice discharge policy. In a small way, my impulse to defend my institution highlights the sometimes uncomfortable professional space health care chaplains occupy. Located between an authorising faith group and the employing institution, chaplains owe a loyalty to both. However, the prior duty to support and advocate for the patient (Francis 2013) may provoke a conflict with either, or both. Uniquely within the NHS, chaplains bear a 'representative role' on behalf of their faith group, and, as such, are accountable to that faith group 'for embodying its ethos and teaching appropriately' (SYWDC 2003: 12). Theologically, ethically and liturgically, this presents a range of potential conflicts. For example, had I agreed to bless Elaine's union with a same-sex partner, I would have been acting contrary to the conventional beliefs and practices of my Baptist faith group, and risked my accreditation; however, refusing to bless the union, no matter how graciously, may have brought me into conflict with the anti-discriminatory policy to which my institution is committed.

Religion hadn't been part of my involvement with Den's family. My decision not to offer to pray after Den had died was made in the moment, and was based on what I knew about Den. Arguably, as prayer and ritual practice are part of my specialty, it would have been quite appropriate to offer to pray: death has always been marked in such ways. Yet I was confident that Den would not want to be prayed over, and it felt important to respect the man he had been. Den had been an orderly man, and, for him, religion had its proper place, being for births, deaths and marriages; the occasional offices that Wesley Carr calls 'brief encounters' (Carr 1985). The encounters with Den and his family typify the many such encounters chaplains have, and while brief, they are not without significance. Births, deaths and marriages focus human fragility, and appropriate rituals, conducted with pastoral sensitivity, address a need to acknowledge that fragility and to find strength in grace. It is to the credit of the NHS that it employs chaplains to attend to such needs.

Conclusion

This case study has focused on an episode of chaplaincy work that aimed to support a family group as they cared for each other and for the person they were losing. As such, it exemplifies a range of chaplaincy interventions and practices: psychospiritual support for a wife, daughter and sister experiencing anticipatory grief; ritual work constructing an atypical service of blessing; bereavement support through preparation for and conducting of a funeral; and multiprofessional liaison with health care colleagues.

This brief commentary portrays the chaplain as possessing symbolic capital, occupying uncomfortable professional space and offering grace in 'brief encounters'. These roles require extremely high levels of skill and personal qualities, not measured by academic or professional qualification alone, and chaplains need not devalue their skill and qualities just because they are so internalised that at times they seem entirely intuitive.

References

Carr, W. (1985), *Brief Encounters: Pastoral Ministry through the Occasional Offices.* London: SPCK.

Christian, R. (2011), *Costing the Heavens: Chaplaincy Services in English NHS Provider Trusts 2009/10.* London: National Secular Society.

Elkins, D.N., Hedstrom, L.J., Hughes, L.L., Leaf, J.A. and Saunders, C.L. (1988), Toward a humanistic-phenomenological spirituality: definition, description and measurement. *Journal of Humanistic Psychology*, 28(4), 5–18.

Francis, R. (2013), *Report of the Mid Staffordshire NHS Foundation Trust Public Inquiry.* London: The Stationery Office. Available online: www.midstaffspublicinquiry.com/report (accessed 16 April 2013).

Nolan, S. (2011), Psychospiritual care: new content for old concepts – towards a new paradigm for non-religious spiritual care. *Journal for the Study of Spirituality*, 1(1), 50–64.

Paley, J. (2008a) Spirituality and nursing: a reductionist approach. *Nursing Philosophy*, 9, 3–18.

—— (2008b), The concept of spirituality in palliative care: an alternative view. *International Journal of Palliative Nursing*, 14, 448–52.

Saunders, C. (1988), Spiritual pain. *Journal of Palliative Care*, 4(3), 29–32.

Speck, P. (1988), *Being There: Pastoral Issues in Time of Illness.* London: SPCK.

SYWDC (2003), *Caring for the Spirit: A Strategy for the Chaplaincy and Spiritual Healthcare Workforce.* South Yorkshire Workforce Development Confederation.

White, G. (2006), *Talking about Spirituality in Health Care Practice: A Resource for the Multi-professional Health Care Team.* London and Philadelphia: Jessica Kingsley Publishers.

PART IV
Military Chaplaincy

Chapter 15

Military Chaplaincy

David Coulter and Giles Legood

Introduction

Today's military chaplains stand in a long line of clergy who have worked outside a parochial or congregational setting. Throughout most of the history of the Church there have been clergy who have ministered alongside people in their times of vulnerability and in their times of strength, in settings that have not been primarily church-based. Over the past two centuries clergy have worked in hospitals, schools, prisons and, in the 20th century, in a wider range of sectors and settings. Whilst there was a massive increase in the numbers of clergy serving with the armed forces during the First World War, the concept of clergy ministering in such a setting is no modern phenomenon. For centuries in Britain clergy have served with and alongside fighting forces.

In this chapter we shall first outline a history of clerical involvement with British fighting forces. In doing so, we shall note the purpose, organisation and differing forms of delivery of ordained ministry to naval, army and air force personnel. As part of this story telling, we shall consider notable examples of sacrificial ministry from 20th-century chaplains of all three Services. The latter part of the chapter will move on to look at some of the lessons identified for chaplaincy by chaplains and others who have reflected on the more recent conflicts in Iraq (Operation TELIC), Afghanistan (Operation HERRICK) and the wider Middle East (Operation KIPION). Finally, the chapter will identify some of the current challenges and strengths for armed forces' chaplaincy in the 21st century as it looks to meet the future religious, pastoral and ethical needs of military personnel.

A History of Military Chaplaincy

The larger medieval households of England often contained regular garrisons of soldiers and these would require the attention of a designated cleric to act as chaplain.[1] Although a decree was passed by the Synod of Westminster in 1175

---

[1] The concept of a single, homogenous 'British' army is a relatively modern one. Chaplains were employed by individual, freestanding regiments until 1796 when a Royal Warrant was issued bringing the Army Chaplains' Department into being.

that no cleric should take up arms or go about in armour, there was no war fought or army raised in England before 1350 which did not have a leading member of the clergy as one of its commanders. As early as 447, Germanus, Bishop of Auxerre, visited Britain and led troops in Wales to a victory over the Saxons and Picts, teaching them, it is said, the war cry 'Alleluia' (Brumwell 1943: 9). Bede tells us that clergy had leading parts to play in other battles in Wales, Chester, York, Scotland and elsewhere.

By the time of the reign of Edward I, however (1272–1307), the age of combative clergy was virtually at an end. Instead, priests accompanied Kings and Knights into battle, including for instance at the Battle of Crecy (1346) where on the eve of battle King Edward III of England retired to his oratory to pray and the next morning rose early to hear Mass and receive communion whilst his army made their confessions and prepared for battle. At the battle three types of clergy are recorded: those acting as the King's confessors and ecclesiastical secretaries; those serving under a baron or other nobleman; and those serving the Welshmen (recorded as those most poorly paid). It is significant to note that these clergy were accompanying the army wherever it went to battle. The chaplains were not remaining on English soil but were travelling to minister wherever their charges went. Thomas Eltham, a chaplain who went to Agincourt in 1414, mentions two classes of chaplains: those 32 belonging to the King's retinue and another class attached to the nobles.

It was not until the late 16th and early 17th centuries, however, that regiments as we might recognise them came to be formed. As they were formed, terms like 'Colonel' and 'Sergeant Major' first came to be used and, significantly for us, the terms 'preacher' and 'chaplain' also begin to appear on the payrolls. The command headquarters of the first national regular army, Cromwell's New Model Army of the 1640s, lists a 'Master Bowles – Chaplain to the Army' (Smyth 1968: 18–19). During the Puritan Revolution it was not only the Puritans who had their own (Puritan) chaplains but the Royalist forces too. The Royalists appointed their own Anglican clergy as chaplains. At the same time those Scottish forces of the Solemn League and Covenant loyal to the King, Charles II, were ministered to by Presbyterian chaplains representing Scotland's established religion. It was Charles II who became the first monarch to maintain a standing army in peacetime. Although the task of appointing a chaplain to a regiment fell to the colonels commanding, such provision was often little more than that of a religious functionary. Like their civilian counterparts, chaplains could absent themselves from their duties and employ a more poorly paid clergyman to carry out their duties for them. One chaplain noted that ' ... the Chaplaincy is generally a kind of sinecure and the care of souls is left to any worthless wretch that will do it at an easy rate. When we lay in one City, the care of four or five regiments was left to an unhappy man, who was an object of common ridicule among the soldiers for his perpetual drunkenness' (Duncan Wright, quoted in Louden 1996: 25).

Such piecemeal and insufficient ministry was abolished in September 1796 when the Army Chaplains' Department was founded by Royal Warrant. The experience of fighting the French in north America and ex-patriots in the War of American Independence had underlined the impressions amongst those responsible for the army's morale that a larger, more permanent and better-equipped chaplaincy was required. On taking office the first Chaplain-General, the Reverend John Gamble, found that 340 regimental chaplains were on leave and so required them to return to their duties by the end of the year or be pensioned off.

Almost all of the chaplains within the new Department were members of the Church of England, although a few were Presbyterians. By 1827 the numbers of Presbyterian chaplains had grown to such an extent that they became a separate branch of the Department. In 1794, Father Alexander MacDonnell became the first Roman Catholic chaplain to serve in the British Army since the reign of James II (1685–1688). Following the Catholic Emancipation Bill of 1829, Roman Catholic chaplains were regularised within the army in 1836 and Catholic troops were permitted to attend Mass in Catholic chapels close to their barracks, provided that their commanding officer approved (mostly these troops served in Irish regiments).[2]

The first known priest to accompany a fleet from Britain was Odo (later Archbishop of Canterbury, who died in 959), who travelled with King Athelstan in the 10th century (Smith 1961: 1). Outside Britain we know that around the year 1000 a priest accompanied the Norse explorer Leif Erikson on a voyage to what we now call north America (Down 1989: 11). The earliest known reference to a priest aboard English *fighting* ships, however, comes from the time of the Second Crusade of 1147 when an expedition set out (which resulted in the capture of Lisbon) with the following in its orders: 'That every ship should have its own priest, and that there should be orders to observe the same practices as in a parish ... That everyone should confess weekly and go to communion on the Lord's Day' (Taylor 1978: 3). During the reign of King John (1199–1216), William de Wrotham, Archdeacon of Taunton, is recorded as being the first 'Keeper of the King's Ships'. This was not a chaplaincy role but an example, like in the armies, of fighting clerics being intimately involved in the life of the military.

During the pilgrimages to the shrine of St James at Compostella in Spain and other places in Europe and the Holy Land, begun in the middle of the 15th century, priests were aboard the ships carrying the pilgrims. In the latter part of the same century priests sailed on galleon ships during what has been called the Age of Discovery. On these journeys they sought both to establish the Church wherever they went and to minister to the sailors and other travellers. In the

---

2   See the chapter 'The First Catholic Chaplains and the Royal Army Chaplains' Department' in Johnstone and Hagerty (1996: 1–20).

military context, however, it was not until the 16th century that chaplains were employed to accompany the fleet with a role which was other than operational, but rather spiritual. In 1626 King Charles I ordered that chaplains should sail on all ships of his naval fleet and in 1653 public worship was made mandatory on all ships of the English navy. By the period 1689–1713 records show that over 700 chaplains were appointed in this time. Names of chaplains show, however, that many appointments consisted of just one voyage and that chaplains also retained their parish benefices whilst serving the navy. This was not the case, however, with the Reverend Alexander Scott, Chaplain of HMS Victory, in whose arms Admiral Nelson died at the Battle of Trafalgar on 21 October 1805. As with chaplains to the various British regiments, there was a high degree of absenteeism amongst the chaplains and widespread hiring of younger clergy to perform the chaplain's role on another's behalf.

Unlike in the army, where we are able to say precisely when the Army Chaplains' Department officially came into being, the command structure within the navy emerged more gradually. Indeed, it may be for this reason that there is much less published material, in book form, on the work of naval chaplains. The first person to be given the title 'Chaplain-Generall [sic] of the Fleet' was William Hodge in 1701. Between 1812 and 1815, John Owen, Chaplain-General of the Army, also served as 'Chaplain-General of the Fleet'. In 1859 the Senior Chaplain at Greenwich Hospital was recognised as 'Head of the Naval Chaplains' and 'Chaplain to the Fleet'. Since 1902 the title and scope of the authority of the navy's most senior chaplain has been established as 'Chaplain of the Fleet'.[3]

Towards the end of the First World War, on 1 April 1918, the Royal Air Force was formed as an amalgamation of the army's Royal Flying Corps and the Royal Naval Air Service. In the first few months of the new Service's life chaplains were borrowed from the navy and army. A Royal Navy chaplain, the Reverend Harry Viener, was seconded to the RAF to create an RAF Chaplaincy Service. Viener became the RAF's first Chaplain-in-Chief. He created a chaplaincy of 60 chaplains, drawn from the navy, army and civilian life. When the war ended the RAF, like the navy and army, reduced in size and so too did its chaplaincy. The RAF had just 29 chaplains by 1919, though this increased to 36 by 1931.

As a Royal Navy chaplain, Viener had originally intended that chaplains should wear uniform without rank (as naval chaplains still do to this day). However, confusion with Church Army officers and uniformed canteen workers led him to think that this solution was unworkable. As a consequence, he produced a compromise in which chaplains would wear a rank relative to the seniority or appointment within the Service. In effect, this meant that chaplains

---

3   For comprehensive lists of holders of these differing posts, together with lists of all chaplains who served in the navy up until 1978, see Taylor (1978: 484–547).

were expected to wear rank for identification and for a position within the RAF hierarchy but explicitly not to exercise executive powers which might separate the chaplain from non-commissioned ranks.

During the interwar years a pattern of RAF chaplaincy emerged which gave it a character different from the chaplaincies in the other two Services. In the army, as we have seen, chaplains have tended to be attached to regiments, following them wherever they are sent and being alongside them in whatever task they undertake. In the Royal Navy, chaplains have tended to be attached to ships and have sailed with the ship's company wherever it is sent. The Royal Air Force, in many respects, has been a more static force. RAF personnel operate from and live at RAF Stations which are, of course, immovable. The model of ministry of RAF chaplaincy, therefore, has for large parts of its history been like that of a parochial model where the community lives, works and socialises in one place. Where RAF personnel have deployed on combat operations, this has meant that some personnel from several stations 'go to war' and whilst a chaplain may go with them it is not necessarily a chaplain who already knows those who are deploying. Whilst Service personnel are away from home, the unit chaplain will still be ministering to those left at home and to the families of those who have deployed.

During the Second World War, the size of the RAF increased to over a million servicemen and women and proportionally the size of the chaplaincy increased (to over 1000 clergy). The vast majority of these clergy joined simply for the duration of war and returned to their civilian ministries thereafter. In a similar vein the chaplaincies of the Naval Chaplaincy Service and the Royal Army Chaplains' Department grew and shrank accordingly.

There is a significant and substantial body of evidence that during both World Wars armed forces' chaplains fulfilled their calling in representing the Church in the heart of the military community. Padre Noel Mellish, aged 35, was an army chaplain on 27 March 1916 when an attack on the St Eloi crater on the Ypres salient was launched. Several enormous mines were exploded under the German trenches and the British troops then attacked. They moved forward and were met by intense rifle, machine gun and artillery fire. The battalion to which Mellish was attached suffered huge losses. Over three days, Mellish repeatedly went out, under machine gun fire, to bring in the wounded. On the first day, without assistance, be rescued 10 wounded men, on the second day he brought back a further 12 and on the third day, with volunteers, he went to rescue the remaining wounded. For this he was awarded the highest award for gallantry, the Victoria Cross.

Padre Geoffrey Harding was an RAF chaplain, attached to a Mobile Radio Unit, who was on the beaches of Normandy on D-Day, 6 June 1944. He won the Military Cross for, in the words of his award's citation, 'his gallantry and disregard for his own safety'. In the carnage of the military engagement that day (there was

a 25 per cent casualty rate for those who landed on the beach), Harding walked
to the neighbouring village, to a house where a number of snipers were located,
and secured some water for those on the beach. He spent all day ministering to
those who were wounded or dying. Years later when being interviewed about
this engagement, which the military named Operation OVERLORD, Harding
remarked, 'someone told me at the time I walked up and down the beach calmly
as if I were walking up and down the aisle in the church, but that was simply due
to the fact that I am constitutionally lazy and refused to be hurried, least of all
by the enemy.'

The Reverend Christopher 'Kit' Tanner, a Royal Navy chaplain, was
aboard HMS Fiji in 1941 when it was bombed by German Junkers and Stuka
aircraft – 370 bombs were aimed at Fiji during the day. When the order came
to 'abandon ship', Kit Tanner moved to the sick bay where there were 60
wounded men. Tanner personally supervised their removal to another ship, the
one whaler which was left in service. 'He was untiring in his ministrations', said
his Captain, 'and forgot nobody'. When the time came for him to jump into
the sea he found that he had a new parish, approximately half a square mile of
choppy Mediterranean. When the men in the sea saw the two remaining British
destroyers withdraw from the scene some of them lost heart and drowned. In
the water, Kit Tanner was a constant tower of strength. He helped men too far
gone to help themselves to the floats. He administered the life-saver's shock
treatment – a well-aimed right hook to the jaw – to a young seaman in the grip
of terrible panic. He assisted a sailor with his arm blown off, who subsequently
survived. He led men in singing and the strains of 'Roll out the Barrel' could be
heard in the night. There were other songs, many of which he had heard sung in
the bar of the Gloucester Rugby Football Club.

Shortly after midnight, cheering started and torches were flashed as it
became clear that HMS Kandahar and HMS Kingston had come for them.
Aboard HMS Kandahar, there were blankets, hot drinks and cigarettes for Fiji's
survivors. Kit Tanner was brought aboard HMS Kandahar but did not relax
from his duties. There were still men in the sea who were too far gone through
exhaustion to grasp the ropes lowered to them from the destroyer. Tanner made
these men his special responsibility. Thirty-four officers and 500 men were saved
out of Fiji's total complement of 700. Nearly 30 of these men owed their lives to
Tanner. No accurate count was possible of the number of times he dived from
HMS Kandahar to bring in yet another man. Finally, only one man remained
to be brought aboard. Despite his exhaustion Padre Tanner made a last effort to
save him and brought him safely on board. When hauled up himself the padre
died within a few minutes, of exhaustion. For these acts of bravery Tanner was
posthumously awarded the Albert Medal.

For generations chaplains have played their part and served with great
distinction, devotion and courage alongside sailors, soldiers and air force

personnel. Modern-day chaplains in the armed forces have responded to a call from God, with the permission of their sending church, to exercise their ministry in the military. To do so they need to be part of a 'profession within a profession'. The Chaplain in Chief US Army in August 2011 wrote:

> We are professional pastors, and we have a total ministry to the entire community. Perhaps more than anyone else, we can provide the leadership, personal openness and acceptance, and professional expertise which commanders need in order to have a positive and healthy environment, a climate of moral responsibility, and community of openness and trust.[4]

In his book *Creative Ministry*, the priest Henri Nouwen addresses the concern between professionalism and spirituality within ministry. Nouwen wrote:

> If a minister wants to be of real help in his contact with people, he has to be a professional with special information, special training, and special skills. But if he wants to break through the chains of our manipulative world, he has to move beyond professionalism, and through self-denial and contemplation, become a faithful witness of God's covenant. (Nouwen 1971: 64)

In a continuum of service and sacrifice, chaplains in the military have demonstrated in peace and in war that they do have a special place and can be professional in the most hostile of environments. They have done so by self-denial and self-sacrifice and been recognised in the services for their faithful witness to the military community.

Lessons Identified – Insights and Reflections of Chaplains Deployed on Operations TELIC and HERRICK: Three Perspectives

The Royal Navy

Deployed naval chaplains often work in singleton jobs with no support from like-minded team members, and as a result are always 'on the job' whilst deployed. It is crucial that appropriate self-care is maintained to help prevent burnout, allow for reflection and an oasis for the spirit. Recent comments from Operation KIPION suggest that there are many in the RN who do not understand the wider contribution a chaplain can make to the life of a ship or unit, beyond

---

[4] Chaplain (Colonel) K.L. Sampson, quoting Chaplain (Major General) Donald Rutherford, Chaplain in Chief US Army, August 2011, *The Armed Forces Chaplaincy – A Profession within the Profession*. Fort McNair National Defense University, 31 July 2013.

worship services, prayers and reactive pastoral care, and need to be educated in the proactive and preventative pastoral work a chaplain can undertake to enhance the holistic care of people.

Ideally a period of shore time will be achievable before the chaplain's next deployment. This should be used to offer pastoral care to the ship's company or unit as they adjust to being back in the UK, whilst allowing the chaplain to unlatch from the ship's company or unit and tie up any loose pastoral ends before deploying again. Deploying in a singleton role carries with it a myriad of emotions and presents many challenges on both a spiritual and personal level. A cultural climate where support and advice is both offered and asked for without hesitation or embarrassment, given and received with grace and compassion, is essential for the development and fulfilment of the chaplain in their role and avoidance of a sense that chaplains are of high value but low priority. Being able to function within the deployed environment with what Leslie Newbiggin calls a 'bold humility' is key not just to identifying lessons, but being able to learn from them.

An example of this bold humility is found during 42 Commando Royal Marines' tour of Afghanistan in 2008. The Reverend Stuart Hallam wrote:

> I gave last rites to Dave and then stood outside the operating theatre and prayed for JT. Adam, the trauma consultant who was working on him, called me in. 'Do you know him, Padre?' 'Yes', I replied, 'very well, he's one of mine and a friend'. 'Then can you come in and hold his head – talk to him ... please, it may help.' I did what he asked without hesitation. I talked and prayed simultaneously.

> For two hours, JT battled for life, the hardest battle he had ever fought, but this battle was one where the overwhelming odds were against him. He didn't really have a chance. Eventually, Adam turned to me and said, 'There is nothing more we can do, it's over to you Stu.'

> I thanked the team for all that they had done and prayed for them and gave the last rites to JT. The operating theatre was awash with his blood but JT just lay there looking utterly peaceful – he was in a better place – certainly a better one than the rest of us ... . (Quoted in Thornton and Thornton 2013: 156)

The Army Perspective

From an Army perspective a chaplain will usually deploy as part of a team – which may have Tri-Service elements – for a period of six months. With pre-deployment training and post-tour leave the operational cycle usually involves a 12-month period. Reserve chaplains usually deploy to a specific unit – such as a medical field hospital – and only occasionally will deploy with their own soldiers. Team cohesion is a key strength and helps to overcome fear and isolation.

> During deployment the need for spiritual resilience was considered to be a key to successful and enduring ministry and the importance of partnering/mentoring/ shepherding of each other is vital. (AFCPB Undated)

> The Post Op Retreat is key to the 'closure' of the Team experience ... and should be conducted in a safe space suitable for decompression and normalisation – especially in terms of renewing the Priestly vocation and life after a long term on Ops. This post tour support is one factor that gives Chaplains confidence for future Ops and builds spiritual resilience. (AFCPB Undated)

A good example of spiritual resilience is found in the relationship between a wounded officer and a non-commissioned Fijian soldier:

> The first round was so close I felt it whistle past my head; the second floored me. I had no time to react. It smashed into my shoulder like a sledgehammer, pulverising bone and tissue. It travelled through my chest, snapping my ribs like matchsticks and macerating a lung. I was picked up by the force and flung several metres through the air, spinning like a ragdoll. (Wiseman 2014: 9ff)

A Fijian lance corporal dashed to help:

> I lay there looking up at the sky, struggling to breathe. The pain in my chest was becoming unbearable and I was dizzy as hell ... I felt useless and helpless ...

The Fijian soldier, Manny,

> lay across my body, using his own armour as a shield for my unprotected body ... and started to pray. He recited the psalms: ' ... and ye though I walk through the shadow of death I shall fear no evil ... '

> He repeated the Lord's Prayer over and over. There was not much else he could do for me medically, but I drew from his great strength and I moved my lips in time with his own, though I did not have the breath to keep up with the words. I reached under him and weakly held the gold crucifix my Aunty Jane had given me before I deployed to Iraq. I held the icon in my bloody fingers. ... (Wiseman 2014: 147)

The Reverend Richard Smith, an army chaplain, writes:

When appropriate, prayer has a power that is hard to define. In those difficult situations of pain and grief, somehow a simple prayer makes available to those present a spiritual well from which they draw solace and comfort. In these moments tears are common. Most of my soldiers are not devoutly religious, but a prayer to God in the midst of shock and grief appears to matter, and matter profoundly. (In Oliver 2013: 140)

The Royal Air Force Perspective

'Timely preparation for deployment is essential and the key to reducing anxiety and allowing a successful deployment' (AFCPB Undated). During deployment it is often recognised that some chaplains would have appreciated someone being identified as a point for open and honest dialogue (within confidentiality guidelines). From a spiritual perspective it is also felt important to identify at an early stage corporate prayer times with other chaplains, other Christians or both. There is also a need for each chaplain to remember why we are there and ultimately who has called us there.

Undoubtedly each chaplain's spiritual robustness is the key to a good and productive deployment. It should be seen as paramount for each chaplain to keep their faith nurtured and healthy prior to, during and after each deployment.

Smith (in Oliver 2013: 146) quotes Rabbi Stephen Roberts and Revd William Ashley Sr, in their book *Disaster Spiritual Care*, that:

It is often the simple presence of a person of God that provides healing and comfort. The ministry of solidarity and accompaniment, of silence in the face of tragedy, of surrender to the God of our understanding, is often the most we can do in such situations. (Roberts and Ashley 2008: xviii)

During the conflict in Afghanistan (Operation HERRICK, 2001–2014) chaplains of all three Services were deployed to be the chaplain attached to the UK Medical Group, most specifically to the hospital at Camp Bastion. Many of the chaplains who carried out this work regard it as one of the most profound times of their ministry. They were moved and changed by what they experienced, for good or for ill. One RAF chaplain, the Reverend Nick Barry, when reflecting on his time at the hospital, talked about the ministry of prayer, presence and proclamation in saying the Prayer of Commendation at the point of death in the hospital's Emergency Department. Echoing the words of the RAF Chaplains' Branch motto *ministrare non ministrari* (to serve, not to be served), Padre Barry recalls the simple but powerful words said to him in conversation with a military nurse. Following the death of yet another soldier, who had died having been brought into the hospital grievously injured, she said 'I'm not religious padre but those words that you say at the moment of death allow us to dare to hope that there might be something better than this.'

This conversation took place in a setting not so dissimilar from a scene from the television programme *MASH*, with the life-saving medical equipment and blood-stained evidence of the fragility of human life all around. Padre Barry noted that he became aware of a

> significant evangelistic component to the words of commendation which are not so easily apparent at, for instance, the sterile, gentle bedside in a nursing home in the UK where death might not be unexpected. Standing on the blood-soaked floor in Bastion hospital there was no clear teaching or preaching, just the liturgical moment where ministry offered a glimpse away from the present location, a glimpse of redemption.

In all three Services the loss of a colleague is felt deeply, especially when that person is killed in action:

> In these situations many soldiers come to the chaplain to speak about how they are feeling. Some speak about regrets, their questions, their fears and their guilt. Others come because they are experiencing grief for the first time and they are not sure whether their emotions and physical sensations are normal. Such conversations are not necessarily religious, but are born out of the Church's desire to care for the soldier's most human needs. Sometimes prayer is appropriate, sometimes not. Some soldiers want to talk about heaven, others suspect there is nothing but darkness. Each soldier, religious or not, uses the chaplain to process his or her thoughts and adjust to a new reality, which sadly often includes the pain of loss and the process of grief. (Smith quoted in Oliver 2013: 143)

The Future

On 26 October 2014, after 13 years in Afghanistan and 8 years of bloody fighting in Helmand that cost the lives of 453 British Service men and women, Camp Bastion, which was once the largest British military base in the world, was finally closed. At its busiest Bastion housed up to 14,000 troops and more than a dozen chaplains. In the height of the fighting there were up to 600 aircraft sorties per day. According to the BBC News the Afghan war cost more than £20bn. Today across the country 6.7 million Afghan children go to school, nearly half of them girls. At the same time health care has improved and life expectancy is longer. The Taliban threat has been substantially curtailed.

With the conclusion of Operation HERRICK, for the British Armed Forces the shift from a long-term war in Afghanistan meant a transition to contingency operations where troops must be prepared to react to crisis around the world, be it overflying Syria; patrolling the Strait of Hormuz (which is considered one of the most strategic, if not the most strategic, straits of water on the planet); providing short-term training teams to the Middle East; or delivering real-time health care and medical support to Ebola victims in Sierra Leone. The range of challenge and threat endures and chaplains of all three services need to be ready and willing to serve alongside.

At the closure of Camp Bastion Brigadier Rob Thompson, the most senior British officer in Helmand, said:

> I think there are three emotions at play. We are proud of what our service men and women have done. We are happy and sad. We are happy we are all going back to our families but we are also sad because we are leaving behind some friends who were courageous on the battlefield. We have made a difference on the streets of Britain and in Afghanistan. This is not defeat or victory. We have an army that is hugely adaptable and can adjust in step as we enter a new campaign.[5]

The challenge for chaplaincy in all three services is how we are to also step up to the mark and prepare for contingency. Inevitably there will be greater joint force commitments where chaplains of all services will serve together. There will also be a great reliance upon Reservist chaplains and pressure upon a diminishing pool of clerical manpower. Questions about humanism and world faith religion will prevail and need to be addressed. So too will the demand from each of the single services for chaplains to serve 'cloth on cloth': the Naval Chaplaincy Service with the RN, the Royal Army Chaplains' Department with the Army and the Royal Air Force Chaplains' Branch with the RAF. More will be asked but more will be given by chaplains who feel called by God to serve alongside those who serve in the Forces of the Crown.

References

AFCPB (Armed Forces Chaplaincy Policy Board) Ops Group (Undated), *Chaplains' Lessons Identified*. Joint Operations Publication.

Brumwell, M.P. (1943), *The Army Chaplain: The Royal Army Chaplains' Department and the Duties of Chaplains and Morale*. London: Adam and Charles Black.

Down, B. (1989), *On Course Together: The Churches' Ministry in the Maritime World Today*. Norwich: The Canterbury Press.

---

[5]   *Daily Mail* online, 26 October 2014.

Johnstone, T. and Hagerty, J. (1996), *The Cross on the Sword: Catholic Chaplains in the Forces*. London: Geoffrey Chapman.

Louden, S.H. (1996), *Chaplains in Conflict: The Role of Army Chaplains since 1914*. London: Avon Books.

Nouwen, H. (1971), *Creative Ministry*. Garden City, NY: Doubleday.

Oliver, S. (2013), *Inside Grief*. London: SPCK.

Roberts, S.B. and Ashley, W.W.C. (2008), *Disaster Spiritual Care: Practical Clergy Responses to Community, Regional and National Tragedy*. Woodstock, VT: SkyLight Paths.

Smith, W.E.L. (1961), *The Navy and Its Chaplains in the Days of Sail*. Toronto: Ryerson Press.

Smyth, J. (1968), *In This Sign Conquer: The Story of the Army Chaplains*. London: Mowbray.

Taylor, G. (1978), *The Sea Chaplains: A History of the Chaplains of the Royal Navy*. Oxford: Oxford Illustrated Press.

Thornton, L. and Thornton P. (2013), *Helmand: The Diaries of Front-Line Soldiers*. Botley: Osprey Publishing.

Wiseman, D. (2014), *Helmand to the Himalayas*. Botley: Osprey Publishing.

Chapter 16

Contextual Issues: War and Peace

Andrew Totten

Introduction

'People tell academics and clergy to look at what the "real world" is like,' wrote
The Reverend Professor John McManners, editor of *The Oxford Illustrated
History of Christianity* and Chaplain of All Souls College. 'But behind their
world is the real world they have forgotten: the battlefield. Here is the ultimate
reason of the social order written in letters of lead and shards of steel' (2002:
217). McManners was not an army chaplain (or 'padre') but an infantry
officer who fought throughout the Second World War. Its brutality affected
him profoundly:

> When we looked over the parapet there were about a dozen dead Germans,
> slashed to bits with grenade fragments and bayonet thrusts. That night, I took
> out one of my few Forces letter forms and wrote to John Brewis, my old tutor
> at Oxford and now Principal of St Chad's theological college at Durham, near
> home. It was to say that, if I ever got back, I intended to be ordained, and I wanted
> him to remind me. (2002: 59)

Wartime experience led to personal commitment but brought McManners's
'conundrum-solving' theology to a close. 'The sight of the dead bodies in the
sandbagged post at Tobruk ended that ... In face of this, you cannot believe in
God, the God of the deists,' recounts his memoir:

> But you can, almost in despair, turn to the God who suffers with his creation,
> accepting the burden of sin that arises from human freedom, and taking it on
> himself. Religious apologetics begin from Jesus on the cross: the Christian life is
> allegiance to him. (2002: 217)

Those remarks are reminiscent of Geoffrey Studdert Kennedy, the padre better
known as 'Woodbine Willie'. For Studdert Kennedy in the First World War, as
for McManners in the Second – and as for more recent military ordinands –
faith remained tenable in conflict only by envisaging God as a fellow sufferer.
The idea, associated with Jürgen Moltmann's *Crucified God* (1972), now seems

to be theological common sense, but it has military roots. Moltmann himself thought *The Hardest Part*, Studdert Kennedy's first book (1919), deserved greater attention than Karl Barth's *Epistle to the Romans*, published around the same time:

> for the theology of the suffering God is more important than the theology of the God who is 'Wholly Other'. What was able to withstand the test of the battlefields of Flanders and created faith even in the hells there was the discovery of the crucified God. (1981: 35)

The crucified God never wielded a bayonet, though. Soldiers do not just become victims, they create them too. With sentimentalism akin to that which views modern British soldiers all as heroes or victims, an overwrought Studdert Kennedy ended up fusing the suffering Christ with his deified Tommy:

> The muddy bloody hero of the trenches is showing us Who is the real King ... Beside the wounded tattered soldier who totters down to this dressing-station with one arm hanging loose, an earthly king looks paltry and absurd ... I only see God in Christ, and these men have shown me – *Him.*
>
> I have seen in them His glory, glory as of the Only Begotten of the Father, full of grace and truth.
>
> I am sure of this God. I know him. I love him. I worship Him. I would die for Him and be glad. (1919: 71–2)

The victimhood of soldiers has a genealogy going back through Shakespeare's *Henry V* to Homer's *Iliad*, but since the Crimean War media coverage has tended to magnify the plight of soldiers. In the Crimea, as in other conflicts, disease took a heavier toll than enemy action, and hospital work dominated chaplains' ministry. That overlap of military and hospital chaplaincy is still valued. When numerous soldiers were being casevaced from Helmand, for example, two consecutive padres at the Queen Elizabeth Hospital in Birmingham, Steven Whiting (army) and Eddie Wynn (RAF), were each appointed MBE. Yet death and injury are inflicted *by* as well as on soldiers. Armed conflict generally entails killing and any military force aims to be better at it than the enemy. Soldiering generates issues for chaplaincy to do not just with the end of life but also the ending of life. Hospital chaplains routinely encounter death, but not institutional killing. British prison chaplains pastor inmates who have killed, but not wardens with the power of capital punishment. Moreover, medical and penal as well as educational institutions have core purposes which (social control critiques notwithstanding) can be readily harmonised with the

Christian impulse to promote flourishing lives. By contrast, padres are located within a state institution whose core business the Church has recurrently found contentious. And the state has the upper hand. Chris Hedges has suggested that 'because we in modern society have walked away from institutions that stand outside the state to find moral guidance and spiritual direction, we turn to the state in times of war ... the institutions of state become, for many, the centre of worship in wartime' (2003: 146). It is a salutary warning for military chaplains, on the boundary of state and Church and civil society, to be mindful of the Gospel as they shape worship, offer care and preach amidst conflict and diminished churchgoing.

The spiritual, pastoral and moral landscape surveyed in this chapter has a Christian focus as that remains the principal form of British military chaplaincy. I write as an Anglican too, mindful that other denominations, not to mention faiths, have their own traditions of reflection on war, as well as different institutional stories by which they have reached accommodation with the state and its resort to force. (The caricature of a generic 'Church of Army' is exactly that.) This chapter deals chiefly with the army against the early 21st century backdrop of Iraq and Afghanistan. It is written in the past tense as British ground combat operations have concluded in both countries, but the profession of the 'parishioners' means many of the issues are perennial. Where otherwise unreferenced, I am drawing on personal experience.

Chaplains, Soldiers and Religion

No word formally describes a padre's 'parish'. However, 'chapel' and its cognate 'chaplain' originated in medieval military labels for the tent that housed, and the priests who carried, the 'cappa' or cloak that was a relic of Saint Martin (Bachrach 2001: 150). Returning to their roots, chapels emerged on expeditionary bases as canvas tents, but within blast-proof walls. Camp Bastion's hospital chaplain as the base was being established in Helmand province observed that 'the church became a chaplaincy centre where people often came along to be alone for a while or to talk to a Padre' (Brown 2007: 62). Civil servants and contractors, a growing presence alongside the military, sought padres out too. Assisted by their quartermasters, successive chaplains furnished each chapel in a traditional style, typically with an altar, lectern, font, benches, denominational service books, votive candle stand, music system and occasionally air conditioning. At outlying bases, which lacked dedicated chapels, the cookhouse or gym would be pressed into service, or soldiers would gather around a focal point like an improvised cross or a shrine to the fallen. Generally speaking, the more austere the location was, the greater the attendance – of both participants and observers. One sunset communion service took place while Muslim soldiers of the Afghan

National Army sat nearby to watch. Tensions on that base eased afterwards, as the Afghans had for the first time recognised their British mentors as being men of prayer too. (The likely response of extremists aside, padres' Christian identity and practice in both Iraq and Afghanistan drew only hospitality and curiosity from religious leaders and their people: it was the occasional officer revealing his atheism who attracted the hostility of locals.)

Many services began with a dozen men standing in a semicircle and grew through word of mouth. Given that commuting between bases was problematic, padres aimed to leave resources in the hands of junior commanders to lead services at significant moments. Video footage shows a sergeant conducting a vigil service for his platoon in the aftermath of a soldier's death, incorporating a eulogy, the 23rd psalm, an act of remembrance, the Lord's Prayer and – in lieu of a blessing – the final words, 'to your duties, fall out'. Eulogies written by younger soldiers not infrequently closed with religious overtones: 'until we meet again at the bar in the sky'; 'sleep well buddy, you finally got your wings!'; 'so rest easy and I'll see you again one day'.[1] Baptisms happened from time to time, but probably many unbaptised soldiers, albeit bearing religious tattoos, received communion as they copied a friend and stepped forward to receive. This bothered some chaplains in terms of ecclesiastical discipline, but was generally resolved by recognising the situation as *in extremis*.

In 2013, 83.9 per cent of soldiers were recorded as Christian, but the figure is in decline.[2] The discrepancy between soldiers' personal beliefs and their stated religion has probably always been sizeable, though. Their historic reputation for godlessness is undeserved (Snape 2005: 236–42), but British soldiers remain sceptical of any official line, be it religious, military or political. General Jonathan Bailey disclosed how a 'senior MOD official', when discussing the description of Britain's military as a 'force for good', explained that 'this branding was legitimate because it was necessary to make the troops feel that they were taking part in morally worthy operations' (Bailey et al. 2013: 6). That was as naive as it was cynical. But soldiers rarely get to test politicians or commanders as they test their padres. The secularist misses a basic point: soldiers have long been dubious about padres' religious body of knowledge. Jesting and testing are hallmarks of the relationship. While tiresome if it dominates the chaplaincy repertoire, banter assists in building bonds of affection and trust. A former Commanding Officer (CO), even while making his case for secular chaplaincy, sensed the risk of wrecking a spiritual ecosystem:

---

[1]   https://www.gov.uk/government/fields-of-operation/afghanistan#fatalities (accessed 10 July 2014).

[2]   https://www.gov.uk/government/uploads/system/uploads/attachment_data/file/280431/2013.pdf (accessed 21 July 2014).

We don't want some clipboard-wielding, Equal-Opportunities-trained, pseudo-Trades-Union-Rep, 'secular chaplain' telling COs how to behave. Neither do I. We already have chaplains who prove that they can perform this sensitive role alongside, but outwith, the chain-of-command giving support and guidance and acting as the focal point for our moral questions and acts of sacred group-bonding. I am merely pointing out that, purely in terms of operational effectiveness, a secular chaplaincy would be better. (Quinn 2014: 54)

Operational effectiveness can certainly mean the difference between life and death in battle (though soldiers may wish to prepare for both eventualities). Equipping, training and planning are crucial. However, engendering effectiveness from within what the military calls the 'moral component of fighting power' is much less tangible, and assessing it is neither neutral nor objective. Anthropologically, the problem is that 'when secular organizations demand sacrifice, every member has a right to ask for a cost–benefit analysis' (Haidt 2012: 257). Moreover, an army can be operationally effective but still experience strategic failure. As in other organisations, 'what seems on first sight to be the solid, defining basis for evaluating organizational and managerial effectiveness turns out to be in large measure a matter of point of view and faith' (Pattison 1997: 32). Padres are nevertheless feeling the obligation to quantify their contribution and effect. Padre Peter King's study of soldiers' religiosity in Helmand is a pioneering example. Over 45 per cent of his respondents carried or wore a symbol of faith (2013: 56). Six of seven chaplains in his focus group 'confirmed a strong demand for religious items' (2013: 22). Three Free Church chaplains 'found such requests challenging ... yet facilitated them despite their own (contrary) understanding or tradition' (2013: 22). Another chaplain observed that 'giving them isn't enough – they often ask us to bless them' (2013: 22). The same chaplain, recognising a need for 'something tangible', decided that every service would be a Eucharist.

'Relatively few Welsh Guardsmen were religious,' noted Toby Harnden (2011: 400), 'but a number became more godly during the tour'. It appears that combat conditions do still prompt religious interest and practice, even if these are likely to prove transient and ambiguous. Soldiers rarely want to give their lives over to a belief system, but they are happy to quarry religion for tangible bits and pieces to add meaning to life and death. In Helmand, a table at each chapel's entrance would be laden with New Testaments, crucifixes and rosaries, prayer cards and 'dog tags' (bearing a religious verse or cross-shaped hole). Such items had to be replenished frequently as soldiers pocketed them without necessarily attending services. Padre Robin Richardson had a cottage industry making pendant crosses for paratroopers out of discarded perimeter wire. Nine thousand cards inscribed with 16 Air Assault Brigade's collect and the 23rd psalm went out during the same tour. The search for peace of mind seemed to be as prevalent as talismanic protection.

Candles acquired significance too, not just with soldiers but also among families back at barracks. At a homecoming service in St Edmundsbury Cathedral, candles representing soldiers who had died were borne to the sanctuary by their best friends to be placed on the altar. Yet candles (and cathedrals too) come at a cost, and difficulties would occasionally surface when budget managers were approached to spend public money on religious items. Such concerns generally dissipated as the value, particularly to the bereaved, became clear. In the meantime, new linkages were being forged between brigades and cathedrals, as well as between chaplains and chapters, and cathedrals seem set to continue fostering in soldiers a sense of religious occasion and awe. This happens in smaller ways too. An injured soldier remarked to a chaplain visiting him in hospital that the sight of his own padre, Nick Todd, wearing clerical robes despite the fierce heat in Helmand (rather than simply draping a preaching scarf over his combats) was almost enough to make him believe in God. Formal dress along with traditional hymns and language possibly helps to 'constitute a worthy tribute to the service of the living or courage of the fallen' (Ball 2013: 128). In the decades ahead, insofar as veterans look to liturgy to make sense of their war experiences, it may need to take this shape.

Sometimes no words are necessary at all. After a soldier was killed by an improvised explosive device (IED), a CO wrote of his padre: 'Antony sits next to me on the short wooden bench. It is comforting to have a priest with Joe. The bible is on the bench between us, its curled, soft-bound edges and camouflaged cover clearly visible' (Harrison 2011: 21). COs felt the loss of men under their command keenly. Repatriation ceremonies could incorporate extracts from eulogies as well as regimental collects but COs sometimes chafed against the centre's efforts to maintain a degree of uniformity. Yet this was also about equal treatment of the dead, regardless of regiment or rank. Chaplains had to accept restrictions on liturgical freedom too. Sermons, for example, were out of place at parades that recurred frequently, with thousands stood throughout in high temperatures. Heat caused one major shift in the repatriation template when it was discovered that the practice of displaying coffins during daytime services was rendering remains unfit for viewing by relatives at home. The outcome saw a separation at Camp Bastion between a vigil service on the parade ground in late afternoon and a 'ramp ceremony' at night as the coffin was borne onto the aircraft, preceded by a padre saying sentences of scripture. Engine noise rendered the words inaudible, but simply the sight of the padre amidst repatriation rituals seemed sufficient, perhaps even becoming a defining image of these campaigns.

Being on the Ground

Ecclesiastes cautions that 'the race is not to the swift, nor the battle to the strong', but young officers in particular can feel that they are impervious to time and chance. Exercising chaplaincy to the swift and strong has to reckon with that aversion to vulnerability. Crucial to this pastoral care is the ability to respond meaningfully. At Camp Bastion a young soldier whose friend had been killed was sent to see a psychiatric nurse as well as his padre:

> The psychologist asked me about my family and growing up and stuff and then about Hammy and what happened when the IED hit Scotty's wagon. I'm not really into God and wouldn't normally go and see the padre, but he was better. He made everything sound so much clearer. He'd been out on the ground as well so he knew what it was like. (Harnden 2011: 399–400)

Being 'out on the ground' informed and lent credibility to Padre Deiniol Morgan's words. It also carried considerable risk. A Main Operating Base in Afghanistan was a relatively safe place, but life became increasingly hazardous as one moved beyond a Forward Operating Base to reach a Patrol Base and finally a Checkpoint, where just a few soldiers might be living. That nomenclature reflects a period when the UK presence, in tandem with a US surge, reached its height. The pastoral challenges and opportunities evolved concomitantly, as they do in all but brief military campaigns, but chaplaincy often comes into its own when improvisation rather than regulation is the order of the day. A lag in policy can cause tensions, though. For example, chaplaincy policy initially barred padres from accompanying soldiers on foot patrols (except where there was a pressing pastoral need to reach a remote base). Intended to protect padres from harm and prevent them from getting caught up in combat at a time when fighting patrols were prevalent, the approach became outdated as districts were secured and patrols switched focus from fighting insurgents to supporting locals. The number of locations also increased exponentially: reaching smaller bases routinely meant walking to them. Above all, when IEDs emerged as the biggest risk in Helmand, padres who walked in their soldiers' footsteps found new depths to ministry amongst them. A policy resolution of sorts was eventually reached, but not without friction between those who wished to keep padres safe and those who wished to unfetter them. It was a minor echo of the First World War, when Kitchener had initially banned chaplains from the front line to avoid them getting in the way and using up resources. By late 1915 the worth of padres sharing their people's dangers was clear to both commanders and men. Studdert Kennedy had advised:

> Live with the men, go everywhere they go. Make up your mind you will share all their risks, and more if you can do any good. The line is the key to the whole business. Work in the very front and they will listen to you; but if you stay behind, you're wasting your time ... Take a box of fags in your haversack and a great deal of love in your heart, and go up to them: laugh with them, joke with them. You can pray with them sometimes but pray for them always. (Quoted in Holman 2012: 165)

That much-quoted passage (with several variants) has become central to chaplaincy rhetoric, but implementing the advice nowadays comes up against 'duty of care' issues concerning the degree of risk to which unarmed non-combatants should be exposed. The Royal Army Chaplains' Department (RAChD) issued its own tentative guidance in the event of a chaplain being killed (Robbins *c*.2007). While stressing that repatriation procedures of the wider military would be followed, the document proposed a 'Chaplaincy Visitor' to liaise between the family and the RAChD. The Chaplain-General would wish to visit the family 'at the earliest opportunity' and would attend the repatriation. A representative of the deceased chaplain's sending church would also be invited to the ceremony, except where numbers would have to be limited, as in 'the event of large numbers of casualties being repatriated'.

Physical dangers aside – and converse to the experience of McManners earlier – battlefields can also put vocation and faith in jeopardy. When training new padres I had reservations over how well their previous ministerial formation had prepared them for Helmand (to which they could soon be deployed). At Amport House (the Armed Forces Chaplaincy Centre) the initial training was extended from four to six weeks to allow for additional ethical and theological reflection on the world they were about to enter. Sandhurst taught them basic skills on a course that was expanded from four to ten weeks. As it transpired, some of those new padres, whose sense of calling had been stirred by coverage of the 'War on Terror', would set an example to more experienced colleagues. Yet some had arrived from civilian ministry with little experience of death in a raw form, let alone the prospect of their own. Padre Christopher Broddle conducted pre- and post-deployment retreats for padres during this expeditionary era. He observed that clergy towards the catholic end of the spectrum were generally more theologically prepared to countenance their death; a few were almost too accepting of it. For some, there were fears of receiving incapacitating injuries or leaving a family bereaved and unsupported. Others wondered how much they could withstand physically as well as spiritually. During one ambush an Afghan interpreter informed me that the Taliban – after they had killed the soldiers – would be especially cruel to the two of us. I recited the *Nunc Dimittis* inwardly and reassured a young soldier who asked what the interpreter was saying. In turn I was somehow consoled that, being among Royal Irish soldiers that day, the last voices I might hear were in the accents of home. A key factor in personal endurance is that degree to which padres feel at home within their regiments: alienation corrodes resilience. A sense of being part of military and chaplaincy tradition can be sustaining too, particularly where literary associations arise. The first hostile shots I heard in Helmand prompted not fear, strangely, but recollection of what C.S. Lewis felt on his initial encounter with battle: 'This is War. This is what Homer wrote about' (1955: 185).

Integrity and Influence

It is often stressed that a disciplined prayer life is crucial on operations, but as Padre Philip Bosher observed in a candid account of his emotions prior to the Iraq War, religious observance can be hurtful as well as helpful:

> At church services words took on new meanings, the language of sacrifice that peppers our liturgy seemed to hit me in the face at every turn of the page. I found myself unable to sing hymns, as I was unsure that I could hold myself together in public ... I attended evensong at the Cathedral, and the choirs that sang and the history of prayer in that building ... began to build the spiritual foundation that was to see me through. I needed to call upon the traditions of my sending church to anchor my spirituality that had suddenly seemed so fragile. Canterbury was to be the last television I saw in the UK: as I boarded the 'plane, it was the day of Rowan Williams' enthronement. (2004: 24–5)

The Archbishop of Canterbury subsequently sent a pastoral letter to chaplains serving in the Gulf. 'There has been a great deal of public discussion about the events now unfolding; the decisions that have been made have been hard choices between different kinds of risk and cost,' he wrote.

> But that is not the focus of this letter and we pray for those who carry the great burden of responsibility for making key judgements in these matters ....

> Few join the armed forces without having thought deeply about the personal cost of service or of the possibility of being put in harm's way and the Church has never shrunk from sending its clergy to serve as chaplains wherever military people find themselves. You stand in a long and honourable tradition of Christians bearing witness to the love of Christ in hard and dangerous places.[3]

---

[3]   http://rowanwilliams.archbishopofcanterbury.org/articles.php/1253/archbishop-pastoral-letter-to-forces-chaplains (accessed 17 February 2014).

Yet a reality of chaplaincy is that not all padres live up to rhetoric about 'honourable tradition' (any more than all army officers do). Moreover, the reality of life in these 'hard and dangerous places' is often mundane – patrolling, 'stagging on', sleeping, cooking and eating, washing and cleaning, keeping fit, writing letters home. 'Incarnational ministry' can be a conceit. In 'bearing witness to the love of Christ', the temptation for the padre, to paraphrase Christopher Swift, is 'to colonize the experience of the [soldier], or build the [soldier's] story into a tool for professional power' (2014: 178). The risk of this very chapter is that it may give the impression of padres constantly engaged in religious activities, or of soldiers suddenly discovering religion en masse. Photographs in particular can promote this perspective (which suits institutional publicity and justification). Avoiding such agendas entails padres finding niches, often among domestic chores, and sharing and responding to situations and conversations as they arise. In his Second World War memoir, Sydney Jary compared platoon life to a 'closed monastic existence' where sufferance, a quiet mind, a sense of the ridiculous, and a reasonable standard of fitness were key qualities (1998: 117). Before the Iraq War, Padre Angus MacLeod received this personal advice from Jary:

> Don't get in the way ... You must exude peace and down to earth common sense. Avoid fuss, drama and acrimony. Soldiers must feel safe with you ... Always be cheerful – no moods – the soldiers will watch you and you will find influence with them far greater than you have yet experienced. You must be a strong soul. (2004: 45–6)

Influence may indeed emerge, but so too can a heightened sense of comradeship, and with it a risk to influence. For that sense of belonging, and indeed the very personality traits that help padres get alongside their soldiers, when coupled with the chaos and disorientation of conflict, can inhibit moral censure and challenge. Following the public inquiry into Baha Mousa's death in British custody in Iraq in September 2003, an 'ethical tool kit' prepared by the BMA recognised that doctors in the armed forces are 'likely to identify closely with, and experience strong loyalty towards, the unit or service of which they are a part'. However, it proceeded to stress that 'doctors' professional obligations require them to prioritise their ethical duties to their patients over and above their responsibilities and loyalties to the military'.[4] *The Report of the Baha Mousa Inquiry* criticised the battalion's padre as well as its doctor. It found that he 'must have seen the shocking condition of the Detainees ... He ought to have intervened immediately, or reported it up the chain of command but, in fact, it seems he did not have the courage to do either' (Gage 2011: 112). Commanders

---

4   http://bma.org.uk/practical-support-at-work/ethics/armed-forces-ethical-decision-making-toolkit (accessed 13 July 2014).

at all levels should nurture their padres as truth-tellers; padres in turn should recognise (contrary to Jary's advice) that there are occasions to get in the way. Particularly in the eyes of the media, the 'key judgements' mentioned by Rowan Williams do not reside just at governmental level.

Michael Burleigh commented that we should 'accept that since wars are going to be around for a long time, we need to be prepared to wage them, while seeking to do so in a just and proportionate fashion, with officers in firm control of men who might be tempted to stray on to the dark side'. He added that 'the job I'd like least is probably that of an armed forces chaplain' (2010: 75). Arresting atrocity must certainly take into account that 'the nature of belonging in armies and armed groups in war is deeply religious and is sometimes more akin to cults than other peacetime institutions' (Slim 2007: 240). Yet modern Christian spirituality is increasingly pacifist. Bringing this to bear on soldiers – labouring the sinfulness of endeavours to which their training is geared – will never encourage reflection on their immediate battlefield responsibilities. The enduring challenge for padres is to commend faith in a way that is meaningful to soldiers and yet keeps combat's dark glamour in check, postponing the point at which men begin to kill for pleasure or out of hatred rather than necessity.

Beyond Theory

Caring for those caught up in war is a prerequisite for worshippers of a suffering God. However, pastoral care at this particular coalface has a moral mineshaft. To restate the preliminary point, soldiers are not simply 'caught up' in war: they also wage it. McManners came to believe the starting point was Jesus on the cross; more fruitful may be the Good Samaritan and his actions had he arrived in time to encounter the robbers. Western just war theory is essentially an extended meditation on precisely this: on how, when an enemy is harming a neighbour, we can nevertheless show love to both. Helping recruits to reflect on what this entails is part of the teaching ministry of padres across the training regiments. However, 'nobody is ever going to invent an ethics class that makes people behave ethically after they step out of the classroom' (Haidt 2012: 90). A sermon may still briefly have that effect, but soldiers' disinclination to embrace godliness is more typical of padres' experience. Soldiers do remain jealous of their reputations, though. Some wish to be feared but few wish to be unloved, and if nurtured without love they may well struggle to show love to neighbours, let alone enemies. Perhaps it is insofar as individual and corporate spiritual support and pastoral care help soldiers to feel they are loved, and that they are accountable *beyond* their groups too, that the moral influence of chaplaincy has its best chance of enduring.

Commencing his magisterial *In Defence of War*, Nigel Biggar noted that his task was 'to think and write out of the place – historical, cultural, emotional, imaginative – that has, with all its many limitations, been given me' (2013: 2). Where chaplaincy is concerned – this book notwithstanding – the task is not academic, but the place remains primary. Shortly after a patrol during which I witnessed bayonets being fixed to engage the enemy, the soldiers asked for a church service. Missile cases served as makeshift pews and an altar. To the liturgy's dominical commands of loving God and neighbour was added the commandment to 'love your enemy'. The men then queued to receive communion. For soldiers and padres who seek to minister to them, just war theory is never just theoretical.

References

Bachrach, B.S. (2001), *Early Carolingian Warfare. Prelude to Empire*. Philadelphia: University of Pennsylvania Press.

Bailey, J., Iron, R. and Strachan, H. (eds) (2013), *British Generals in Blair's Wars*. Farnham: Ashgate Publishing Limited.

Ball, J. (2013), 'O Hear Us When We Cry to Thee': Liturgy in the Current Operational Context. In Todd, A. (ed.), *Military Chaplaincy in Contention. Chaplains, Churches and the Morality of Conflict*. Farnham: Ashgate Publishing Limited, 113–32.

Biggar, N. (2013), *In Defence of War*. Oxford: Oxford University Press.

Bosher, P. (2004), A personal account of going to war. *Royal Army Chaplains' Department Journal*, 43, 24–7.

Brown, D. (2007), Herrick IV – a wilderness experience. *Royal Army Chaplains' Department Journal*, 46, 61–6.

Burleigh, M. (2010), Is God on our side? Morality in World War Two (an edited version of the Annual Basil Liddell Hart Lecture). *Standpoint*, November.

Gage, W. (chairman) (2011), *The Baha Mousa Public Inquiry Report Volume III*. London: The Stationary Office.

Haidt, J. (2012), *The Righteous Mind. Why Good People are Divided by Politics and Religion*. London: Allen Lane.

Harnden, T. (2011), *Dead Men Risen. The Welsh Guards and the Real Story of Britain's War in Afghanistan*. London: Quercus.

Harrison, A. (2011), 'Flight of an Angel'. *Royal Army Chaplains' Department Journal*, 50, 21–2.

Hedges, C. (2003), *War Is A Force That Gives Us Meaning*. New York: Anchor Books.

Holman, B. (2012), *Woodbine Willie: An Unsung Hero of World War One*. Oxford: Lion Books.

Jary, S. (1998), *18 Platoon*. Bristol: Sydney Jary Limited.

King, P.W.S. (2013), *Faith in a Foxhole?* Unpublished thesis for MTh in Chaplaincy Studies, University of Cardiff.

Lewis, C.S. (1955), *Surprised by Joy*. London: Geoffrey Bles.

MacLeod, A. (2004), 'That which is most personal, is most universal'. *Royal Army Chaplains' Department Journal*, 43, 45–8.

McManners, J. (2002). *Fusilier: Recollections and Reflections 1939–1945*. Norwich: Michael Russell Publishing Ltd.

Moltmann, J. (1981), *The Trinity and the Kingdom of God*. London: SCM Press.

Pattison, S. (1997), *The Faith of the Managers: When Management Becomes Religion*. London: Cassell.

Quinn, L. (2014), What has God got to do with military capability? *British Army Review*, 160, 46–57.

Robbins, S. (c.2007), *Procedures to be Followed in the Event of an Army Chaplain Being Killed on Operations*. Upavon: Ministry of Defence Chaplains (Army).

Slim, H. (2007), *Killing Civilians: Method, Madness and Morality in War*. London: Hurst.

Snape, M. (2005), *The Redcoat and Religion. The Forgotten History of the British Soldier from the Age of Marlborough to the Eve of the First World War*. London: Routledge.

Studdert Kennedy, G.A. (1919), *The Hardest Part*. London: Hodder and Stoughton.

Swift, C. (2014). *Hospital Chaplaincy in the Twenty-First Century. The Crisis of Spiritual Care on the NHS*, 2nd edition. Farnham: Ashgate Publishing Limited.

Chapter 17
Case Study

Asim Hafiz

Introduction

This case study brings together two strands of my work as the Muslim (civilian) Chaplain to the military. The first strand is my work to increase understanding within the Armed Forces, in society at large and in British Muslim communities of the important and committed role of Muslim personnel serving in the Armed Forces. The second strand is the pastoral, moral and spiritual care I offer to those men and women. The two strands met in the particular role I exercised following the death of LCpl Jabron Hashmi, the only Muslim member of the Armed Forces to be killed in Afghanistan, on 1 July 2006 (to whom this chapter is dedicated).

Promoting Understanding

In 2005 *The Muslim News* advertised a vacancy for a Muslim (civilian) chaplain to the military. It was a pivotal move by the Ministry of Defence as until then all military chaplains were either Christian or Jewish. The recruitment of the Muslim chaplain to the military was done alongside the recruitment of the Buddhist, Hindu and Sikh civilian chaplains to the military. This paved the way for military chaplaincy in the UK to begin to contemplate and reflect on pastoral care and religious practices of military personnel from a multifaith perspective.

At the time I was in my third year of service as a prison chaplain at HMP Wandsworth, having previously worked as a health care chaplain. I raised awareness amongst my Muslim colleagues in many sectors of this new role in another important institution in British society. To my surprise, the response I received from my Muslim peers was not at all favourable. 'You can't work for the military because all they do is kill people', 'You are not allowed to work for an organisation that is killing other Muslims in Iraq and Afghanistan' and 'There are no Muslims in the military' are just some of the responses I received.

Though others were hesitantly supportive of this new role they were not prepared to apply and serve in this very 'misunderstood' sector of the British establishment. I was shocked at the resistance and it was this that made me more resolute to consider the idea of being a chaplain to the military. My role would not be about condoning or condemning war whilst working with soldiers, rather about being there for the human being at times of difficulty and need. Often, when talking about my role as an Imam to the British Armed Forces, I would say, 'just because one joins the military that does not mean that the person loses his or her soul or spirit'. All this created in me a sense of responsibility and duty to God and society and a kind of calling. So I prayed, applied, waited for God to decide what he wanted me to do, and was appointed.

What convinced me to pursue a vocation in the Armed Forces was the knowledge that there were Muslims serving within the British military who were willing to defend and protect Britain and its people – all people in Britain. The defence and protection of people's lives and property, and the promotion of justice and fairness, are all Islamic ethics. So for me, there was no contradiction in being a chaplain for the Muslims serving within the military. It was important that, just as other personnel, they also had access to religious, spiritual and pastoral support and guidance from their own faith perspective.

Within months of taking up my post it was clear that a key challenge was the small number of Muslims within the military, who were spread out across the world. Many did not know that there were other Muslims in the military, there was no opportunity to meet each other and it was difficult to develop a community of the 'faithful' in order enhance spirituality, learning and camaraderie.

I first addressed this by introducing the annual Armed Forces Moral and Spiritual Development Course at Amport House and the annual Armed Forces Eid Gathering.

Secondly, as part of a dynamic and long-term approach, I set up the vision of founding a group which would be able to meet the special needs of Muslims serving within the military and veterans. This was to be done with the best interests of the Armed Forces at the core of the group. This group functioned on an ad hoc basis until October 2009 when it was officially inaugurated as the Armed Forces Muslim Association (AFMA) by the then Chief of the General Staff, General Sir David Richards, who very kindly agreed to be its founding patron. Many argued that AFMA was divisive as it separates the Muslims in the military from the rest, that it distinguishes between people in an organisation where uniformity is so crucial. It encourages personnel to be 'Muslim' soldiers, sailors and airmen rather than just soldiers, sailors and airmen. Though I can appreciate these concerns, in my opinion AFMA was not about division but rather cohesion through creating awareness, building bridges, enhancing well-being/welfare and increasing networking amongst Muslims in the military. AFMA was about building confidence, boosting morale and encouraging retention. AFMA would reinforce the moral and spiritual values which the

Armed Forces promote through their core values and standards, while also enabling personnel to be both a 'good British Muslim' and a 'good British soldier'.

Given the suspicion of the Armed Forces in some parts of the Muslim community, I hope that AFMA will be able to bridge the gap between the Armed Forces and the Muslim community and be a reminder that HM Forces are as integral to British society as are other British institutions such as the Police Force, the Fire Service, Ambulance Service, the NHS and other emergency services. They are there to serve this nation as whole, including the Muslim community. And their training and professionalism allow the British population, including the Muslim community, to roam the streets of Britain without fear, freely and securely; to sleep confidently and comfortably at night knowing that they and their families are safe and that no illegal power will come and invade this country; and that if protection is needed it will be there. It is exactly the training the Armed Forces receives which protects the freedoms that we have in Britain, including the freedom to be Muslim.

Further, nationalism and patriotism are values that are compatible with Islam and Islamic teachings. There is a famous Islamic saying in Arabic '*Hubbul watan minal eeman*' – 'the love of your nation is part of your faith'. Islam allows Muslims to practise their faith within the context in which they find themselves. It doesn't matter whether they are a majority or a minority in that country. It is for this reason that Imam Shafi, a great Muslim jurist and theologian of the 8th century, rewrote a whole thesis when he moved from one region to another, taking into consideration the particular circumstances and context of the Muslims living there. Nationalism and patriotism for the greater good was also practised by the Holy Prophet Muhammad amongst the various faith communities in Madina in 7th-century Arabia in order to create unity and security amongst the community.

A second initiative came in July 2014 when the newly appointed Secretary of State for Defence, Michael Fallon, launched the Armed Forces Muslim Forum (AFMF). As the Imam and Islamic Advisor to the Armed Forces I helped set up this new apolitical body, which seeks to build a positive and better relationship between the British Armed Forces and the British Muslim communities through dialogue, conversation and collaboration. The initiative was conceived in the aftermath of the murder of Drummer Lee Rigby which unfairly projected a view that British Muslims do not support their Armed Forces and are hostile towards them. AFMF is not about engaging in the politics of conflict and the use of force, but rather it is about recognising the values and principles according to which the men and women in our Armed Forces commit themselves to the defence and security of our country and *all* its people – it is about the human aspect of our service personnel. The motto that was selected for AFMF was 'Celebrating Service – Commemorating Sacrifice', with a view to representing the service and sacrifice of our Armed Forces both past and present. The Forum has five objectives:

- Develop and sustain positive relationships between the British Muslim community and their Armed Forces;
- Support the Armed Forces in improving understanding of Islam and Muslims in Britain and around the world;
- Work collaboratively to educate civil society as to the nature and purpose of the Armed Forces;
- Exchange ideas and views on topics of mutual interest and act as a platform for dialogue and consultation;
- Highlight and formally recognise the current and historic contribution of Muslim service personnel to UK society, fostering mutual pride and appreciation.

Muslim Pastoral, Spiritual and Moral Care

The second strand of my work, the support provided for Muslim personnel, is rooted in pastoral care, despite a common perception that Imams do not play a significant role in pastoral care and that it is not a key element within the role; in fact, there is a strong tradition of pastoral care and support in Islam for the vulnerable and needy.

Reasons for this misunderstanding include the tradition that Muslim communities have received their spiritual and pastoral support from familial and communal structures and arrangements, which has meant that formal 'religious professionals' were not required to meet and fulfil these needs, as is the case for various faith communities (Gilliat-Ray et al. 2013: Chapter 2). The motivation of the Muslim community for caring for others comes from the Islamic ethic, that the well-being of everyone in society is everyone's duty. A further factor is that pastoral care as a distinct topic has not been included in the training of Imams in Britain.

However, exactly the same factors that enabled chaplaincy to flourish in Christianity, such as urbanisation, technology and social and professional mobilisation and industrialisation, generated a demand on Muslim communities to provide pastors who would take on the role of chaplain (ibid.). Yunus Dudhwala has described this development:

> In an ever changing world where individual priorities have taken over collective responsibilities, a new tradition of Muslim chaplaincy is evolving... With the increase of materialism which in turn has decreased the time people can give to others, this new tradition of Muslim Chaplaincy will only increase. (Dudhwala 2006)

Therefore since the late 1990s we have seen a considerable increase in government-funded posts for Muslim chaplains, particularly in the prison service. Nevertheless, even with this rise, 'Muslims as a whole are only just catching on to the idea of Chaplaincy' (Siddiqui 2007: 45). It is clear that there is a need for Muslim chaplains and that there has been a significant increment in their employment in all sectors, although on a very small scale in the military.

As for Imams, as religious leaders they should be an embodiment of the teachings of the Qur'an and their role model and motivator is the Prophet Muhammad, just as he is for all Muslims. Both of these tenets exemplify the need to provide pastoral and spiritual care to the people that are in your care.

The two most oft-mentioned qualities of God in the Qur'an are mercy and compassion, which are virtues all Muslims are required to practise. Further, the Prophet encouraged Muslims to exercise compassion on all humanity regardless of faith, culture or origin.

There is no contradiction for a Muslim chaplain in providing pastoral care in sector ministry; actually it is very welcome (Gilliat-Ray 2008: 145).

Therefore, serving as a Muslim chaplain to the military, regardless of all the opposition I received, was a moral and godly thing to do. The Prophet Muhammad acted as a pastor to his disciples at a time of war and conflict. He shared with them in their challenges and difficulties. There is an excellent example of him getting alongside his congregation during the Battle of the Trench and helping them dig the trench to ward off the enemies. When his companions shared with him that they had tied a rock to their stomachs to relieve the pain of hunger, he lifted up his shirt and showed them that whilst they had one rock attached he had in fact tied two rocks to his stomach due to the severity of hunger and lack of food.

The Prophet Muhammad also maintained oversight of the morality of the soldiers that he led and cared for. Any kind of unethical behaviour during war and conflict was totally forbidden. An example is when Usama ibn Zayd, a companion of Muhammad, killed a man who claimed to be surrendering as he believed he only did so to save his own life. Prophet Muhammad held him to account about this behaviour and reprimanded him and challenged him to explain how he had judged the man's true intentions (*Bukhari*).

Muslim military leaders too were not only concerned about their soldiers' spiritual and pastoral care but their morality in conflict. Abu Bakr, the first caliph of Islam, ordered his men:

> Stop, O people, that I may give you ten rules for your guidance in the battlefield. Do not commit treachery or deviate from the right path. You must not mutilate dead bodies. Neither kill a child, nor a woman, nor an aged man. Bring no harm to the trees, nor burn them with fire, especially those which are fruitful. Slay not any of the enemy once they have been captured. (Aboul-Enein and Zuhur 2004: 22)

The central focus of spiritual, pastoral and moral care in the above Islamic examples aligns me with the role of military chaplains, described on the Royal Army Chaplains' Department's website:[1] spiritual support, both publicly and privately, at every level of the Army; pastoral care at home and abroad; moral guidance through formal teaching, counsel and personal example.

LCpl Jabron Hashmi

One of the most difficult pastoral events I have ever had to deal with occurred within months of my assuming the role of Muslim Chaplain to the Armed Forces in 2006. It clearly illustrates the way in which I work both to provide support for Muslim personnel and their families and to improve understanding of their role in the Armed Forces, including within Muslim communities and publicly.

On 1 July 2006, 24-year-old LCpl Jabron Hashmi became the first and only British Muslim soldier to be killed in action in Afghanistan. He was hit by a rocket-propelled grenade in an attack by the Taliban. Jabron was then only one of a few hundred Muslims serving in the British military and his death gained major media coverage. Jabron felt privileged to serve the Army and his country as a British Muslim. His decision to join at a time when the British Armed Forces were engaged in Muslim countries was a courageous and selfless act.

It was my role to support his family during this terrible time, which was both a great honour and a huge responsibility. Unlike other bereavements the unique circumstances surrounding Jabron's death magnified the situation. There would be members of his own community who would question his sacrifice and the nobility of his actions. His mother was obviously devastated and the feeling of abandonment and heartache for the whole of Jabron's family was palpable. Ironically, at the same time, there was a realm of spirituality in the whole experience which brought everyone together – and closer to God.

Jabron was born in the Pakistani city of Peshawar, just 40 minutes from the Afghan border. His family explained how he was 'excited' to be returning to the region where he grew up. His brother Zeeshan said,

> As a British Pakistani who was Muslim first and foremost, he felt he had a privileged position which he must utilise. In this day and age most of the problems are as a result of misunderstanding of each other's culture, and Jabron understood that. By committing himself to join the British Army and then by going to Afghanistan as a soldier, he knew he was best placed to perhaps bridge those gaps.

---

[1]   www.army.mod.uk/chaplains/chaplains.aspx (accessed 14 April 2015).

The media declared Jabron to be the first British Muslim soldier to be killed in the 'war on terror'. He was portrayed as 'a British Muslim, a British hero', whilst others judged him, unjustly, a traitor and an enemy who deserved to suffer, be isolated and die.

In Islam, as in Christianity, suffering is unavoidable in this worldly life. The Prophet Muhammad's companions believed that to be close to God one needed to experience some sort of hardship. The Qur'an says:

> Be sure we shall test you with something of fear and hunger, some loss in wealth or lives or the fruits (of your toil), but give glad tidings to those who patiently persevere ... They are those on whom (descend), blessings from God, and Mercy, and they are the ones that receive guidance. (Surah 2.155–7)

Having spent nearly a year on deployment to Afghanistan working alongside the British and US military across the country I saw at first hand the effects of conflict.

War is the most dreadful experience. Regardless of which element of the machine and manifestation of war you are part of, it is no doubt the most horrible expression of humanity. Even though in many instances it becomes a necessary act of violence for a noble and positive cause, its brutality cannot be denied. It does not matter which side of the divide one belongs to – the suffering and pain does not spare anyone, including the innocent bystander and civilian who has no interest in any of the warring factions. Islam gives permission to go to war, as long as it's for a just cause. Terrorism is not Islam's view of war, despite what some people claim. Eliminating persecution, oppression and injustice, and establishing peace and harmony, are the reasons Islam allows war. Nonetheless, there is no war without suffering and sacrifices, whether it is the soldier, his opponent, his family or the people he is trying to protect. However, what makes the experience significant is for what and why the suffering is endured. Chaplains do not necessarily help answer this question but they may help to frame the question properly in the first place.

For me, central questions are: Where is God in all this anguish? How does one gain comfort, solace and maintain a sense of purpose in the midst of such sacrifices? For me, one answer is that God is in the purpose that these individuals died for and in the comrades they've left behind. To sacrifice for something positive and good is a value that all faiths are able to adhere to. Sacrifice is an ethic that doesn't stand alone, but is underpinned by numerous other values which allow us to make the right choices, in the right place, at the right time. The stories of Abraham, Moses, Jesus and Muhammad, and that of Jabron, teach us that in order to preserve and promote the values and principles that one believes in, sacrifices, and on occasion tough sacrifices, will have to be made.

Pastoral Challenges

Pastorally, Jabron's death raised a number of chaplaincy and theological questions for me and the Army Chaplain's Department too. The death of a British Muslim soldier during operations was probably something we had not encountered since the Second World War. How would his faith needs be met when we only had one Muslim Chaplain to the Forces and at that time he was UK based? How would his faith be represented publicly but also within his regiment? How would his faith fit into the existing structures that were predominantly established for a Christian soldier? The first hurdle, at a time when there was only one Muslim Chaplain to the Forces, was how would Jabron's faith be represented in an operational environment where theoretically no British Muslim chaplain was deployed, especially during vigil and ramp ceremonies, where the chaplain provides a focal point for acts of remembrance and prayer. Fortunately, during Jabron's repatriation from theatre, the first Canadian Muslim chaplain was posted at Kandahar Airfield and was able to step in to represent his faith at this important time. It was either a coincidence or divine intervention that he was available. In 2014 I met the Canadian Muslim chaplain who presided over Jabron's ramp ceremony. Meeting him provided me with a sense of completion to my pastoral involvement in Jabron's case. Every attempt was made to hasten Jabron's repatriation from Afghanistan, with the military authorities advocating that every minute that his return was being delayed beyond 24 hours would be in violation of his religious needs to be buried within a day. This would also trouble his family who are a devout Muslim family. However, it was understood that repatriating the deceased from a conflict zone was not an easy task and that he would be repatriated as soon as was safely possible.

Another challenge occurred when I was told by the Royal Army Chaplains' Department that I would not be allowed to stand on the tarmac and pray for Jabron as his body was dismounted from the aircraft at RAF Brize Norton. The view was that a senior chaplain regardless of his or her faith would represent the chaplaincy department on the tarmac. It would be useful to note that all senior chaplains in the Army are Christian. I suggested that it would be be fitting for a Muslim chaplain to be present, in line with Jabron's faith, but also to respect Jabron's family, who would also be present. I was told that the chaplain did not represent his faith when receiving the deceased but rather he represented the chaplaincy department. I therefore requested that all visible signs of Christian symbolism be removed from the chaplain. The response I received was that he cannot because he is a Christian chaplain. Eventually, I did go on the tarmac with a Christian chaplain and Jabron was not the only soldier to be repatriated that day. Had a Muslim chaplain not been able to receive Jabron that day I feel proper respect and dignity would not have been demonstrated to him and his family.

Coffins of fallen soldiers when being repatriated are always draped in the Union Jack. It was interesting to listen to a discussion taking place about how Jabron's coffin might be draped. The issue was not that it was draped in the Union Jack but it was about how it was draped. For some, the way it was draped represented the Christian cross and they were worried that this might be offensive to Jabron and his family if it was seen as such. For me, this highlighted some deep but detailed religious and spiritual questions people were discussing during this emotive moment and how taken-for-granted forms of symbolism shape perceptions and behaviour.

Organising Jabron's memorial service was another rewarding experience. Jabron was killed alongside comrade Cpl Peter Thorpe. Both were repatriated together and a joint memorial service was held for them at the Defence Intelligence and Security Centre (DISC) in Chicksands. I worked closely with the padre there to create an order of service that could be encompassing of both the Christian and Muslim faiths. There was some sensitivity about how such a service would take place in the chapel at DISC. How would the religions be intertwined in this service? In the end it was to be a joint service which would have specific Christian parts and reserved Muslim parts. The padre and I thought we had done a good job in amalgamating our parts but an email from Jabron's brother Zeeshan, who had also served in the Army, made it clear that the first draft of the order of service in his view did not meet Jabron's religious needs at all. His email made me reflect on the purpose of the memorial service. Was it for the deceased or his family who are Muslim? Was it for his comrades who are predominantly Christian? Or was it for all of them? The email also made me aware of the significance of this service for the Muslim community. The service needed to offer a supportive context for all these groups to remember Jabron and his comrade. And it was important that the Armed Forces be seen to do this with respect for the two faiths represented.

Ultimately, the memorial service was very well received. Everyone was moved by the synergy and respect that the Christian chaplain and I demonstrated in valuing and honouring the memories of two individuals whom everyone in the church dearly loved and missed; two brave individuals who had paid the ultimate sacrifice. Both of us remembered them in our own traditions in a way that brought people together. Regardless of the terms we used people knew what we meant and felt.

But that's what padres do. They create pastoral environments and spaces where people, beliefs and feelings can come together to be understood. They rarely have the right answers during war, where it is difficult to comprehend and perceive God, but they will certainly help in forming the right questions.

References

Aboul-Enein, H.Y. and Zuhur, S. (2004), *Islamic Rulings on Warfare*. Strategic Studies Institute. Darby, PA, Diane Publishing Co.

Dudhwala, Y. (2006), *Building Bridges between Theology and Pastoral Care*. Lisbon Consultation, European Network of Health Care Chaplains. Available at: http://enhcc.eu/lisbon06.htm (accessed 29 November 2014).

Gilliat-Ray, S. (2008), From 'Visiting Minister' to 'Muslim Chaplain': The Growth of Muslim Chaplaincy in Britain, 1970–2007. In Barker, E. and Richardson, J. (eds), *The Centrality of Religion in Social Life*. Aldershot: Ashgate.

Gilliat-Ray, S., Ali, M.M. and Pattison, S. (2013), *Understanding Muslim Chaplaincy*. Farnham: Ashgate.

Siddiqui, A. (2007), *Islam at Universities in England: Meeting the Needs and Investing in the Future*. Report submitted to Bill Rammell MP, Minister of State for Lifelong Learning, Further and Higher Education.

PART V
Prison Chaplaincy

Chapter 18

Prison Chaplaincy

Helen Dearnley

I was in prison and you visited me. (Matthew 25:36)

Introduction

The door slammed shut, the sound of metal upon metal echoing eerily as I sat on the bunk, in the cell. I looked at the door, the closed gateway to freedom, and realised that there was no keyhole on the inside, this really is prison ... but I'm the chaplain and I can get up and walk away when I choose to do so, those I serve can't.

Prison chaplains form an integral part of Her Majesty's Prison Service; in 1773 an Act of Parliament enabled Justices of the Peace to appoint and pay salaries, not exceeding £50, to chaplains from the established Church to serve their local prisons (Noblett 1998: xxxi). As the years have passed, the role of the chaplain has evolved and the personal heritage of each chaplain now covers a wide range of faiths and denominations, but their core purpose, to serve those incarcerated by the courts by valuing their whole person, body and soul, remains the same.[1] This chapter seeks to open the door on the day-to-day life of a prison chaplain, reflecting on the varied roles and responsibilities they hold.

The Prison Context

Prison is a unique environment where few want to be, and yet all sectors of society are represented: young, old, rich, poor, male, female; all crimes are represented

---

[1] HM Prison Chaplaincy Statement of Purpose: NOMS [National Offender Management Service] Chaplaincy is committed to serving the needs of prisoners, staff and religious traditions by engaging all human experience. We will work collaboratively, respecting the integrity of each tradition and discipline. We believe that faith and the search for meaning directs and inspires life, and are committed to providing sacred spaces and dedicated teams to deepen and enrich human experience. By celebrating the goodness of life and exploring the human condition we aim to cultivate in each individual a responsibility for contributing to the common good. We will contribute to the care of prisoners to enable them to lead law-abiding and useful lives in custody and after release. Agreed by the Chaplaincy Council and the Chaplaincy Senior Management Team, September 2003.

from fraud to murder, shoplifting to terrorism offences; and sentences last from just a few days or weeks to the rest of an individual's natural life.

'On 23 May 2014, the prison population in England and Wales was 84,305, of whom 3,826 were women. Between June 1993 and June 2012 the prison population in England and Wales increased by 41,800 prisoners to over 86,000.'[2] These figures[3] provide an uncomfortable challenge for all who work in the Criminal Justice System, a challenge magnified when the reoffending statistics are considered.[4] These figures arguably place a responsibility upon chaplains and all prison staff to consider how their work engages with the rehabilitation of offenders, and with desistance[5] (as explored in Chapter 19, by Mike Kavanagh).

Prison chaplaincy has a variety of facets including the contextual: many prisoners experience different types of prison during their sentence and chaplains also move within these institutions. Statutory requirements provide another facet: induction, health care, segregation and discharge visits. Pastoral encounters may contain reflection on concerns: past, present and future. Finally, when the gates are opened there is a facet of care expressed in through-the-gate support/community chaplaincy. Each of these facets will be reflected on in this chapter.

In the light of the additional challenge which the reoffending and desistance figures provide, effective chaplaincy seeks to discern and respond to the humanity of each individual prisoner, when many of them do not recognise their own human value, in an environment that by its very nature removes the basic human rights of physical freedom and close personal relationships (Jewkes 2007: 123ff).

As an Anglican chaplain my own understanding of what it means to discern humanity in another is shaped by faith stories such as Jesus' encounter with the Samaritan woman at the well,[6] who as an outsider, a foreigner and a woman would have been used to being treated as less than human. Yet in her encounter with Jesus she is spoken to, she is given the opportunity to be the giver as well as the one who receives when Jesus asks her for a drink, and through this encounter she is connected to her community who come to hear Jesus because of her story.

---

[2]   Prison Reform Trust Bromley Briefing, Summer 2014.

[3]   As a percentage of the population, amongst the highest in Europe.

[4]   Prison Reform Trust Bromley Briefing, Summer 2014: 46 per cent of adults are reconvicted within one year of release. For those serving sentences of less than 12 months this increases to 58 per cent. Over two-thirds (67 per cent) of under 18 year olds are reconvicted within a year of release.

[5]   The role of faith in desistance is compellingly explored in Tom O'Connor and Jeff Duncan's (2011) research.

[6]   John 4:1–42.

This is the action of God who walked the earth as a human being, in Christ, who sat with a woman and spoke to her, who saw her for who she was and offered her life and the possibility of reconnection with her community. Trying to follow the example of Christ, I seek to bring his compassion to my encounters with those in prison. Despite the high ideal it seems to be it is often the simplest of acts, just as it was with Jesus asking for water, which unlocks the humanity of another.

One such occasion occurred when I was called to visit a young man, Paul,[7] who, despite his previous release beginning with every promise of a fresh start, had just re-entered prison. After knocking on the door I entered his cell. He was sitting on the corner of his bed, wiping the dirt off his white trainers. I asked him, 'Why are you doing that?' He replied poignantly, 'I aint gonna see mud or grass again for ages miss, seeing it breaks me up.' His words hung in the air for a few moments. What could I say? He was right. His new sentence meant that it would be some time before he saw the world again through unincarcerated eyes. We talked some more about his family, his hopes, his dreams upon release; as he spoke, the trainers got cleaner.

There are 120 prisons in England and Wales, each ministered to by a multifaith chaplaincy team, supported by and accountable to a Headquarters Adviser, who in turn reports to the Head of Faith Services (Chaplain General). Nearly all prisons have a Managing Chaplain[8] appointed specifically to lead and manage the team of chaplains and chaplaincy volunteers and to ensure delivery of religious provision. Whilst this chapter is written from a Christian perspective, chaplains and volunteers from other faith traditions will bring their narratives and their understanding of faith to this ministry.

Prisons are divided by their security category, the highest security being a category A prison[9] and the lowest security being a category D prison.[10] Which prison an offender resides in will depend upon their security classification, the courses they need to undertake to reduce their risk of reoffending and, where possible, their home location.

---

[7] All names and some narrative details are changed throughout the chapter to ensure the anonymity of those involved.

[8] 2013 saw, as part of a National Offender Management Service restructuring, chaplaincy roles being formally graded alongside their Prison Service colleagues. As a result, a Managing Chaplain is regarded as the same grade as a Band 7 Governor who would often fulfil roles such as head of function (or deputy head of function in larger more complex prisons), and a Chaplain is regarded in the same way as a Custodial Manager (formerly known as Principal Officers) who usually manage around 15 staff and are responsible for a department or wing.

[9] For example, HMPs Belmarsh, Whitemoor and Full Sutton.

[10] For example, HMPs Sudbury, Leyhill and Hollesley Bay. Further information on each prison can be found at www.justice.gov.uk/contacts/prison-finder (accessed 15 April 2015).

Some establishments, often referred to as 'locals',[11] have as their core role the reception of prisoners direct from court. Other prisons may have particular areas of expertise: HMPs Whatton and Bure are specialist establishments holding only sex offenders, HMPs Glen Parva and Feltham are Young Offender Institutions holding prisoners up to the age of 21, HMPs Foston Hall and New Hall hold only female prisoners. Other establishments like HMPs Ranby and Wayland follow the working prison agenda,[12] seeking to provide each prisoner with a 40-hour working week. Furthermore, establishments like HMPs Leeds, Lincoln and Chelmsford are also now additionally designated as resettlement prisons seeking to ensure that the vast majority of offenders are released from prisons in, or close to, the area in which they will live.[13]

Whatever the nature and purpose of the establishment, the core roles of the chaplains are the same. However, the nature of the ministry can be very different. A chaplain serving in a local prison, whose primary function is to serve the courts, may only have an average of a few days to support those in their care, some of whom will be sentenced, others will be on remand, and therefore innocent until proven guilty, each undergoing the often traumatic transition from being in the community at breakfast and incarcerated by teatime. The average stay in a local prison can be counted in weeks, with the prisoner either being released or transferred to another establishment to continue their sentence. Chaplains in local prisons never know who may walk through the door; all sections of society are represented, from members of the House of Lords (Archer 2002) to the homeless (Taylor 2006, White and McDowall 2011).

In contrast, chaplains serving in establishments where 'lifers' (James 2003) are incarcerated will have many years to walk alongside those in their care, requiring great patience and resilience. Although there are obvious differences when working with the variety of offender groups, the possibility of a transformational humanising encounter remains the same.

Statutory Duties

The 1952 Prison Act enshrines in law the statutory duties of a Prison Chaplain. These tasks, which must be undertaken every day, are incorporated into the Prison Rules and are explained in detail in the Prison Service Instruction (PSI) for

---

[11]   For example, HMPs Exeter, Doncaster and Leicester.
[12]   http://one3one.justice.gov.uk/ (accessed 3 May 2015).
[13]   www.justice.gov.uk/transforming-rehabilitation/resettlement-prisons (accessed 15 April 2015).

Chaplaincy (PSI 51/2011).[14] There are four statutory duties: induction interview, health care visit, segregation visit and discharge interview.

The induction interview: entering prison on the wrong side of the bars is often through its very nature a distressing and dehumanising experience (Noblett 1998: 3). The reception 'process', however professionally undertaken by staff, is the absolute point of no return to freedom. It is my perception that those arriving fall into three broad categories, the violent[15] – those who enter prison literally fighting all the way, the returner – those who have been through the system before and know what to expect, apparently trapped in a revolving door between prison and freedom, and the first timers who have arrived in prison across the ages (B.2.15 1924, Woodward 2007) outwardly showing a mix of bravery (real and acted) tinged with the fear of the unknown. All groups are seen by chaplains within a set timeframe, usually within 24 hours of arrival.

The challenge for the chaplain conducting these interviews, which are undertaken individually and in private, is to see behind the presenting emotion and respond to the humanity of that individual. The induction visits themselves vary hugely from those who want only functional information as to how the institution operates to those who need to be heard and to receive support that begins to form a relational understanding.

In responding to the human situation chaplains find themselves listening to those suddenly facing a 20–25-year sentence before being considered for parole, or those who have had a significant life event, hearing they are going to be a parent or that a relative is dying or having just started a new job, now find themselves facing a sentence. Often there is huge regret, self-recrimination and anger, chaplains are alongside, able to support and advise in the rebuilding of family lives, or the coming to terms with an irretrievable relationship breakdown.

Most, if not all, chaplains can tell stories of prisoners who present as angry and frustrated but, when alone with the chaplain, drop the hard exterior and poignantly share their fears and dreams. Chaplains in this instance provide a 'safe space', acting not only as a conduit of information and support but also as a representative presence of God who in the vulnerability of this encounter responds to their broken humanity.

Most often those who work in local prisons never know the effect of their 'reception' ministry, seeds are sown and the harvest reaped elsewhere in the prison estate, and yet when the stories are fed back to you, through other prisons or by the prison receiving a letter from freedom, the power of this ministry of welcome should not be underestimated.

---

[14]   This document can be read in full at www.justice.gov.uk/downloads/offenders/psipso/psi-2011/psi-51-2011-faith-pastoralcare.doc (accessed 15 April 2015).

[15]   A violent offender could be either a first timer or returner; however, responding to their needs is a distinctive challenge.

The door to the interview room closed and the man broke down in tears, a story of months of remaining 'strong' for his family was told. His offence was historic but time had caught up with Peter – he admitted that he deserved to be in prison, he understood what he had done wrong and without justification, reflected on why he had acted in the way he had many years ago; however, despite his family sticking by him, what he could not see was how he would survive four years in prison. He spoke at length that evening, about his family and his fears, and arrangements were made by prison officers and medical staff to provide additional support for him for as long as he required it.

He agreed to help himself by keeping busy; as part of that, he asked to attend church again, something he had stopped doing in childhood. After this initial period of crisis he became a regular in chapel, finding there 'space and a true freedom inside'. A few weeks later he had moved to another prison. Peter is now released but at his discharge interview he recalled how the chaplain's response at his induction interview broke his determination to take his own life. In this example, the chaplain is a fulcrum, acting as listener and holder of the past on one hand and holder of future hope on the other. This pivotal place of transformation is one where the prison chaplain is frequently privileged to minister.

The challenge for all prison chaplains as they go around their daily statutory duties is to maintain their own humanity, avoiding the dangers of institutionalisation and disillusionment, which can lead to visits becoming merely routine, and ensuring that they remain (as long as the prisoner permits it) meaningful encounters.

Along with a Governor and medical professional, chaplains are the only non-uniformed staff prisoners will meet with each day when they are separated from the prison community through their actions. Segregation is regarded as one of the hardest places to serve time; 'bang up' is constant with the exception of one hour's exercise and time to mop and clean the cell. It is the chaplains' role in these visits to develop an appropriate relationship with the prisoner that builds trust and fosters engagement and reflection. This is not always easy, particularly when on occasion there needs to be three or five officers present to enable the chaplain to be kept safe, or when the prisoner is on dirty protest, making conversation at even the most basic level a real challenge!

The third daily statutory duty is to visit the health care unit. Mirroring in lots of ways any other hospital visit, the health care round is one where chaplains are able to support those who find themselves seriously ill, physically or psychologically, within the prison environment. Whilst these visits are always pastoral, sometimes they take on a deeper significance as the chaplain supports a prisoner through the last days of their life, a challenging time for anyone, but even more so if you are incarcerated and away from, and in some cases rejected by, family and former friends.

The final statutory duty is the discharge visit. Every prisoner before their release has the opportunity of seeing a chaplain to talk about their hopes and fears for the future and to seek support for their often complex resettlement needs, for example by providing an introduction to an appropriate faith community on the outside. Prison chaplains often minister in conjunction with community chaplaincy schemes;[16] such schemes provide an additional layer of support, matching prisoners before they are released with mentors, who will support them through the gate and in their first challenging months of freedom, journeying with them as they rebuild their lives practically and emotionally.

The challenging reality is that for many who leave prison, their return is sometimes only days or weeks away. I personally have on several occasions said goodbye to a prisoner one day and met him on induction again two days later. When the prison door revolves so fast it is imperative for the chaplain to remain resilient and to hold on to the hope and belief that one day the situation may be different.

Pastoral Care

Resilience is key to effective prison ministry as chaplaincy behind bars, walls and fences is sometimes isolating (with chaplains often, because of the commitments of the role, feeling cut off from their faith communities), often challenging (dealing daily with people who in the main do not want to be there and are at varying degrees of acceptance of their sentence, or waiting to be sentenced), occasionally frightening, and always surprising.

At the heart of prison chaplaincy is the understanding that chaplains are there pastorally for prisoners and staff of all faiths and none. To achieve this they must be present in all the daily grind of prison life, they must be available to laugh when others are laughing and to carry the tears when the pain becomes unbearable, they should be found in the most difficult of places, when unfolding events are uncertain and frightening, they should be available, ready to listen and to encourage. Above all, prison chaplains should be approachable, they must never proselytise,[17] but through their words and actions they shine as advocates for their faith, and their faith communities.

A chaplain in any prison is called not to judge but to challenge to change through word and action (Fennessey 2002, Atherton 1987), providing 'hope for

---

[16] Further information on community chaplaincy can be sourced through www.communitychaplaincy.org.uk (accessed 15 April 2015).

[17] PSI 51/2011.

the journey'[18] to desistance; this is not easily achieved and requires deep rooting in a personal faith tradition and a close self-awareness.

The front page of the Prison Officer's Association magazine *Gatelodge*[19] for April 2010 showed an ordinary terraced street with the words 'Fraudster, Burglar, Drug dealer, Rapist, Paedophile, Murderer, Terrorist', highlighting how prison staff of all ranks, grades and departments work in a particularly challenging environment with many prisoners who have been incarcerated to protect society from their actions, all located in one place for staff to support their rehabilitation back into the community. A chaplain's role is to support the staff as well as the prisoners, remembering that it is not just the front-line staff who need support but all grades; some may not even meet prisoners face to face but may have to spend considerable time reading their case histories, which can be both graphic and disturbing.

Effective pastoral care should form the heart of any prison chaplain's duties across the prison environment. It is a ministry of availability – an effective chaplain will rarely seem too busy to stop and listen to the concerns of those inside its gates; however, the nature and depth of such care will depend on the particular needs of the prisoner and staff population at a particular time, which as in any ministry can ebb and flow, necessitating that the chaplain moves between proactive and reactive models of ministry as required.

Pastorally, a chaplain may be found in the middle of any extraordinary event in the prison; be it a death in custody, a concerted indiscipline (riot), a hostage situation or an act of serious self-harm it is part of the chaplain's responsibility to provide support for all staff and prisoners affected.

Forming part of the chaplain's pastoral role is the difficult task of informing a prisoner that a friend or a member of their family has died. This responsibility illustrates many of the core pastoral skills a prison chaplain requires. Alongside the practical complexities of confirming that the death has occurred (there are many attempts to seek revenge on prisoners by making hoax calls about such matters), the chaplain must ensure their own safety during the conversation and the safety of the prisoner after the news has been imparted. Breaking the news requires compassion and skill, supporting an individual who is then practically helpless to affect change or support their wider family, requires dedication and compassion; journeying with someone who is mindful that their actions may have made the life of the deceased harder, requires patience and wisdom. Additionally, a prisoner may not wish to, or may not be permitted to, attend the funeral service in the community; in these circumstances it falls to the chaplain to provide an alternative 'space' for the prisoner to reflect about the life of their loved one.

---

[18]   'Hope for the Journey' was the Prison Chaplaincy conference slogan in 2011.
[19]   www.poauk.org.uk/index.php?gatelodge (accessed 15 April 2015).

Multifaith Working

Sixty-nine per cent of prisoners declare themselves as being of faith.[20] The last 15 years have seen a transformation in multifaith chaplaincy. Modern Prison Service chaplaincy embraces a multifaith and multidenominational approach to ministry. This multifaith working is arguably rare in its quality and in the depth of its effective integration and outworking. This is in contrast to the position found by Beckford and Gilliat (1998) who reflected that multifaith chaplaincy was not present and that prison chaplaincy was in fact Anglican chaplains acting as 'brokers' (Beckford and Gilliat 1998: xii) for other faith groups. However, Todd and Tipton (2011: 37) reflect, 'Chaplaincy now better serves and reflects the needs of a multicultural community and is thus an important resource for the contemporary Prison Service and its populations'.

The current multifaith chaplaincy teams are the outworking of a challenging, sometimes painful and very significant journey that the Prison Service has faced ahead of many of its European and international counterparts. The ministry has evolved from purely Anglican to a multidenominational Christian ministry to one which actively embraces the breadth of the major world religions.

This journey to inclusive multifaith chaplaincy teams took time, to the extent that historically relations with 'non-Christian' faiths had been negatively impacted. The Prison Chaplaincy Service lost some credibility and the religious needs of 'non-Christian' prisoners were arguably long overdue in being met. After recognising the need to evolve, a substantial programme of work was implemented under the leadership of the then Chaplain General, the Venerable William Noblett, which led to a 'paradigm shift' (Noblett 2009: 42ff) of structures and attitudes within the service so that prison chaplaincy could begin to develop on a more inclusive basis to provide fair and equitable provision across the faith traditions. Although the journey to inclusivity always continues, most recently with the recognition of the Rastafarian faith in 2012, multifaith working is now structurally embedded within Prison Service Chaplaincy.

PSI 51/2011 requires that 'Chaplains and Chaplaincy Teams must be appointed to meet the needs and reflect the faiths make-up of the prison population.' Prison chaplains are either: employed, on a full- or part-time basis; sessional, working a limited number of hours as required; or volunteers. This breadth of appointment opportunity creates a diverse group of chaplains all with different needs and expectations which the Managing Chaplain (who can be recruited from any faith tradition) must facilitate and enable in such a way as to permit full team integration into the wider prison. This is undeniably a challenge which is hard to achieve, particularly if an individual chaplain only

---

[20]   A full breakdown of prisoner faith demographics can be found at www.parliament.uk/briefing-papers/SN04334.pdf (accessed 15 April 2015).

attends the prison for three hours a week to support a numerically small faith community, and for volunteers who often have very specific roles and yet need to appreciate the wider context in which they are working.

The chaplaincy team within each prison is required to minister to each faith group that is present there; this work in the field is supported by Faith Advisers to the Prison Service. Faith Advisers are senior representatives of their communities who together form the Chaplaincy Council and whose role it is to support chaplaincy teams by recruiting and endorsing appropriate chaplains and by advising the headquarters team in faith-related matters, including contributing to the PSI guidance materials which underpin all aspects of prison chaplaincy. Together, chaplains and chaplaincy HQ advisers working with the Faith Advisers must seek to ensure that each prison does not just have the appropriate faith demographic of chaplains but also has the practical spaces and resources for each faith group to meet for worship and prayers.

This has necessitated the adapting and sharing of religious spaces, a sharing that many have found challenging as they explore what it feels like to have no permanent home.

In larger establishments, the chaplaincy department will be responsible for a large multifaith space, with neutral decoration and with easily movable furniture to facilitate Friday prayers for Muslim prisoners. In some prisons this space will be designated as a Muslim prayer room; a smaller multifaith room easily adaptable to the needs of the faith groups which use it, often in such spaces there are wall displays for each faith hidden by curtains when not in use; and a chapel which all Christian denominations will share.

In smaller establishments one room is used for all faith groups (often this space has historically been the chapel), necessitating teams to transform the room from mosque on a Friday to chapel on a Sunday to a temple on Monday, and so forth. Such rearrangement involves more than simply furniture removal but requires within all chaplains a deep understanding of hospitality and compromise. A shared multifaith room on Good Friday can be a poignant place to be. It is easy to perceive why the journey to truly multifaith spaces has not always been easy, as each chaplain wrestles with the needs of their own community alongside the potentially conflicting needs of their brothers and sisters of other faith traditions. However, over the last decade or so when chaplaincy teams have worked through this transition of space they have been at the forefront of true multifaith working, and in so doing chaplains have continued to provide the much-needed 'safe sacred spaces' (Todd and Tipton 2011: 36) for prisoners and staff. Furthermore, in so doing they have additionally borne witness to a powerful model of collaboration and partnership as opposed to competition. In this sense many chaplaincy teams within the prison environment now act as examples and inspiration for the wider community.

It is the responsibility of the Managing Chaplain, supported by the Faith Advisers, to ensure that each faith community represented within the prisoner faith demographic is enabled to have one hour of corporate worship and additional religious instruction each week; in addition, it is good practice for the faith minister to be available to provide pastoral care for their devotees. It is a challenging task ensuring that there is appropriate provision across all faith traditions, as it is habitually difficult to recruit appropriate faith chaplains in areas where prisons are situated away from particular faith communities; additionally, there are sometimes real challenges encouraging people within all faith traditions to become prison chaplains. For those of all faiths who do join, the opportunities to care, to educate and to transform lives should not be underestimated.

As ministers of faith each chaplain is responsible for leading their weekly faith services and for providing the opportunity for a faith-based class, to enable participants to question and to develop a greater understanding of the teachings of their faith and its outworking in their daily lives. Through effective worship and teaching, which enables prisoners within a supportive environment to explore remorse and repentance, to develop a moral code and to belong to an accountable community, it is possible on occasions to see lives truly transformed (Taylor 2006, Woodward 2007) – these glimpses of transformation are both personally rewarding and inspirational for all.

Sometimes a prisoner's faith journey is slow and methodical, on other occasions a single experience acts as a catalyst. In this respect faith is arguably one of life's experiences which connects in a very similar way whether we are 'on the out' or serving in prison. Theologians have spoken about faith as being the same as the light of a candle which remains constant but appears brighter when life is at its darkest. In prison this holds true also: when the darkness of life is most apparent faith can be seen most strongly, held on to, returned to or reached out for.

Chris had only been in prison for a couple of weeks; his sentence, which was his first, would last only a few months. When we first met he was relatively ambivalent to his situation, determined to keep his 'head down to get on and get out'. The next time we met, however, the situation was very different. I had to tell Chris that his young child had been in an accident and was lying critically ill on life support in intensive care. The doctors had asked that I explain his child was not expected to live for more than a few hours. The different disciplines within the prison worked together so Chris could attend the hospital, and at his request I accompanied him and the escorting staff. We arrived in time for Chris to witness the hospital chaplain perform an emergency baptism service. Chris had some time with his child before returning to prison. Serving time took on a whole new meaning for Chris that day, and I saw afresh the broken humanity of one in my care. We sat together in his cell and at his request we prayed, something he had not done in years, then we waited. Every hour I would ring the hospital and update Chris, waiting to hear the shattering news that his fight had been lost, trying to support Chris alone and isolated from his family. Here the role of chaplain became a human symbol of God's presence: watching, waiting, being alongside him and his family in the darkness. It was two days later when we received the miraculous news that Chris's child was out of danger ... Chris came to chapel that Sunday for the first time since his childhood and afterwards promised himself that he would do so again ... he wrote to the prison months after his release to say he was still attending church every week.

Over the last few decades prison chaplaincy has evolved into an effective multifaith organisation, with each team managed by chaplains from across faith traditions, working together and frequently sharing sacred spaces. Prison chaplains in 2014 continue to have a distinctive role in prisons[21] providing both a practical and symbolic dimension to prison life as faith 'experts', teachers and deliverers of pastoral care and as 'symbols of morality and humanity' reassuringly connected to the 'outside world' (Todd and Tipton 2011: 25ff).

Being a chaplain in the Prison Service is both a privilege and an awesome responsibility. When I first began my ministry as a prison chaplain, the late Bishop John Austin when preaching at my licensing service told me that I had a responsibility to be aware of the humanity of everyone and to demonstrate God's love wherever and whenever I could.

As an Anglican chaplain, belief in the incarnation, God who came as one of us in Christ and walked about amongst us, is at the heart of my faith – God who lived our humanity and in so doing opened the possibility of human life in all its fullness to each and every person.

Discerning and responding to even the deepest hidden humanity of the toughest and most dehumanised offenders is at the heart of prison chaplaincy; I believe that with it reoffending will be reduced and desistance become a much greater possibility.

References

B.2.15 (1924), *Among the Broad-Arrow Men*. London: A & C Black Ltd.
Archer, J. (2002), *A Prison Diary by FF8282*. London: Macmillan.
Atherton, R. (1987), *Summons to Serve*. London: Cassell Publishers.

---

[21] This distinctiveness is explored in depth in Andrew Todd and Lee Tipton's report *The Role and Contribution of a Multi-Faith Prison Chaplaincy to the Contemporary Prison Service* (Todd and Tipton 2011). Many of the findings of this research are replicated in the larger US study commissioned by the Pew Forum, *Religion in Prisons: A 50 State Survey of Prison Chaplains* (Pew Research Center 2012).

Beckford, J.A. and Gilliat, S. (1998), *Religion in Prison: Equal Rites in a Multi-Faith Society*. Cambridge: Cambridge University Press.

Fennessy, C. (2002), *A Time to Serve*. London: St Pauls Publishing.

James, E. (2003), *A Life Inside*. London: Atlantic Books.

Jewkes, Y. (ed.) (2007), *Handbook on Prisons*. Cullompton: Willan Publishing.

Noblett, W. (1998), *Prayers for People in Prison*. Oxford: Oxford University Press.

—— (2009), *Inside Faith: Praying for People in Prison*. London: Darton, Longman and Todd.

O'Connor, T and Duncan, J. (2011) The sociology of the humanist, spiritual and religious practice in prison: supporting responsibility and desistance from crime. *Religions*, 2(4), 590–610. Available at: www.mdpi.com/2077-1444/2/4/590 (accessed 15 April 2015).

Pew Research Center (2012), *Religion in Prisons – A 50-State Survey of Prison Chaplains*. Available at: www.pewforum.org/2012/03/22/prison-chaplains-exec/ (accessed 15 April 2015).

Taylor, R. (2006), *To Catch a Thief*. Weybridge: New Wine Press.

Todd, A. and Tipton, L. (2011), *The Role and Contribution of a Multi-Faith Prison Chaplaincy to the Contemporary Prison Service*. Available at: http://stmichaels.ac.uk/assets/pdf/Todd-and-Tipton-2011-Report-on-Prison-Chaplaincy.pdf (accessed 17 April 2015).

White, A. and McDowall, I. (2011), *Tough Talk*. Milton Keynes: Authentic Media Limited.

Woodward, B. (2007), *Once an Addict*. Milton Keynes: Authentic Media Limited.

Chapter 19

Contextual Issues: Justice and Redemption

Michael Kavanagh

Believing in Change: The Contribution of Prison Chaplaincy

St Irenaeus, the 2nd-century Bishop of Lyons, wrote, 'The Glory of God is a human being fully alive'. To live life cherishing each moment and being fully alive can give a very different sort of 'buzz' from that which many offenders describe as part of their experience; it can release prisoners from a life of crime. Prison chaplaincy contributes to that release by enabling prisoners to see themselves differently, to truly value their own lives so that they can come to value the lives of others: to live full lives themselves and not to mar the life living of others.[1]

New Identities: From Offender to Being a Person 'Made Good'

The seven pathways from offending have been key in developing an approach to reducing reoffending that takes seriously offender needs. They include accommodation, education/training/employment, health, drugs and alcohol, finance/benefit/debt, children/families and attitudes/thinking/behaviour. By identifying an offender's needs explicitly and objectively, interventions and support can be put in place to meet those needs and thereby reduce risk. But a moment's reflection on our own lives, if looked at in terms of the risk/need principle, reminds us that we are more than the sum of our deficiencies. People are not criminals all the time (to paraphrase Archbishop William Temple, 'No one is a criminal and nothing else.'), they are capable of other and better ways of acting. But many prisoners get trapped in a criminal identity that supports offending through a variety of cognitive and social props. Although addressing risk and need can be part of building a new identity, key to sustaining this is a new narrative that brings it all together, and a supportive social group to sustain this new identity. This is why some prisons have opted for an informal 'Eighth

---

[1]   This chapter celebrates the work of chaplains in all prisons, the support of the Chaplaincy team in HQ and the inspiration which has come from the prisoners who have shared their stories. I also wish to thank Liz Bird, Lynette Emmanuel and the 'Belief in Change' Communities at Channings Wood and Risley prisons for helping me to Believe in Change.

Pathway' called spirituality or faith but which could be renamed 'Bringing it all Together'. This connects with 'Belief in Change', an accredited offending behaviour programme which is being piloted in Risley prison, a case study of which is described below.

Multifaith prison chaplaincy[2] can be key in helping people develop and support a new identity, a new narrative bringing together the often fractured parts of a person's inner world that means that they have not been fully alive. In this way work within chaplaincy contributes to the goal of reducing reoffending and supporting the journey of desistance, the journey away from crime.

Shadd Maruna, one of the pioneers of the idea of desistance, has explored in detail the factors that support people living positive, crime-free lives. Among these he has looked at the role of faith. He coined the phrase 'knifing off' (Maruna and Roy 2007, Maruna et al. 2006) to describe the way in which some offenders were able to establish a new identity through faith. They would talk in terms of being given a fresh start, a new beginning, a fresh identity that meant they were no longer defined by the person that they were – their criminal identity had been knifed off. This process needs to be handled with care as people do need to learn from their mistakes and not use 'knifing off' as a cover for not addressing some of the issues that led them into offending. Offending behaviour programmes, education and skills training as well as deepening faith all contribute to prisoner rehabilitation. But the key idea in Maruna's study is that faith gave people a chance at a new start, freed them to see themselves differently and not be chained to a past identity.

The other crucial finding in Maruna's work is the importance of resettlement into a supportive faith community for those who have come to faith or rekindled their faith whilst 'inside'. Coming to faith, or the renewal of an existing faith practice, whilst 'inside' can be key to good prison adjustment (see Burnside et al. 2005), but on its own does not have a huge impact on reoffending rates. But if 'faith inside' is combined with a supportive faith community on the outside, which in reality means a group of people who will support the person's new identity, then a significant impact on reoffending may be seen. Before reflecting further on resettlement, it is important to consider religious conversion in prison.

Every so often the press runs a story about forced conversions, especially to Islam. But when religious conversion is looked at carefully and appreciatively, as in the work of Alison Liebling (Liebling et al. 2011), a richer understanding of conversion emerges. Especially for prisoners who have long sentences, conversion is actually about discovering a new sense of meaning which makes sense of the past, offers a new way of seeing the future and of establishing a new, pro-social identity. Spiritual practice gives order to the day, the week and even

---

[2]   Chaplaincy teams comprise chaplains reflecting the faith/denominational breakdown of the prison.

the year, marked as it is by fasts and festivals. Being part of a group of people who practise their faith can give real hope and support. Although much work has looked at conversion to Islam, the principles apply to people who convert to other faiths in prison. Buddhism and Paganism are two interesting cases in point, as many people who come to practise these on the 'inside' were not part of such communities on the outside.

Social Capital: Relationship and Resettlement

To sustain the changed sense of self that comes about through conversion or renewed faith practice, through-the-gate work is crucial. Whilst the Christian community has been engaged in this work for many years as a result of having had people in prison, for other faith communities this work is relatively new. Coming to terms with having members of their community in prison can be challenging, bringing as it does for some a sense of shame both to the community and to the family.[3]

Imaginative work is being done in this area recognising that a 'one size fits all' model is not going to work because different faith communities have different shapes. Some examples will illustrate this and underline the importance for 'prime providers' in the Community Rehabilitation Companies under *Transforming Rehabilitation*, to find ways of engaging with faith communities to ensure that the added value that faith can bring to desistance can be realised. As mentioned, although there are some lifelong Buddhist practitioners in jail, especially foreign nationals, most come to Buddhist practice on the inside. This, combined with the fact that many local Buddhist groups meet in people's homes, poses particular resettlement challenges. Responding to this, the Buddhist prison chaplaincy, Angulimala, which is based at the Forest Hermitage near Warwick, is working in partnership with NOMS to develop a project called 'Let Go'. The hope is for the Forest Hermitage to be a place where ex-offenders can attend groups to build on the practice that they developed on the inside, to make retreat to deepen practice and to join a web-based community of practice to keep them engaged and motivated when facing challenges. This is a stepping stone to joining a local group in due course.

Within the Muslim community, charities are growing to address housing needs, mentoring and capacity building within the community to encourage

---

[3]   At present, 'through-the-gate work' is undergoing an enormous change with the creation of Community Rehabilitation Companies (CRCs) which, alongside a newly created National Probation Service (NPS) will manage offenders, assessing them at the start of their sentence and planning their release as well as contributing to their sentence plans whilst they are in custody as set out in *Transforming Rehabilitation: A Strategy for Reform*, Ministry of Justice, May 2013.

volunteering so that ministry to prisoners and ex-prisoners becomes more embedded in the community as a whole. Capacity building within local faith communities has been the goal of a number of events organised by the Wormwood Scrubs Community Chaplaincy. Presentations to introduce the through-the-gate work have been held in a Sikh Gurdwara, Hindu temple and mosque as well as in the local Anglican church. The aim is to attract mentors from across the faith communities and to raise awareness among those communities who are still coming to terms with having to face the fact that numbers of their young people have been caught up in criminal activities.

The Jewish community is very supportive of people on release but focuses on looking forward rather than revisiting past failures. The Sikh Gurdwara is a natural base for providing support to vulnerable people and to resettle prisoners, incorporating as it does not only community events as well as faith teaching but the common kitchen, the Langar. For Hindus, the temple can also be a source of support as prisoners seek to reintegrate and sustain the Hindu practice that has helped them on the inside. The Pagan community, like the Buddhist, often have meetings in homes, though some are in more public spaces. It is exploring ways to develop guidelines to keep both the ex-offender and the community safe, but is also developing mentoring schemes to support pagan prisoners on release. The Janus project being pioneered by the Pagan Federation is an example of a particular faith community developing a model that can be used inclusively to support prisoners from across all religious traditions and none. A key organisation that helps groups to develop this work is the Community Chaplaincy Association. There is a strong sense of collaboration based on the recognition that many Churches have already developed good practice guidelines relating both to child protection and resettlement and so groups will work together to build on best practice. Following the recognition of Rastafarian practice in prison in 2012 there is now guidance for Rastafarian 'groundation' and 'reasoning'[4] to take place in prison and resources to help people relatively new to the faith to learn about key concepts such as 'livity'. This roughly means lifestyle and is holistic, covering diet (many Rastas are vegan), clothing and personal hygiene, and can help people both to use their time in prison productively but also begin to imagine a different sort of life outside that is marked by service to others and recognising and using personal gifts.

Chaplaincy is well placed to respond to the challenges posed by *Transforming Rehabilitation* and Resettlement Prisons as chaplains always work as part of an external faith community, having to be authorised by that community to work

---

4   'Groundation' or gathering is Rastafarian community worship and will include drumming, the use of shakers, chanting and prayers. 'Reasoning', which may take place as part of groundation or alone, is based on the principle 'each one, teach one' and allows for critical reflection on ideas – written or oral, e.g. a passage of scripture.

in prison. The specification underpinning much chaplaincy work, PSI 51/2011 *Faith and Pastoral Care of Prisoners*[5] has two mandatory outputs recognising the centrality of this work. They relate to contact with chaplaincy for prisoners prior to release and ensuring links are maintained with external faith and community groups. There is also the opportunity for community-based faith leaders who may have supported the prisoner before conviction to offer support and, where appropriate, to assist in reintegration upon release.

To summarise, discovering or rediscovering a religious faith or a new sense of meaning and purpose can help to integrate other experiences and influences of rehabilitation in the prison. This is an eighth 'bringing it all together' pathway which recognises that we are more than the sum of our deficiencies. This sense of a new identity is supported through engagement with faith-based community groups coming into the prison – volunteers who believe that change is possible making it more possible for the prisoners to believe this of themselves and thus help to sustain a new self narrative. Whilst this process assists in prison adjustment, it can also impact on reoffending if it is combined with through-the-gate support and an engaged faith community upon release.

Post Traumatic Growth and the Statutory Duties: Possibilities of New Identities

The idea of 'post traumatic stress' is well known. But recent work in psychology is exploring why some people seem to go through traumatic experiences but come through them stronger and more resilient. The term 'post traumatic growth' has been coined for this phenomenon (Joseph 2012). What seems to make the difference is enabling people to be real about the feelings they experience as a result of what has happened to them. It is also important that they have time to explore the meaning of the experience – in other words, to allow a new sense of identity to coalesce around the experience – for example, enabling a person to grow from a sense of being a 'victim' into a new identity as a 'survivor'.

Imprisonment for most is a traumatic experience – even for those who may have served a number of sentences and certainly for those receiving long or indeterminate sentences. Within prison life itself there can also be traumatic experiences: the loss of a loved one outside, or the experience of violence or bullying on the inside. The statutory duties of the chaplaincy, enshrined in the 1952 Prison Act and developed in the present PSI 51/2011, require chaplains to visit daily new receptions, those who are in segregation or cellular confinement,

---

[5]   Prison Service Instruction (PSI) 51/2011, *Faith and Pastoral Care of Prisoners*, Ministry of Justice, updated 18 November 2013, which contains both mandatory outputs and guidelines for faith practice in a series of annexes.

those in health care facilities and those preparing for release, as well as those identified as being at risk of self-harm. Chaplains are well placed to be part of the process of turning stressful experiences into opportunities for growth and the development of a new sense of meaning. This requires that prisoners are given time to reflect and that 'doing the stats' for chaplains should never become a tick box exercise. Too much is at stake – such visits may be the window of opportunity a person needs at a liminal moment in their life to see things afresh and begin or reinforce a journey of change. The value of the chaplain in supporting prisoners at such moments of crisis is brought out in Chapter 18 by Helen Dearnley. It was also picked up in the interviews undertaken as part of the NOMS-sponsored research into prison chaplaincy undertaken by the Cardiff Centre for Chaplaincy Studies (Todd and Tipton 2011). A governor commented:

> The chaplains of today are not here to judge or convert anyone, or anything like that, they are just here to talk to and give prisoners support. (Todd and Tipton 2011: 23)

In the same study, two prisoner comments are also illustrative:

> I find that when I am at my lowest ebb ... I always know there is someone in the chapel I can talk to. (Todd and Tipton 2011: 29)

> I suppose at the end of the day this place (chaplaincy) and the chaplains make the prison a less painful place, you know, like there is less hurt as a result of being here. (Todd and Tipton 2011: 29)

Developing Internal Capital

In the literature on desistance the idea of internal capital relates to the development of self-esteem, self-efficacy, a healthy sense of shame, and elements of regret, hope and emotional self-management. Looking at faith practice in prison through this lens helps to frame such activities in ways that link them to supporting the journey of desistance. All faith traditions affirm the worth of human beings – those espousing reincarnation recognise that being born as a human gives a unique opportunity for spiritual practice and so raises the possibility of liberation from the wheel of death and rebirth. For faiths that do not see the world in this way there is an acknowledgement of the value of the person. St Irenaeus' words, quoted above, are one example from within the Christian tradition.

Given that prisoners' low self-esteem can have a negative effect on their motivation to change, being part of a community that affirms a person's intrinsic worth can be an important corrective. Volunteers from outside communities can be especially helpful in this process as prisoners recognise that they come entirely by choice and can see their value affirmed through the consistent support they receive. In a personal comment to the author a prisoner who was leaving the high security estate after many years put down his personal change as being bound up with the faithful support and interest of a volunteer who had visited him as part of an outside faith group over many years. The volunteer had given his time freely and saw the person rather than the crime and recognised the possibility of change before even the prisoner himself. Participation in rehabilitation programmes, attendance at chapel and faith classes were also important, but it was this lasting pastoral, freely given relationship that had been key in allowing a new sense of self to emerge. In her work on a volunteer, faith-based reintegration programme in America, Ruth Armstrong (2014) echoes this anecdotal insight by exploring how trust placed in an ex-prisoner by a volunteer can be a factor in enabling and supporting change and desistance from crime. Similarly, in his book *The Good Prison*, Gerard Lemos (2014) comments on the importance of relationships that foster the journey of change by broadening it to include a number of people who impact on the prisoner:

> As far as offenders are concerned, if they go to prison, they will, like it or not, have to trust lawyers, prison officers, probation officers, chaplains and teachers – hosts of people who, contrary to their previous experience, should be available, reliable and willing to help. Their chances of rehabilitation are significantly enhanced by the capacity to build and benefit from relationships of trust with authority figures that can help, as well as represent role models, advocates and, above all, *a sense of possibility*. (Lemos 2014: 29, my italics)

Faith traditions also encourage a sense of personal responsibility which can be allied with an experience of support. So taking responsibility for actions in the past need not simply be crushing but can lead on to an understanding that the future may offer new possibilities and that guilt and regret/repentance should be followed by a commitment to change. Braithwaite's (2006) distinction between disintegrative and reintegrative shaming is helpful. Shame within the context of remorse, regret, apology and forgiveness can allow the offender to move on and develop a new sense of hope for the future. In this way shame can be reintegrative and part of a journey of reconciliation and is integral to the way such feelings are managed in the context of faith practice. Where these elements are not present and shame is reinforced by the community this can lead to a greater sense of alienation and strengthens ties to a peer group who support a criminal rather than pro-social identity. The support of both a 'higher power', to use the language of Alcoholics Anonymous, and of chaplains and volunteers on the inside, and a faith community on the outside furthers this process.

Religious Education

Religious education classes are crucially important to develop a rounded understanding of the faith tradition both for prisoners discovering a faith and those who are renewing their beliefs. They can also be opportunities to make links with other elements of the prison regime to give a new sense of purpose and direction. One interesting example is the notion of 'right livelihood' found in Buddhism or the idea of 'works' in Rastafari. Both ideas make explicit the link between faith practice and work or productive activity. This can lead to a new sense of motivation for work or education in prison as it provides a way of seeing this as an extension of spiritual practice rather than simply as another part of the regime. Work may also be seen as reparative, a making good for the harm done to the victim and community. A new sense of meaning can bring a deeper engagement and support a new narrative so prisoners see themselves as able to contribute to society in a positive way in the future.

In spite of articles in the press focusing on the role Muslim chaplains play in combating violent extremism in prison and some of the challenges this brings, the reality is that the majority of Muslim prisoners are not in for terrorism-related offences. To assist Muslim chaplains in providing good faith foundations for prisoners HMPS has developed a teaching course called *Tarbiyah*. It is described in this way in the introduction: '*Tarbiyah* is all about growing, increasing, education and learning, being nurtured and developed but in every goodly aspect so it is wholesome and comprehensive.'[6]

With modules relating to social responsibility, tolerance, trust and honesty, links are made between the faith and being a good citizen. Widely misunderstood ideas such as jihad are addressed in a way that emphasises the way they can lead someone to be a more devout Muslim contributing to a just society rather than lending support to an ideology that can foster violent extremism. Jihad itself is seen as struggle in a way that parallels and reinforces work a prisoner may be doing to address deficiencies in the realm of attitudes/thinking and behaviour as part of an offending behaviour programme:

> Jihad an-nafs is the struggle against evil ideas, desires and powers of lust and anger, placing all of them under the dictates of reason, faith and obedience to God's commands and finally, purging all evil ideas and influences from one's soul.[7]

---

6   *I2i 'Islam to Iman', The Tarbiyah Programme*, Ministry of Justice National Offender Management Service HMPS, Introduction, p. 1.

7   *Tarbiyah* programme, Module 5, p. 7.

Corporate Worship, Prayer and Meditation

All traditions teach a variety of methods for prayer and meditation. This can be key in supporting emotional self-management. Discovering ways of dealing with anxiety or frustration may not be the prime purpose of learning to pray or meditate but it can be a helpful adjunct to support other techniques learned through interventions. Spiritual traditions speak of *practice* and underline the need to persevere rather than seeing such approaches as 'quick fixes'. Different traditions will use different words, but the idea of spiritual practice as journey can be especially helpful. Works such as *Pilgrim's Progress* build into the narrative the journey as a series of challenges and setbacks which provide a parallel interpretation of the human journey of life. Desistance encourages a mindset that honours the distance travelled on the journey to stopping offending as well as the binary measure of whether the person has reoffended or not. So it is important to notice that progress for an offender may mean less frequent offending and less serious crimes and this may well indicate that the person is making progress to giving up crime altogether. This can be something a chaplain can bring out in the context of the reception visit when someone may be feeling that they have 'failed'. Some faiths ritualise 'moving on' after setbacks, for example through the practice of the sacrament of confession within some Christian traditions. Shadd Maruna (2011) has argued for the value of exploring how ritual can help in the process of re-entry into society following a period of imprisonment as a means of strengthening the sense of new beginnings and new opportunities that can come with release. Some Christian chaplains anoint with oil and pray with prisoners as they go out and invite members of the prison congregation to do so as well. This may strengthen the sense of possibility that comes with release. In the author's experience, such prayer is often accompanied by repentance for past failures and prayer for their victims and their families.

Interestingly, research into the psychological effects on practices rooted in the spiritual traditions underline their wisdom. Seligman's (2011) development of the 'Three Blessings Exercise' in which people are encouraged to give thanks in a structured way at the end of each day echoes the 'attitude of gratitude'[8] fostered across the faith traditions and has been shown to be as effective as a course of antidepressants. A trail involving compassion training showed it increased altruism and changed the neural response to suffering as demonstrated on MRI scans (Weng et al. 2013). A recent study (Bilderbeck et al. 2014) evaluating the effects of yoga in prison demonstrated statistically significant effects on a variety of measures summarised as follows: 'Together these results suggest that yoga has

---

[8]   Zig Ziglar, www.ziglar.com/newsletter/july-13-2010-edition-28 (accessed 15 April 2015).

beneficial effects on subjective wellbeing and mental health, as well as enhancing cognitive–behavioural functioning'.

The work of Burnside et al. (2005) in summarising a variety of studies of faith-based programmes has also underlined the value of faith practices in enabling prison adjustment as demonstrated by numbers of adjudications as well as measures of well-being.

Whilst such studies in no way 'prove' the value of a spiritual practice or the value of chaplaincy in a custodial environment, it is encouraging to see evidence that the personal accounts people give of the impact of chaplaincy activities are mirrored by formal research findings.

The corporate dimension of worship or meditation in prison is especially important in providing an experience of a pro-social community where implicit norms of behaviour are enacted – the community being marked by mutual respect and accountability. The meeting after worship/meditation for refreshments is an extension of this process – give and take, listening, support are all built up week by week and also provide a grounding for the behaviours expected from a faith community outside prison. It is important that the experience of worship inside in some ways parallels what people can expect on the outside so that if they join a faith community upon release it is in some ways familiar.

As well as religious texts, chaplaincy can provide other inspirational but not always explicitly religious books which encourage resilience and a new sense of identity. Jo Simpson's *Touching the Void* – a book and a film – can help discussion about getting through against the odds. Similarly, the film *The Way*, which is based on the idea of pilgrimage, provides insights into coming to terms with loss that can be a key factor in the stories of many offenders. Even the recent best-selling book *A Street Cat Named Bob* (Bowen 2012) can be used to provide a sense of hope and a belief that things can be different:

> There's a famous quote I read somewhere. It says that we are all given second chances every day of our lives. They are there for the taking, it's just that we don't usually take them.

This can help sustain motivation and give a new way of approaching each day in a positive rather than negative light. Allied with stories that inspire, that give a sense that things can be different, is inviting ex-offenders who have 'made good' to come and share their stories – the ups and the downs and how they faced and overcame challenges. They can help people to see themselves as capable of change and able to write a new chapter in their story.

Seekers, Pastoral Care and Liminality

The 2011 census recorded that whilst formal religious affiliation is declining, an interest in the 'spiritual' is increasing. This trend is likely to be reflected in the prison population. If this is combined with the experience of prison as 'liminal' and a moment where post traumatic growth can occur, then chaplaincies need to provide opportunities for offenders to come and explore what is on offer to make sense of their experiences and offer a way forward. It can be especially valuable where humanists are part of the chaplaincy team. Including them can help some prisoners whose new sense of themselves may not involve a 'higher power' but rather a renewed sense of faith in human potential to do good and of the dignity of human being apart from any notion of transcendence.

Many chaplaincies run 'open days' where prisoners can come and ask questions and explore ideas in a non-threatening and supportive environment. Such opportunities can also introduce the chaplaincy itself as a place of reflection that can be especially valuable at a time of loss or change. The research into multifaith chaplaincy already mentioned (Todd and Tipton 2011) identified the value of the chaplaincy as a different kind of place within the prison where it was possible to think, reflect and consolidate, especially when people were coming to terms with loss. Even people of no particular faith tradition find the opportunity to be quiet and light a candle, perhaps on the anniversary of death, to be helpful as a way of marking time passing. Such space is also valued by staff.

This research into chaplaincy also underlines the value of the pastoral care provided by chaplains outside their statutory duties. What was distinctive in the eyes of the interviewees was that although it was recognised that chaplains themselves frame their ministry in religious language, such care was not simply 'God talk'. Instead, the care provided had an exploratory and person-centred quality to it. This provided the opportunity to make sense of events in a way that could allow new possibilities to emerge:

> The Chaplain, you know, they help me escape prison. Not just this prison *but my own prison*, you know? You can trust the Chaplain, you know. Tell them stuff you wouldn't tell no one else. (Todd and Tipton 2011: 30, my italics)

Looking to the Future

This chapter has demonstrated how chaplaincy contributes to the wider aims of NOMS in relation to reducing reoffending, resettlement as prioritised through *Transforming Rehabilitation* and ensuring decency and equality within prisons. There are nevertheless challenges looking forward, as enunciated in the recommendations in the Cardiff report. Space does not permit a full exploration of these but a few are worthy of particular comment. At the time of the report the concern was expressed that chaplaincies across the estate had the quality of being 'idiosyncratic franchises'. As part of a wider restructure, the previous Chaplain General, William Noblett, negotiated and developed a restructured Chaplaincy HQ to both assure the delivery of chaplaincy services in line with the PSI whilst also encouraging a responsivity to the local context through a network of HQ Advisers whose yearly visits include 'user voice', incorporating a prisoner focus group as well as an appreciative inquiry questionnaire and meeting with the whole chaplaincy team to ensure equality of provision and a sense of belonging for all team members – employed and sessional. The praxis of multifaith working, a paradigm shift for chaplaincy, is now well established (Noblett 2009), but is not taken for granted. A regional training programme run in 2012 for chaplains from across all the traditions included the opportunity for groups to engage in Scriptural Reasoning[9] and also to explore models of ministry as understood by different traditions to enable open and honest communication about both commonalities and differences. Training has also picked up the value of 'humanitarian pastoral care' articulated by interviewees, so the 'Pastoral Care and Counselling Course' delivered to chaplains is structured with an eye both to the crisis intervention and longer-term pastoral care that is part of the contribution to the wider care of prisoners in establishments.

Prison chaplaincy is an enormous privilege but is also challenging working with people with multiple needs. The importance of chaplains maintaining links with their own faith community, maintaining their own spiritual practice and developing strategies to maintain resilience is emphasised in the Starting Out course for new chaplains that also covers the practicalities of prison ministry. All training is delivered in a multifaith context which allows for mutual learning and exploration helping to equip people for their work within the context of multifaith teams. A final comment from the research made by one chaplain illustrates the potential for chaplaincy teams to model inclusive community that will inspire prisoners following discharge:

> One of the most powerful acts of faith I can be seen to do in this prison is walking on the wings side by side with my Muslim colleague having a good laugh. That is very powerful and it is interfaith dialogue in action. (Todd and Tipton 2011: 23)

---

[9]   Scriptural Reasoning allows members from different faith communities to share texts on a similar theme in a collaborative way with an introduction to the text being followed by a discussion comparing insights – further information can be obtained via the link to the University of Cambridge's Interfaith Programme: www.interfaith.cam.ac.uk (accessed 15 April 2015).

A Case Study: The 'Belief in Change' Programme[10]

Many of the ideas discussed in this article form the basis of a faith-informed reintegration programme 'Belief in Change'. A pilot of the programme has been running at Risley. It was commissioned by NOMS Chaplaincy, developed through European Social Fund grant funding and has been accredited by the Correctional Services Accreditation Panel. It is multifaith and aimed at medium to high risk male offenders aged between 25 and 40 – although some older offenders who are part of the community have found it helpful in giving them a new way of seeing the past and planning a different future.

The programme is holistic and offers a range of experiences that invite offenders to change – Figure 19.1 illustrates. It is community based, but is not a closed community, encouraging participants to try out their new skills and insights through engaging with the wider prison. It also allows participants to engage in productive activity that can be seen as reparative. The 'Belief in Change' programme also draws on the idea of retreat found in spiritual traditions. For the duration of the programme participants in some sense 'come away' from their previous experience of prison and are encouraged to reflect personally through the keeping of a journal. They also reflect together on what it means to be a community through morning meetings which include inspirational talks from participants or outside speakers as well as dealing with the nuts and bolts of living together.

In addition to daily community meetings there is peer support and restoration groups. These give participants and staff different ways of dealing with things that happen within the community itself and to develop new strategies for dealing with conflict or disagreement. Each participant also has 16 hours of personal coaching to develop a Life Plan in preparation for release, and the support of mentors and volunteers from the outside community. Like a retreat experience, there is an explicit focus on re-entry so the work and progress made during the programme is not lost through inadequate preparation for the challenges that will be faced either through re-entry to another wing in the prison, moving to Cat D conditions or on release.

There are also 42 hour-long 'Lifeskills Sessions'. Many of the sessions in the six modules – Preparing to Change; Relationships; Health and Wellbeing; Productive Living; Parenting and Family Life; Resources and Social Networks – are based on stories and practices introduced from across the faith and humanistic traditions to encourage reflection and the growth of resilience. Stories of people 'making good' encourage participants to see themselves both as able to change and to make a difference. This allows a new sense of narrative and the developing

---

[10]   Bird, L., Kavanagh, M. and Emmanuel, L. (2010), *The Belief in Change Programme*, Crown Copyright, National Offender Management Service.

a new future self that complements work on the Life Plan. Another theme of the programme is the idea of legacy, which is key to the idea of a changed narrative and identity. Participants are invited in various ways – choosing their inheritance tracks based on the Radio 4 feature, plotting their life journey, reflecting on what their memorial might be when they die – to own their past but also to see that they have a role in shaping their future that can free them to pass on positive memories and inspiration as someone 'made good'.

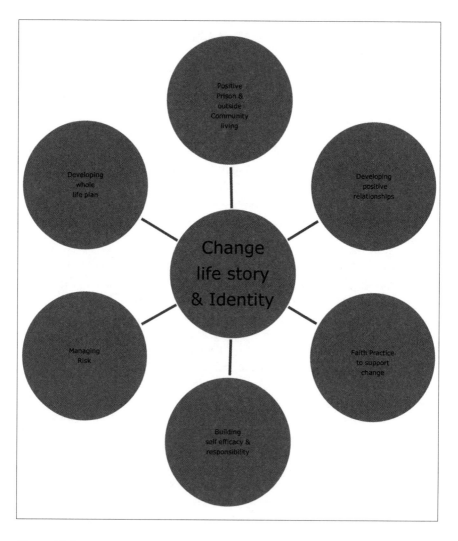

Figure 19.1

'Bringing It All Together'

As one of the 'Belief in Change' participants put it, 'Believing in Change makes change possible.' He was saying that when people believe in him as someone capable of change, then he is more able to believe in this for himself. Chaplains and chaplaincy volunteers as well as other prison staff are such Believers in Change. Through spiritual practice, prisoners are able to begin to frame a new narrative to help them desist from crime. The process incorporates a variety of practical tools that help build resilience and the capacity to overcome failure as well as to celebrate success. With the added value of through-the-gate work and a supportive faith community upon release, such new narratives can be sustained and the possibility of a positive legacy becomes real.

References

Armstrong, R. (2014), Trusting the untrustworthy: the theology, practice and implications of faith-based volunteers work with ex-prisoners. *Studies in Christian Ethics*, August, 299–309.

Bilderbeck, A., Farias, M. and Brazil, I. (2014), Psychological and cognitive benefits of yoga among UK prisoners. *Prison Service Journal*, May, 36–42.

Bowen, J. (2012), *A Street Cat Named Bob*. London: Hodder and Stoughton.

Braithwaite, J. (2006), *Crime, Shame and Reintegration*. Cambridge: Cambridge University Press.

Burnside, J., Loucks, N., Adler, J.R. and Rose, G. (2005), *My Brother's Keeper: Faith-Based Units in Prisons*. Cullompton: Willan Publishing.

Joseph, S. (2012), What doesn't kill us. *The Psychologist*, 25, 816–19.

Lemos, G. (2014), *The Good Prison: Conscience, Crime and Punishment*. London: Lemos and Crane.

Liebling, A., Arnold, H. and Straub, C. (2011), *An Exploration of Staff–Prisoner Relationships at HMP Whitemoor 12 Years On*. Cambridge Institute of Criminology Prison Research Centre. Available at: https://www.gov.uk/government/uploads/system/uploads/attachment_data/file/217381/staff-prisoner-relations-whitemoor.pdf (accessed 15 April 2015).

Maruna, S. (2011), Reentry as a rite of passage. *Punishment & Society*, 13(1), 3–28.

Maruna, S. and Roy, K. (2007), Amputation or reconstruction. *Journal of Contemporary Criminal Justice*, 23, 104–24.

Maruna, S., Wilson, L. and Curran, K. (2006), Why God is often found behind bars: prison conversions and the crisis of self-narrative. *Research in Human Development*, 3, 161–84.

Noblett, W. (2009), *Inside Faith: Praying for People in Prison*. London: Darton, Longman and Todd.

Seligman, M.E.P. (2011), *Flourish: A Visionary New Understanding of Happiness and Well-being*. New York: Simon and Schuster.

Todd, A., and Tipton, L. (2011), *The Role and Contribution of a Multi-Faith Prison Chaplaincy to the Contemporary Prison Service*. [Monograph]. Available at: http://stmichaels.ac.uk/assets/pdf/Todd-and-Tipton-2011-Report-on-Prison-Chaplaincy.pdf (accessed 17 April 2015).

Weng, H.Y., Fox, A.S., Shackman, A.J., Stodola, D.E., Caldwell, J.Z., Olson, M.C., ... Rogers, G.M. and Davidson, R.J. (2013), Compassion training alters altruism and neural responses to suffering. *Psychological Science*, 24(7), 1171–80.

Chapter 20

Case Study

Rosie Deedes

Introduction

Prison chaplaincy, like ministry in many other contexts, is reactive, shaped by the environment and the needs of the community in which it is located. As prisons vary in category and make-up, so the chaplain's role changes accordingly. In a local prison where prisoners arriving straight from court may be traumatised by coming to prison for the first time, chaplains offer crisis support. In a resettlement prison, from which prisoners are about to be released, the pastoral need may be to encourage prisoners to prepare for life on the outside; a long term prison may be helping an older population face the possibility of dying in prison. However varied the context, the position of the chaplain within the institution remains largely the same. Prisons are secular organisations, but like the armed forces, there has traditionally been a strong chaplaincy presence, and generally the chaplaincy department is considered to have a unique and valuable role to play (see Todd and Tipton 2011).

This case study of one chaplain's ministry draws on my own experiences in several different prisons since 1999. It identifies some key features of the contemporary context of prison chaplaincy and explores different dimensions of the reactive, but distinctive, pastoral care offered by chaplaincy.

A Changing Context

I write as an ordained Anglican priest, but operate as a member of a team. Prison chaplaincy in the past decade has been at the forefront of cross-denominational and multifaith working (see Todd 2011, Todd and Tipton 2011, Gilliat-Ray et al. 2013). Sacred spaces are shared, not only with all shades of the Christian community, but by other faiths. In HMP Isle of Wight, for example, I worked closely with my Muslim colleague to find a way of making the large chapel in Albany suitable for the Muslims to use for Jummah prayers on a Friday. This involved creating screens, made by prisoners in our woodwork workshop, which would separate the back area of the chapel from the sanctuary, so that the Christian symbols were obscured and therefore would not cause offence to the Muslims who now pray there. The toilet area accommodates ablution facilities for the Muslims, and the vestry now contains prayer mats as well as communion artifacts and vestments for Roman Catholics, Anglicans, and Free Church colleagues, and yoga mats!

The effective collaboration of a diverse team in chaplaincy is essential for the credibility of the department. If chaplains are seen to work together they challenge the negative, hostile and sometimes extremist views of prisoners who through prejudice, ignorance or lack of opportunity have considered people of faiths different to their own as enemies (see further Todd 2013). Staff in prison may also hold strong views about religion and religious people. Chaplains may be the first people of faith colleagues have encountered, so when we demonstrate a willingness and enthusiasm about working with others from different traditions and perspectives we are challenging these negative perceptions.

In 2010, soon after arriving in Albany prison, I started a Faith Forum, where nominated prisoners of faiths represented in the prison meet monthly to discuss faith matters. This way, as chaplain to a majority faith, I can support and hear the needs of the minority faith groups, and enable them to hear the concerns of each other. At each of these meetings prisoners chair and take minutes. There is a moment of silent reflection before beginning and the meeting concludes by shaking hands in the Quaker tradition. At each meeting a member of the forum presents some aspect of their faith to the others, so we all learn the meaning and significance of faith in its many forms from each other. At any meeting there are likely to be representatives from Hindu, Sikh, Buddhist, Jewish, Muslim, Christian (RC, CofE and Free Church), Pagan, Church of Jesus Christ of Latter Day Saints, Quaker, Rastafarian, Spiritualist and Jehovah's Witness. It is hard to imagine such a diverse gathering being possible in many other situations.

The Faith Forum was so valuable that we soon established it on the other prison sites of HMP Isle of Wight, in Parkhurst and Camphill. We have also organised, through the forums, an annual Festival of Faith Music, when each faith group takes a five-minute slot to share some aspect of their faith using music as the main medium. This is now an established part of the calendar of events for the prison to which local dignitaries are invited. Demonstrating religious harmony in any setting is powerful, but enabling prisoners to contribute is both constructive and groundbreaking. And it also helps to restore in them a sense of self-worth and is, therefore, part of their rehabilitation.

Pastoral Care in Context

In this multifaith context, one of the daily pastoral duties of a member of the chaplaincy team remains to visit those in the hospital wing.[1] In HMP Holloway,

---

[1]   One aspect of the statutory duties of the chaplain, enshrined in the 1952 Prison Act.

when I was there, this unit held about 25 women, many of whom were suffering from mental health conditions, as well as some who were physically unwell. Often women who had self-harmed or who were intent upon harming themselves were kept in this location where the supervision by nurses as well as officers was greatest. There were many occasions where a woman was deemed so at risk of killing herself that there was a member of staff located outside the door of her cell 24 hours a day, monitoring the woman's every move. Whilst the hospital wing could at times seem more like Bedlam or Broadmoor, and although frequently it was a place of possibly the greatest concentration of tragedy in the country, it was also a place of great care and collaboration between many different disciplines, and also between the patients themselves.

It was probably in this most challenging of environments that I learned the most about pastoral care, and my own limitations. Just as you cannot problem-solve in prison, neither can you save people, however much you might want to, or think you should try. People in prison have very little control over their environment; they are told when to get up, what to eat, when to go to their room. For many, this absence of control is probably the most painful of all the conditions they have to deal with in prison, and some will go to extreme lengths to regain what they feel has been taken away from them.

One young woman, Lisa (all names have been changed), a highly intelligent graduate, had spent much of her recent life testing out her environment, and pushing herself to the limits of rational behaviour. When she arrived in Holloway, she was in a wheelchair having thrown herself off a bridge. She also had a catheter. She had been diagnosed with an untreatable personality disorder, and had been told by a psychiatrist that she would be dead by her mid 20s. It is hard to fathom the impact of such a diagnosis on her already disturbed and damaged psyche, and no amount of pastoral care, however well intentioned, would have addressed these complexities. The general consensus for those that got to know Lisa was that she did not want to die but she sought to control her environment by whatever means possible. She refused to eat. She repeatedly removed her catheter, choosing to lie in her own urine and excrement rather than to use the facilities offered to her. Often when I would visit her, she would be lying on the floor, refusing to communicate, in clothing provided by the prison which could not be torn up and made into a ligature. Why someone would prefer these conditions to the more humane conditions of the rest of the prison is hard to fathom, and perhaps can only be understood in ontological as well as psychological and spiritual terms. I could not answer the why of her behaviour, and I could not offer her a solution to it either, so what was my role as chaplain?

Paul Tillich (1952) talks of the 'courage to be', and so much of pastoral ministry in extremis, is being rather than doing: being a presence, being alongside, being available. Often on my daily visits I would stop at Lisa's doorway, and if she was not looking or responding verbally, I would simply introduce myself, and say hello, and say I was happy to talk with her if she felt ready or wanted to. Then I would stay for a few minutes, in silence if necessary, move on and tell her I would see her tomorrow. Eventually there came a turning point when Lisa chose to communicate. This was certainly not down to one person's input, and is always a joint effort, not least from the patient. It is hard to recall the how and why of the change; I suspect Lisa herself would not be able to explain it, and as with many extremely damaged individuals hers was not always a smooth path to recovery; self-sabotage, low self-esteem, and habitual behaviour often mean that someone reverts to destructive patterns because they are more familiar and 'comfortable'. Lisa taught me the importance of being faithful, of being trustworthy, and of never giving up on someone. I recall telling her frequently that I didn't accept that people couldn't change, and that if God doesn't give up on us, then why should I?

The I–Thou of Pastoral Care

In all pastoral situations, in my experience, there is a giving and taking between those involved. The person seemingly being ministered to becomes the minister, and the teacher becomes the pupil. Often I found myself wondering what was expected of me in a particular situation, only to discover that the prisoner led the way, and gave me the role which they required me to take. What I have also discovered is the reciprocity of care in any situation, and the give and take in any encounter. This is the 'I and Thou' relationship of Martin Buber (1958), which I always experience and look for, and which I will always feed back to the person with whom I am currently engaged. Prisoners, who have had everything taken away from them, can also lose their sense of self-worth and dignity, feeling: What do I have to give to anyone any more? In acknowledging to that person that I have received something from them, that they have taught me something, which I will then use in my future ministry with whoever else I encounter, I hope to remind them, and reawaken in them, their capacity to give.

HMP Isle of Wight has the highest number of deaths in custody of any prison in the country. Most deaths are from natural causes and many are associated with older age. My pastoral encounters with older prisoners helped me to accompany one younger prisoner, Sam, who was dying, and in journeying with him, he taught me how to journey with others. I told him once that I hoped I would write about him one day. He would be delighted to know that I have told his story and will continue to do so when other opportunities arise.

Sam was in outside hospital when I first met him. He had been there for a few days under investigation for his condition. I realised after an hour's visit that here was someone who liked and needed to talk. His biggest fear was that he would be told he had cancer. Shortly after this visit his fears were realised.

In the weeks that followed I accompanied Sam through the process of coming to terms with his diagnosis and the inevitability of his death. Initially he was tempted to fight back emotionally, to be the horrible, angry individual he used to be. After all, he was dying, what was the point in being nice any more? He would still die at the end of it. Feeling angry is a response to loss. But whereas for most of us this would be understood and allowed for, for Sam to act on these feelings would have been dangerous. I told him he had a choice: how he wanted to die. He couldn't change the fact that he was dying, but he could die well, and be respected and affirmed in that, or he could revert to old ways, and die bitter and lonely too.

Sam made that choice. He died well, with great courage, and dignity, and most of the time good humour. But he struggled to stay on this track. It is so easy to slip into old habits, to feel sorry for oneself, to think the world owes one a favour, to wish to 'curse God and die'. But as Sam said, if he did that, then what has the struggle of his time in prison been for? What would all the therapy, the reflection, the offending behaviour courses have really done for him? Did he not owe it to himself, and to those who had helped him on the way to face this latest challenge as the new Sam, rather than the old?

Sam was 35. He had been in prison for 20 years. He told me that he came to believe, after about 10 years in prison, that he would never be released, but he still had that hope within him that he might. His early life was characterised by violence, physical abuse and emotional paucity. He was, in his own words, out of control. The catastrophic result of this situation was that he murdered a close family member. Twenty years on, after years in secure children's homes, prison institutions and secure mental hospitals, Sam grew up. Sometimes old patterns of thinking would emerge again, but now he recognised them, and fought to shrug them off.

Little did any of us expect that the greatest test of Sam's new outlook on life would come, not from the fact of his dying, though that of course brought many challenges, but from facing his victims. Sam had had no contact with his family since his court appearance where he had been sentenced to life in prison. As far as he was concerned his family hated him, and wished him dead. However, when he was told that he was dying, Sam was given the option to inform his family of his circumstances; he chose this option, and one of our Family Liaison Officers made contact with them through the probation service. Sam and I had many long and involved conversations about his family, and his feelings towards them. He was reflective, empathic, and mature about them and himself, but he had no notion of how they had been in the intervening years. It was a momentous occasion when after an exchange of letters between them, they had their first phone call, and even more so when they asked to come and visit.

Sam and I prepared for this visit by talking. It was clear to me that Sam was still very fearful of his father, a big man who had been a drinker, and violent in his parenting. Would his parents and siblings wish to kill him for what he had done? When I met Sam's parents in the visits hall just prior to their visit, Sam's parents were equally fearful. Would he still be the angry uncontrollable teenager they had left in care? Did he still harbour murderous thoughts towards them? It was as if each side had an image of the other which had been frozen in time, and neither had any concept or hope that people can change in the intervening 20 years.

Because of my pastoral relationship with Sam, he asked me to stay for this visit with his family, partly for protection, and also because he needed to reflect on this experience afterwards. It was one of the most moving and memorable experiences of my ministry, and it brought some measure of healing and reconciliation to most of the family members who participated. Sam saw his Dad as an infirm, vulnerable and softer individual. His parents saw Sam as a mature, reflective and humbled young man. Sam's Mum said to him that he would always be her little boy.

The sadness of this situation was that there was not more time available to build on the reconciliation of this visit. But perhaps it is not just quantity of time that matters, but the quality of it. Though there were subsequent letters and phone calls, and though the family hoped to visit again after Christmas, we had to invite them to visit before this, as Sam's condition deteriorated rapidly. By the time the visit was arranged, Sam had already slipped into an unresponsive sleep. Though he managed once to open his eyes, and seemed to acknowledge his parents' presence, Sam could no longer communicate with them, though of course they could with him. I encouraged Sam's Mum to give Sam permission to go, as I felt from my previous experiences of him that this would ease his dying. It was an agonising moment for Sam's mum, to let go of her son, but she did so with such courage and graciousness, saying that her child who had died at Sam's hands would be waiting to receive him. This was such a moment of forgiveness and absolution, which no one other than Sam's mother could have offered. Sam did not regain consciousness, and died shortly after this visit. I took his funeral.

Holding Hope

A chaplain needs to be flexible and adaptable. Having left Sam's final family visit I then ran to the chapel to lead the Christmas carol service with 70 prisoners and outside guests! As a chaplain, it is also vitally important to be spontaneous, and to recognise and seize the opportunity to have a meaningful conversation with someone if the moment presents itself. On most occasions when I leave my office with a list of people I intend to go and see on B wing, I return having seen many people, none of whom I set out to! Few people will formally request to see a chaplain, and certainly staff will rarely do so, but by giving the appearance of having time, and being willing to make time for someone you might encounter on a corridor, or in an office, conversations may emerge which are of importance and value. Sometimes it is just by smiling, and greeting people as one passes that people become conscious that you are a person who is approachable and trustworthy, and after three years of greetings, there might be an opening for a more significant conversation. In a busy local such as Holloway, where the average length of stay when I was there was 28 days, I learned quickly that each encounter with a prisoner is significant, for you might see her one day, and the next she would be moved on to another establishment, or get bail if she was on remand. It is interesting that the Prison Service has recently developed the strapline "Every contact matters"; I suspect chaplains have known this for ever!

One of the other daily statutory duties for chaplains is to see all the new prisoners within 24 hours of their arrival. Most new arrivals in Holloway were seen the morning after their first night in prison. They were often in shock, disorientated and distressed. Frequently they were unable to put into words how they were feeling, though often they were very tearful. The purpose of these visits was to reassure the prisoner that there are people in the prison there to support them, and to listen. Coming to prison can strip prisoners of their self-esteem, and leave them feeling extremely vulnerable and lost. Hopefully, after the indignities of coming into prison for the first time, having to hand over all your property and being strip searched, seeing a friendly face can help women or men coming to prison for the first time to come to terms with their situation and find a way of coping.

Women coming to prison often have very low self-confidence already. Helping women imprisoned for the first time to find their voice, to know how to deal with other prisoners and with staff, to feel less isolated and to find methods of coping and adapting were the essential elements of most of my pastoral conversations. With the support and encouragement of a counsellor and a probation officer, I developed an accredited course, First Timers in Custody, which used the dynamic of a group, lasting for six weeks, one afternoon a week, to address these concerns. This was organised and facilitated by the chaplaincy team and it became an important part of the support network within that particular women's prison, HMP Downview; it also demonstrated the contribution chaplaincy can make beyond the realms of practising and supporting faith development.

As a chaplain I have seen many women first timers distraught, despairing, believing they cannot go on. I have seen them adjust to imprisonment over the weeks and months, and find ways of making the situation bearable and in some cases positive. This is the kind of message which I have given to someone who is feeling hopeless, and it will be reinforced by other prisoners who act as peer supporters, and listeners (Samaritan-trained prisoners) who will also meet the new arrivals.

The role of chaplains must be to hold on to hope, both for and with individuals and within the institution. This is not always easy in an environment where cynicism can dominate, and it can be made harder by the indifference, ignorance or hostility many in society feel towards prisoners and prisons. Hope is not false jollity providing a quick fix or unrealistic solutions. Hope is being able to maintain and encourage a sense of perspective and of valuing prisoners as individuals; it is recognising the importance of those who work in prison who all play a part in enabling prisoners to change.

To be a chaplain in a prison requires a diverse set of qualities and gifts. It is not for those who wish to problem-solve, see quick results or who like to feel in control. The infrastructure of the institution; the bureaucracy of the organisation; the complexity of the procedures; the constant changes of policy and direction; the constraints, financial and otherwise of working in a public service can in themselves be debilitating. Coupling this with the chaos, harm, vulnerability, violence, sin and shame we deal with on a daily basis means that chaplaincy in this context is not for the faint-hearted or easily overwhelmed.

I believe that chaplaincy in prison is a calling. It is ministry which is real, raw, diverse, illuminating, enlightening, humbling, stimulating, unpredictable, diverse and challenging. Chaplains in prison need to have their feet on the ground, their eyes on their keys, and their lives fixed on God. They must keep their sense of humour as well as their sense of perspective; they must be able to engage with everyone, and be able to let go of them too. They must be resilient, compassionate and self-aware. I have always held Matthew 10.16 in mind in thinking about my own role as a prison chaplain: 'Be wise as serpents and as gentle as doves!'

I have on my desk a postcard with a panel of the Quaker tapestry depicting the following quotation from a Quaker, Harvey Gillman. It resonates with my own sense of vocation to this ministry, and reminds me of one of the fundamental principles of prison chaplaincy: to look for the good in people and help them rediscover this for themselves.

> I believe there is that of God in all people though sometimes it is hard to find. Punishment ought to be a way of helping people to realize the hurt they are doing to this sense of worth in themselves and in others.

References

Buber, M. (1958), *I and Thou*, transl. R.G. Smith. New York: Charles Scribner's Sons.

Gilliat-Ray, S., Ali, M.M., and Pattison, S. (2013), *Understanding Muslim Chaplaincy*. Farnham: Ashgate.

Tillich, P. (1952), *The Courage to Be*. New Haven, CT: Yale University Press.

Todd, A. (2011), Responding to Diversity: Chaplaincy in a Multi-Faith Context. In M. Threlfall-Holmes and M. Newitt (eds), *Being a Chaplain*. London: SPCK, 89–102.

—— (2013), Preventing the 'neutral' chaplain? The potential impact of anti-'extremism' policy on prison chaplaincy. *Practical Theology*, 6(2), 144–58.

Todd, A. and Tipton, L. (2011), *The Role and Contribution of a Multi-Faith Prison Chaplaincy to the Contemporary Prison Service*. Available at: http://stmichaels.ac.uk/assets/pdf/Todd-and-Tipton-2011-Report-on-Prison-Chaplaincy.pdf (accessed 17 April 2015).

PART VI
Education Chaplaincy

Chapter 21
Education Chaplaincy

Jeremy Clines

Introduction to Education Chaplaincy

The Area Covered

Education chaplaincy, in its past and present forms and across all learning ages, is a broad area to describe and interpret. There are many ways in which education chaplaincy has been understood and how it has fulfilled its purpose. This chapter covers the following matters in relation to education chaplaincy:

1. An introduction to education chaplaincy;
2. Versions of contemporary practice;
3. Contemporary practice: exemplars and challenges;
4. Future developments.

The term 'education chaplaincy' is used to describe any chaplaincy work sited within an educational setting, including child and adult education at all levels. The focus of this chapter pays most attention, first, to my own context of England and Wales, and second occasionally references Scotland and Northern Ireland too, which are similar, but where education and the church are funded and governed differently.

The consequences for education chaplaincy are affected by the settlement between religion and state in Britain and Northern Ireland compared with the multiple chaplaincies for different religions and beliefs that are present at many universities in the United States of America. This chapter describes a context that has seen its education chaplaincy provision mainly shaped and predominantly funded by churches and church foundation institutions. Multi-religious chaplaincy settings are increasing but the Christian frameworks within which these developments occur have a large impact on how chaplaincies are operated.

The Context and Settings of Education Chaplaincy

The types of situations in which chaplaincy occur are exceptional in relation to other sectors because:

  i. there is a long-standing openness within education to engage with matters of religion, faith and belief;

 ii. requirements for chaplaincy in education are less prescriptive than military, hospital and prison settings;

iii. the principal support – apart from the small but significant contribution of Jewish chaplaincies in higher education – has occurred from the Christian churches or Christian foundation institutions;

 iv. the speed with which chaplaincies have become multi-religious has been rapid, recent (since 2000), and in nearly all cases dependent on volunteers from the institution or local community.

The public discourse of the academy has at all points in its history included religion in its learning and dialogue at elementary and secondary levels and in higher education (HE). This is in part because of the origins of the university and the school system that were wedded to the church.

Although much provision has, to date, been Christian, such provision has predominantly been understood as inclusive of people of all faiths and beliefs. This type of work regards chaplaincy ministry to 'be unconditional, non-judgmental, open-minded and able to value the spiritual tradition of others in a non-partisan way' (Swinton 2011: 19). This is in contrast to an alternative and more exclusivist approach that sees chaplaincy as a further opportunity for religious instruction from one perspective, which hopes to persuade people into religious faith or sustain them within an established mode.

The efforts to involve and value students and staff of the world religions has been particularly evident since 2000 but had begun in the 1980s and 1990s (Gilliat-Ray 1999). Further incentives and challenges have been provided by more recent religion and belief legislation, which has a range of consequences in further education (FE) and HE learning settings and has also created challenges for schools.

Because chaplaincy has not been a mandatory requirement (except in certain church foundation institutions) there has been a much wider scope regarding what can be embodied and how a chaplaincy might develop in a way that is context specific. Because the existence of chaplaincy has been dependent on funding, the vast majority of the shaping of such services has been done by Christians in employed positions.

In academic year 2012 there were:

- 4,265,000 FE institution participants in England and Wales in 2010/11 (Bolton 2012: 20, Table 7);
- 5,007,000 pupils at public sector 'elementary/primary' schools in the whole of the UK in 2012 (Bolton 2012: 15, Table 1);

- 3,856,000 at public sector 'secondary' schools in the UK in 2012 (Bolton 2012: 16, Table 1);
- 564,000 children at independent schools in England and Wales in 2012 (Bolton 2012: 17, Table 4);
- 2,340,275 enrolled in UK HE institutions (HEIs) in 2012/13 (HESA 2014).

Almost 90 per cent of HEIs do have a chaplaincy (Clines 2008: 4), and around half of FE colleges (Education Division 2014a). In FE and HE most of these have representatives from at least some of the world religions, as is explained later. A tiny proportion of state schools have some kind of chaplaincy (see, for instance, Treagle 2011). In fewer instances, these represent a wider variety of beliefs. Nearly all church primary schools have a Christian minister with some responsibility (e.g. the parish priest), but not usually a chaplain. Most independent schools with a church foundation will have also have a Christian chaplain. About 50 per cent of FE institutions have chaplaincies too, which are usually multi-religious.

The History of Chaplaincy Provision

Chaplaincies have been organised in an ad hoc way in each type of setting. These locations include:

- state, fee-paying and private schools;
- schools with/without Christian Foundations;
- FE colleges;
- other colleges of education;
- HEIs;
- church or Christian HEIs;
- HE colleges based in a larger HEI;
- other settings, secular or religious in nature.

Many current forms emanate from the long-standing involvement of the Christian church in education of people of all ages. After Roman times the church in England founded English schools from the end of the sixth century CE (Lawson and Silver 1973: 1–11). Many more schools were established after 1066 CE, and by 1500 CE a few universities had also been founded in England and Scotland (Lawson and Silver 1973: 12–84, Edgar 1893: 2). Wherever a lay minister or clergy person has been appointed to serve a learning community then we can understand this work as an early example of education chaplaincy. Schools that are not faith based are the least well provided for, then FE colleges, but nearly all HE settings have a chaplaincy (Clines 2008: 8).

The provision of elementary and secondary education for the poor began with enthusiasm from the late 18th century. However, it was a set of parliamentary Acts in the 1830s and the influence of the church, both Anglican and non-conformist, that led to the churches establishing systems for teacher training and school provision from 1840 to 1870 (McGregor 1991: 1–10).

Because it was the churches that provided the schooling, in nearly all instances the school would be a parish (or chapel) school. The priest or minister from the church would have a role in the school, so provision was different but parallel to that of a school chaplain. From these earliest times to the present, it is not that a priest was legislated for, but rather that a church school was established where a parish ministry existed.

Schools with a church foundation, independent of the parish systems (which are commonly called both 'public' and 'private' schools) would legislate for a chaplain in their instruments and articles in a pattern that followed the Oxford and Cambridge custom. It is such independent schools where 'the majority of school chaplains' are based (Lindsay 1999: 118).

The absence of automatic chaplaincy provision in state schools arose because they were funded by the then newly founded local authorities. These schools began as a result of the Elementary Education Acts of 1870 to 1893 (for 5 to 14 year olds). Further education began (originally in technical colleges) as a result of the Local Government Act of 1888 and the subsequent Technical Instruction Act (1889) and Local Taxation Act (1890) that provided adequate financing for education (Pratt 2000: 12).

All of these locally organised, state-funded schools and colleges did not have a religious requirement to their foundation, although at primary and secondary level Christian religious instruction has been part of the structure of the learning programme, as well as a daily act of worship, up to the present day. This means that where chaplaincy happens it is more likely to be multi-religious in these settings (though prior to 2000 chaplaincies would have nearly always been exclusively Christian).

The scale of FE colleges and the significance of their chaplaincies, where they exist, is difficult to overestimate since more 16 and 17 year olds are at FE colleges than in a school sixth form, and these colleges also provide adult education, vocational courses, employability opportunities and many foundation degrees, as well as a range of degree-level courses too. That they are multi-religious has been an exemplar to chaplaincies in school and HE settings.

The Basis for Current Provision

The requirement for a chaplaincy may be stated in the founding documents (for example, the instruments and articles) of an organisation. This pattern is repeated in the history of independent schools, prisons and some church foundation schools and HEIs. It is almost entirely the case in state schools, church schools, FE colleges and HEIs that there is no requirement or statute requiring a chaplaincy.

Many chaplaincies in HEIs and FE colleges were established by a mutual arrangement between churches and the institution, with funding coming predominantly but not exclusively from the churches and physical space usually being provided by the institution. Some institutions, particularly in HEIs, also have Roman Catholic and Jewish chaplaincies established as independent entities by the respective faith organisation investing both in property and staff to run the facility.

In the 1960s and 1970s some visionary HE chaplaincies were established to serve different Christian denominations with a joint centre, and, exceptionally, universities in Lancaster and Guildford opened multi-religious chaplaincies. By 2008 the majority of chaplaincies had made some multi-religious arrangements, usually via prayer facilities, volunteers representing different beliefs and working with student faith societies (Clines 2008: 8–24).

More recently many institutions that have opted to have chaplaincies (rather than them being required as part of their foundation) have come to recognise the essential responsiveness provided to questions of religion and belief as part of the organisational concern for equalities. This is usually a consequence of a more thorough attention being given to ensuring a set of robust standards for student and pupil support and pastoral care, which has subsequently resulted in chaplaincies being asked to become more multi-religious. At times the chaplaincy may be in place for the benefit of student learners, but commonly the pastoral care provided is for all members of a learning organisation (as well as its alumni, potential new members, former staff and visitors).

The most rapid expansion of education chaplaincy in the last two decades has been in FE chaplaincy: 'almost 50% of all FE colleges that have chaplaincies have established them in the past 10 to 15 years' (Limb 2007: 40). Although some chaplaincy had been done, historically, by local clergy (Archbishops' Council 2002: 4) and ecumenically (ibid.: 5), newer developments have borrowed, in part, from a Health Service model (and other sectors) as well as from the latest developments in HE chaplaincy.

'In the space of a few years, college chaplaincy had advanced from being a marginalized activity in a marginalized sector to an institution whose value to individuals, to colleges and even, to the fulfillment of national policy, had been acknowledged' (Healey 2007: 268). These newer ideas in FE were to establish multifaith chaplaincies as a response, to transform the approach to religion and belief identities and to think in more contemporary terms about 'spiritual moral social and cultural development' by talking instead of 'values, belief and faith' (Limb 2007: 1). This was as a direct response to the government White Paper (Limb 2007: 2).

New arrangements have also occurred in church secondary schools (for 11–18 year olds). Historically, some would have had a chaplain, replicating the independent schools' arrangements, while others have depended on the minister of the local church. Recent changes mean that there are a rapidly growing number of church secondary schools and accompanying that an increase in the number of chaplaincies (Archbishops' Council Education Division 2014).

Beyond the work of chaplaincies, it is vital to note that the historic shape of student support in HE in Britain has been influenced, predominantly, by the Christian pastoral care provided in an Oxford or Cambridge college by the Church of England chaplain 'with strong moral and religious overtones' (Earwaker 1992: 103). This notion has been promulgated by tutors offering pastoral support and by early examples of Student Services departments. More recent critique of existing models of 'pastoral care' in HE have asked for a more inclusive and less 'paternalistic' version of support services for students (Earwaker 1992: 106).

Where chaplaincies are established without Christian foundations in the institution, there is evidence within HE that there is a 'greater flexibility' in the way an institution 'responds to diversity' (Gilliat-Ray 1999: 44) that is not focused on a Christian purpose or goals of Christian mission.

The church continues to see its contribution to chaplaincy as a way for the church to be present with significant groups from society in terms of age profile and numbers; Shilson-Thomas argues for the pertinence of a Christian presence in HE chaplaincy settings because 'with 44 per cent of people aged between 17 and 30 entering higher education, it seems self-evident that this is where the Church needs to be' (Shilson-Thomas 2011: 32).

Versions of Contemporary Practice

Typical Features: Models and Roles

Typical models of chaplaincy include some or all of the following features:

- Christian foundation and a multifaith identity;
- Christian worship and Muslim prayer;
- belonging to or provided for the institution;
- more recent examples of multi-religious chaplaincies;
- part of the learning process (e.g. chaplains who teach).

As mentioned earlier, the usual history of provision in institutions that have existed for more than three decades is that a Christian lay or ordained minister or ministers have been the initial people to organise and staff the chaplaincy.

A large majority of chaplains being Christian, and of these many being Anglican, results in a predominant understanding that the chaplaincy has responsibility for all members of the institution, not just those of the minster's particular denomination. In the Church of England this is understood, theologically, as a priest being licensed by their bishop with the 'cure of souls'; the care for all persons in their area or place of service. More recently a post-holder may have been a coordinator with a responsibility to coordinate a team of volunteers representing a variety of world religions and other belief positions.

Excluding Oxford and Cambridge, 95 per cent of salaried chaplaincy staff in HEIs are Christian (Clines 2008: 13) and among all staff, voluntary and paid, 78 per cent are Christian (ibid.). Although some HE chaplaincies had begun to title themselves 'multifaith' by 2008, the majority had not (9 called 'multifaith', 79 'chaplaincy' and 14 other names; Clines 2008: 8). Since a quarter of chaplaincies (26 per cent) did not have any voluntary staff, it means that 74 per cent of chaplaincies had more than one religion represented in the staff team (Clines 2008: 5).

Usually, role descriptions will include the need to provide pastoral care and, where acts of worship take place, some responsibility for leading and organising these occasions will fall to the chaplain or chaplaincy. Chaplains are commonly allocated a specific share of pastoral responsibility, or given a commitment to work within a wider team of staff providing support for students or pupils. Many HE chaplains are situated within Student Services to reflect the overlapping and collaborative ways in which an HEI will support students.

Learning institutions have a range of freedoms in determining their ethos and identity. Models for chaplaincies, although heavily influenced by Christian ministry, differ from those deployed in more general Christian ministry, but there are overlaps. When those responsible for shaping models for ministry were asked for their emphases for ministry, it was the heading 'practical theologian' that came first on the seven-item list rather than the 'manager', which came last (Bunting 1993: 19). From the more developed options Bunting offers, 'the competent professional' is probably the one that is most readily translatable into an HE setting. Despite this, 'there is no one clear set of ideas, practices, theologies or principles underlying Christian chaplaincy practice in the UK' (Gilliat-Ray et al. 2013: 167). Rather, 'chaplaincy theory, theology and practice in different institutions has been ad hoc' (Gilliat-Ray et al. 2013: 168).

In chaplaincy settings, models are varied in ways that reflect the institutional life and the history of how chaplaincy work has been practised in that particular setting. Chaplains and chaplaincies, especially in Christian settings, may have seen their work as involving some of the following elements:

- to gather a congregation for worship;
- as a religious 'stepping stone' in a liminal context;

- an information and resource base for enquirers;
- adopting a person-centred, reactive approach;
- multiple chaplaincies for many religions/beliefs;
- an integrated team (either ecumenical or multifaith);
- a Christian team plus a wider, voluntary group;
- a proactive ministry contributing to institutional life.

Many of these approaches can be used in combination and some of them are effective even as a singular approach.

A contribution to the broader organisational life may also feature in a chaplain's role and gives opportunities for collaborative working. Responsibilities can include: serving on committees, helping with social programmes, engaging with institutional ethics committees or dialogues, participating in fundraising, and contributing to learning and teaching programmes.

When compared to chaplaincies in other sectors, it is reasonable to surmise that the functions and duties of an education chaplain are likely to be, on average, less prescriptive than those of chaplains in prison, military or health care settings. This is because these other settings have more specific and prescriptive functions in their organisational purpose when compared to learning institutions.

Experiences of Compulsory Chaplaincy

Because of the influence of the church on state education (including religious education and a Christian 'daily act of worship') many have childhood memories (and even some HE students prior to the 1970s) of compulsory chapel as a fundamental part of both their experience of education and Christianity, and this is perpetuated in a range of settings.

More typical though, now, especially in FE and HE settings, are chaplaincy formats that seek to be person-centred and determined to travel to where people are based rather than expecting everyone to arrive at an act of worship that is provided for everyone – see, for instance, the Church of England reports on changes in FE and HE chaplaincy: Limb (2007) and Archbishops' Council (2002).

Within schools, social and organisational conformity means there can be pressure to opt in, especially for those with an unclear or minority belief identity. This can be particularly discomforting for those wanting to explore or who see others provided with specific provision (for example, Muslim alternatives) compared to their own circumstances. Social inclusion within a faith-based school setting provides challenges for pupils, teachers, parents, school boards and chaplaincies (see Donlevy 2002: 102).

Contemporary Practice: Exemplars and Challenges

Exemplars from Higher Education Chaplaincy

Recent times have brought modernised versions of chaplaincy that have, with predominantly all Christian staff (and a predominance of Christian funding), meant changes to the culture, ethos and purpose of a chaplaincy. Change has been more limited where the foundation of the organisation has been Christian (see above). At best, though, chaplaincies have understood the distinctive contribution they can make to the spiritual formation both of the individual and the institution.

Institutions (however traditional), especially in HE, have quickly learned that the increase in global travel has meant that a chaplaincy can offer a vital service, promoting understanding and dialogue. At a more functional level too, chaplaincies have become more important because the learning institution has seen a broader range of advantages than in the past for a chaplaincy helping to meet a range of developmental needs for a wider variety of students.

Chaplaincies have a history of responsiveness to personal development and community cohesion. Even before the current need and aspiration for improving inter-religious and cultural understanding, chaplaincies were in the lead when it came to earlier questions of global education. In a section entitled 'Education for World Citizenship', Shockley (1989: 118) recognises the particular role chaplaincies can play in global education: 'Campus ministries are strategically placed to serve a catalytic function in bringing together university resources on issues of international significance' (Shockley 1989: 119). On ethnic minority concerns, again, Shockley speaks of a present continuous and future imperative need: 'Every campus unit serving a white majority campus should continually ask itself what it can do to serve the welfare of ethnic minority students' (Shockley 1989: 122).

In exploring how faith communities have become more engaged in HE chaplaincy, in 2008 seven (whole-day) practice dialogues were set up for HE chaplaincy practitioners. They comprised many religious and belief perspectives as well as university managers and leaders, to explore some substantial elements of the shape of education chaplaincy work (Clines 2008: 27–64). Seventy-six practitioners (Clines 2008: 5) participated on the following topic areas:

- the place of voluntary staff in a chaplaincy team;
- issues of space provision for a chaplaincy service;
- the ethics and principles of interfaith working;
- Christian theology of chaplaincy in a multifaith setting;
- chaplaincy contribution to institutional mission and vision;
- the importance of faith communities as HEI stakeholders;
- student faith societies and chaplaincy relations.

A significant finding from this was that the variety of types of people's needs – dependent on their religion, belief and other characteristics – means that to provide a fair level of provision requires the ability to think in terms of 'dynamic equivalence' between a multiplicity of needs and service users (Clines 2008: 29).

The third section of the same report presented practice narratives, which both described and analysed how chaplaincies were engaging in practice that related to a multi-religious and pluralist context. The variety of responses, fashioned to face contemporary multi-religious and inter-religious challenges, showcased how effective chaplaincies can be in their particular contexts in devising new and creative ways to run a service that engages the students and staff of an HEI (Clines 2008: 65–108).

Developments in FE Chaplaincy

The research, commentary and advice provided on FE chaplaincy provision (see, for instance, Archbishops' Council 2002, NEAFE 2005, fbfe 2007, Limb 2007) has advocated for a multi-religious and multi-faceted basis for chaplaincy provision:

> There is considerable variety in the chaplaincies in existence across the country. It is not a 'one-size-fits-all' approach. Rather, chaplaincies determine their own approach depending on local circumstances, size of institutions and the capacity of local faith communities. (fbfe 2007: 7)

This advice has recognised that when provision is publicly funded, it must address the variety of religion and belief identities of students and that the basis for establishing chaplaincies must be qualitatively different. The following statement from fbfe offers new purposes and, more fundamentally, justifications that FE colleges may need to draw up to bolster confidence in providing a chaplaincy that does more than replicate existing Christian models of provision:

> Multi-faith student support comes in a variety of shapes and sizes, and is known by many names: multi-faith chaplain, faith adviser, padre and so on. There is a clear need for any faith-based support in educational institutions such as FE colleges, funded mainly by the public purse, to value all faiths and beliefs. Whilst it is recognised that the concept of chaplaincy has a Christian heritage, many areas in the public sector, such as prisons, universities, hospitals and courts now refer to the notion of multi-faith chaplaincy on the basis that this is not exclusively Christian, but rather seeks to serve the needs of the whole institution and people of all faiths and belief. It is clear from consultation with the FE sector that the term 'multi-faith chaplaincy' is also now the most appropriate one for use in the FE sector as it most accurately reflects the nature of the multi-faith student support

given in practice. For these reasons, we called this guide *Multi-faith Chaplaincy: A guide for colleges on developing multi-faith student support*. (fbfe 2007 : 6)

This provides a progressive basis for establishing chaplaincies from which the broader sector (and other sectors) can learn.

Currents in School Chaplaincies

Schools chaplaincy has changed, especially with the significant increase in academy schools. The more traditional versions of schools chaplaincy (Lindsay 1999) from the independent schools sector now have a new companion, with the rise to a total number of 198 Church of England maintained secondary schools and academies (Archbishops' Council 2014: 3). Eighty per cent of the schools that responded to the survey reported having a chaplaincy, just over half of these made full-time appointments (the response rate was about 35 per cent so the data cannot be taken as an accurate picture across all such schools). Later, recent publications in this area are identified, but quantitative and qualitative data on changes to provision is lacking.

Multifaith Spaces

An increasing number of education chaplaincies, especially in FE and HE, have a responsibility for multifaith spaces that are being put into new buildings, or the reconfiguration of existing estate. Such spaces can create a sense of inclusion, and bring three types of benefits, providing 'bridging, bonding or linking forms of social capital' (Hewson and Brand 2011: 8). Although this may 'facilitate links to (and between) dissimilar individuals', it also can play into an interpretation of chaplaincy and religion as a homogenised space that becomes isolated from the rest of the learning institution.

Additionally, the spaces themselves can, by being profoundly neutral, offer a 'theatre of the absurd' backdrop, a genre that was initiated and typified by Samuel Beckett's play *Waiting for Godot* where people in limbo wait for a person or entity or circumstance they don't understand but name 'Godot': the irony of multifaith space is all too apparent to Crompton:

> inside a windowless multifaith room we are in limbo, like the non-place where the action of a Beckett play occurs. (Crompton 2013: 492)

Such a peculiar dynamic needs exploration across the different sectors. Educational chaplaincies will do well to remain attuned to the risks of their purpose being characterised by the architectural emptiness a multifaith space creates.

Recent Literature

Apart from the remarkable groundbreaking work of Gilliat-Ray (1999) on religion, chaplaincy and universities and the more wide-ranging study on chaplaincy by LeGood (1999), very little else was written on HE chaplaincy before Robinson (2004). Then the specific studies of Roman Catholic chaplaincy by McGrail and Sullivan (2007) and Muslim chaplaincy by Siddiqui (2007), and the snapshot report on *Faiths in Higher Education Chaplaincy* (Clines 2008) were the last studies on the area. However, the Guest et al. (2013) project does produce an analysis of Christian students' perspectives on Christian chaplaincy with some of their own commentary.

The careful work that has been facilitated by NEAFE and subsequently by fbfe (National Council of Faiths and Beliefs in Further Education) has strengthened the position of FE chaplaincy and informed policy decisions. The research efforts, though, are relatively small in number, with the thesis of Healey (2007) remaining unpublished.

Schools chaplaincy in Britain and Northern Ireland has received the least attention. James Norman's edited volume (2004) from an Irish context demonstrates how substantial work can be gathered together on education chaplaincy at primary and secondary level. It would be beneficial if efforts, building upon Glackin (2010) and Treagle (2011), were made for the different provisions of school chaplaincy in the rest of Britain and Ireland – see also O'Malley (2008) and Pohlmann (2013) for perspectives from North America.

On the broader themes of Christianity and education, which has heavily informed how chaplaincies have operated, the debt is with John Henry Newman (1976) who explores the shape of the university and the marriage between belief and academic enquiry. It is this area of Christian theological thinking that has informed how an ethic for multi-religious chaplaincy has developed within an education context.

This is, currently, articulated as a Christian commitment to shaping public life, not simply for the benefit of the Church's own members but rather a faith-based 'Christian case for pluralism in public policy', because of the 'nature of faith' and 'the purpose of the state' (Chaplin 1997: 62–71).

Such interest in religion in a pluralist public life cannot ignore the pitfalls. Hauerwas sees the manifold risks in a positive embracing of religious pluralism as a singular idea that 'declares nations, cultures and religions obsolete' (Hauerwas 2007: 64). This version of pluralism is about perpetuating 'western global dominance' by creating a 'presumption' by people who are pluralist that 'they are in control of the world in which they find themselves' (ibid.). Rather, the need is 'to find a way to negotiate our religious differences' (Hauerwas 2007: 65) so that 'we are not doomed to reject one another out of fear' (Hauerwas 2007: 74). This pressure is where chaplaincies, in becoming relabelled as 'multifaith', may at worst be perceived to simply be reinforcing a pluralist agenda where in fact, at best, such settings are the place where the negotiating of difference can happen intrinsically.

Both Higton (2012) and Rowan Williams suggest such faith and the university can be mutually transforming:

> faith has the opportunity of constantly varying and challenging conversation with the styles of human learning, so that its language has every opportunity of being tested and refreshed ... Faith separated from the life of intellect is no longer a human activity, but belongs in the bleak 'post-human' world of totalitarian captivity. (Williams 2005: 35)

Where Higton is interested in an Anglican theology of the university, Williams is wanting to draw on broader and more pluralist themes of faith and belief.

It would be both simplistic and hazardous to hope chaplaincies are the places where, in education settings, the shape of religion in public life is expressed. Simplistic, because religious expression occurs not only where religious provision is made, but where religious people are learning while believing: it is across the breadth of learning, research and enquiry that both intellectual life and belief develop.

It is vital to note that Christian theology argues for its own faith identity as being central to the university (see Higton 2012: 129–31, 139ff, 253) since it is this type of philosophy that continues to be a dominant feature of the justification for the funding of chaplaincy by the vast majority of funders, that is, the churches. Higton concludes that 'the chaplain, the Christian union, the chapel: *if* they do their job properly, they call the university to its highest good at the same time that they witness to that good's penultimate nature' (2012: 253).

If chaplaincies are pictured as the only place or the best place for learning and belief to intersect, this would risk chaplaincies becoming repositories of religion that become isolated from the rest of institutional life, once more privatising faith and taking it out of the public sphere (Clines and Gilliat-Ray, 2015: 235).

These specifically Christian theologies of religion in the public realm have a parallel that arises beyond religion or the academy and is evidenced within a sociological analysis of society. Adam Dinham describes this as a new attention to religion in the public sphere: 'faith is back in the public space' (Dinham 2009: 3). Dinham sees how, despite the predictions of religious decline, 'religious faith has nevertheless remained a hugely significant social phenomenon and has come to be dominated by policy perspectives which see faith groups as rich in resources that can be put to general use' (Dinham 2012: 9).

This can lead to a very positive positioning of chaplaincy within an educational setting, but it does come with a further pitfall, which arises – as with chaplaincy in any setting – from the crises that arise within the context.

In education, at all three levels, challenges provoked by changing in funding criteria and budget cuts combined with repeated changes to curriculum for 5–18s creates a complex crisis. In HE, where measures of success and funding shift repeatedly, it is described as a 'triple crisis' (Amaral and Magalhaes 2003) that goes to the very heart of institutional identity. These distortions of the HE learning environment have, according to Gerald Loughlin, been about the marketisation of the university with 'university education ceas[ing] to be about the formation of informed and critical sensibilities, and bec[oming] a means for maximizing earning potential' (Loughlin 2004: 121). Chaplaincies may be valued, newly, for their contribution, but may be misvalued – in the contexts where all provision is measured in a reductionist way – missing the quality of educational spirit such a department can produce.

Future Developments

Suggested Models for Development

There are many –at times conflicting – ways that chaplaincy can be modelled. If an institution was seeking to provide a full and coherent structure to provide for the needs and requirements of all religions and beliefs then a chaplaincy (or chaplaincies) can only ever be a subset of religion and belief services within an organisation. That doesn't mean, necessarily, that new structures need to be invented, but rather that the responsibility for responsiveness to religion and belief requires an institutional attentiveness, not a chaplaincy which becomes a locus for all such matters.

Futurology and Education Chaplaincy

There are three obvious reasons for change in education: politics and the funding of education, technology and the means of education and, third, paradigmatic shifts in how the university is imagined. The review of spiritual and moral development in FE and the framework arising for multifaith chaplaincy show how a sudden shift in the interpretation of a field of education – via new government policy – can change the fabric of chaplaincy work:

> Much of the policy guidance that was offered by the Labour Government on religious matters before the 2010 election was also heavily influenced by the perception that universities were at risk of being used as sites of religious 'radicalisation', particularly of young Muslims, and other matters around extremism, religion and belief. (Dinham and Jones 2012: 187)

This means that the need for effective chaplaincy provision has become more of concern for HEI leaders, governors and managers. If schools will imitate FE in taking moral and spiritual education down a more inclusive track, that will require a pastoral support service that is more multi-religious and responsive to religious and belief identities, which would be a very significant shift.

Conclusion

The influences on shaping and forming chaplaincy in education create distinctive and different purposes and trajectories compared to the wide variety of chaplaincy work across other sectors. Within education chaplaincy the varieties of shapes and models evidence the fluctuating and developing context where chaplaincy is now esteemed in many places where it has not been previously. Internal and external critiques of education chaplaincy are in short supply and it will benefit this sector if further energy is given to assessing the history, development and future of this work.

References

Amaral, A. and Magalhaes, A, (2003), The triple crisis of the university and its reinvention. *Higher Education Policy*, 16(2), 239–53.

Archbishops' Council (2002), *Pillars of the Church: Supporting Chaplaincy in Further and Higher Education*. London: Board of Education of the Archbishops' Council.

Archbishops' Council Education Divison (2014), *The Public Face of God: Chaplaincy in Anglican Secondary Schools and Academies in England and Wales*. London: Church of England Archbishops' Council.

Bolton, P. (2012), *Education: Historical Statistics*. London: House of Commons Library, Social and General Statistics.

Bunting, I. (1993), *Models of Ministry: Managing the Church Today*. Cambridge: Grove Booklets.

Chaplin, J. (1997), Christians and the Public Realm. In Shortt, J. and Cooling, T. (eds), *Agenda for Educational Change*. Leicester: Apollos, Stapleford House Educational Centre, 59–71.

Clines, J. (2008), *Faiths in Higher Education Chaplaincy*. London: Board of Education.

Clines, J. and Gilliat-Ray, S. (2015), Religious Literacy and Chaplaincy. In Dinham, A. and Francis, M., *Religious Literacy in Policy and Practice*. Bristol: Policy Press, 235–54.

Crompton, A. (2013), The architecture of multifaith spaces: God leaves the building. *The Journal of Architecture*, 18(4), 474–96.

Dinham, A. (2009), *Faiths, Public Policy and Civil Society*. London: Palgrave Macmillan.

—— (2012), *Faith and Social Capital after the Debt Crisis*. London: Palgrave Macmillan.

Dinham, A. and Jones, S.H. (2012), Religion, public policy, and the academy: brokering public faith in a context of ambivalence? *Journal of Contemporary Religion*, 27(2), 185–201.

Donlevy, J.K. (2002), Catholic schools: the inclusion of non-Catholic students, *Canadian of Education / Revue canadienne de l'*éducation, 34, 101–18.

Earwaker, J. (1992), *Helping and Supporting Students: Rethinking the Issues*. Buckingham: (Society for Research into Higher Education) Open University Press.

Edgar, J, (1893), *History of Early Scottish Education*. Edinburgh: J. Thin.

Education Division, Church of England Board of Education (2014a), *Chaplaincy for the FE Sector*. Available at: www.churchofengland.org/education/colleges-universities/fe/chaplaincy-for-further-education.aspx (accessed 16 April 2015).

fbfe (National Council of Faiths and Beliefs in Further Education) (2007), *Multi-faith Chaplaincy: A Guide for Colleges on Developing Multi-faith Student Support*. London: Learning and Skills Council.

Gilliat-Ray, S. (1999), *Higher Education and Student Religious Identity*. Exeter: Department of Sociology.

Gilliat-Ray, S., Ali, M.M. and Pattison, S. (2013), *Understanding Muslim Chaplaincy*. Aldershot: Ashgate.

Glackin, M. (2010), *Presence in Pilgrimage: An Exploration of Chaplaincy in Catholic Secondary Schools in England and Wales*. Saarbrücken: Lambert Academic Publishing.

Guest, M., Aune, K., Sharma, S. and Warner, R. (2013), *Christianity and the University Experience: Understanding Student Faith*. London: Bloomsbury Academic.

Hauerwas, S. (2007), *The State of the University: Academic Knowledges and the Knowledge of God*. Oxford: Blackwell.

Healey, D.G. (2007), *Colleges, Values and the Place of Chaplaincy*. University of Sheffield: unpublished thesis submitted for the degree of PhD, School of Education.

Hewson, C. and Brand, R. (2011), *Multi-Faith Space: Towards a Practice-based Assessment*. Paper presented at the International RC21 Conference 2011, Session 14: Religion and Urban Space. Available at: www.sed.manchester.ac.uk/architecture/research/mfs/documents/Hewson-Brand-RC212011.pdf (accessed 16 April 2015).

Higher Education Statistics Agency (HESA) (2014), *Higher Education Student Enrolments and Qualifications Obtained at Higher Education Institutions in the United Kingdom for the Academic Year 2012/13.* Available at: https://www.hesa.ac.uk/sfr197 (accessed 16 April 2015).

Higton, M. (2012), *A Theology of Higher Education.* Oxford: Oxford University Press.

Kavanagh, D. (2012), The University as Fool. In Barnett, R. (ed.), *The Future University: Ideas and Possibilities.* Abingdon: Routledge, 101–11.

Lawson, J. and Silver, H. (1973), *A Social History of Education in England.* Abingdon: Routledge.

LeGood, G. (ed.) (1999), *Chaplaincy: The Church's Sector Ministries.* London: Cassel Company.

Limb, A. (2007), *Making Space for Faith: Values, Beliefs and Faiths in the Learning and Skills Sector. A Report on the National Enquiry into Opportunities for Spiritual and Moral Development in Further Education.* London: National Ecumenical Agency in Further Education (NEAFE).

Lindsay, D. (1999), Schools. In LeGood, G. (ed.), *Chaplaincy: The Church's Sector Ministries.* London: Cassel Company., 117–23.

Loughlin, G. (2004), The University Without Questions: John Henry Newman and Jacques Derrida on Faith in the University. In Astley, J., Francis, L.J., Sullivan, J. and Walker, A. (eds), *The Idea of a Christian University.* Milton Keynes: Paternoster, 113–31.

McGrail, P. and Sullivan, J. (2007), *Dancing on the Edge – Chaplaincy, Church and Higher Education.* Chelmsford: Matthew Jones Publishing.

McGregor, G. (1991), *A Church College for the 21st Century? 150 Years of Ripon and York St John.* York: The Ebor Press.

Maxwell, N. (2012), Creating a Better World: Towards the University of Wisdom. In Barnett, R. (ed.), *The Future University: Ideas and Possibilities.* Abingdon: Routledge, 123–38.

NEAFE (National Ecumenical Agency in Further Education) (2005), *Faiths and Further Education: A Handbook towards a Whole-College Approach to Chaplaincy for a Pluralist Society.* London: Learning and Skills Council (LSC).

Newman, J.H. (1976), *The Idea of a University: Defined and Illustrated,* fully annotated edition. London: Oxford University Press.

Norman, J. (2004), *At the Heart of Education: School Chaplaincy and Pastoral Care.* Dublin: Veritas Publications.

O'Malley, D. (2008), *School Ethos and Chaplaincy.* Bolton: Don Bosco Publications.

Pohlmann, D. (2013), *School Chaplaincy: An Introduction.* Oregon: Mosaic Press.

Pratt, J. (2000), The Emergence of the Colleges. In Smithers, A. and Robinson, P. (eds), *Further Education Reformed.* London: Falmer Press., 56–68.

Robinson, S. (2004), *Ministry Among Students: A Pastoral Theology and Handbook for Practice*. Norwich: Canterbury Press.

Shilson-Thomas, H. (2011), Selwyn and Newnham Colleges, Cambridge. In Threlfall-Holmes, M. and Newitt, M., *Being a Chaplain*. London: SPCK, 30–33.

Shockley, D. (1989), *Campus Ministry. The Church Beyond Itself*. Louisville, KY: Westminster/John Knox Press.

Siddiqui, A. (2007), *Islam at Universities in England: Meeting the Needs and Investing in the Future*. Leicester: The Markfield Institute.

Swinton, G. (2011), The Grey Coat Hospital and Westminster City School. In Threlfall-Holmes, M. and Newitt, M., *Being a Chaplain*. London: SPCK, 18–20.

Treagle, D. (2011), *Fresh Experiences of School Chaplaincy*. Cambridge: Grove Books.

Williams, R. (2005), Faith in the University. In Robinson, S. and Katulushi, C. (eds), *Values in Higher Education*, Castle-Upon-Alun, Vale of Glamorgan: Leeds University and Aureus, 24–35.

Chapter 22

Contextual Issues: Learning and Human Flourishing

Garry Neave

Introduction

> To generalize is to be an idiot; to particularize is the alone distinction of merit.
> (Blake 1814)

So W.G. Hoskins (1955) began his seminal work uncovering the rich tapestry underlying the visible landscape. It is a commonplace that the contemporary educational landscape is undergoing a series of substantial changes and it is valuable for those involved in chaplaincy to have a deeper awareness of the nature of those changes and a more nuanced sense of their deeper connections and evolution.

A teacher or lecturer coming to the end of their professional career will perhaps have 40 years of service and is likely to have entered the profession in or around 1974. That profession had certainly not been static or unchanging but had enjoyed substantial stability over those decades.

Structures, Staff and Subjects

Among the major features of this stable educational landscape was the position of Local Education Authorities (LEAs), who were responsible for the overwhelming majority of maintained schools, colleges and polytechnics, including the shape and range of local provision; determined policy through their Education Committees; and administered the system through authority-wide services.

It is perhaps the steady weakening of the role of LEAs that has captured most attention, notably through the Academies programmes initiated under the stewardship of Lord Adonis and given much greater momentum under the coalition government, where they were seen as the principal solution to almost intractable problems of school improvement. The talismanic quality of academisation, to both its proponents and detractors, makes it less than simple to come to a clear view about the cost and value for money of the initiative, its impact on pupil performance and social mobility and its effects on other areas of provision. What is not in doubt is the seismic shock it has delivered to the structures through which maintained schools were provided and through which they were accountable.

Staff were previously almost entirely employed by LEAs on terms and conditions which were nationally agreed and famously codified and captured in successive editions of the *Salaries and Conditions of Service for Lecturers in Further Education* (the Silver Book): the national collective agreement between NATFHE, the lecturers' trade union, and employers. Previously incorporated into contracts of employment, the Further and Higher Education Act (1992), saw the replacement of these national terms and conditions with those negotiated locally. In the majority of LEAs, the Table of Establishment for a school or college followed a precise formula, which could and often did also set out minutiae such as the number of telephone extensions that a college of a given size was allocated. In one large tertiary college in the early 1980s, the Principal was required to obtain a counter-signature for all cheques in excess of £50 from the relevant Area Education Officer.

However, the scope and content of the curriculum was largely left to institutions and their LEA to shape, and the Department of Education and Science was reluctant in principle to interfere with those local decisions. The key examinations for most pupils were the GCE Ordinary and Advanced Level subjects offered by the, fiercely independent, Examination Boards, which in turn were associated with the universities from which they took their origins. Guidance upon the examination syllabus could be bracingly concise: that for GCE A Level History in 1974 was essentially a list of possible topics, not covering two sides of A5, along with a set of past papers and the previous years' Chief Examiner's Reports. It is worth emphasising that there was no National Curriculum until 1988 (Flude and Hammer 1990) and that even when introduced, its contents remained more fluid than is sometimes imagined.

For those pupils outside of the 25 per cent of the ability range for which O Level was designed, the Certificate of Secondary Education catered for those of the next 55 per cent of the ability range, with a growing use of teacher-assessed coursework, which in turn was being adopted outside of those subjects – such as art – where practical or skills-based tests were a long-established feature.

In technical colleges and in many secondary modern schools a wide variety of vocational courses were used, often accredited through a professional body associated with the industry or commercial sector in which their students would be seeking employment.

Over this system, ministers could and did exercise influence – often to a significant degree – and were responsible for a whole range of regulatory functions expressed in Circulars, as well as shaping financial settlements and the parameters for pay policy. Her Majesty's Inspectors of Schools (HMI) brought a very high degree of intellectual rigour to their task of evaluating the quality of provision, although inspections did not follow a rigid timetable and it was possible to pass much of one's career without being subject to a visit from HMI.

The use of data was also highly variable between and within schools and colleges, in part because of the absence of nationally set and benchmarked assessment instruments and in part because the task of collecting and analysing data still relied heavily upon paper-based systems. One statistical return, universally if unoriginally known as Form 7 (after its official reference number) was a detailed annual record of a wide range of pupil-related and institutional data. However, its major weakness as a management tool was that it was usually submitted some 6–12 months after the year to which it related and the data it contained were not usually published for a further six months.

It is easy to fall into a Rousseau-like reverie about this past landscape, smiling indulgently at its more idyllic features ('imagine, a whole career without an Inspection') or more astringently critiquing its apparent casual disregard for practice that seems absolutely central today, such as hard data on pupil performance. That would be an important mistake for two reasons.

First, far from being a torpid, placid and dull place, the educational landscape has been teeming with innovation, controversy and development for much of the period since the 1970s. To take only one example, the lack of a National Curriculum undoubtedly led to random chance affecting student experience – many a child will have 'done' Stone Age Man or The Romans each time they moved school. However, the absence of high levels of prescription also generated the School Mathematics Project, Nuffield Science, The Schools Council History Project 14–16, Jerome Brunner's Spiral Curriculum and a whole host of other innovations.

Secondly, many of the educational developments since the late 1990s that are accepted as a given feature of the new landscape are prefigured in some earlier form – or are best understood as a reaction against those developments. For those, such as chaplains to schools and colleges, who need to understand the context within which they work more deeply than merely being able to put names to its major features, having a grasp of 'what lies beneath' gives them a surer grasp of an extraordinarily rich and complex educational world. It may also help them understand the tensions and conflicts that are found in startling profusion and which can both enable creativity and stifle innovation. It is to these tensions that we now turn.

Navigating the Landscape

Follow the money

At least according to the film *All the President's Men*,[1] to understand a complex series of linked events, the best thing to do is to follow the trail of the cash. Funding mechanisms are one of the most powerful system levers in education – and indeed in many public services – and schools and colleges are no exception.

In overall terms, by 2020, the government is expected to spend about £90 billion a year on education, of which about £7.5 billion will go into further education (FE) and sixth form colleges. Whilst plainly a substantial sum, representing just over 12 per cent of current tax revenue, it is worth noting that welfare and pensions are expected to account for about £160 billion and health for £133 billion in 2015.

It is also important to understand the longer-term pattern of education spending. According to the Institute of Fiscal Studies (IFS), from the mid 1970s through to the mid 1980s, education spending was largely constant in real terms. This was then followed by a real-terms increase until the late 1990s.

However, over the period from the mid 1970s through to the late 1990s, there was a gradual decline in education spending as a share of national income, so that it reached around 4.5 per cent of national income by the late 1990s. There are two notable exceptions to this pattern: during the recessions of the early 1980s and early 1990s, education spending temporarily rose as a share of national income as a direct result of the concurrent reductions in national income.

Since the late 1990s, education spending has risen substantially. Between 1999–2000 and 2009–2010, education spending rose from 4.5 per cent to 6.4 per cent of national income. Under the previous Labour government, the fastest-growing areas of education spending were capital spending on schools, early years spending and further education spending (Brady et al. 2013). Public spending on higher education grew the most slowly.

During the most recent recession, the percentage fell back slightly to 6.2 per cent of national income in 2010–2011, although there was a notable increase in education spending as a share of national income. This partly results from the sharp drop in national income, but it also reflects continued growth in the real-terms level of education spending.

However, in addition to the 'austerity constraints' currently affecting public services, most informed commentators anticipate further real-terms cuts between 2015 and 2020, although it also appears likely that the severity of cuts will differ. The IFS calculates that current spending on schools will see the smallest real-terms cut (about one per cent in total) and this prediction appears

---

[1]	*All the President's Men*, Walter Coblenz, 1976.

consistent with the spending pledges recently expressed by both Conservative and Labour education politicians during their 2015 election campaigns.

The areas seeing the largest real-terms cuts are expected to be against current spending on higher education (40 per cent in total) and capital spending (more than halved; Association of Colleges 2014). However, reforms to tuition fees will increase total resource spending – via public and private contributions – on higher education, and university leaders have spoken openly of their fears of the impact of the anticipated level of reductions. Spending on the early years and youth services is expected to be cut by over 20 per cent in real terms in total. Planned cuts to age 16–19 education spending are likely to be of a similar magnitude, and the Association of Colleges has estimated that cuts of between 20 and 30 per cent in government funding are entirely possible. These cuts will be taking place as the education leaving age (formally referred to as the Raising of the Participation Age) is fully implemented, which is likely to make the pressures on individual providers even greater.

A Perfect Storm: Reforming the Curriculum and its Assessment

Whilst the period up to the 1970s saw considerable curriculum innovation and the development of new families of qualifications, especially in vocational programmes, the speed and scale of change accelerated rapidly from 1997. The introduction of Curriculum 2000 was overtly designed to make qualifications more accessible to a wider cohort of students than their precursors, to give less weight to terminal examinations in favour of modular assessment, to incorporate ways of measuring attainment that did not assume the use written examination papers and, particularly at A and AS Level, to encourage greater breadth of study.

A similar series of reforms attempted to achieve comparable improvements in vocational provision, often driven by the laudable goal of ensuring that 'practical' and 'academic' subjects attracted similar levels of public esteem and employer recognition. The rock on which many of these attempts foundered was that – largely set by political imperatives – of maintaining the 'gold standard A Level' as the benchmark against which all other qualifications would inevitably be judged. Colleges in particular saw a succession of new qualification frameworks, many of which appeared indistinguishable in practice and some of which were too short-lived to be implemented.

Into this mix came the rapid rise in importance of high-stakes testing, by which is meant the rigorous use of public examination data to make judgements about the quality of a school or college. The stakes are high for the student taking the test, assessment or examination, and get higher as opportunities become fewer in a skills-based economy for those without the required qualifications. However, as noted below, the stakes are also high for the institution, since if its students underperform against quantitative benchmarks, their school or college is likely to lose funding, to be subject to more intensive external intervention and to see a number of its leaders pursuing what is left of their careers elsewhere.

Schools and colleges are highly adaptive organisations – contrary to the oft-painted picture of them being slow and cumbersome entities. In particular, their leaders are adept at responding to new regulatory and other demands, such as those posed by high-stakes testing. Synergistically, this adaptability linked with the undoubted wish of government to see measurable improvement in pupil performance and the acute awareness of business opportunities facing the large companies which the awarding bodies and examinations boards had now become.

It is temptingly easy to describe the process which then unfolded in the most unflattering and cynical terms: headteachers and principals seeking to game the system, with the active help of the commercial assessment industry and the collusion of politicians whose reputations required signs of the very improvements they had sought. Indeed, one Labour Minister (Estelle Morris) resigned on the basis of a particularly critical improvement target not having been reached, even if her reasons for resigning were characteristically more honest and personally self-critical than others suggested.

However, it is clear from the statistical evidence gathered by examination boards and the Qualifications and Curriculum Authority that pupil performance in externally set and marked tests, for example at Key Stages 2 and 3 and in public examinations at GCSE, AS and A Level, did improve in the period up to 2010. In particular, the percentage of pupils obtaining five GCSE grades A–C (or their equivalent vocational qualification) rose rapidly, including in areas of significant previous underperformance.

With the election of the coalition government in 2010, a powerful agenda for change was rapidly enacted. One key element in that agenda was the assertion that the much-vaunted improvement in examination scores had fatal flaws: briefly summarised, it was argued that much of the improvement was due to skilful gaming of the system by schools and colleges and in any event, even if the improvement was real and substantial, we were already trailing behind other nations, whose pupil performance far outstripped the UK's.

The medicine prescribed for this ailment was a major review of the curriculum and the assessment systems associated with it. Under Professor Alison Wolf, a rigorous and searching scrutiny took place of vocational qualifications, which commanded the unusual combination of political, sector and business support for its recommendations (Wolf 2011). In particular, the importance of qualifications having real currency for their students – for example, in fitting them for their intended future profession – was widely accepted as requiring significant reductions in the number and shape of the colossal number of qualifications then available.

Almost inevitably, the proposals affecting the National Curriculum at ages 4–19, including GCSE and A Level, provoked a high degree of conflict. In part, they were seen as seeking a reversion to a model of a 1950s curriculum that many professionals opposed, and in part the scale and pace of change was – or seemed – relentless. A further factor was the approach taken by the then Secretary of State, which combined personal courtesy with an invincible conviction of the importance of these – and other – radical policy changes in reversing decades of social exclusion, inadequate education and declining competiveness in world markets.

Whilst a number of changes have been slightly deferred because of the practical or logistical complexities of implementation, there is no doubt that schools and colleges have experienced a very intense period of curriculum change and uncertainty. In 2015–2016, a number of these changes come fully into force, against very unforgiving timescales and, as noted above, at a time of very marked fiscal constraint. The timetable for the 2015 general election also posed major potential problems for the planning and implementation of reforms to the GCSE and A Level examination cycle.

An Inspector Calls

The theme tune for the TV series *Mastermind* is the wonderfully evocative 'Approaching Menace'. According to at least one FE principal, both the title and its associations come to mind when the Office for Standards in Education (OFSTED) crops up in conversation.

As noted in the introduction, for many years HMI provided Parliament – and ministers, officials, LEAs, headteachers, principals and others – with evaluations of educational provision of great depth and rigour, based on their wide experience and professional independence.

However, they did not form a quasi-regulatory body for individual institutions, or for the quality of services in children's services or by local authorities. Although deep, HMI inspections were carried out at relatively long intervals and their reports were not invariably or systematically published.

In part, that was also due to the absence of accessible national data on pupil performance, published in a format that enabled comparison between schools, including those in an area such as an LEA or between schools of a particular type or with comparable pupil cohorts. Individual LEAs had carried out some of this statistical work, notably the Inner London Education Authority, with its seminal study by Rutter and colleagues entitled *15,000 Hours* (Rutter et al. 1979). Similarly, academic institutions had considerable expertise in analysing pupil and school data, for example in the correlation between socio-economic factors and educational outcomes or the impact of different teaching methodologies on pupil performance.

The first attempt at publishing this data took place in 1992 and was part of the Citizen's Charter. The principal reason behind the publication of league tables (as they are almost universally known) was to enable parents to exercise their choice of school for their sons and daughters in a more informed way. Since 1992, they have become, in the memorable phrase of Mike Baker, long-serving BBC Education correspondent, 'as powerful a weapon of control as the medieval thumbscrew' (Baker 2007).

One of the consequences of making these data available – and now almost on an industrial scale – was to bring together the emphasis on high-stakes testing and a political conviction that much more rigorous and frequent inspection was a powerful lever for school improvement. In consequence, OFSTED was created in 1992 and its remit successively extended to include provision from early years settings to the Children and Family Court Advisory and Support Service (CAFCASS).

Sir John Harvey-Jones used to say that a good way of getting to the heart of an organisation's culture was to ask what would get a person fired in that company. There is no doubt in the mind of many school or college leaders that what they might colloquially term 'failing your OFSTED' will bring serious consequences for the institution and probably for its leadership in some cases.

We Don't Do God

Alastair Campbell's famous press conference remark conveys the nervousness about the place of faith and belief in national politics and also, though that was not its original context, about its place in educational institutions more generally.

Yet even a casual scrutiny of school and college websites rapidly identifies frequent statements about the institution's ethos, its mission, its values, its wider purpose for those whom it serves and its place in the community.

Leaving aside the distinctive ethos of schools with a designated religious character, and of the small number of sixth form colleges with a Roman Catholic foundation or heritage, it is helpful to identify some of the areas that go beyond a purely instrumental view of educational mission or purpose.

At a formal level, all schools and colleges are required to provide a broad and balanced education that will equip their learners for the future, including their social, moral, cultural and spiritual development.

In the past, that provision has often been organised through a tutorial and enrichment programme and through extracurricular activities (such as sport, music, art, dance or drama). In schools, the non-statutory requirement to provide personal, social and health education (PSHE) along with sex and relationships education (SRE) and citizenship has often been the framework for this wider view of developing pupils as individuals.

At the same time, schools and colleges have duties and responsibilities under equality and diversity legislation, most comprehensively under the Equalities Act 2010. For many groups, this legislation has been a powerful vehicle for tackling discrimination and for encouraging much greater diversity among the college community, although progress is sometimes strikingly uneven.

It is also crucial to realise that pupils and students do not leave their faith at the gate, and the same goes for staff and parents or governors. As the work of the NUS and the National Council of Faiths and Belief in FE (fbfe) has demonstrated, earners welcome and highly value the opportunity to discuss major life issues, especially where this is carried out in a respectful and sensitive way. Fbfe's own publications, such as *Challenging Voices* (fbfe 2012), also show how such opportunities open up wider discussions about the curriculum itself and about the nature and character of the school or college culture.

In this context, the discussion about 'British values' is one which has yet to properly unfold, bounded as it is by a requirement to actively promote these being incorporated into national standards for teachers, into statutory guidance, into the OFSTED Inspection Framework and a range of other government initiatives and programmes, predominantly those aimed at combating violent extremism.

Finding Meaning in the Landscape

So far, we have been sketching out some of the features of this rich and complex landscape, which ranges from colleges with 60,000 students aged between 14 and 93 and budgets bigger than some small local authorities, to primary schools with a single, all-age class of 17 learners aged 4–11.

In this final section, we offer some suggestions about navigating around the less familiar parts of this landscape and some pointers about the langue and preoccupations of those who work or learn there.

It's not all about the money – but a lot is!

In understanding how chaplaincy provision can be provided most effectively, and in ensuring that schools and colleges understand what it can offer – and what it cannot or should not offer, a grasp of financial reality is exceptionally valuable. As noted above, schools and colleges face a significant period of deep financial pressures: their largest expenditure is on staff (perhaps between 65 and 80 per cent of their budget, with much of the rest committed to facilities and resources for learning). They scrutinise every single item of expenditure and may have had to make large staffing reductions in the last few years. They need chaplains who understand that and can be creative about the use of time and resources.

Equally, a large school or college will have a substantial budget; at one level, a decision about budgets is a decision about the importance of something. As George Lansbury used to remark, 'the language of socialism is the language of priorities' – and so it is highly advisable for chaplains and those who support them to seek to really understand what this school or college is trying to prioritise and what effects that might have upon the provision.

It's almost always to do with numbers

In contrast to many faith-based organisations, including perhaps the majority of English churches, schools and colleges live by the numbers – enrolments, attendance, examination results, deprivation indices, fee income, staffing costs, lettings income, … . As serving chaplains know, they are also increasingly target driven and are very focused on clear and effective planning, which delivers agreed goals and levels of service. Managers and leaders will naturally expect to know an idea has been well thought out, sensibly costed and contributes to what the school or college is trying to achieve, especially its most important priorities.

It is important to stress that the best school and college leaders are very strongly driven by their values and seek to make their institutions far more than the stereotypical exam factories or skills production lines. A really imaginative, creative idea can have a lot of persuasive impact – schools and colleges are full of people who are problem-solvers, highly resourceful and welcoming to something that will genuinely benefit their learners. The task for chaplains is to find those people and engage in a really thorough and purposeful way.

It's always to do with students and pupils, even when it's not

It is sometimes the case that schools and colleges seem to pride themselves in being hard-nosed, results-focused institutions in which winners never quit and quitters never win. If you are working in that environment, one of the most valuable things a chaplain can do is to try to see what underlies that kind of culture and how you can set priorities that you can work with and where you can do so with integrity.

For example, a college or school may respond to issues that are pupil-voice or customer feedback generated, as this may affect satisfaction ratings. Another institution may be preoccupied with compliance in equality and diversity issues or with achieving particular recruitment targets. Yet another may be deeply concerned about engaging with its local community and uncertain as to how this might be done in an area where there are strong faith communities and no obvious structure for staff to consult and build its outreach work.

It's always to do with values, even when it's not

In general, once you get beyond social politeness, most of those who work in schools and colleges are very candid about wanting to make a difference to the people who attend their institutions. Staff may feel constrained by the culture, they may have had difficult experiences that have left them bruised or tired, or they may be just plain fed up. Those who work in professions such as nursing and teaching will often have encountered a kind of cultivated cynicism into which is easy to be seduced and which acts as a safety valve and, as Isabel Menzies-Lythe noted, a defence system against anxiety (Menzies 1960).

One way into this culture is through careful and sensitive listening. It is through such attention that one can find the anchors in the values that people hold most deeply, especially once they are able to speak about them more openly around you. Chaplains can then pose to themselves the questions: Which of those values connect with you and the work you are trying to do? Which can you prompt, encourage, help give voice to and express in a language which the school or college can understand and which makes sense to them?

For those looking for recent examples of such conversations, the recent leadership report published by the 157 Group and fbfe (Gannon 2014) is a rich source. In essence, the report is based on a set of interviews with college principals about the values and beliefs that make them lead their colleges the way they do. Some are religious and others aren't, but all have in common a willingness to make their values explicit and – as far as they are able – to spell out what they feel that means in practice for their own leadership and the direction of their college.

It's always to do with change, especially when everyone tells you it's not

Perhaps the most important stereotype to be aware of is the one that confidently asserts that most – possibly all – teachers are resistant to change and oppose anything new and unfamiliar. You will indeed find people who take that approach in teaching – and probably in accountancy, plumbing, aero-engineering, retailing, quality control, street cleansing and surgery.

Schools and colleges are centres of change – the class you taught before morning break behaves completely differently at 3.00 pm and Year 11 are a different proposition from the same group in Year 7. The brilliant session you ran yesterday on silver service with BTEC Hospitality Group 1 was such a disaster with Hospitality 2 today ...

Staff may be sceptical of something that looks a lot of work for nil gain, or doesn't seem matched to their students' needs or might leave them handling issues they do not feel confident about as tutors.

That does not mean chaplains should be afraid to suggest something the staff have never done before, especially if you are putting yourself out to make it work. To put it in a quotation often attributed to Ernest Rutherford, 'we have run out of money, so we'll have to start thinking'.

It's not about you, even if you think it might be

In contrast to many other categories of school and college staff roles, the pathway to chaplaincy is immensely varied. In taking up a chaplaincy role, it can be hard to avoid framing it in terms of one's own hopes, intentions, plans and aspirations. That is entirely natural and the institution will have expectations – as it would with any other comparable role – that the chaplain will be proactive in setting out what is needed.

The danger, especially for those unfamiliar with educational institutions as systems, is that the chaplain misses the opportunity to put her or his own anxieties to one side and instead to spend time actually listening to what people say or don't say, what they enjoy or get frustrated about, observing just what happens in this place and what people seem to be concerned over.

At a concrete level, it can be enormously helpful to take every chance you can to join in, always in a natural and unforced way: one chaplain's breakthrough moment was being a member of the kitchen clearing crew in a college training restaurant!

Finally, regardless of one's own faith community or belief system, those who provide chaplaincy services need above all to resist the idea that they are there to bring values to a place that doesn't have them already. That also implies that chaplains need to take their time earning the right to challenge those values, especially if the chaplain does not know why this particular school or college works in that way.

References

Association of Colleges (2014), *The Department for Education Budget after 2015*. London: Association of Colleges. Available at: https://www.aoc. co.uk/sites/default/files/The%20Department%20for%20Education%20 budget%20after%202015.pdf (accessed 3 February 2015).

Baker, M. (2007), *League Tables: Only Half the Story*. Available at: http://news. bbc.co.uk/1/hi/education/6257063.stm (accessed 3 February 2015).

Blake, W. (1814), Annotations to Sir Joshua Reynolds's Discourses. In Erdman, D.V. (ed.), *The Complete Poetry and Prose of William Blake*, revised edition 1988. New York: Anchor Books.

Brady, M., Coffey, A., Fitgerald, A., Gambaro, L. and Ts, T. (2013), *Labour's Record on Education: Policy, Spending and Outcomes 1997–2010*. London School of Economics.

fbfe (2012), *Challenging Voices*. Available at: www.fbfe.org.uk/wp-content/files_mf/1385639548REsilience_FE_booklet_Challenging_Voices_PDF_final.pdf (accessed 3 February 2015).

Flude, M. and Hammer, M. (eds) (1990), *The Education Reform Act, 1988: Its Origins and Implications*. London: Routledge.

Gannon, A. (2014), *The Leadership of Teaching, Learning and Assessment by Governors*. London: 157 Group. Available at: www.157group.co.uk/sites/default/files/documents/157g-120-leadershipofteaching.pdf (accessed 16 April 2015).

Hoskins, W.G. (1955), *The Making of the English Landscape*. London: Hodder and Stoughton.

Menzies, I. (1960), A case study in the functioning of social systems as a defence against anxiety. *Human Relations*, 13(2), 95–121.

Rutter, M., Maughan, B., Mortimore, P., Ouston, J. and Smith, A. (1979), *15,000 Hours: Secondary Schools and their Effects on Children*. Shepton Mallet: Open Books.

Wolf, A. (2011), *Review of Vocational Education – The Wolf Report*. London: Department for Education and BIS. Available at: https://www.gov.uk/government/uploads/system/uploads/attachment_data/file/180504/DFE-00031-2011.pdf (accessed 20 September 2013).

Chapter 23

Case Study

John Caperon

Education Chaplaincy, Church Policy and Schools' Chaplaincy

Education chaplaincy is described generically in the previous chapters; here the aim is to explore as a case study of educational chaplaincy one specific context in which that chaplaincy is significant – schools, and particularly secondary schools in England. Much of what follows will of necessity have to generalise from very many individual instances. In order to provide a degree of specificity, however, I shall draw on the practice of four schools – an independent boarding school of Christian foundation (School A) and three Church of England state-maintained academies (Schools B, C and D) – in order to illuminate current practice. I shall also examine both the origins of school chaplaincy and some of the current pressures bearing upon it.

It is worth noting at the outset that the national Church displays some policy uncertainty in relation to chaplaincy in schools. Although the origins of schools chaplaincy in England lie in the private sector of education, where many schools – clearly Anglican – still employ chaplains as senior members of staff, the Church is a significant institutional stakeholder in the state-maintained system of education, with some 200 secondary schools sponsored by dioceses. A kind of socio-political embarrassment could account for the Church's policy uncertainty. Though English private (often called 'public') schools – teaching a mere seven per cent of the school population – are currently still seen as a leading force for educational excellence, there has been an understandable reluctance in the Church of England to identify too closely with these schools at the expense of the Church's own educational enterprise in the state-maintained Church schools sector. Some in the Church would raise objections to private education on the grounds that it caters for the offspring of the privileged and produces unfair social and economic advantages for its alumni. The irony is, though, that it is in the private schools that chaplaincy has been, and still possibly is, most deeply rooted.

A further irony: it is in secondary schools generally that educational chaplaincy may be currently growing most rapidly, at a time when other chaplaincies, including those in higher education, have been under threat of cutback. The burgeoning academies programme, pursued under governments across the spectrum and set to continue, has involved the extension of the Church's stake in the school system as both 'fresh start' and 'takeover' academies have been sponsored by diocesan boards of education, increasingly through 'multi-academy trusts' (MATs). It now seems clear that new Church academies are being encouraged by the national Church to invest in chaplaincy. At the same time, there is rapid growth in the number of national and local charities and church groups which are funding and providing a new version of chaplaincy – perhaps 'para-chaplaincy' – in non-Church schools. This appears to be an era of dynamic development and change in schools' chaplaincy which is happening so rapidly that it is difficult to chart accurately.

The Origins of Chaplaincy in Schools: A Continuing Tradition

The beginnings of school chaplaincy can be traced to the mediaeval era, when the Church's educational power was extensive and monopolistic. Schools were associated either with monastic establishments, or with clerical or royal initiatives: Westminster (originating in the 12th century but re-founded under Elizabeth I), Winchester (founded 1382) and Eton (founded 1440) are famous instances. Oddly, all these institutions are today private schools charging high fees despite their origins in charitable concern for 'poor scholars'. It is unclear when exactly the role of chaplain emerged as differentiated from that of teacher, but the educational practice of these schools was intensely religious, if not precisely monastic, as in the regime at Westminster in the early 17th century (see Drury 2013: 53–70).

By the 19th century, an emergent school chaplaincy role existed. Thomas Arnold, the century's most influential educationalist, added the role of chaplain in 1831 to his headship at Rugby school, thus taking responsibility for the spiritual and moral life of the institution, which he clearly rated above the intellectual (Newsome 1961: 28). By midcentury, the role of chaplain was clearly established as a powerful moral and spiritual influence in the private schools: the chaplain would conduct Anglican worship, and be a leading moral contributor to what became the 'public school ethos' (Parker 1987). By the early 20th century, the values and ethos of the 'public school' had extensive provenance and the place of 'chapel' in school life was central.

This tradition continues. School A, established in the 19th century, is graced with a fine gothic chapel which is the 'sacred space' where the weekly school Eucharist is celebrated with impressive ritual and a significant degree of participation by the 13–18-year-old co-ed pupils. A large choir adds high-quality traditional church music, homilies are characterised by a degree of intellectual and spiritual challenge, and a high proportion – some two-thirds – of the student congregation will voluntarily receive the sacrament or a blessing. The chaplain –

an Oxford graduate and former parish priest – presides, and evidently has the respect and affection of the school community. His role includes a substantial teaching commitment; his lessons in a mainstream subject provide the context for him to establish relationships with pupils and to gain intellectual credibility among them. The chaplain is seen by pupils as a key member staff – he embodies both care for the individual, and the faith which is at the heart of the school's corporate identity. In many respects – given changed social relationships since the 19th century – he plays a role which would be recognisable to pupils of a former era.

The Tradition Developed: State-Maintained Schools

Following the 1944 Education Act, which established the late 20th century version of the 'dual system' of county and voluntary schools (Maclure 1965: .222), school chaplaincy along public school lines began to be replicated in the (new) Church state-maintained secondary schools. By no means all Church secondary schools appointed chaplains after 1944, but the common public school pattern of a chaplain who might also be head of religious education (or 'Divinity', in traditional public school parlance) appears to have been echoed in many Church-maintained school chaplaincies.

By the end of the 20th century, therefore, school chaplaincy was a feature of several parts of the school system. Broadly, all the old English public schools had Anglican chaplaincy provision, with some of the more high-status schools developing multifaith provision alongside their traditional, resident Christian chaplaincy: Eton College is an example of a school with Christian, Muslim, Jewish and Hindu chaplaincy. In the public school context, chaplaincy may be seen as a core aspect of their 'traditional' educational values, although in some schools it now exists alongside the more contemporary-styled provision of a counselling service.

Roman Catholic secondary schools in England, both private and state-maintained, seem to take the provision of chaplaincy as educationally axiomatic, and dioceses as well as the church nationally through the Catholic Education Service produce clear policy and practice guidelines for school chaplaincy. The late 20th century decline in the numbers of priests and religious sisters, though, means that many Roman Catholic maintained schools now have female lay chaplains, which in turn means that the central act of catholic worship – the Mass – is less often celebrated, by a visiting priest.

In Church of England state-maintained secondary schools and academies the picture is mixed. Some employ chaplains (lay or ordained) on a full-time basis with no teaching commitment; others employ the traditional chaplain/teacher model; others have visiting chaplaincy provided by a local clergy person or a group of local clergy, sometimes set up ecumenically; some employ 'Christian youth workers' in a chaplaincy capacity; yet others have no school-provided (and financed) provision but rely on local charities or churches to provide occasional visiting 'para-chaplaincy' services. It is currently unclear what faith provision is being made in Church of England secondary schools for the personal and faith needs of pupils of other faith groups. The picture, in brief, is very diverse, and no single, clear rationale appears to be at work.

School Chaplaincy in the 21st Century: Initial Research

An apparent lack of interest in school chaplaincy evinced by the institutional Church of England, and the absence of any relevant research data, prompted in the early years of the new century the first empirical research into this ministry. The Bloxham Project, a non-denominational educational charity dedicated to the support of school chaplaincy predominantly in the private school sector undertook a research programme from 2009 to 2011, whose impulse was to explore 'the nature, extent and effectiveness' of school chaplaincy in Church of England secondary schools.

The Bloxham research programme (carried out in collaboration with the Oxford Centre for Ecclesiology and Practical Theology, OxCEPT, based at Ripon College Cuddesdon, Oxford) published its initial report in 2011 (Caperon 2011). Drawing on an extensive literature review and a series of scoping interviews to set its parameters, the research encompassed a series of in-depth interviews with Anglican school chaplains in all types of secondary school, both private and state-maintained; a national online survey of all identifiable serving chaplains in Church of England schools – some 400 contacts; and focus-group interviews with students in a cross-section of these schools. In all, the research revealed a fascinating picture of the state of school chaplaincy in the early 21st century, which will be set out in the coming paragraphs.

School Chaplaincy: Diversity and Function

School chaplains themselves represent a highly diverse group, ministering in divergent contexts, but with a common sense of specific vocation to this ministry. In contexts ranging from the most prestigious private schools with their rolling acres and noble chapels to cheaply constructed, post-war state-maintained Church schools set in run-down council estates, there appears to be a common core to the ministry of school chaplaincy. Centring on two functional roles, the pastoral and the liturgical, but with four further functional dimensions identifiable as the spiritual, missional, prophetic and pedagogic, school chaplaincy is carried out by a diverse range of ministers. These encompass male and female, early- and late-career, lay and ordained people with a broad spectrum of ecclesial backgrounds and outlooks and of theological and ministerial training.

A glance at Schools B, C and D will exemplify this diversity. School B is set in an inner-city context with a widely mixed-heritage and vibrant student body. The chaplain is an Anglican priest, formerly active in a high-status profession and having served as an inner-city curate before taking on the chaplaincy. His role includes no subject-teaching, but much of his time is dedicated to developing the religious literacy of pupils through assemblies and through curricular initiatives. In ecclesial terms, he is in the catholic Anglican tradition, with its legacy of profound theological thought. School C is set in a suburban context, with a less diverse but still substantially mixed-heritage student body. The chaplain is a former youth worker, now a trained teacher of a mainstream subject, whose ecclesial home is in the liberal tradition of open Anglicanism. Among his challenges as a lay chaplain are working with pupils whose own fundamentalist church background confronts his approach, and developing with local clergy the school's Eucharistic practice in the small, uninspiring chapel. School D is set in a prosperous town context, with a mostly white, middle-class student body; the chaplain is a female priest with a background in an evangelical parish and an enthusiasm for counselling, in which she is a qualified practitioner. She brings a gentle but clear identity to her role – leading worship in the school's fine chapel as well as pastorally supporting individual staff and students.

Given this diversity, the commonality of school chaplains' concerns is distinctive. Their sense of specific calling to work both with the young – their prime focus – but also with all others comprising the extended community of the school – teachers, support staff, parents, governors – can be compared with the traditional notion of the parish: a defined geographical community and sphere of ministry. The school 'parish', however, is an associational entity, defined by its core activity – education – which is the reason for the school's existence. This extension of chaplaincy to the whole school community makes it an 'extensive' rather than 'intensive' ministry, and it may be helpful to see it as 'utility-extensive' (Percy 2013: 43), that is, a ministerial sphere where 'membership' of the pastoral community is ascribed rather than chosen, so that it is assumed that all are included within the sphere of care.

And it is clearly pastoral care that school chaplains put first. This may mean in some contexts a particular concern for the troubled pupil, for whom the chaplain may be both support and advocate. It may mean visiting parents to support and reassure when their child has been injured, or worse. It can mean supporting teacher colleagues under stress; and in some contexts it may involve a weekly meeting with the head to offer counsel and encouragement. In some schools there is a clear and collaborative relationship between chaplaincy and the school's other 'pastoral' provision – in School A the chaplain and professional school counsellor are close colleagues, and in School D the chaplain works in the context of the school's 'student services' team. Pastoral care in school chaplaincy is the disinterested, practical and inclusive concern for any person in need or distress, and given the turbulence of the teenage years, there is no shortage of clients.

High on school chaplains' list of priorities is their liturgical role as worship leaders: a special priority for School A's chaplain. In contexts (usually private schools) where the chapel is central to school life, chaplains will probably lead daily services, either for the whole school or for a section of it, and there may be further provision for voluntary worship. In other contexts (say state-maintained Church schools) the chaplain may act as worship and assemblies coordinator, as in School B, arranging rotas and providing material for assemblies led by other staff, as well as leading worship personally. The chaplain's challenge is to make school worship accessible and meaningful for students and staff, an experience of genuine spirituality, through creating the conditions in which the presence of God may be experienced.

Apart from the core foci of pastoral care and liturgy, school chaplaincy has other functions, as indicated above. Spiritual leadership within the school community devolves on the chaplain, and it is for him or her to provide a spiritual perspective which others may not at first discern. Similarly, there is a missional function which involves representing the life of faith, a call, in the words of Archbishop Robert Runcie, to: '[n]ourish those of the faith; encourage those of other faiths; challenge those who have no faith' (Dearing 2001: 4). There is also a prophetic function, 'speaking truth to power', which may involve the chaplain calling his or her colleagues to a better way of being or doing; and the chaplain will also be a person who has a teaching function – as someone who teaches about faith or as someone who has a specifically catechetical role – particularly in those schools where the rite of Confirmation is administered as part of the school's own routine as an avowedly Christian community: both Schools A and C offer this, something no longer confined to the private sector.

School Chaplaincy: Identity and Presence

Beyond all these functional aspects of the school chaplain's role, however, is a more ontological dimension: the chaplain's personal being as someone whose presence and role both express and embody the truths of the Christian gospel. School chaplains speak of a 'ministry of presence', where being is more significant than doing, where incarnation or embodiment is what counts. In this understanding, chaplains may be seen to ' ... occupy that strange hinterland between the sacred and the secular, the temporal and the eternal, acting as interpreters and mediators, embodying and signifying faith, hope and love' (Percy 2006: 188).

As people of faith, chaplains in school are deeply counter-cultural in an age of public secularity, and when the young are decreasingly likely to be members of a church – unless the school can be seen in effect as a kind of 'prime ecclesial community'. At the same time, chaplains are promoters of a Christian understanding of the world, offering access to spiritual capital, being agents of religious socialisation, and through the provision of worship – and especially Eucharistic worship – extending the 'chain of memory' which is the ongoing reality of the community of Christian faith through the ages (see Hervieu-Leger 2000).

These core research insights into school chaplaincy are, importantly, reinforced by pupil focus groups. Questioned about the role and function of chaplains, school pupils are clear about the pastoral priority of chaplaincy, about its spiritual leadership function, about the chaplain as a leader and enabler of worship. Further, they show an insightful grasp of the notions of identity and presence. The chaplain 'makes faith present' in the school community, and is seen as a role model for Christian character and behaviour: he or she incarnates and exemplifies faith through presence. As to identity, pupils seem clear that what counts is not so much the functional tasks undertaken by a chaplain, but the person the chaplain is: 'it's his "-*ness*", who he is, his essence, his being', reported a pupil in School C.

This emphasis on the person lies at the heart of school chaplaincy, a form of ministry – perhaps like all others – strongly dependent on the personal nature, character and disposition of the individual minister fulfilling the role at any one time. Both chaplains and pupils see a link between this understanding and the exemplar ministry of Jesus. 'How Jesus was with people' was stated as a ministerial model by School B's chaplain; and School C's chaplain was described by pupils as a 'kind of mini-Jesus': an insight which may both encourage and chasten the practising chaplain in a school community.

School Chaplaincy in the 21st Century: Further Dimensions

The Bloxham/OxCEPT research focused solely on what might be thought of as 'institutional' chaplaincy: that is, chaplaincy provided by the schools themselves as an aspect of their Christian educational mission and offered – as described above – to the whole, extended school community. Another way of describing such chaplaincy is to think of it as 'embedded', a term helpfully suggested by Paul Ballard to suggest that the chaplain in an institution works within, but is ultimately loyal to values beyond, the institutional context (Ballard 2009). What has been characteristic of school chaplaincy in the early 21st century is that even while 'embedded', institutional chaplaincy has been growing, other distinctly different styles have also burgeoned.

One example of new developments in school chaplaincy – not without relevance to this country, despite its distance – is an Australian government initiative to fund the provision of what might be called 'visiting' chaplaincy in state secondary schools across the country, with lay or ordained chaplains recruited from local church communities. This development implies an understanding of 'chaplaincy' at some distance from the institutional, embedded model just described, but an initial research report on the scheme concludes that it has been positively received by school principals as beneficial. Visiting chaplains have been especially valued for supporting troubled pupils in secondary schools, as a kind of pastoral last resort, supporting the school when its available professional resources have been exhausted. At the same time, it is a kind of chaplaincy which also concerns itself with wider social issues: one vignette from the report cites a chaplain working with a group of immigrant mothers to develop their practical cooking skills (Hughes and Sims 2009).

The Australian experiment prompted interest in school chaplaincy in at least one para-church organisation in the UK. Scripture Union, an interdenominational evangelical Christian charity '[u]sing the Bible to inspire children, young people and adults to know God' (Scripture Union 2014), has taken a clear interest in fostering and supporting a related style of visiting chaplaincy in schools. Again, though, this is an understanding of chaplaincy somewhat different from the institutional pattern. The organisation's overtly evangelistic aim is distinctive, and it appears that the main thrust of its support is towards an understanding of chaplaincy for schools that may be best described as 'para-chaplaincy', one involving youth-work-trained workers in developing pastoral relationships with pupils on an ad hoc and visiting basis.

Para-chaplaincy: An Alternative to the Embedded Model

Scripture Union is one of several organisations of evangelical provenance now actively either initiating or supporting this new style of chaplaincy. Another is the Luton Churches' Educational Trust (LCET), which has developed a strong local reputation and whose work has been favourably reported in the international Roman Catholic journal *The Tablet* (see Curtis 2011). LCET describes itself ' ... as first and foremost a local project, set up by a group of forty-five churches in 1993, to reconnect the Christian community with young people and make a positive difference to their lives ... '. The diversity of LCET's work, encompassing courses to build self-esteem and reduce self-harm among teenagers, the support of religious education in local schools, and offering re-integration courses for excluded pupils, in addition to providing visiting chaplaincy for schools, appears clearly prompted by 'a desire to see Christ's message of hope and justice expressed to and among young people' (Luton Churches Educational Trust 2014).

What, then, are the features of this new, visiting 'para-chaplaincy'? It is essentially an externally provided chaplaincy, where the chaplain is separate from the institution; the chaplain's understanding of faith is shaped not by the school's ethos or its formal ecclesial identity but by the sponsoring church or charity from which he or she is sent. There may well be no formal contract between school and provider setting out either the chaplaincy role or the expectations of it on either side. It is occasional, in that visits may be irregular or ad hoc, perhaps in part responding to a particular situation or to the perceived needs of pupils. It is, as indicated above, usually carried out by younger, lay people probably trained in Christian youth work rather than in theology and ministry. It is focused especially on the pupil members of the school, in an attempt to respond to their social, personal and spiritual needs, rather than being a service to the whole community. In short, its focus is on the pastoral and missional aspects of the school chaplain's role described above.

Para-chaplaincy is offering a distinctly different style and kind of ministry. Its assumptions may well derive from a view of the world, and of the relation between 'Christ and Culture' (see Niebuhr 1951), different from that held by embedded, institutional chaplains: it appears to be rooted in a more conservative, and less optimistic, theology than that which seems to animate more traditional chaplaincy. The noted army chaplain of the First World War, Geoffrey Studdert Kennedy, advised: 'Live with the men, go where they go'. There may be a sense in which the para-chaplain is motivated rather to encourage pupils to share his or her life – including its rootedness in the Church – than to share their lives, however. A Christian outreach agenda appears to be at the core of para-chaplaincy, whereas institutional chaplaincy appears to be impelled by a more straightforwardly and disinterestedly pastoral impulse with little overt sense of an evangelistic motivation.

The Identity of Chaplaincy in Schools: Contested and Unresolved

It will be observed, though, that both these stances have authentically Christian pedigrees; in missiological terms, they can be seen to represent the different standpoints of a 'creation-centred' or a 'redemption-centred' impulse in theology (Bevans 1992: 16). Given this, the question inevitably arises, what should be understood by the term 'chaplaincy' in relation to schools, or indeed more widely in the educational context? One approach would be to consider the occupational group of professional school chaplains – those specifically employed as such by their institutions and represented by my chaplains A, B, C and D – as representing the norm, the base model. If this view is taken, then the chaplaincy role as described by the Bloxham/OxCEPT research may be seen as what school chaplaincy 'really' consists of. In this understanding, chaplaincy would indeed be, as has been suggested above, ministry rooted in a 'utility-extensive' model.

However, it may also be argued that formal employment arrangements have little to do with the actuality of what 'chaplaincy' is, especially in the light of the growth of the alternative 'para-chaplaincy' style. It is equally arguable that this new and dynamic practice has an equal validity as chaplaincy, and that it could be seen as a pastoral response to a perception of an increasingly secularised youth, detached from the teaching of the Christian faith, spiritually and morally rootless. Para-chaplaincy may thus be seen as targeted to meet this situation, rooted in contrast to embedded chaplaincy, in a 'market-intensive' model of ministry. In effect, this means that chaplaincy in schools currently has a contested identity; what is meant by 'chaplaincy' in the school context is unclear, and the ministerial practice of those embracing varying understandings of chaplaincy may differ not just in emphasis but in underlying motivation, and in theological impulse.

Given that schools are the context in which the young may be most likely to encounter a formal ministry of the Church – a church from which, as research conducted by Lancaster University and YouGov indicates (available at: http://cdn.yougov.com/cumulus_uploads/document/mm7go89rhi/YouGov-University%20of%20Lancaster-Survey-Results-Faith-Matters-130130.pdf; accessed 23 May 2015), generational distance increases with youth – the identity of chaplaincy in schools is hugely significant. This makes all the more puzzling the national Church's apparent uncertainty about this aspect of educational ministry. A ministry which has its origins in the private schools, but which has now spread widely to Church of England schools and academies, and is now being augmented, complemented or possibly even challenged by the new para-chaplaincy, deserves to be taken seriously as never before.

References

Ballard, P. (2009), Locating chaplaincy: a theological note. *Crucible*, July–September, 18–24.

Bevans, S.B. (1992), *Models of Contextual Theology*. Maryknoll, NY: Orbis Books.

Caperon, J. (2011), *School Chaplaincy: What Does Research Tell Us?* Cuddesdon: The Bloxham Project and OxCEPT.

Curtis, C. (2011), Kindling for the spiritual fire. *The Tablet*, 3 September, 45.

Dearing, L. (2001), *The Way Ahead: Church of England Schools in the New Millennium*. London: Archbishop's Council.

Drury, J. (2013), *Music at Midnight: The Life and Poetry of George Herbert*. London: Allen Lane.

Hervieu-Leger, D. (2000), *Religion as a Chain of Memory*. Cambridge and Maldon, MA: Polity.

Hughes, P. and Sims, M. (2009), *The Effectiveness of Chaplaincy: As Provided by the National School Chaplaincy Association to Government Schools in Australia*. Perth, Australia: Edith Cowan University.

Luton Churches Educational Trust. (2014), *LCET webpage* [Online]. Luton. www.lcet.org (accessed 21 January 2014).

Maclure, J.S. (1965), *Educational Documents: England and Wales 1816 to the Present Day*. London: Methuen & Co Ltd.

Newsome, D. (1961), *Godliness and Good Learning: Four Studies on a Victorian Ideal*. London: Cassell.

Niebuhr, H.R. (1951), *Christ and Culture*. New York: Harper & Row.

Parker, P. (1987), *The Old Lie: The Great War and the Public-School Ethos*. SLondon and New York: Hambledon Continuum.

Percy, M. (2006), *Clergy: The Origin of Species*. London and New York: Continuum.

—— (2013), *Anglicanism: Confidence, Commitment and Communion*. Farnham and Burlington, VT: Ashgate.

Scripture Union (2014), *Scripture Union website* [Online]. Milton Keynes: Scripure Union. www.scriptureunion.org.uk (accessed 21 January 2014).

Conclusion

Andrew Todd, Mark Cobb and Chris Swift

This handbook has sought to contribute to and develop a systematic understanding of the developing phenomenon of chaplaincy, as a contribution to what is emerging as a field of study in its own right. It has done so in a number of ways. First, it offers an up-to-date picture of the world of chaplaincy, especially within the United Kingdom public sector, which makes clear the continuing public significance of this aspect of religion in public life within a changing political context. Secondly, it provides a rich interdisciplinary reflection about chaplaincy. And thirdly, it advances understanding of how chaplaincy can be further established as a field of study, both in terms of research methodology and critical theoretical reflection. This conclusion identifies the book's major contributions in each case, but also identifies next steps in the development of chaplaincy studies.

The Public Significance of Chaplaincy

In the sections of the book that focus on chaplaincy in particular contexts, the initial chapters in each section and the case studies offer a concentrated collection of insights into chaplaincy as it is now, written from within the field.

These and other chapters identify a range of core practices, rooted in the historic strength of chaplaincy – pastoral care developed through 'brief encounters' (seen, for example, in the case studies offered by both Nolan and Deedes). This role has both been located by chaplains within, and provided occasion for, a wider faith practice – the religious and spiritual roles of chaplains. At numerous points (including in the chapter by Gilliat-Ray and Arshad) the book has charted the development of this role from historically Christian practice, dominated by Anglicanism, to a multifaith practice with reduced, or at least changing, inequalities between faiths and denominations, for both practitioners and their 'clients'.

The accompanying development is of chaplaincy explicitly directed towards, or providing for, those who would not identify themselves as religious, but for whom the label 'spiritual' has some utility, as a way of capturing questions of meaning and identity, and informal or individual ritual practices, for example, those associated with memorialisation. This area, sometimes expressed as 'generic' chaplaincy or spiritual care, has been a particular subject for debate in health care. For example, (as considered by Swift) the question of chaplaincy provision for those who do not identify themselves as religious has been a specific matter of debate in relation to the NHS England (2015) guidelines for chaplaincy, and one which connects with NHS England's overarching aims of promoting equality and reducing health inequalities.

Further areas of practice considered here may be captured as the 'expertise' of chaplaincy. Some areas of expertise are context specific, developed as chaplains deepen their understanding of the organisation(s) they serve and contribute directly to the 'mission' of those organisations, be it education, health, security, justice or commerce. But some areas of expertise cross contextual boundaries. One such historic area of practice for chaplains has been their moral role, which can vary from being a critical voice for human well-being in an organisational setting to an explicit role of moral formation (as discussed by Totten). Sedgwick, in his chapter, addresses this area directly in his discussion of how chaplains can promote the good.

Alongside this continuing role, an emerging area of expertise for many chaplains is that of the 'subject-matter expert' in all things religious. In an era of increasing diversity of faith and belief, and lower levels of 'religious literacy', the chaplain may become a convenient source of information and insight concerning the needs of patients of particular faiths, or the risk associated with particular religious beliefs. More creatively, this expert knowledge may contribute to new approaches to public practice, as discussed by Kavanagh in his consideration of chaplaincy's contribution to reducing reoffending and the resettlement of prisoners, and the development of social capital.

Alongside the above roles, and often underpinning them, another one whose significance has become prominent is that of the chaplain as entrepreneur. This skilful negotiation of political complexities in the interests of developing chaplaincy is apparent in a number of chapters (such as the case study by Asim Hafiz), and is discussed by Hewson and Crompton, in their chapter, in relation to chaplains and multifaith spaces.

These dimensions of the contemporary practice of chaplaincy illustrate its continuing significance within a changing public context. In the United Kingdom chaplains continue to be mostly members of faith communities whose role is carried out in organisations and settings whose primary aim is not to be a faith community, but rather to deliver health, education or justice; to offer retail or commercial services; to exercise government; etc. But the political context in which these chaplains make their public or social contribution has changed markedly.

Foremost amongst those contextual changes is the legal and public policy frameworks shaping contemporary chaplaincy. As Billings and Cranmer make clear, the rights framework rooted in Article 9 of the European Convention on Human Rights, which enshrines the right to manifest one's religion or belief, and in the 2010 Equality Act which identifies religion and belief as a 'protected characteristic', is highly significant. Increasingly, seeing religion or belief as a right, and as an area to be addressed by equality legislation and policy, is replacing older public frameworks, such as establishment. And whereas the historic justification for chaplaincy, rooted in Anglican establishment, appears to be a mixed blessing, open to critique like other areas of historic privilege, the newly established public duty to promote equality may perhaps be opening up opportunities for chaplains to inform, contribute to, and even shape this area of public life.

With such opportunities come emerging responsibilities for chaplains, especially (as Billings points out) to address the question of equality directly. This includes addressing the continuing inequalities of multifaith provision: the persistent question of who acts as broker within a chaplaincy for those of different faiths and beliefs; the distribution of resources across faith and belief groups; and the inclusion of new groups (including new religious movements and humanists).

A further key aspect of the changing context, which surfaces to some extent in the preceding chapters, is the area of risk and security. A proper concern for vulnerable people is prominent in the public sector and has reshaped the practice of all those who work in it, including chaplains. The question of being safe to practise is addressed particularly by Paterson in his consideration of the importance of supervision. A more hidden question in this book is that of the chaplain's contribution to security, particularly in relation to government concerns about 'extremism'. It is an issue touched on by Clines and Kavanagh and considered elsewhere by Todd (2013). Given the expectation that chaplains will be expert in matters of religion, an existing concern in educations and prisons that chaplains will monitor religious behaviour, and increasing concern about the risk of 'extremism' in education (illustrated by OFSTED interaction in 2014 with schools in Birmingham and East London), it may be that security questions will become more prominent in the near future for chaplains.

Developing the Study of Chaplaincy

Given the above, the study of chaplaincy has the potential to increase understanding of its significance, for and amongst practitioners, academics and wider audiences, including faith communities and others concerned with religion in public life. So as well as demonstrating changes in practice and context, this book also makes the case for developing the study of the field of chaplaincy to keep up with those changes.

One of the challenges therefore is to work beyond the existing parameters of study and reflection on chaplaincy, which historically has been significantly practitioner-led. Meeting that challenge is about locating understanding of chaplaincy within wider understandings of the context of chaplaincy, and about locating the inherited disciplinary approach to the study of chaplaincy within a wider range of academic approaches. It is also about drawing in new conversation partners (not least from the academic community) while continuing in dialogue with chaplains themselves, and their supporting organisations.

The historic strength of chaplaincy studies has been in the field of practical theology and ethics. The former discipline continues to act as a crucial foundation for chaplains in their hermeneutical role, as they seek to connect their faith tradition with their work in different settings. It continues to be put to good effect, not least in this volume by Swinton and Kelly, in relation to a theology of health, and by Totten in his consideration of the reality of a Christian chaplain engaging with the question of just war. But practical theology remains a language of chaplaincy (and primarily of Christian chaplaincy) not necessarily shared by others in a multifaith, secular context.

Ethics has been another discipline drawn on by chaplains, which offers a mediating language and the possibility of dialogue amongst those of different ethical perspectives (including secular ones, as discussed by Sedgwick); but it elucidates only one dimension of the role of chaplaincy. In order to locate those disciplines within a wider field, what is needed is a developing range both of ways of mapping chaplaincy within its social context and of theoretical perspectives which interpret the map. Studying chaplaincy needs to be about establishing an interdisciplinary field of study, which can both elucidate a complex phenomenon and stimulate dialogue amongst those who engage with chaplaincy from quite different perspectives and frames of reference.

The Research Agenda

As McSherry and Kevern argue, this necessarily involves developing a more sophisticated range of methodological approaches to the study of chaplaincy, within an enhanced research environment. Research approaches from the social sciences can contribute to establishing a properly empirical dimension to chaplaincy studies (in place of a tendency to the anecdotal, which was an inherited weakness, characteristic of a number of approaches to theological reflection). At the same time, as Slater argues, chaplaincy-focused research needs to hold the balance between an interpretative–relational emphasis, characteristic of qualitative research and amenable to chaplains' self-understandings, and an empiricist, or positivist, approach, that may become allied with public demands for evidence-based practice and value for money.

Again as McSherry and Kevern argue, an important aspect of the deployment of such methodologies needs to be the observation and interviewing of a wider range of people connected to chaplaincy than just chaplains; in particular, managers, service users and stakeholders. This approach is adopted, for example, by Todd and Tipton (2011) in relation to prisons (referred to here by Kavanagh); and was employed historically by Wilson (1971), but it is rare still. Creating an enhanced environment for such methodological development must also include paying attention to research methods and skills training for chaplains themselves; recruitment and training of research students; the carrying out of funded research projects, and employment of suitably qualified researchers; and establishing working relationships across academic disciplines and communities.

Interdisciplinary Critical Reflection

Accompanying increased methodological sophistication, and also supported by an improved research environment, should be the development of the range and depth of theoretical approaches to interpreting the map of chaplaincy. To this end, the present volume has deployed a range of disciplinary approaches to chaplaincy, including psychology (Watts), law (Cranmer) and consideration of space (Hewson and Crompton).

At the core of theoretical reflection on a phenomenon that is centrally about the significance of religion and belief need to be sociology (including the sociology of religion), ethnography (and understandings of human culture) and politics (including both political science and political philosophy). Thus, for example, political philosophy locates debate about chaplaincy within the debate about religion, liberal democracies and public reasoning; understandings of ritual, from ethnography, contextualise chaplaincy's engagement with the 'sacred'; and chaplaincy may be both contextualised by, and critique, understandings of secularity, secularism(s) and secularisation.

Billings demonstrates the value of locating chaplaincy within a nuanced understanding of public policy. And Pattison develops a sophisticated theoretical reflection on chaplaincy as distinctive expression of religion, embodying religious sacralities that are negotiated by chaplains and new within the field of religion and belief.

Such approaches, especially Pattison's, provide language for what is arguably a crucial next step in chaplaincy research and reflection. Interdisciplinary theoretical frameworks and sophisticated and rigorous methodological approaches to chaplaincy research, especially those which engage users and commissioners of chaplaincy as well as chaplains, prepare the ground for a more thorough examination of the public impact of chaplaincy. This is vital and largely unexplored territory. Slater's warning about the dangers of positivist approaches, and their potential for being co-opted by those simply concerned with cost efficiency, stands. But there is value in being able to demonstrate that chaplaincy (and religion more widely) has public capital value, and to be able to elucidate the way in which chaplaincy is valued as social, symbolic and cultural capital, and therefore economically (Bourdieu 1986, discussed in Todd 2015).

To What End?

To borrow the central ethicist's question, identified by Sedgwick in his chapter, what good should such an area of study seek to promote? The proximate goal of the emerging field of chaplaincy studies might remain, to deliver robust, research-led education and professional development for chaplains, not least by working with them to locate their reflection on practice on a broader and more developed methodological and theoretical canvas.

This might be underpinned by an academic goal, that of knowledge creation and transfer, especially a nuanced, critically reflective map of the phenomenon of chaplaincy and of the way it is constructed and understood. To fulfil this goal, and thus become a more established field, will require action and resources (as already hinted at above), including: an active national and international research network of scholars exploring this field; a coherent programme of seminars and conferences; a concerted exercise to agree a consensus on the road map that chaplaincy studies should follow, say, for the next five years; a strategic and organised approach to funding applications across the major centres of chaplaincy studies, nationally and internationally; and growing chaplain-researchers through access to research training programmes.

But the primary good sought by those who study chaplaincy must be to engage in public dialogue, both *about* the contribution of religion and belief to public life (in and through the work of chaplains), including the theological contribution, and *as part of* that contribution. That places the public impact of research in this area beyond the academic community, in both faith community and secular settings; and within a dialogue involving chaplains, their organisations and managers, policy makers and those responsible for the governance not only of chaplaincy, but of religion in public life.

Final Reflections

This volume has presented multiple accounts of chaplaincy and the ways in which it is understood and conceptualised through various disciplinary lenses and within specific contexts. This approach aims to make chaplaincy less obscure and more intelligible but in turn requires us to consider how these accounts have been framed and what interpretations have been applied. In attempting to describe and explain chaplaincy we therefore need to be mindful of what has been omitted, obscured or partially rendered. The caution here is both an acknowledgement of the constraints of this volume and an invitation to engage in critical reflection on a practice and body of knowledge that is itself entangled in much wider fields of enquiry and debate. In studying chaplaincy we therefore need to acknowledge the inherent internal and external dynamics of the subject generated through the dialectics of the sacred in the personal and organisational circumstances that chaplains engage with and mediate.

Chaplains often operate at points of human transition that are most evident in the significant events of the life cycle that manifest the full spectrum of human experience from profound suffering to overwhelming joy. These are moments in the flux of life that can confirm or question the normative realities by which people orientate their lives and may therefore amplify, transform or threaten sacred experiences, inspiration, meanings and values. In response chaplains will support the individual's narration of events within a wider context of sacred narratives, symbols and ritual, typically drawing upon the resources of their own religious tradition. This is most evident, and perhaps most distinctive, when marking the transitory nature of life and addressing human mortality:

> Most important for delineating religion, religions mark and cross the *ultimate* horizon of human life. Other cultural trajectories—for example, art, music, and literature—can mark and traverse the boundaries of the natural terrain and the limits of embodied life. These other cultural forms, however, usually do not appeal to superhuman forces or map cosmic space—and they do not offer prescriptions about how to cross the ultimate horizon. (Tweed 2006:76)

Boundaries are also a feature of chaplaincy in the more mundane forms that constitute organisations and institutions. Chaplains span religious and secular organisations because of their membership of the former and practice in the latter, and in so doing they become fluent bilinguists and benefactors of the accommodation afforded by a liberal politic and a moderate form of secularity. In the UK chaplains exist in public institutions because of the public good that they profess to serve and their ability to address the sacred without recourse to an uncompromising religious ideology. However, this relationship is not without contention particularly from those on one hand who wish to pursue more absolute forms of a secular state, and on the other, who claim there is insufficient equality of religions and inadequate participation of religious minorities. Whilst these tensions are expressed at the national level in the political and legal systems it is at the local level that organisations and chaplaincies have to make sense of practical and representational issues for the pluralistic communities they support. Chaplaincy at its best can therefore be viewed as a working demonstration of what is possible in such contexts where there is a commitment to serve the sacred aspects of life in its many forms.

The various dynamics we have outlined indicate how chaplaincy is a highly contingent practice because of where it is situated and what it serves, and this in turn requires forms of enquiry that can make practical and theoretical sense of a lively discipline and context. There is no doubting that chaplaincy has much to learn from scholarly activity in related subjects but we also suggest that there is warrant for the particular study of a profession that addresses matters of religion and spirituality within the public places and organisations that chaplains serve. This gap in our knowledge to date is perhaps more remarkable given that on a daily basis large sections of the public will interact with such organisations that are entrusted with significant powers and duties to enable society to function and to promote human goods such as learning and health. This suggests we have a long way to go before we can answer questions such as: what does the presence of chaplains in such organisations tell us about the nature of the sacred in the routine and profound moments of life; and how do chaplains make sense of and respond to the many forms of the sacred that are expressed and experienced by the public?

A final set of questions in a volume devoted to the study of chaplaincy concerns chaplains themselves and the public purposes they serve. Here we discover further gaps in our knowledge principally around two interrelated themes: one pedagogical and the other contextual. Firstly, to what extent do we understand the distinctive capacities, capabilities and practices required by chaplains to fulfil their roles effectively, and what are the educational and formative processes that can cultivate the development and formation of chaplains? Secondly, do diverse contexts require chaplains to adopt distinctive practices or specific approaches, and is there a set of learning and practices that chaplains hold in common, such as interpersonal communication and prayer? Questions such as these illustrate how much we have to learn about chaplains and the generative potential of chaplaincy studies for the scholarly community, the community of practice and the public sphere.

References

Bourdieu, P. (1986). The Forms of Capital. In J.E. Richardson (ed.), *Handbook of Theory and Research for the Sociology of Education*. New York: Greenwood Press, 241–58.

NHS England (2015), *NHS Chaplaincy Guidelines 2015: Promoting Excellence in Pastoral, Spiritual & Religious Care*. Available at: http://www.england.nhs.uk/wp-content/uploads/2015/03/nhs-chaplaincy-guidelines-2015.pdf (accessed 16th May 2015).

Todd, A.J. (2013), Preventing the 'neutral' chaplain? The potential impact of anti-'extremism' policy on prison chaplaincy. *Practical Theology*, 6(2), 144–58.

—— (2015), Religion, security, rights, the individual and rates of exchange: religion in negotiation with British public policy in prisons and the military. *International Journal of Politics, Culture and Society*, 28, 37–50.

Todd, A.J. and Tipton, L. (2011), *The Role and Contribution of a Multi-Faith Prison Chaplaincy to the Contemporary Prison Service*. Research report to the National Offender Management Service. Available at: http://stmichaels.ac.uk/assets/pdf/Todd-and-Tipton-2011-Report-on-Prison-Chaplaincy.pdf (accessed 17 April 2015).

Wilson, M. (1971), *The Hospital – A Place of Truth*. Birmingham: University of Birmingham Institute for the Study of Worship and Religious Architecture.

Index